THE COMPLETE
SPANISH
COOKBOOK

Pulpitos en Salsa de Almendras y Ajo (top), p.112; Calamares Rellenos en Salsa de Ajo (front). p.114.

THE COMPLETE
SPANISH
COOKBOOK

Jacki
Passmore

Little, Brown and Company
Boston • New York • Toronto • London

A LITTLE BROWN BOOK

Published in conjunction with Lansdowne Publishing Pty Ltd
Level 1, Argyle Centre, 18 Argyle Street, The Rocks NSW Australia 2000

First published by Weldon Publishing 1991
Reprinted 1992, 1993
Reprinted in paperback for Little Brown 1995,
This (abridged) edition reprinted in 1997, 1999

© Copyright: Lansdowne Publishing Pty Ltd 1991, 1997
© Copyright design: Lansdowne Publishing Pty Ltd 1991, 1997

ISBN 0 316 87717 4
A CIP record for this book is
available from the British Library

Copy Editor: Patricia Connell
Designer: Warren Penney
Photographer: Mike Hallson
Photographer's Assistant: Peter Waddington
Typeset in Australia by Adtype Graphics, Sydney in Schneidler
PRINTED IN SINGAPORE

Little, Brown and Company (UK)
Brettenham House
Lancaster Place
London WC2E7EN

WEIGHTS AND MEASURES

We have tested these recipes using standard
American cup and spoon measurements,
and have applied the following conversion.

3 cups = (750 ml/24 fl oz)   1 cup = (250 ml/8 fl oz)
1 quart = (1.14 l/40 fl oz   1 tablespoon = (15 ml/1/2 fl oz)
$\frac{1}{2}$ cup = (120 ml/4 fl oz)

CONTENTS

INTRODUCTION

The dramatic landscape of Spain's sweeping plateau, fringed by rocky coastlines, reflects a history as turbulent, romantic and eventful as any to be found in Europe. This vibrant land occupies the bulk of the Iberian peninsula, curving into the Atlantic Ocean south of France, the rectangle of Portugal's land hugging its western periphery and the blue waters of the Mediterranean lapping its southern shores.

Pivotal are the distinctive plateaux juxtaposed on sweeping flat plains that are the countryside of the central provinces of old and new Castile, and legendary La Mancha. To the south is Andalusia, and southwards from there, where the Mediterranean narrows to the neck that is the Strait of Gibraltar, the famed resort strip of Costa del Sol announces the province of Granada. Extremadura, to its west, follows the Portuguese border northwards. Murcia and Valencia curve northeastward around a brilliant Mediterranean coastline to meet with Catalonia, which occupies the northernmost Mediterranean region of Spain. Its offshore partners, the Balearic Islands are clustered southwards on the same latitude as the city of Valencia. Landlocked Aragon wraps around the upper reaches of Valencia and Catalonia, steeply mountainous at either end and irrigated by the basin of the Ebro, one of Spain's largest rivers. Northwards again are La Rioja and Navarra and, in the far northeast, the Basque Country, abutting southeastern France in the forest-clad Pyrenees and in that corner of the Atlantic coast where the Bay of Biscay might also be known as the Gulf of Gascoyne. Westwards along the coast are Asturias and Cantabria, which neighbor the provinces of Old Castile and León to their south, and hugging their western reaches and the northern border of Portugal is Galicia. We have followed this geographical pattern of the provinces in the layout of this book.

Spain is a many-faceted country, and its complexity intrigues. It's a land of extremes, of passion and spirit, of strongly held ideals, of a physical beauty that astounds, and of monuments that at once humble and amaze the viewer by their sheer number, age, size and artistry. Spain is a country of tremendous variation in landscape and terrain, in climate and culture. At 200,000 square miles, it's a much larger country than it would appear on a map, yet still smaller than Texas. Its people, numbering around 38 million, are of many types and backgrounds. They are proudly parochial or impressively sophisticated, always charmingly hospitable, and with physical characteristics revealing their richly blended ancestry. It's a country of many tongues, with four main languages — Basque, Catalan, Galician and *Castellano* (Castilian) — and many dialects. You may visit armed with your guidebook and parrot-phrasing of "useful" sentences only to find that *Castellano* is the second language in many parts. Spain's cuisine reflects all of these elements. It's intensely traditional and regional, yet today's chefs are boldly inventive, experimenting with new ingredients in age-old formulas, and new themes with foods that have been used for centuries.

The Spanish love to eat; they do it often, in quantity and with obvious relish. *Desayuno* (breakfast) is usually light — hot chocolate or coffee with *churros*, featherlight strips of freshly fried dough, or toast or pastries. (Eggs, bacon and cereal are for the hotel dining room.) At around 11 a.m. it's coffee again, with sweet buns. At 1 p.m., when shops and offices close for the afternoon break, many might slip into a bar for a quick drink and a nibble of *tapas* before heading home for siesta or meeting friends in a restaurant for lunch. *La comida* (lunch) is to most Spanish people the main meal of the day. It is taken at leisure somewhere between 2 and 3 in the afternoon. It will be at least a 3-course meal, usually beginning with soup and bread or rolls followed by a fish or vegetable course and then a substantial main course. Dessert and coffee invariably follow, although the fashionable set may choose to take these at another restaurant. And of course there's wine! Little wonder that businesses do not begin trading again until around 4 p.m. And that is rather arbitrary; being "on time" is not high on the priority list here.

But the day's eating is only half through. *Merienda* — the Spanish answer to the British "afternoon tea" — means tea or coffee, cakes or pastries and light snacks taken in coffee shops and cafeterias at around 5 p.m. Then, as business closes for the evening somewhere between 7 and 9 p.m., it's back to the *tapas* bars for a drink and nibbles. When I'm in Spain I usually don't get past this part of the ritual; after living in Asia for a large part of my life, I like the concept of "grazing" on many different types of small dishes and the thought of a 3- or 4-course supper after 10 p.m. is a challenge my digestive system has yet to accept readily. But at around this time, just when elsewhere one might be considering calling it a day, the restaurants once again open to an enthusiastic clientele for *la cena* (dinner/supper), again a 3- or 4-course production. The Spanish enjoy soups and often start a meal with one, but they also like egg dishes, simple fish courses such as a poached trout or a grilled fillet, salads or vegetables as first courses. In Spain the "three vegetables and meat" style of main course is not standard. You are more likely to receive your vegetables as a separate course, and the main course on its own with perhaps one vegetable as a garnish. After the evening meal, you might move on to another restaurant or coffee house for the sweet course and coffee.

If a country's eating habits are a reflection of the nation's character, then the Spanish are indeed an ebullient and fun-loving race.

A LONG AND COLORFUL HISTORY

Spain's long history encompasses seven hundred years of occupation by the Romans, until a 5th-century invasion by the Visigoths ended in a reign that overlaid a Teutonic tone to the country's culture and lifestyle. In 711 came the Moors from northern Africa across the Mediterranean. Sweeping old ways before them in the central and southern part of the peninsula, they brought a sense of immense grandeur to the country, with their Caliph Abd-ar-Rahman III ruling from the magnificent city of Córdoba.

During this splendid era Spain prospered to become the leading light in the arts, in architecture and in learning for the whole of Europe. Most of her great cities were established during this opulent phase of her history, and the construction of immense castles throughout the central plains brought her the name Castilla or Castile. At this same time, the western coastal strip was given as a fiefdom to Count Henry of Burgundy by the incumbent Alfonso I of Castile. It later derived the name Portugal from the northernmost fief, the Comitatus Portaculenis, which extended around the old Roman seaport of Portus Cale, present day Oporto, now recognized as the birthplace of port wine.

As Spain's Umayyad dynasty disintegrated into factional fighting, the caliphate split into a number of independent and hostile Moorish kingdoms. The Christian kings who had maintained a stronghold in León, in central-northern Spain, were able to usurp power and form Spain into two great kingdoms, León and Castile.

DISCOVERING THE NEW WORLD

In 1469, the marriage of Princess Isabella of Castile to Prince Ferdinand of Aragón initiated developments that made Spain into a great world power. These far-sighted rulers financed exploration overseas, resulting in Spain's ascendancy as a colonial empire of immense wealth and importance. Christopher Columbus' discovery of the West Indies led the conquest of many foreign lands. By the 16th century, Spain was the richest and most powerful of the European countries, with colonies established in the West Indies, Cuba, Mexico, Central America and the greater part of South America, Florida and the Philippines. It was in this same era that Portugal, competing in the colonizing stakes, appropriated through the efforts of Bartholomew Días and Vasco da Gama the Indian state of Goa, the vital Malaysian port city of Malacca (Melaka), and the legendary "Spice Islands" — the Moluccas in present-day Indonesia — as well as establishing lucrative trade with China, Japan and many parts of Africa.

FOOD FROM AFAR

The American-Mexican connection was to have as great an impact on the life and times of the Spanish people, and on their cuisine, as did the occupation of the Moors. As each majestic galleon returned from the New World, its cargo revealed seeds and seedlings native to southern and central America to plant on home soil. Sweet and hot peppers and tomatoes thrived, destined to become the focal point of Spanish cooking. Already almond groves proliferated, introduced by the Romans and loved by the Moors, plus sugar cane, oranges, grapes and saffron. Dried beans, some native others imported, began to make a significant contribution to the diet. The simple cuisine of roasted meats, of grilled seafoods, of *ollas* (stewpots) filled with game and local *verduras* (leafy vegetables) incorporated the new ingredients to begin the evolution of the cuisine that continues today as classic Spanish cooking.

WHAT IS SPANISH CUISINE?

The rocky hillsides of greyish soil and sparse vegetation in many parts of the country are more conducive to the growing of olive trees and grapes, the grazing of sheep and goats than the fattening of beef cattle or growing of cultivated crops. The high plains are subject to vast climatic changes from winter through summer, so crops have been tailored to suit the conditions. Here the rural landscape is dominated by row upon row of smiling sungold faces of sunflowers, expansive acreages of wind-riffled wheat and vast crops of onions and garlic. What animals are reared, mostly pigs and calves, are killed for the kitchen while small and usually cooked simply by roasting or braising.

Availability of ingredients always dictates the development of a cuisine, so we see quite different emphasis in the various provinces of Spain. The coastal regions enjoy an abundance of seafood in immense variety. To the north, there are large cold-water fish, eels, gigantic crabs and a wealth of mollusks. The Mediterranean provinces have an equally delicious choice — red mullet, crayfish, mussels and much more. The Spanish are inordinately fond of *embutidos*, all kinds of cured pork. The prime choice is *jamón de Jabugo*, an air-cured ham similar to the Italian prosciutto or Parma ham. It is sliced to stuff into crisp rolls, nibbled in *tapa* bars and introduced into all kinds of cooked dishes. *Jamón ibérico*, the native black pig, once provided most of the pork, and makes the finest of ham. Today's heavy demand has meant cross-breeding to meet requirements, and quality is maintained by a strictly applied award of *denominaciones de origen* introduced by the Ministry of Agriculture. *Chorizo*, a spicy cured sausage heavily impregnated with paprika and garlic, is eaten like salami or simmered in stews, or with rice and beans to bring its unique flavor to the dish. The best and chunkiest is *chorizo de Salamanca*, with *chorizo de Pamplona* favored by those who like a finer texture. Pork is also made into many different styles of fresh sausage in the various regions, the Catalan *butifarra* being one of the best, while more substantial and intense in taste are the dark blood sausages called *morcilla* based on savory rice.

Game meats, popular since early times, continue as an important food source in Spain. Rabbits are tender and subtle of flavor. A brace of game birds — quail, pheasants, pigeons, woodcocks, partridges — are hunted for the *olla* (stewpot), with the sport so keen that signage indicating hunting restrictions is posted on most rural properties. The Spanish like adventurous combinations in their food. Meats are mixed with poultry or game birds, or with seafood. Eggs are added to a meat or fish dish. Sweet fruity tastes are found in savory sauces. Spicy chili, pungent cumin introduced by the Moors, and wondrously fragrant saffron insinuate themselves onto the palate in many dishes. The Spanish love of garlic, and of peppers sweet and hot, red and green, transcends all regional differences. Their enthusiastic use in so many different dishes, with such surprising variation in taste and effect, is what above all gives Spanish food its national character. It is a down-to-earth cuisine, based on good basic ingredients and simple preparations that should create few problems for your kitchen.

SPAIN TODAY

Present-day Spain portrays a less ostentatious image than it enjoyed in those early times. Its fortune linked with its colonial power, times changed as history intervened to sever the repressive colonial domination of foreign lands and people. Spain continued as a unified country with as disparate a group of people as any one country could boast. Throughout Spain the people, the landscape, the language and the cuisine display distinct and unique regional characteristics that we have dealt with in depth in each of the regional chapters of this book.

MADRID, LA MANCHA AND NEW CASTILE

MADRID, CASTILLA LA NUEVA Y LA MANCHA

South of Madrid is Castilla–La Mancha, the land of Don Quixote and his windmills. The knight errant has not been forgotten here, his honor preserved at a charming inn near the rural town of Puerta Lápice, where his statue in bronze presides over a courtyard and tavern little changed from the time Cervantes took inspiration for his great tale there. Some of the silo-shaped, whitewashed windmills remain. A few are entrusted to the state as museums and others house restaurants on the tourist route, but most have crumbled, like the dreams of Cervantes' hero, into the dust of this bleak landscape. La Mancha is the land the Arabs described as Al Manchara, dry and flat. It's over 1200 feet above sea level, windswept and extreme in climate, with blistering summer heat and biting winter cold. It's a land of vast fields of wheat, of sunflowers, of green and luscious crops under heavy irrigation, of purple-hued saffron crocus fields as far as the eye can see, and of enormous flocks of goats and sheep.

The province of Toledo, just south of Madrid, is the region that most typifies La Mancha. The old city of Toledo, fortified by wall and river bend, is now the crafts center of Spain — home of silversmiths, swordsmiths, woodworkers and metal-workers, and artists following the tradition of El Greco. It is a city where one enters a time warp, for building regulations are such that all inner-city construction must be of the old style. The narrow, cobbled streets wind past buildings completed four hundred years ago, abutting ones finished only months ago; you can hardly tell which is which. Here you can look through darkened doorways into dusty workshops where lutes are lovingly shaped by octogenarians, or into the studio of a young artist glazing pottery in revolutionary new ways, or into a restaurant kitchen where the *cocido* bubbles, and where braces of *perdices* and *conejo* hang near the chimney. La Mancha is partridge country and Toledo restaurants offer them in endless different ways, one of the classics a simple braised dish in thin gravy with the slight tartness of cabbage and onions. The birds are also marinated and simmered in vinegar, *en escabeche*, to serve hot or cold.

Ciudad Real sweeps south to the Sierra Morena, with Andalusia on its southern slopes. Its heart is the wine town of Valdepeñas, where the wines are as straight-forward as the people who make them. Cuenca to the southeast makes little of a culinary contribution, but its cliff-hanging houses enthrall the visitor.

Guadalajara sounds as romantic as it looks. It is a land of medieval castles perched high on craggy mountains, of ancient villages tucked into the hillsides. Its cooking, too, is the simple style of old, food of the hunters and shepherds.

The harsh climate has created an uncomplicated cuisine, distinct in flavor, sustaining and satisfying, food they call *fuerte* — which translates as "strong" or "bold." There are nose-teasing, hearty stews of meat from the trap with beans and root vegetables, going under names like *gachas*, *galianos* or *gazpachos* (pluralized *gazpacho* means a game soup-stew, not Andalusia's famous cold soup). *Migas* is yesterday's coarse bread fried in olive oil with salt pork and sausages, and of course garlic. Roast meats emerge fragrant from brick ovens to eat with *pisto*, a dish of braised peppers, tomatoes, aubergine (eggplant) and zucchini (courgette) akin to the Catalan *samfaina*, but derived from the Moorish *alboronia*, the *chakchouka* of North Africa.

There are strongly flavored cheeses like the grandmother of them all, *queso manchego*, to eat with wines of Valdepeñas. There is the bold taste of *bacalao*, the nuttiness of *garbanzos*, the gaminess of wild birds and rabbit. There are sweets around which legends have been built. *Mazapán de Toledo* is said to have originated in the 13th century, when nuns of the San Clemente convent faced the prospect of a bread shortage by improvising small loaves from ground almonds and sugar syrup. This original marzipan proved to be too firm and rich to enjoy as a staple, but it tasted wonderful — so the convent adopted a tradition of training its nuns to cook *mazapán*. Toledo is still Spain's major producer, molding it in a host of different classic shapes from bite-size nuggets to gigantic serpents and mythical beasts. The *mazapán* is quickly baked in a very hot brick oven, then glazed with a sugar syrup, while tracings of white sugar frosting decorate the larger forms. Other lighter-than-air confections enjoyed in these parts are *roscos*, doughnutlike cakes that may be plain or frosted, unfilled or dripping with a creamy filling, and *flores manchegos*, which are enormous "flowers" of a thin batter that is cooked on a hot oiled iron. They are dredged with fine sugar which, coupled with their own fragility, makes them a challenge to eat.

Reigning over this region is Spain's capital, Madrid, an autonomous region of its own, and home to a massive population whose chief concern, it would seem, is eating. From *churros* and coffee for *desayuno* (breakfast) to that last cup of hot chocolate on the way home late in the evening, life seems to be dominated by the table. And what magic comes from the kitchens of this stylish city. Almost four hundred years ago Madrid began to earn her reputation as a culinary mecca. Resident royalty demanded the best, importing some of the finest European chefs to prepare it. From early times taverns and high-class restaurants flourished, listing ingredients and dishes from all over the country on their menus. Beside their own classics of *cocido madrileño* and the supreme tripe dish, *callos a la madrileña*, are *parrilladas* of meat or shellfish and *zarzuela* from Catalonia. There are superb *paellas* to rival any from Valencia, and *cochinillo asado* in the style of Sepúlveda and Segovia. Cascades of the freshest of seafoods, like classic still-life paintings of a forgotten age, tempt eye and palate from icy display cases. Hams deck the ceilings of *tascas*; delicatessens lure with jars of white asparagus, cheeses in myriad shapes and tastes, *chorizo* and *salchichón* from every part of the country, tubs of olives, jars of oil. The bars are smoky, lively, always packed. The *tapas* of Madrid are legendary. Some specialize in just a few items done superbly; others go for the big impact, one restaurant listing almost eighty different types. The old section of the city has the sort of atmosphere that lures tourists all through the year, with narrow streets of tiny old-world shops, butchers and egg merchants, *pastelerías* and stationers, barbers and tobacconists. Bars and restaurants are everywhere, spilling onto the sidewalks of cobbled streets, encroaching into lanes, facing onto impressive squares thronged with people. The air is heady with food smells, exhaust fumes, all-pervading cigarette smoke and spirited conversation. Here you may eat a *plato del día* (plate of the day) of steak, eggs and chips, of rice and grilled lamb, of veal stew and rice for a few pesetas — *cocina típico*, local specialties at a casual outdoor restaurant. Or perhaps you'd prefer to go to one of the city's many quality restaurants, tucked away from the hubbub of everyday. Behind closed doors in elegant settings, discreet waiters offer the finest of Spanish wines, magnificent classic dishes and elegant *nueva cocina*, the new wave of Spanish cooking.

SOPA DE PATATAS Y ALMENDRAS
LEEK AND POTATO SOUP WITH ALMONDS · SERVES 4

3 medium potatoes, peeled and cubed (about 1 lb/500 g)

4 cups/1 l/1 qt water

salt

2 slices white bread, crusts trimmed

$2\frac{1}{2}$ tablespoons ground blanched almonds/almond meal

$1\frac{1}{2}$ cups/400 ml/13 fl oz chilled chicken stock

2 leeks (white parts only), rinsed and chopped

1 tablespoon unsalted butter

white pepper

4 sprigs dill or mint

1 tablespoon chopped toasted almonds

Boil the potatoes in the water with a little salt until very tender. Drain, reserving 2 cups (500 ml/16 fl oz) of the liquid. Soak the bread and almond meal in the stock to soften. Cover and refrigerate. Sauté the leeks in butter for 1 minute, then cover and cook very gently for about 10 minutes or until tender. Purée the potato in a food processor and remove. Purée the leeks, bread and almond meal; do not overprocess. Add to the potato purée with the chicken stock and season to taste with salt and pepper. Pour into soup bowls and garnish with herbs and the chopped nuts. Serve chilled.

SOPA DE AJO
GARLIC SOUP

SERVES 6

This simple soup is one of the foundation stones of the Spanish cuisine. In its most basic domestic form, *sopa de ajo* began as a concoction of crushed garlic, crumbled stale bread and olive oil in hot water, but it has evolved to encompass many regional and individual interpretations. While the original is to many still the only way to cook it, being great for warming and cleansing the blood, combating colds and aiding the digestion, in different hands *sopa de ajo* becomes a masterpiece of subtlety and blending of flavors. Madrileños like it with paprika. In coastal Málaga a fish stock is the base. In Navarre a gelatinous stock made from a calf's foot gives an added richness and roundness of flavor. The mixture can be liquid, or thick and dryish. The bread can be soggy or crisp. You can add a tomato if you like. I enjoy it with a coating of egg.

8 cloves garlic, peeled

$\frac{1}{4}$ cup/60 ml/2 fl oz olive oil

8 very thin slices coarse country-style bread, crusts trimmed

$1\frac{1}{2}$ teaspoons sweet paprika

6 cups/1.5 l/1$\frac{1}{2}$ qt veal or chicken stock

salt and pepper

3 eggs

chopped parsley

Fry the whole garlic cloves in oil until they are very well colored and the flavor has impregnated the oil, then discard. Fry the bread until crisp. Remove and set aside. Add paprika to the oil and fry briefly, then add the stock, salt and pepper and bring to a boil. Break up the bread, return to the soup and simmer for about 10 minutes. Transfer to an ovenproof serving dish. Beat the eggs and pour slowly into the soup without stirring; they should rise to the surface. Place in a preheated 450°F/220°C/Gas 8 oven until the eggs have cooked to a firm layer on top. Sprinkle parsley on top and serve at once.

Variation: If preferred, transfer the soup to individual covered ramekins and break a whole egg into each. Cook in the oven until the eggs are firm. Alternatively, stir beaten egg into the soup to give the soup a creamy consistency.

Gazpachos Manchegos
GAME HOTPOT

SERVES 6

Nothing at all like the cold pepper and tomato soup of Andalusia, the *gazpachos* (plural) of the central plains is a meat or game soup with mild mushrooms, herbs and saffron. *Torta*, an unleavened flour and water bread cooked on a hot stone, is its traditional partner. Half is crumbled into the pot, the rest torn into pieces and dunked into the broth. A coarse country-style bread can replace it.

1 young hare or rabbit, cleaned

salt and pepper

$\frac{1}{2}$ cup/60 g/2 oz all-purpose (plain) flour

$\frac{1}{2}$ cup/120 ml/4 fl oz olive oil

2 medium onions, chopped

1 cup/90 g/3 oz wild mushrooms, sliced (optional)

6 cloves garlic, chopped

3 oz/90 g smoked or cured ham, finely diced

1 large tomato, peeled, seeded and chopped

1 large green bell pepper (capsicum), seeded and cut into strips

6 cups/1.5 l/1½ qt water

2 sprigs thyme

2 sprigs rosemary

1-inch/2.5-cm cinnamon stick

12 saffron threads

Cut the hare or rabbit into chunks or bite-sized pieces and season with salt and pepper. Coat lightly with flour and fry in oil until evenly colored. Push to one side. Fry the onions until colored, then the mushrooms (if used) with garlic for 2 minutes. Add ham, tomato and peppers and fry for 2 to 3 minutes, then add the meat, herbs and cinnamon with additional salt and pepper. Bring to a boil, cover and simmer for 2 hours, adding extra water as needed. Grind saffron with 2 tablespoons of the hot broth and add to the pot.

Variation: Substitute a mixture of small birds and rabbit for the hare.

Torta

4 cups/500 g/1 lb all-purpose (plain) flour

1 teaspoon salt

Mix flour and salt with enough cold water to make a soft but not sticky dough. Knead into a smooth, round shape. Cook on a preheated hot metal oven plate or on top of an electric griddle on a very low setting until cooked through, about 45 minutes. Tear half the bread into small pieces and add to the soup, break the remainder to serve on the side.

Cocido Madrileño

MADRID HOTPOT   SERVES 8–10

This classic dish is loved by the Madrileños. Like all *cocidos*, it is now more commonly a *pueblo* (village) dish, the housewife putting it on in the *olla* to cook as she goes about her domestic chores. There are many different types of *cocido* or "one-pot" dishes. In Catalonia a similar hearty one-pot meal is known as *escudella de pagès*, and in Galicia as *caldo gallego*. The classic from La Mancha, beloved of Don Quixote and his faithful companion Sancho Panza, is known as *olla podrida*. The meal is served as three separate courses: the rice or noodle soup, the meats over the beans, and cabbage and sausage on the side. For special occasions, tiny meat dumplings may also be added to the pot.

1½ cups/270 g/9 oz dried garbanzos (chickpeas), soaked overnight

6 oz/180 g smoked bacon

1 pig's foot/trotter

4 x 2-inch/5-cm pieces veal or beef shank/shin (about 1 lb/500 g)

1 stewing chicken (boiling hen)

4 oz/120 g salted *tocino* or cured ham

4 oz/120 g *morcilla* or blood sausage

1 bay leaf

1 bouquet garni (bunch of mixed dried herbs)

12 cups/3⅓ l/3 qt water

4 potatoes, peeled and cubed

2 leeks, cleaned and sliced

3 carrots, peeled and thickly sliced

2 medium turnips, peeled and cubed

½ cup/90 g/3 oz short-grain/round white rice or broken fine egg noodles (vermicelli)

salt and pepper

10 oz/300 g *chorizo* sausages

3 cups/300 g/10 oz chopped cabbage

2 tablespoons olive oil

Drain garbanzos and place in a very large pot. Cut bacon into 3 pieces. Blanch pig's foot, shank and chicken quickly in boiling water, drain and add to the pot with the *tocino, morcilla* and herbs. Add the water, bring to a boil, reduce heat and simmer for 4 hours. Add potatoes, leeks, carrots and turnips and simmer another 40 minutes.

Remove and debone the meat. Cut all the meat into slices or bite-sized cubes. Strain 6 cups of the soup into another pan and add the rice or noodles, bring to a boil and simmer for about 25 minutes or until very tender (pasta will take less time). Add salt and pepper to taste. Return sliced meat to the pot and season.

Prick the sausages with a skewer to prevent their skin from bursting. In another pot cook the sausage and cabbage with 1 cup water for 6 to 8 minutes over medium heat. Drain and slice the sausage. Heat the olive oil and fry sausage and cabbage for 2 to 3 minutes, then season to taste.

To serve, pile the garbanzos into a deep serving dish with the vegetables. Arrange the sliced meats on top. Pour on remaining broth. Serve the rice or noodle broth as the first course, the garbanzos and meat, and the sautéed sausage and cabbage as the main courses. A spicy garlic and tomato sauce can be served on the side (see page 274).

Callos a la Madrileña

TRIPE MADRID STYLE

SERVES 4–6 (*TAPA*)

Callos a la madrileña is popular as a *tapa* in Madrid, where it is served in small dishes to be eaten on little wooden picks. Like the Chinese, the Spanish sensibly add complex flavors and plenty of spiciness to tripe dishes, making them tempting enough to lure even the most dedicated avoiders of offal dishes.

1 lb/500 g veal shank/shin

1 pig's foot/trotter

1 bay leaf

2 medium onions, chopped

6 whole black peppercorns

1 whole clove

1½ lb/750 g tripe

3 cloves garlic, sliced

2 tablespoons olive oil

6 oz/180 g *chorizo* sausage, sliced

2 oz/60 g *tocino* or other cured ham

1 tablespoon sweet paprika

1 cup/250 ml/8 fl oz dry white wine

2 teaspoons tomato paste

1 fresh hot red chili pepper, seeded and chopped

1 sprig fresh thyme

1 sprig fresh parsley

1 *morcilla* or other blood sausage, about 3 oz/90 g, sliced

Blanch the veal and pig's foot in boiling water and drain. Place in a large pan and cover with water. Add the bay leaf and half the onion, the peppercorns, clove and tripe. Bring to a boil, reduce heat and simmer, partially covered, for 2 hours. Strain the stock into another pan. Remove meat from the veal shank and cut into small pieces. Set aside. Cut tripe into 1½-inch/5-cm squares. Place the shank bone and pig's foot in the stock and add the tripe. Sauté the remaining onion and the garlic in the oil for 2 to 3 minutes, add the *chorizo* and *tocino* and fry for another 2 to 3 minutes. Add the paprika and cook for a few seconds, then add the wine and tomato paste. Stir to mix well, then pour over the tripe and add the chili and herbs. Cover and simmer for 1 hour.

Remove the shank bones and discard. Remove the pig's foot, scrape off skin and cut the meat into small pieces. Return shank and pork to the pan and add the *morcilla* sausage. Simmer for another hour, or until the tripe is very tender. Add salt and pepper to taste. Serve hot.

Albóndigas de Ternera con Salsa de Tomate

VEAL MEATBALLS IN TOMATO SAUCE · SERVES 4 (*TAPA*)

4 oz/120 g lean veal, diced

2 oz/60 g chopped ham

2 oz/60 g chopped salted *tocino* or smoked bacon

pinch each of salt, pepper and nutmeg

2 eggs*

2 tablespoons all-purpose (plain) flour

1 cup/120 g/4 oz fine dry breadcrumbs (optional)

1 cup/250 ml/8 fl oz olive oil

1 recipe fresh tomato sauce (page 274)

Place the meats with seasonings in a food processor and grind to a smooth paste. Add 1 egg and process briefly, then form into small balls and coat lightly with flour. Dip into beaten egg and roll in breadcrumbs, if used. Fry in the oil until golden brown and cooked through. Drain. Heat the tomato sauce, add the meatballs and serve.

*Only one egg is needed if the meatballs are not to be coated with crumbs.

Sesos en Adobo

MARINATED BRAINS · SERVES 4 (*TAPA*)

Tender lambs' brains steeped in a wine marinade are served on toothpicks as a *tapa*. Little chunks of liver can be done in the same way, simmered in the marinade as below and then sautéed in oil.

12 oz/375 g lambs' brains

1 cup/250 ml/8 fl oz water

½ cup/120 ml/4 fl oz dry white wine

1 tablespoon white wine vinegar

1 bay leaf

1 medium onion, thinly sliced

1 small carrot, peeled and sliced

1 clove garlic, slivered

3 black peppercorns, cracked

1 large dill pickle (gherkin), sliced

Place the brains in a saucepan with cold water to cover and bring to a boil. Remove from the heat and allow to cool to room temperature. Drain the brains, pick off any fragments of skin and cut each brain into quarters. Place in a non-aluminum saucepan and add the 1 cup water and remaining ingredients. Set aside for 20 minutes, then bring to a boil and simmer for 2 minutes. Again allow to cool in the liquid. When cold, remove with a slotted spoon and place on a plate of shredded lettuce. Pierce each with a toothpick on which is a sliver of dill pickle.

Albóndigas de Ternera con Salsa de Tomate (left), opposite; Roscos (bottom left), p.30; the other dishes are rice soup, cabbage and sausage, and a side dish of spicy tomato sauce

Chanfaina a la Castellana (top), p.29; Pisto Castellano (front), p.22

CROQUETAS DE BACALAO

SALT COD CROQUETTES   MAKES ABOUT 30 (*TAPA*)

Popular throughout Spain and equally in Portugal, these tasty little bites of *bacalao* are served by the portion on small plates in *tapas* bars. They are best straight from the oil, when they will be crisp on the surface and delectably tender inside. Nowadays many *taberna* proprietors enjoy the convenience of microwave heating — sadly to the detriment of many of their dishes, this one, I think, included.

1 lb/500 g prepared *bacalao*
(page 266)

1 cup/250 ml/8 fl oz milk

1 lb/500 g potatoes, peeled and cubed

salt

$\frac{1}{4}$ cup parsley leaves

1 small onion, peeled and quartered

2 cloves garlic, peeled

white pepper

2 cups/250 g/8 oz fine dry breadcrumbs

deep frying oil

Place the *bacalao* in a saucepan with the milk and enough water to just cover. Bring to a boil and simmer for 8 to 12 minutes or until the fish is very tender. Drain, reserving the liquid. Flake the fish with a fork, discarding skin and bones. In the meantime, boil the potatoes in lightly salted water until very tender. Drain. In a food processor chop the parsley finely, add onion and garlic and chop finely. Add the potatoes and *bacalao* and process to a smooth paste. Add a very little of the reserved liquid if the paste is too dry. Season with pepper and check for salt. Form the mixture into walnut-sized balls and roll in breadcrumbs. Chill for 2 hours. Heat about 10 cm/ 4 inches oil in a wide pan and fry the croquettes in batches of 10 until golden brown.

GAMBAS AL PIL-PIL

SHRIMP (PRAWNS) IN SIZZLING SAUCE   SERVES 6 (*TAPA*)

A favorite dish in *tascas*, the shrimp are served in *cazuelitas* so hot that they are *pil-pileando* (sizzling) when they get to the table.

$\frac{1}{2}$ cup/120 ml/4 fl oz olive oil

2 cloves garlic, very finely chopped

1 small fresh hot red chili pepper, seeded and finely chopped

$\frac{1}{2}$ teaspoon paprika

24 fresh peeled shrimp (prawns), deveined

Heat 2 *cazuelitas* in the oven and add the oil, garlic, chili and paprika. When the oil is very hot, put in the shrimp and toss over direct heat for a few seconds. Take to the table with crusty bread, standing the hot dishes on little wooden plates to prevent damage to the table. Allow the dish to cool slightly before eating.

PISTO CASTELLANO
BRAISED PEPPERS AND AUBERGINE
SERVES 6–8

Serve with roast meats and *patatas a la panadera* straight from the baker's oven.

3 large red bell peppers (capsicum)

2 large green bell peppers (capsicums)

2 medium eggplants (aubergines)

1 medium onion, finely chopped

$\frac{1}{2}$ cup/120 ml/4 fl oz olive oil

3 cloves garlic, finely chopped

1 large sun-ripened tomato, peeled, seeded and chopped

1 teaspoon chopped fresh oregano

1 teaspoon chopped fresh thyme

$\frac{1}{2}$ teaspoon chopped fresh rosemary

salt and pepper

1 tablespoon finely chopped parsley or mint

Roast the peppers in a hot oven or over a flame until the skins are well blackened and blistered, but take care they do not become charred. Roast the eggplants in the same way until they are very soft and the skin is loose and dark. Wrap in a kitchen towel for a few minutes, then peel. Cut peppers and eggplant into wide strips. Sauté onion in the oil until golden. Add garlic and cook briefly, then add the tomato and herbs and cook for 2 to 3 minutes. Add the peppers and eggplant and cover the pan tightly. Cook very gently for about 15 minutes. Season to taste and stir in half the chopped parsley or mint. Garnish with the remainder.

PATATAS A LA PANADERA
POTATOES FROM THE BAKERY
SERVES 6–8

When a large roast is cooked in the baker's giant brick oven, there is usually a tray of potatoes roasting beside it. They can be simply rubbed with lard or meat drippings, or brushed with olive oil, roasted until the surface is crisp and golden, and then tossed with salt, finely chopped garlic, pepper and paprika. Or they can be done in this delicious way.

6 very large potatoes, peeled

1 medium onion, very thinly sliced

$\frac{1}{2}$ cup/120 ml/4 fl oz olive oil

$\frac{3}{4}$ cup/180 g/6 oz butter (optional)

2–4 cloves garlic, slivered

1 bay leaf

$\frac{3}{4}$ teaspoon dried thyme, crushed

1 teaspoon sweet paprika

salt and pepper

1 cup/250 ml/8 fl oz beef or veal stock

Thinly slice the potatoes and layer in a greased baking dish with the onion. Mix the oil and melted butter, if used, with the garlic, bay leaf, thyme, paprika, salt and pepper and pour evenly over the potatoes. Pour the stock down the side of the dish so it does not disturb the seasonings. Cover and bake in a preheated 375°F/190°C/ Gas 5 oven for about 1 hour, or bake covered for 40 minutes, uncover and cook until the potatoes are tender and the tops are crisped and brown.

Cebollitas Con Pasas
BABY ONIONS WITH RAISINS   SERVES 4

These little glazed onions, cooked with raisins until almost caramelized, are a superb accompaniment to roasted meats.

$1\frac{1}{2}$ lb/750 g small onions, peeled

2 medium tomatoes, chopped

$\frac{1}{2}$ cup/120 ml/4 fl oz red wine vinegar

$\frac{1}{3}$ cup/90 g/3 oz sugar

$\frac{3}{4}$ cup/110 g/$3\frac{1}{2}$ oz raisins

1 bouquet garni

$\frac{1}{4}$ cup/60 ml/2 fl oz virgin olive oil (or butter)

salt and pepper

Combine all ingredients in a casserole. Cover and cook in a 350°F/180°C/Gas 4 oven for 1 hour, stirring from time to time and adding a little extra liquid if needed.

Pollo en Escabeche
MARINATED CHICKEN   SERVES 4–6

The Arabs left many artistic and culinary legacies in Spain. Among them was the technique of *escabeche*, which comes from an old Persian word for "pickle" or "acidulate". The Spanish originally used it to preserve fish and small marinated fish; *sardinas en escabeche* (see *Tapas*) are still one of the most popular *tapas*. But they tried *escabeche* also with great success on small game birds, and in the following way on chicken. It features on the menu in many restaurants in Madrid, although it is more a specialty of northern Old Castile. Use any prepared game bird, such as pheasant, guinea fowl or partridge, in the same way.

3 lb/1.5-kg chicken

$\frac{1}{4}$ cup/60 ml/2 fl oz olive oil

3 cloves garlic, peeled

1 teaspoon black peppercorns

1 bay leaf, crumbled

1 teaspoon salt

$2\frac{1}{2}$ cups/650 ml/21 fl oz dry white wine

$\frac{3}{4}$ cup/180 ml/6 fl oz white wine or cider vinegar

1 lemon, sliced

Cut the chicken into 4 pieces. Dry with paper towels and fry in the oil until lightly colored without allowing the surface to become crusty. Transfer to a non-aluminum pan and add the remaining ingredients. Bring just to a boil, then reduce heat to very low and simmer for at least 1 hour. Allow to cool, then place in an earthenware or glass dish, cover with plastic wrap and chill. Serve cold with a little of the cooking liquid.

SALMOREJO DE PERDIZ A LA TOLEDANA
PARTRIDGE BREASTS IN EGG CUSTARD   SERVES 4

The *salmorejo* of Toledo is a creamy custard partridge pâté that is served with roasted partridge breasts. But *salmorejo* also describes a tart sauce of vinegar, pepper and oil, and the thick puréed *gazpacho* typical of Córdoba. Nor should it be confused with the dishes called *al salmorrejo* of Aragón, which include several fascinating combinations of local sausages and ham, eggs and asparagus or other vegetables.

4 small oven-ready partridges

salt

1 small onion, quartered

1 small carrot, peeled

1 bay leaf

1 sprig fresh thyme

3 eggs, beaten

pinch of freshly grated nutmeg

pepper

1 tablespoon olive oil

1 small onion, very finely chopped

4 sets partridge giblets

1 cup/250 ml/8 fl oz dry white wine

pinch of chopped fresh thyme

1 teaspoon chopped parsley

Remove the full breast and wing sections from the birds, then slice off the wings. Skin and bone the wings, chop the meat and set aside. Lightly sprinkle the breasts with salt and place skin on a rack in a roasting pan. Set aside. Remove legs and thighs; skin, bone, chop and mix with the wing meat. Place carcasses in a pan with a large pinch of salt. Cover with cold water. Add the quartered onion, carrot, bay leaf and thyme and bring to a boil. Simmer for 20 minutes, then strain the stock; set aside.

Purée the chopped leg and wing meat in a food processor, adding 1 cup/250 ml/8 fl oz of the stock. Add the eggs and nutmeg and season with salt and pepper. Pour into a greased baking dish and set in a roasting pan with warm water to come halfway up the sides of the dish. Place in a preheated 400°F/200°C/Gas 6 oven with the breasts and cook for about 20 minutes or until the breasts are cooked and the custard is set. Remove from the oven and keep warm.

Sauté the chopped onion in the oil and reserved giblets in the roasting pan until well browned. Add the wine, $\frac{1}{2}$ cup/120 ml/4 fl oz reserved stock and the thyme. Season with salt and pepper. Boil briskly until well reduced. Arrange the breasts on the custard, pour the sauce over or serve separately. Garnish with parsley.

PERDICES ESTOFADAS A LA TOLEDANA
CASSEROLED PARTRIDGE TOLEDO STYLE   SERVES 4

2 good-sized oven-ready partridges

2 cloves garlic, chopped

salt

½ cup/120 ml/4 fl oz olive oil

1 tablespoon butter

1 large onion, finely chopped

¾ cup/60 g/2 oz chopped cabbage

½ cup/120 ml/4 fl oz dry white wine

large pinch each of ground cinnamon, oregano and paprika

½ teaspoon black pepper

1 teaspoon mild mustard

1 tablespoon sherry vinegar

2 slices white bread, crusts trimmed

oil for frying

Cut the partridges in halves. Grind garlic and salt together and rub into the birds. Brown the partridge in a *cazuela* in the oil and butter. Add the onion and brown well. Add cabbage, wine, spices, pepper and mustard and stew gently for 1 hour. Add vinegar and cook briefly, then add water as needed to make a sauce. Check seasoning, adding salt and pepper to taste. Cut the bread into triangles and fry in the oil until golden. Serve the partridge with the fried bread. A casserole of baby onions often accompanies this dish.

CAPÓN RELLENO CON ALCACHOFAS
CAPON STUFFED WITH ARTICHOKES AND MEATS   SERVES 8

1 capon or plump chicken, about 4½ lb/2.1 kg

12 oz/380 g finely ground (minced) veal

12 oz/380 g finely ground (minced) pork

1 small onion, finely chopped

1 clove garlic, finely chopped

1 tablespoon olive oil

6 pitted prunes, soaked in 2 tablespoons dry sherry

8 cooked/canned baby artichokes, quartered

salt and pepper

1 egg

⅓ teaspoon dried oregano

⅓ teaspoon dried thyme

Bone the capon or chicken and finely chop any loose pieces of meat, plus the meat from the drumsticks. Mix with the other ground meats. Sauté the onion and garlic in olive oil until softened. Mix with the meats. Drain and roughly chop the prunes. Add prunes, sherry, artichokes, salt and pepper, egg and herbs to the meats and mix thoroughly. Stuff the boned birds with the mixture and secure the opening with thin metal skewers.

Place on a rack in a roasting pan and add 1 cup water. Roast in a preheated 350°F/180°C/Gas 4 oven for 1 hour without turning. Increase the heat to 395°F/190°C/Gas 5 and roast a further 20 minutes, basting several times. Let stand for 10 to 12 minutes before slicing thickly, or allow to cool and chill to firm up, then slice thinly to serve with salads.

COCIDO DE TERNERA CON GUISANTES

BOILED VEAL WITH PEAS
SERVES 6–8

The Spanish, I have found, have a fondness for peas, a vegetable that we do not often include in our meat dishes. When I discovered this recipe I almost decided to exclude it from this book as I judged, untried, that it would be dull beyond belief. I was unexpectedly surprised at the depth of flavor that comes from the peas and carrots and the exquisite texture and tenderness of the meat. It has become a family favorite.

4-lb/2-kg veal roast, preferably shoulder

salt

$\frac{1}{2}$ cup/120 ml/4 fl oz olive oil

1 large onion, chopped

1 large carrot, peeled and diced

6–8 cloves garlic, chopped

2-inch/5-cm cinnamon stick

1–2 bay leaves

$\frac{1}{2}$–1 teaspoon black peppercorns

2 medium tomatoes, peeled and chopped

$1\frac{1}{2}$ cups/400 ml/13 fl oz dry white wine

$1\frac{1}{2}$ cups/400 ml/13 fl oz veal stock or water

1 teaspoon chopped thyme

2 teaspoons chopped parsley

2 cups/350 g/12 oz green peas

cornstarch/cornflour

Trim the roast and rub with salt. Brown well in the oil, then remove. Brown the onion and carrot well, then add the garlic and cook briefly. Return the roast and add the spices, tomatoes, wine, stock and herbs. Bring to a boil. Reduce heat, cover and simmer for about 2 hours or until the veal is very tender, turning occasionally.

Boil peas separately in lightly salted water; drain. Remove the meat and set aside, keeping warm. Boil the sauce briskly to reduce, thickening if needed with cornstarch mixed with cold water. Adjust seasoning and add the peas to the sauce. Slice meat and arrange on a serving plate; pour the sauce over.

Variation: This is equally delicious with sliced asparagus, green beans or baby artichokes instead of peas.

CHULETAS DE TERNERA A LA CASTELLANA

VEAL CUTLETS CASTILIAN STYLE
SERVES 4

3 cloves garlic, mashed

12 small veal cutlets

salt and pepper

1 tablespoon olive oil

Spread the garlic evenly over the cutlets, then season with salt and pepper. Brush lightly with olive oil. Arrange on a rack in a roasting pan. Roast in a 450°F/230°C/Gas 6 oven for 10 minutes, then turn and roast the other side until cooked to preference. Separately roast small cubes of potato with plenty of pan drippings and serve with the cutlets, with *pisto manchego* on the side.

CORDERO ASADO A LA MANCHEGA
ROAST BABY LAMB

SERVES 6

Whole baby lamb is traditionally spit roasted, or cooked over a fire of dried vine shoots in the huge brick ovens of the local bakery. This works equally well in a domestic oven.

5- to 6-lb/2.5- to 3-kg prepared baby lamb*

salt and pepper

$\frac{1}{2}$ cup/120 g/4 oz softened lard

2 cups/500 ml/16 fl oz dry white wine

3 bay leaves

2–3 sprigs fresh thyme or rosemary

4 cloves garlic, chopped

1 medium onion, finely chopped

1 tablespoon all-purpose (plain) flour

2 tablespoons cognac or dry sherry

1 cup/250 ml/8 fl oz veal stock

1 tablespoon chopped parsley

Rub lamb with salt, pepper and softened lard. Place on a low rack in a baking pan and roast in a preheated 400°F/200°C/Gas 6 oven for 20 minutes. Add the wine, herbs, garlic and onion and roast at 375°F/190°C/Gas 5 for a further 25 to 40 minutes, basting frequently with the pan juices. Check for doneness by piercing the thigh with a skewer; it should insert easily, with only thin, clear juices escaping.

Remove meat from the pan and keep warm. Remove the rack and place pan on the heat. Skim off fat and simmer the pan liquids to reduce, if necessary. Sprinkle in the flour and scrape up all of the pan drippings. Add cognac and cook over high heat, stirring, for a few seconds, then add the veal stock and enough water to make gravy to taste. Adjust seasoning; strain. Add the parsley. Carve the lamb at the table, serving the gravy separately.

*Have your butcher supply a whole baby lamb split underneath along its length so it can be spread flat to cook. Otherwise use one or two legs of lamb, deboned and spread flat.

Tip: Roast whole small eggplants (aubergines), small red or green bell peppers (capsicums) and peeled onions in the pan or separately to serve with the lamb.

ATASCABURROS
CASSEROLE OF RABBIT

SERVES 4

2½-lb/1.2-kg oven-ready rabbit

black pepper

½ cup/60 g/2 oz all-purpose (plain) flour

¼ cup/60 ml/2 fl oz olive oil or softened lard

1 medium onion, thickly sliced

2 whole heads garlic, unpeeled

5 large sun-ripened tomatoes, peeled, seeded and chopped

1 cup/250 ml/8 fl oz dry white wine

2 tablespoons cognac or dry sherry (optional)

2 bay leaves

1 sprig each fresh thyme and oregano

2-inch/5-cm cinnamon stick

1 teaspoon salt

1½ teaspoons sweet paprika

Cut the rabbit into serving pieces, season with pepper and coat with flour. Fry in the olive oil in a *cazuela* or other heatproof casserole until well colored. Remove and keep warm. Fry the onion with whole unpeeled garlic for 3 to 4 minutes, then add the tomatoes, wine and cognac and bring to a boil. Simmer until the liquid is well reduced. Return the meat with bay leaves, herbs, cinnamon, salt and paprika. Add water to barely cover and bring to a boil. Cover and simmer over low heat or in a preheated 350°F/180°C/Gas 4 oven for about 1½ hours until the meat is very tender, stirring from time to time. Remove garlic before serving.

Tip: Cooking this dish in advance and reheating when needed brings out extra flavor. Beef or a small leg of lamb can be substituted for rabbit.

A dried hot red chili gives the flavor added emphasis.

GARBANZOS A LA MADRILEÑA
GARBANZOS (CHICKPEAS) WITH CHORIZO

SERVES 4–6

1½ cups/270 g/9 oz dried garbanzos (chickpeas), soaked overnight

2 medium onions, chopped

4 cloves garlic, minced

1 teaspoon baking soda (bicarbonate of soda)

12 oz/350 g *chorizo* sausage, sliced

2 tablespoons olive oil

2 teaspoons chopped parsley or other fresh herbs

salt and pepper

Drain garbanzos. Place in a saucepan with half the onion and garlic, the baking soda and 4 cups (1 l/1 qt) water. Bring to a boil, reduce heat and cook uncovered over very low heat for about 3 hours or until the garbanzos feel tender but not mushy when squeezed between finger and thumb; cooking time can vary widely depending on the age of the beans, so check after 2 hours. Drain well.

Sauté remaining onion and garlic in the olive oil for 3 to 4 minutes, then add chickpeas and chorizo and sauté a further 2 to 3 minutes. Add parsley with salt and pepper to taste. Serve hot.

Variation: This dish is quite delicious with 1 cup/120 g/ 4 oz chopped spinach added after the onions have been sautéed.

CHANFAINA A LA CASTELLANA
PIG'S LIVER CASTILIAN STYLE

SERVES 4

Chanfaina is a tender stew of meat cooked in red wine. Its counterpart in Portugal is known as *chanfana*. The strong taste of pig's liver goes well this way. Traditionally, this style of *chanfaina* contains both tender cubes of congealed pigs' blood, as well as the liver. As it's often difficult to obtain, the blood has been omitted from this recipe, although if you have access to a Chinese butcher you may find it there. If so, add some, cut into small cubes, in the last five minutes of cooking.

1¼ lb/650 g pig's liver

½ cup/120 ml/4 fl oz milk

¼ cup/60 ml/2 fl oz olive oil

1 medium onion, sliced

3 cloves garlic, chopped

2 large tomatoes, peeled, seeded and chopped

1 cup/250 ml/8 fl oz red wine

1 tablespoon sweet paprika

½ teaspoon cayenne pepper

1 bay leaf

1 beef bouillon (stock) cube

1 tablespoon red wine vinegar

2 teaspoons finely chopped parsley

Cut the liver into bite-size cubes and place in a glass dish. Pour in the milk and set aside for 20 minutes. Drain the liver and dry with paper towels. Fry in the oil to seal all surfaces. Push to one side and sauté the onion and garlic in the oil until softened but not colored. Remove from the pan.

Add tomatoes and cook for about 8 minutes. Return the liver and onions and add the wine, paprika, cayenne, bay leaf and crumbled bouillon cube and cook over moderate heat for about 15 minutes. Sprinkle on red wine vinegar and parsley before serving.

TORTILLA CAPUCHINA
OMELETTE WITH ASPARAGUS AND POTATOES

SERVES 4

2 medium potatoes, peeled and sliced

1 medium onion, thinly sliced

3 tablespoons olive oil

1 cup/60 g/2 oz fresh breadcrumbs made from country-style bread

8 slender fresh asparagus stalks, cooked and chopped*

salt and pepper

5 eggs, beaten

Sauté potatoes and onion in 2 tablespoons oil until they are soft enough to break up with the edge of the spatula. Add the breadcrumbs and asparagus and mix well. Add seasonings and eggs. Lightly oil an omelette pan with remaining oil. Heat to moderately hot and pour in the mixture. Cook, gently shaking the pan and firming up the sides of the omelette with the spatula. When golden brown underneath, invert onto a plate and cook the other side. Cut into wedges to serve.

Tip: Well-drained canned asparagus pieces can be used.

Variation: A popular dish in Toledo is *tortilla a la magra*, a potato tortilla topped with a slice of grilled meat.

TORRIJAS
FRIED SUGARED BREAD

SERVES 4

$\frac{3}{4}$ cup/180 ml/6 fl oz sweet sherry or Málaga wine (or milk)

8 slices two-day-old bread, crusts trimmed

3 eggs, beaten and strained

$1\frac{1}{2}$ cups/400 ml/13 fl oz flavorless vegetable oil

$\frac{1}{2}$ cup/120 g/4 oz superfine sugar*

$1\frac{1}{2}$ teaspoons cinnamon

Sprinkle the sherry evenly over the bread and let stand for 10 minutes. Dip bread into beaten egg and fry until crisp and golden on both sides. Drain and cover with sugar and cinnamon. Serve at once.

Torrijas can be drizzled with honey instead of coating with sugar.

ROSCOS
DOUGHNUT CAKES

MAKES 24

These doughnutlike buns come in many forms. Some are fried, others baked. They may be sugar-frosted, toffee-dipped or plain.

1 cup/250 ml/8 fl oz flavorless vegetable oil

1 tablespoon aniseed

4 cups/500 g/1 lb all-purpose (plain) flour

$\frac{1}{4}$ teaspoon salt

1 cup/250 ml/8 fl oz dry white wine

$\frac{1}{3}$ cup/90 g/3 oz sugar

3 medium eggs, well beaten

confectioners' (icing) sugar or frosting (below)

Frosting:

$\frac{1}{2}$ cup/120 g/4 oz superfine sugar

2 teaspoons lemon juice

2 tablespoons water

1 egg white

1 tablespoon confectioners' (icing) sugar

Heat the oil and aniseed together in a small saucepan for 5 minutes, then let cool. Sift the flour and salt into a mixing bowl. Add the wine, aniseed oil and sugar and mix lightly. Gradually add the egg, beating with a wooden spoon to form a smooth dough. Turn out onto a lightly floured board and knead until the dough is smooth and elastic. Cover with plastic wrap and let stand for at least 2 hours. Divide into 24 pieces and roll each out into a thin sausage shape. Twist into rings and pinch the ends together. Place on a greased and floured baking sheet. Bake in a preheated 375°F/190°C/Gas 5 oven for about 20 minutes or until the buns feel dry and springy on the surface. Remove to a cake cooling rack.

Dissolve the sugar in a small saucepan with lemon juice and water. Cook until it forms a syrup, then cool. Beat the egg white until stiff, pour on the syrup in a thin stream and beat in, adding the confectioners' sugar. Spread the prepared frosting over the cakes.

MAZAPÁN DE TOLEDO

Marzipan Toledo Style   SERVES 12

1½ lb/750 g very finely ground
almonds

¾ teaspoon almond extract
(essence)

3 cups/750 g/1½ lbs superfine sugar
(preferably vanilla sugar)

3 egg whites, lightly beaten

Gently heat the almonds, almond extract and sugar together until warm enough to knead into a smooth paste. Blend in egg whites. Form into the desired shapes with the fingers or press into molds. Arrange on a greased baking sheet and bake in a preheated 300°F/150°C/Gas 2 oven until the *mazapán* feels dry.

Tip: The *mazapán* can be glazed by dipping into sugar syrup and briefly toasted under a hot grill to brown the tops.

Mazapán is also made into large shapes that are decorated with sugar frosting. Melt 1 cup/250 g/8 oz superfine sugar in a pan and when cool stir in one small egg white, stiffly beaten. Pipe onto the marzipan.

BUÑUELOS DE VIENTO

"PUFFS OF WIND"   MAKES 24

These little fritters are as lightweight as puffs of wind. They can be filled with cream or a conserve such as *membrillo* (quince) or *melocotón* (peach). They are at their best on the day they are made.

2 large eggs

½ cup/120 g/4 oz superfine sugar

2 tablespoons cold water

¼ cup/60 ml/2 oz virgin olive oil

finely grated rind and juice of ½
lemon

1½ cups/180 g/6 oz all-purpose
(plain) flour

1½ teaspoons baking powder

2 cups/500 ml/16 fl oz olive or
vegetable oil

superfine sugar or confectioners'
(icing) sugar

In a mixing bowl whisk the eggs, sugar and water together until light. Add the oil and lemon and mix in well. Sift in the flour and baking powder and stir in. Cover the bowl and set aside for 30 minutes.

Heat frying oil in a deep pan until almost smoking, then reduce heat slightly. Drop tablespoonfuls of the batter into the hot oil, no more than 5 at a time, and cook until puffed and golden brown. Turn once only, cook the other side and then remove with a slotted spoon. Drain on a rack covered with paper towels. Dust thickly with sugar.

Tip: When cold, the *buñuelos* can be slit open at one side and filled with sweetened whipped cream.

EXTREMADURA AND ANDALUSIA

EXTREMADURA Y ANDALUCÍA

Spain is a land of dramatic contrasts, and Andalusia contributes much to that image. The people are dark-eyed and feisty, vital, carefree, romantic. This is the land of the bullfight, of the *plazas de toros*, brilliant white circular constructions with red-edged balconies, of giant roadside silhouetted billboards of the black fighting bull. This is the land of the grape and olive, for little else can thrive in much of this parched region, where often the soil is better suited to baking into terracotta tiles and bricks than for the planting of seed. But olives thrive in small village landholdings and in massive plantations extending over hundreds of acres. Andalusia is today a major force in the olive oil industry, her olives — particularly meaty *manzanillas* — prized. And grapevines draw on the harsh soil to produce grapes with the distinct flavor that makes the genuine *jerez* (sherry), and drink in the strong Andalusian sunshine to turn sugary sweet for Málaga's unique *dulce de málaga* wine, the best of which is as smooth and velvety as a tokay.

Andalusia is the Spain of guidebooks — white-splashed stucco cottages hung with pots of blooming geraniums, spectacular Moorish palaces, gargantuan Christian cathedrals whose architecture shows an Islamic influence. Its cities were home to great poets and writers; people of history books like Christopher Columbus; and storybook characters like Carmen the ultimate temptress and the ghoulishly practical Barber of Seville. Andalusia is the whole of southern Spain, in it the provinces of cosmopolitan Seville, Cádiz, Huelva, Málaga, bountiful Granada, arid Almería, high-perched Jaen sloping up the Sierra Morena to meet with Castile. The gypsies are still there, bargaining cotton lace and trinkets with the tour groups, bartering armfuls of wild asparagus or a brace of trapped partridges, tending their goats near their tunnel-cave homes on the hills behind Granada's spectacular Alhambra palace. It's a place of pink-stockinged *matadores*, molded into embroidered jackets and thigh-clinging pants, of the whoosh of ruffled skirts and stamp of bootshod flamenco dancers, of guitars and song. Tourists throng to Andalusia for its famous beaches on the golden Costa del Sol, where names from travel brochures become reality — Marbella, Málaga, Torremolinos — and the seafood is exquisite.

The southern tip of Spain is so close to Morocco you feel you could almost touch it. The fullest extent of the Moorish occupation was felt here. Caliph Abd-ar-Rahman III chose Córdoba as his capital, building around him a city of such splendor that for several centuries it was considered the grande dame of Europe. He sponsored culture and learning — the enormous university of Córdoba high above the red-tiled roofs of the city continues the tradition of excellence that began there in those opulent times. He patronized the arts and architecture, giving to Spain monuments and palaces of incomparable beauty and magnificence. And he brought an exotic Arab influence to the cuisine, especially the desserts that use almonds, figs, and egg yolks by the score in caramel-rich custards they call *tocino de cielo*, translating curiously something like "bacon of the heavens." Orange groves were planted for decoration and their heady fragrance, the bitter juice of these "sevilles" flavoring sauces and savory dishes.

Sevilla is today's capital, a city of baroque charm arrayed along the banks of the Guadalquivir. Though the city is 100 miles inland, the river is wide and deep enough to allow shipping to Seville, which became a major trading port centuries ago after the discovery of the Americas and the trade that ensued. Seville is a magic city where old meets new, where nightlife never ceases, where the bustle of the *barrio de Triana*, the old gypsy quarter, contrasts with the tranquility of the river where holidaymakers paddle rowboats. Seville has a multitude of restaurants, many of them serving *tapas*, and among the best are the little *banderillas* of skewered meats or tidbits. The idea came from the Moors, a scaled-down version of their kebabs on a skewer. *Tortillas* always feature as *tapas*, and in Andalusia they have perfected the classic *tortilla española* packed with potato, but they also have one that to my taste leaves all others far behind: *tortilla andaluza de cebolla* is an almost-sweet concoction of eggs and caramelized onions. Masterful! And with tapas a glass of chilled sherry, for here it is drunk not warm as an aperitif in the English tradition, but well chilled. Sherry is used for cooking too, and many of the region's finest dishes have a sauce based on a *fino* or *amontillado* sherry. It's splashed into soups and sauces, though even better for this is a sherry vinegar of brilliant intensity. Wines too are used for cooking, the intensely flavored white Pedro Ximénez being partnered magically with sweet monkfish and raisins.

Granada has been blessed with the best of everything — its feet lapped by the Mediterranean, its head in the clouds atop the Sierra Nevada, Spain's highest mountain range. Snowcapped through winter and lushly forested in summer, it hosts that splendid home of kings, the precious jewel of craftsmanship and beauty that is the red-walled Palace of the Alhambra. The cuisine is diverse and sophisticated in its subtle blends and overtones. *Tortilla al Sacromonte* is perfection, a delicate omelette of lambs' brains and *criadillas* (testicles) served on San Cecilio's day. Further upland, Córdoba offers a menu suited to more robust tastes, of game stews and marinades, of lamb and kid — the latter cooked *al ajillo*, with masses of garlic, to drink with *montilla* wines.

Extremadura joins Andalusia where the Sierra Morena tracks westwards to Portugal, and follows the Portuguese border northwards to León, with Castile on its eastern flank. Arab influence is equally evident here in the monuments and the dishes of Badajoz. But it is also shepherd country, and many dishes created in the fields have moved to the kitchens, bearing the appelation "de pastor." There are basic bread and water soups; there are "shepherd's breadcrumbs," *migas*, crumbs from yesterday's loaf fried in olive oil and garnished with the fare at hand — a few grapes, a strip of ham, an egg. There are *calderetas*, lamb stews deliciously uncompromising, and heartwarming casseroles of beans, sausages and tripe. This sparse land is *conquistador* country, many of those legendary figures originating in these parts. And it has another claim to fame, a gastronomic one. In the 16th century, the monks of the Alcantara Monastery in Cáceres, in the heart of Extremadura, compiled one of the world's first cookbooks. Two centuries later this prize was snatched up along with the booty garnered during the Napoleonic invasion, to turn up later in Paris amongst the culinary elite of the day. Escoffier's classic game bird dish *al modo de Alcántara*, in which pheasant or partridge is marinated and roasted in port with a dozen or so whole truffles, was said to have come from this chronicle, as did the soup *consumido*, which entered the French classic cuisine as consommé.

GAZPACHO SEVILLANO
SEVILLE STYLE GAZPACHO   SERVES 6

1 green bell pepper (capsicum), seeded and chopped

1 medium onion, chopped

1–2 cloves garlic, peeled

$\frac{1}{2}$ cucumber, peeled, seeded and chopped

3 large sun-ripened tomatoes, peeled and seeded

6 toasted blanched almonds

1 large slice white bread (crusts trimmed), soaked in water and squeezed dry

1 teaspoon salt

1 tablespoon chopped fresh herbs (preferably parsley and mint)

$\frac{1}{2}$ cup/120 ml/4 fl oz virgin olive oil

6 cups/1.5 l/1$\frac{1}{2}$ qt ice water

3–4 tablespoons sherry vinegar

Place the vegetables and 1 cup/250 ml/8 fl oz water in a food processor or blender and process briefly until smooth. Strain through a nylon sieve into a soup bowl. Process the almonds, bread, salt and half the herbs to a paste, adding the oil. Add some of the ice water, then strain into the puréed vegetables and add the vinegar and remaining water. Chill thoroughly.

Variations: Additional green peppers, olives, onion, cucumber and tomato, cut into very small dice, as well as chopped hard-boiled eggs and croutons of day-old bread fried in olive oil, are served separately to be added to taste.

GAZPACHO

The Arabs provided the fundamentals of *gazpacho*, and the Andalusians embellished it with peppers and tomatoes from the New World to make the classic cold soup the world has come to love. But there are endless other variations. *Ajo blanco de Málaga* begins with soaked white bread, ground to a snowy-smooth white soup with garlic and almonds, then pops in fat white grapes to surprise and delight the diner. Some are thick, like the one from Córdoba they call *salmorrejo de Córdoba*; some have diced ingredients; others are smooth and creamy. There's even a *gazpacho* like a game-hunters' hotpot packed with meaty chunks.

SALMOREJO CORDOBÉS
GAZPACHO ANDALUCIA   SERVES 6

This is a specialty dish from Córdoba, where they chose to name it *salmorejo* instead of *gazpacho* — perhaps because its vinegary taste is reminiscent of the sauce which goes by the same name. An unusual dish from Toledo featuring roasted partridge breasts floating in a delicate custard is also called Salmorejo. (The recipe can be found in the chapter on Madrid, La Mancha and New Castile.) In Aragon, quite different dishes go by the name *al salmorrejo* and comprise interesting combinations of eggs with vegetables or sausages and meats.

2 large green bell peppers (capsicums)

1–2 cloves garlic, chopped

1 teaspoon salt

3 slices white bread (crusts trimmed), soaked and squeezed dry

4 large sun-ripened tomatoes, peeled, seeded and chopped

3 tablespoons olive oil

2 tablespoons sherry vinegar

6 cups/1.5 l/1½ qt ice water

2 hard-boiled eggs, finely chopped

1 large orange, peeled and finely chopped

1 cup/60 g/2 oz toasted croutons

Cut peppers into small squares and place in a mortar, food processor or blender with garlic and salt. Crush or chop finely, then add bread, tomatoes and olive oil and process until smooth. Add the vinegar and ice water and stir in egg and orange. Sprinkle with croutons and serve.

GAZPACHO EXTREMEÑO
ICED SOUP IN THE EXTREMADURAN STYLE   SERVES 6

Using the recipe above for *salmorejo cordobés*, substitute 3 small raw eggs for the tomatoes, and add extra olive oil. Season with salt and pepper.

Ajo Blanco con Uvas
WHITE GARLIC GAZPACHO WITH GRAPES
SERVES 4–6

This startling but sophisticated dish originated in Málaga from the concept of the most humble *gazpacho* of bread, water, olive oil and vinegar. Huge local green table grapes give the tangy, creamy soup a touch of sweetness. Innovative cooks have their own interpretations of this classic, and one I particularly enjoy is *ajo blanco malagueño con melón y pasas*, replacing the grapes with melon balls and plump raisins.

4 thick slices (6 oz/180 g) country-style white bread (crusts trimmed), soaked in water and squeezed dry

1 tablespoon sherry vinegar

1 cup/150 g/5 oz blanched almonds

3–4 cloves garlic, chopped

$\frac{1}{2}$ cup/120 ml/4 fl oz olive oil

4 cups/1 l/1 qt ice water

1 cup/150 g/5 oz peeled white grapes

Place bread in a dish and sprinkle with vinegar. Let stand 2 to 3 minutes. Grind almonds in a food processor with garlic and olive oil until pastelike. Add the bread and half the water and process until smooth and creamy. Press through a nylon sieve and add remaining water. Chill thoroughly. Divide grapes between four chilled bowls and pour in the soup.

Sopa de Picadillo
QUICK SOUP
SERVES 4

A quick family soup to serve the day after a *cocido*, made from the juices of the pot — usually a rich ham, chicken or beef stock. You simply add chopped "little bits" — toasted croutons, fried cubes of bread, diced egg, cooked potato, rice or pasta, ham. Add a splash of sherry and a sprig of fresh herbs; mint is usually the choice, but parsley will do just as well.

4 cups/1 lt/1 qt stock

2 slices white bread (crusts trimmed), diced

$\frac{1}{4}$ cup/60 ml/2 fl oz olive oil

2 hard-boiled eggs, chopped

3 tablespoons very finely diced cured ham, or $\frac{3}{4}$ cup/120 g/4 oz chopped *jamón de York* (cooked ham)

1 tablespoon dry sherry (optional)

4 mint leaves

Heat stock to boiling. Fry the bread until golden in the oil, then remove with a slotted spoon. Divide bread, eggs and ham among 4 soup bowls. Season the stock with sherry, adding salt and pepper as needed. Float on some of the olive oil if liked. Pour into the bowls and add a mint leaf to each. Serve at once.

Ajo Blanco con Uvas (top), opposite; Huevos a la Flamenca (front), p.41

Rape a la Malagueña (top), p.45; Rape al Pedro Ximénez (front), p.44

WIN	LOSE				
WE	THEY	WE	THEY	WE	THEY

P.P.C. (UK) Ltd.

RTILLA

shes in Spain. It is no relation to the flat corn
me probably came from there, as it dates back
firm golden disc, usually about $1\frac{1}{4}$ inches/3 cm
s, the most popular being the simple *tortilla*
any time of the day. Sandwich a thick slice in
a, serve it with salad for lunch, pack it in a
eakfast or by itself as a first course. The classic
ender, with perhaps a little onion. But *tortillas*
ftovers such as chopped spinach, ham, offal,
eas, onions or seafood.
with patience and a good pan — light enough
ick coating or an interior well seasoned to
out perfect *tortillas* after two or three tries.

SERVES 2–4 (6 AS *TAPA*)

s probably eaten more than any other kind. Purists
thers prefer the extra flavor of a little onion.

60 ml/2 fl oz of the olive oil in a wide pan
the potatoes in the pan. Cook over low to
t until potatoes can be easily pierced with
t 10 minutes. Remove. Fry the onion until
ed, scraping the pan to incorporate any chips
t in it. Return the potato and chop with a
well mixed with the onions.

s in a large bowl with seasoning. Add the
re and blend well. Heat remaining oil in an
pan until it begins to smoke. Pour in the
omelette mixture and cook over fairly high heat, shaking
the pan frequently and running a spatula around the
edge to loosen from the sides of the pan, until the
omelette is almost firm. Place a plate over it and invert
the pan onto the plate. Slide the omelette back into the
pan and cook the other side until firm. Turn out and
cut into wedges. Serve hot or cold.

TORTILLA AL SACROMONTE
OMELETTE "AL SACROMONTE"   SERVES 4

8 oz/250 g veal sweetbreads

¼ cup/60 ml/2 fl oz olive oil

4 oz/120 g *jamón serrano* or other cured ham, finely chopped

1 tablespoon chopped parsley

6 eggs, beaten

salt and pepper

Prepare the sweetbreads following the directions for *mollejas de ternera al oporto*, on page 187. Cool and slice thinly. Sauté in 2 tablespoons of the oil until lightly colored, than add the ham and sauté briefly. Mix sweetbreads, ham and parsley with the beaten eggs and season to taste.

Heat the remaining oil in an omelette pan or nonstick pan and pour in the mixture. Cook over moderate heat, running a spatula around the edge of the *tortilla* to loosen the edge. When golden brown underneath, invert onto a plate and slide back into the pan to cook the other side until omelette is firm all through. Cut into wedges and serve warm.

MIGAS DE PASTOR
SHEPHERDS' "BREADCRUMBS"   SERVES 4

Originating in rural Extremadura but enjoyed in most parts of Spain, this makes a great breakfast or snack. Almost the daily meal of shepherds who had to eat what they could hunt, carry with them or pick from local farms.

1 lb/500 g two-day-old crusty peasant-style bread*

1¼ teaspoons salt

4 cloves garlic, finely chopped

¾–1 cup/180–250 ml/6–8 fl oz olive oil

4 thin slices *jamón serrano* or other cured or smoked ham

4 spicy sausages

½ cup/75 g/2½ small black olives

4 eggs

1 cup/150 g/5 oz white grapes

Slice crusts from the bread and tear the bread into small pieces. Place in a strainer and dip into cold water; drain well. Sprinkle with salt, cover with a cloth and set aside for several hours to soften.

Fry the garlic in the oil until well colored, then add the bread and fry to a rich gold. In the meantime, separately fry or grill the ham and sausages, then warm the olives in the same pan. Fry the eggs until the whites are firm with the yolks still soft. Heat grapes by dipping into boiling water. Pile the bread and garlic in the center of four plates. Place an egg, a slice of ham and a sausage on top and surround with the olives and grapes. Serve at once.

*Preferably from a coarse-textured country loaf.

Variation: A simpler version of this dish uses just the spicy sausage and eggs.

Huevos a la Flamenca
GYPSY EGGS

SERVES 4

¾ cup/180 ml/6 fl oz olive oil

2 large potatoes, peeled and cubed

4 thin slices *jamón serrano* or other cured ham, cut into narrow strips*

1 medium onion, thinly sliced

2 large sun-ripened tomatoes, peeled, seeded and sliced

1 small red bell pepper (capsicum), seeded and sliced

12 green beans, halved crosswise

12 slender green asparagus stalks, halved crosswise

1 tablespoon tomato paste (optional)

salt and pepper

1 *chorizo* sausage, sliced

4 large eggs

2 teaspoons chopped herbs (parsley, thyme, marjoram)

Heat the olive oil in a shallow ovenproof sauté pan or paella pan and sauté the potatoes until golden on all sides. Pour off about ⅔ of the oil, add the ham and onion to the pan and cook over medium heat for 2 to 3 minutes. Add tomatoes and cook to soften, then add peppers, reserving some for garnish. Add beans and asparagus and cook over low heat until vegetables are almost tender, stirring carefully with a flat spatula once or twice. Mix tomato paste with a little water and pour over the dish. Add salt, pepper, herbs and the sliced sausage and cook another 2 to 3 minutes. Make 4 depressions in the mixture and slide in the eggs. Arrange reserved peppers on top. Bake in a preheated 350°F/180°C/Gas 4 oven for about 12 minutes or until the eggs are just cooked. Garnish with remaining peppers and serve at once.

*Thinly sliced prosciutto is excellent in this dish. Cut into short strips and add to the vegetable mixture before placing in the oven.

Variation: Huevos a la flamenca can be cooked in individual ramekins to serve as a first course or supper dish. Cook the vegetables and ham as above, and spoon into small ovenproof dishes. Break an egg on top of each and decorate with the sliced sausage and peppers. Bake for about 10 minutes.

Foie Gras con Uvas
GOOSE LIVER WITH GRAPES

SERVES 4

8 oz/250 g fresh goose livers

2 tablespoons butter or extra-virgin olive oil

2 tablespoons dry sherry

¼ cup/60 ml/2 fl oz veal stock

¾ cup/110 g/3½ oz seedless white grapes, peeled

salt and pepper

Thinly slice the livers and sauté in the butter or oil until they just change color. Remove and keep warm. Deglaze the pan with the sherry and boil until evaporated. Add the stock and boil until well reduced, adding the grapes, salt and pepper to taste. Spoon over the livers and serve at once.

ALBÓNDIGAS CON SALSA DE JEREZ
MEATBALLS IN SHERRY SAUCE
SERVES 4

1 lb/500 g very finely ground (minced) veal

4 oz/120 g cooked ham, finely ground (minced)

3 oz/90 g *jamón serrano* or other cured ham, very finely chopped

1 small onion, peeled, very finely chopped

1 clove garlic, peeled, mashed

$\frac{1}{2}$ cup/30 g/1 oz fresh breadcrumbs

1 egg

1 tablespoon chopped parsley

1 teaspoon finely chopped mint

salt and pepper

$\frac{3}{4}$ cup/90 g/3 oz all-purpose (plain) flour

2 cups/500 ml/16 fl oz olive oil

Sauce:

1 medium onion, peeled, very finely chopped

2 tablespoons olive oil

1 clove

1 bay leaf

$\frac{1}{2}$ teaspoon black pepper

$\frac{1}{2}$ cup/120 ml/4 fl oz dry sherry

$\frac{1}{2}$ cup/120 ml/4 oz veal stock

Place the veal and ham in a mixing bowl and add the onion, garlic, breadcrumbs and egg. Mix well, sprinkle on the parsley and mint and add salt and pepper. Work into a smooth paste, then form into small balls. Coat lightly with flour and fry in hot oil until the surface is golden. Remove with a skimmer and set aside.

In another pan sauté the onion in oil until golden. Add the clove, bay leaf and pepper and put in the meatballs. Pour in the sherry and stock and cover. Place in a preheated moderate oven 360°F/180° C/Gas 4 to cook for about 40 minutes. Add a little water to the pan if the liquid is absorbed. Serve in the pan.

ALBÓNDIGAS CON VINAGRETA DE MOSTAZA
MEATBALLS WITH MUSTARD VINAIGRETTE
SERVES 4–6

1 recipe *albòndigas* (above)

1 medium onion, thinly sliced

1 tablespoon finely chopped parsley or mint

1 recipe *salsa vinagreta* (page 274)

1 tablespoon whole-grain mustard

Prepare and cook the albóndigas and allow to cool. Place in a glass or ceramic dish and scatter onion rings and chopped herbs on top. Prepare the *vinagreta*, then whisk in the mustard to make a creamy sauce. Pour over the meatballs and serve.

Cazuelitas de Espárragos Trigueros

LITTLE CASSEROLES OF WILD ASPARAGUS   SERVES 6

Wild asparagus — *espárragos amargueros* — with its long, thin green stalks, has a characteristic slightly bitter flavor. *Espárragos trigueros* grows naturally among wheat crops, taking its name from its habitat — *trigo* or wheat. Apart from the wild variety, Andalusia is one of the best regions for asparagus-growing in Spain, the other being La Rioja, particularly for the plump, creamy white asparagus enjoyed throughout Europe. Young green or white fresh garden asparagus or, in a pinch, canned white asparagus can be used for this first course or light meal, and I have also experimented successfully with peeled broccoli stems (which Chinese cooks often substitute for asparagus), and with baby green beans.

48 stems (2 bunches/$1\frac{1}{2}$ lbs/750 g) *espárragos trigueros* or other asparagus

1 teaspoon salt

$\frac{1}{2}$ cup/120 ml/4 fl oz olive oil

1 slice white bread, crusts trimmed

2 cloves garlic, finely chopped

1 tablespoon sweet paprika

black pepper

1 tablespoon red wine vinegar

6 eggs

1 teaspoon finely chopped parsley

Trim the asparagus and cut into 2-inch/5-cm lengths. Cook in boiling salted water for 4 minutes; drain. Heat the oil and fry bread until golden. Remove, then fry the garlic until lightly colored. Add the paprika and pepper. Transfer contents of the pan to a food processor, breaking up the bread into small pieces.

Process to crumbs. Divide the asparagus among 6 small earthenware ramekins and sprinkle with the crumbs. Drizzle on the vinegar and break an egg over each. Sprinkle with parsley. Bake in a very hot oven for about 5 minutes or until the eggs are just set. Serve at once.

Zanahorias Con Vino de Málaga

CARROTS WITH SWEET WINE   SERVES 4–6

Here carrots are glazed with the syrupy sweet wine of Málaga. A good sweet sherry or Marsala can be substituted.

$1\frac{1}{2}$ lb/750 g carrots, peeled and thinly sliced

salt

1 very small onion, finely chopped

3 tablespoons olive oil or butter

$\frac{1}{4}$ cup/60 ml/2 fl oz Málaga wine, sweet sherry or Marsala

2 teaspoons finely chopped parsley

Boil the carrots in lightly salted water until just tender. Drain. Sauté the onion in the oil or butter until lightly golden. Add the carrots and sauté for a few minutes. Add the wine and cook gently until it is absorbed. Stir in the chopped parsley.

RAPE AL JEREZ
MONKFISH IN SHERRY SAUCE

SERVES 4

Despite its lack of visual appeal, monkfish (or anglerfish, as it is also known) has a lobsterlike texture and sweet, rich flesh that invites interesting flavor combinations.

4 monkfish steaks or sea bass fillets, each about 180 g/6 oz

2 tablespoons olive oil

¾ teaspoon salt

black pepper

¼ cup/30 g/1 oz flaked almonds

½ cup/120 ml/4 fl oz medium or pale dry sherry

2 teaspoons chopped parsley

Arrange the fish in a buttered oven dish and sprinkle evenly with all remaining ingredients except parsley. Cover with aluminum foil and bake in a 375°F/190°C/ Gas 5 oven for about 20 minutes. Sprinkle with parsley and bake uncovered until the fish can be easily flaked with a fork.

RAPE AL PEDRO XIMÉNEZ
MONKFISH IN SWEET SHERRY

SERVES 4

Between Málaga and Montilla are the vineyards where the white Pedro Ximénez grapes grow. They are used to make a pleasing dry white wine, or are sun-ripened into the intensely sweet red-brown berries that produce a definitive style of sherry, which can be as concentrated as a tokay. Pedro Ximénez sherry and sun-dried raisins are both used in this dish; if the sherry cannot be obtained, substitute another good-quality sweet sherry.

1½ lb/750 g monkfish (anglerfish) pieces

salt and pepper

½ cup/60 g/2 oz all-purpose (plain) flour

1 medium onion, chopped

⅓ cup/90 ml/3 fl oz olive oil

½ cup/90 g/3 oz raisins

½ cup/120 ml/4 fl oz *Pedro Ximénez* sweet sherry

¾ cup/180 ml/6 fl oz fish stock

1 teaspoon chopped parsley

Slice the fish crosswise into 2-inch (5-cm) pieces. Sprinkle with a little salt and pepper and coat lightly with flour. Sauté the onion in 1 tablespoon of the oil until lightly colored and softened; add the raisins and fry to soften. Remove. Fry the fish in the remaining oil until just colored on both sides. Return the onion to the pan, add sherry and season with salt and pepper. Cook over high heat to reduce the liquid. Add the fish stock, reduce heat and simmer gently until the fish can be easily flaked with a fork, about 12 minutes. Transfer to a serving dish and sprinkle with the parsley.

Rape a la Malagueña
MONKFISH MÁLAGA STYLE

SERVES 4

A nut sauce similar to the classic Catalan *romesco* also features in Andalusian cuisine.

2 tablespoons hazelnuts

1½ lb/750 g monkfish pieces, skinned

salt and pepper

½ cup/60 g/2 oz all-purpose (plain) flour

1 cup/250 ml/8 fl oz olive oil

1 medium onion, finely chopped

2 cloves garlic, chopped

2 medium tomatoes, peeled, seeded and chopped

1 tablespoon finely chopped parsley

2 tablespoons blanched almonds

½ cup/30 g/1 oz fresh breadcrumbs

6 saffron threads

½–¾ cup/120–180 ml/4–6 fl oz hot fish stock or water

Toast the hazelnuts in a pan or a hot oven. Place in a cloth and rub to remove skins. Set aside to cool. Cut the fish into thick slices. Season with salt and pepper and coat lightly with flour. Fry in the hot oil to seal all surfaces. Remove and set aside. Fry the onion and garlic until golden, then add the tomatoes and cook until soft and pastelike. Season to taste. Purée in a food processor, if desired. Add half the parsley, then spread half the tomato sauce in a greased casserole and arrange the fish on top. Cover with the remaining tomato sauce. Fry the almonds and hazelnuts with breadcrumbs in olive oil until golden brown. Transfer to a mortar or food processor and grind to a smooth paste. Place saffron in mortar with a few drops of the hot stock and crush to bring out the color. Add to the almond mixture with the remaining stock. Pour over the dish and bake in a preheated 350°F/180°C/Gas 4 oven for about 15 minutes. Sprinkle with remaining parsley and serve.

Pez Espada Frito
FRIED SWORDFISH STEAKS

SERVES 4

4 swordfish steaks, about 7 oz/ 200 g each

4 cloves garlic, finely chopped

½ cup/120 ml/4 fl oz olive oil

juice of 1 large lemon

¾ cup/90 g/3 oz all-purpose (plain) flour

2 teaspoons chopped parsley

sliced lemon and orange

Place the swordfish steaks in a flat dish and add the garlic, 2 tablespoons of the olive oil and lemon juice. Marinate for 15 minutes, then turn and marinate a further 10 minutes. Drain and coat lightly with flour. Fry in the remaining oil for about 3 minutes on each side. Garnish with chopped parsley and the sliced lemon and orange and serve with boiled potatoes.

Variation: Cut the fish into cubes and thread onto oiled skewers with pieces of onion and bell pepper (capsicum). Marinate, then grill over charcoal until done.

URTA A LA ROTEÑA
BAKED PORGY
SERVES 6

Fish and potatoes are frequent partners in the Spanish cuisine and often come with a sauce based on sweet or hot peppers. Fished in the Gulf of Cádiz and to a lesser extent in other parts of the Atlantic and Mediterranean, *urta* is an unusual carnivorous fish of the *dentex* family, related to red bream. This dish comes from Rota on the other point of the bay from Cádiz.

2 lb/1 kg *urta/pargo* (porgy/bream) fillets, skin on

salt and pepper

½ cup/60 g/2 oz all-purpose (plain) flour

2 large onions, very thinly sliced

⅓ cup/90 ml/3 fl oz olive oil

4 cloves garlic, sliced

3 medium tomatoes, peeled, seeded and sliced

1 red bell pepper (capsicum), seeded and chopped

1 hot red chili pepper, seeded and chopped

1 bay leaf

1 small cinnamon stick

Season the fish with salt and pepper and coat lightly with flour. Set aside. Sauté the onions in half the oil until lightly colored. Remove half the onion and spread in a casserole. Add garlic to the pan and fry briefly, then add tomatoes and peppers with chili, bay leaf and cinnamon stick and cook until reduced to a thick sauce, about 20 minutes. Sauté the fish in the remaining oil and arrange over the onions with the sliced potato on top. Strain the sauce through a sieve, pushing as much through as possible. Discard bay leaf and cinnamon stick. Pour sauce over the dish and bake in a preheated 350°F/180°C/Gas 4 oven for about 25 minutes, or until the potato is tender.

BOQUERONES
FRIED BABY ANCHOVIES IN OLIVE OIL
SERVES 6

In Andalusia tiny fish are enjoyed as an appetizer, *tapa* or quick snack. *Boquerones* are anchovies, small silvery fish of the herring family which proliferate in the southern Spanish waters. When caught at only a few inches long, they are delicious eaten fresh or marinated as *tapas*. Floured and fried *boquerones*, pinched together at the tails in little bouquets, accompany a vegetable pasta dish known as *Fideos a la Malagueña* (see page 51).

30 small whole *boquerones* (sardines or sprats), cleaned

salt and pepper

1 cup/120 g/4 oz all-purpose (plain) flour

1 cup/250 ml/8 fl oz olive oil

3–5 cloves garlic, peeled

Rinse and dry the fish. Season and coat lightly with flour. Heat the oil in a wide pan. Make a slit near the tail of one fish, pinch the tails of 4 other fish together and push through the slit, pinching together. Hold firmly and place in the oil so that they stick together as the oil seals the flour. Cook the remaining fish in identical groups. Lift out carefully, drain and serve with lemon halves and crusty bread.

FAISÁN MODO ALCÁNTARA
PHEASANT ALCÁNTARA STYLE   SERVES 4

One of the earliest cookbooks to chronicle the dishes of Spain was written by the monks of the monastery of Alcántara in Cáceres. This prized publication found its way into France following the Napoleonic invasion and was used in the creation of several classic French dishes. The extravagance of the original recipe, with its dozen truffles, makes it impossible to reproduce in most households, but I find that dried morels provide their own distinct flavor and something akin to the earthy aroma of the truffles.

2 medium pheasants, hung 3 days

salt and pepper

5 duck livers

2 tablespoons lard or clarified butter

10–12 dried morels or other dried mushrooms, soaked

3 cups/750 ml/24 fl oz tawny port

1 teaspoon finely chopped parsley

Clean and dress the pheasants and season well inside and out. Place in a glass dish. Season the livers with salt and pepper and brown over high heat in half the lard or butter. Mash to a paste. Drain half the mushrooms, slice and simmer in the port for 10 minutes. Remove with a slotted spoon and mix with the mashed liver, then spread inside the pheasants and truss with wooden poultry skewers or butchers' twine. Pour the port over the birds, add the whole morels and cover the dish. Let stand in a cool place for 3 days, turning occasionally.

Drain the pheasants, reserving the marinade. Season with salt and pepper and place on a low rack in a roasting pan. Brush with remaining melted lard and add half the marinade. Roast in a preheated 350°F/180°C/Gas 4 oven for about 50 minutes. Add the remaining marinade, without the morels, and roast another 20 minutes, or until the pheasants are tender. Remove the birds, cut in halves and place on a serving platter. Add the whole morels to the pan and boil until sauce is well reduced. Season to taste. Pour over the birds and garnish with chopped parsley.

Pato a la Sevillana

SEVILLE-STYLE DUCK

SERVES 6

2 ducklings, 4 lb/2 kg each

2 tablespoons olive oil

1 large onion, sliced

2 tablespoons all-purpose (plain) flour

2 cups/500 ml/16 fl oz dry white wine

2 bitter Seville oranges, thickly sliced

2 sprigs parsley

1 small bay leaf

1 large carrot, peeled and cut into 6 pieces

salt and pepper

cornstarch/cornflour (optional)

6 oz/180 g large green olives, pitted and coarsely chopped

Cut the ducks into serving pieces. Heat oil in a heavy casserole and brown duck evenly, cooking in several batches. Remove and keep warm. Brown the onion very well in the same oil, then drain off excess oil, sprinkle on the flour and cook lightly. Add the wine and cook, stirring, for 2 minutes. Return the duck to the casserole. Add the oranges, parsley, bay leaf and carrot with a little salt and water to barely cover. Cover the casserole and cook in a 350°F/180°C/Gas 4 oven for about $1\frac{3}{4}$ hours or until duck is very tender.

Skim off the fat from the surface of the dish and save for another use if desired. Remove the duck. Strain the sauce into another pan and thicken, if needed, with a paste of cornstarch and cold water. Season to taste, add the olives and warm through. Serve sauce over the duck.

Gallo de Campo a la Jerezana

CHICKEN IN SHERRY SAUCE

SERVES 4

2 lb/1 kg chicken pieces

1 bay leaf

$\frac{1}{2}$ teaspoon salt

3 cloves garlic, peeled

6 black peppercorns

1 large onion, chopped

1 medium onion, sliced

1 small dried red chili pepper

$1\frac{1}{2}$ teaspoons sweet paprika

2 teaspoons chopped fresh oregano

$\frac{3}{4}$ cup/180 ml/6 fl oz dry sherry

1 cup/150 g/5 oz small green olives

2 teaspoons chopped parsley

2–3 tablespoons cornstarch (cornflour)

Place the chicken skin upwards in a heavy large saucepan. Add the bay leaf, salt, garlic, peppercorns and chopped onion. Add cold water to almost cover, then bring to a boil, cover tightly and simmer for about 30 minutes. Turn the chicken. Add the sliced onion, chili, paprika and oregano and cook a further 25 minutes. Add sherry and olives with half the parsley, stir and cook a further 8 to 12 minutes or until chicken is completely tender.

Transfer chicken pieces to a serving plate. Mix the cornstarch with a little cold water, stir into the sauce and cook, stirring, for 1 to 2 minutes to thicken. Add salt and pepper to taste. Pour sauce over the chicken and garnish with the remaining parsley. Serve with boiled white rice flavored with butter and saffron.

COCIDO EXTREMEÑO
CASSEROLE OF GAME WITH GARBANZOS AND SAUSAGE   SERVES 8

The names *pote, olla, escudella, puchero* and *cocido* are interchangeable, representing the great meal-in-a-pot dishes that are the backbone of Extremadura's cuisine. A variety of meats, vegetables and legumes make this fabulous hotpot a nourishing family meal, which began in the kitchens of the upper classes but is now more likely to be found bubbling on the hearth of *pueblo* kitchens. Each region has its own style, using ingredients typical of the area. Some are served straight from the pot, others presented as an impressive three- or four-course meal. See also *Olla Podrida* (page 201).

1 cup/180 g/6 oz dried garbanzos (chickpeas), soaked overnight

1-lb/500-g ham hock

2 lb/1 kg veal or beef shank/shin

2 oven-ready pigeons, Cornish hens (spatchcock) or guinea fowl

1 large onion, peeled and halved

2 bay leaves

2 sprigs fresh thyme

1½ teaspoons salt

2 cloves garlic, chopped

3 large potatoes, peeled and cubed

2 cups/180 g/6 oz shredded cabbage or other vegetables such as spinach, collards or beet greens

½ cup/90 g/3 oz short-grain/round white rice

8 oz/250 g *chorizo* sausages

8 oz/250 g *morcilla* or other blood sausage

2 large tomatoes, peeled, seeded and chopped

2 teaspoons tomato paste

1 dried hot red chili pepper

black pepper

Place the garbanzos in a large pan with the ham hock and veal or beef shank and water to generously cover. Bring to a boil, reduce heat and simmer for 2 hours. Cut the poultry into quarters and blanch in boiling water; drain. Add to the pot with half the onion, the bay leaves and thyme. Add salt and enough hot water to cover generously. Bring to a boil, then reduce heat and simmer, tightly covered, for about 1½ hours or until the garbanzos and meat are tender.

Discard the ham bone. Add garlic, potatoes, cabbage, rice, whole sausages, tomatoes, tomato paste and the chili; add more water if necessary to maintain the consistency of a thick soup. Cook for 25 minutes, then remove sausages and slice thinly. Bone the birds and remove meat from shanks. Return to the pot and heat through. Season with additional salt, if needed, and plenty of black pepper.

Variation: Use chicken or rabbit instead of the game birds. Several slices of dried smoked ham can be used instead of the ham hock. Dice them and return to the pot after cooking.

OLLA GITANA

"GYPSY STEW"

SERVES 8

An *olla* is a large stewpot made from iron or earthenware, tapering slightly at the top and with a looped handle on either side. A chunky stew, usually made with dried beans and fat pork, cooked in this pan is also known as an *olla*.

1 cup/180 g/6 oz dried white beans (haricots) or garbanzos (chickpeas), soaked overnight

1½ lb/750 g meaty pork ribs

10 cups/2.5 l/2½ qt water

2 medium potatoes, peeled and diced

2 bay leaves

1 medium onion, chopped

2–3 cloves garlic, chopped

⅓ cup/90 ml/3 fl oz olive oil

4 oz/120 g squash or pumpkin, peeled and diced

2 small firm pears, peeled and chopped

1½ cups/300 g/10 oz sliced green beans

1 bunch Swiss chard or turnip/beet greens, rinsed and chopped

2 slices day-old bread, crusts trimmed

¼ cup/30 g/1 oz blanched almonds

¼ teaspoon powdered saffron

salt and pepper

1 tablespoon red wine vinegar

Place the soaked beans and pork ribs in a pan with the water. Bring to a boil and simmer for 2 hours. Add potatoes and bay leaves and cook for another 30 minutes. Fry the onion and garlic in a little of the oil until very well colored. Add the onion mixture and squash to the *olla* and cook for 15 minutes, then add the remaining fruit and vegetables and simmer a further 15 minutes. Fry the bread and almonds in the remaining oil until golden. Grind to a thick paste, then add the saffron and stir mixture into the soup. Season to taste and simmer 5 to 6 minutes. Stir in the vinegar just before serving.

FIDEOS A LA MALAGUEÑA
PASTA WITH VEGETABLES

SERVES 6–8

1 lb/500 g *fideos* or spaghettini

3 medium potatoes, peeled and cubed

⅓ cup/90 ml/3 fl oz olive oil

2 small red bell peppers, seeded and chopped

2 cloves garlic, chopped

1 cup/180 g/6 oz green peas, cooked and drained

salt and pepper

chopped parsley

Boquerones (page 46)

Boil the pasta in salted water until tender. Drain. Sauté the potato in half the oil until tender. Set aside. Sauté the peppers and garlic in the remaining oil until softened. Add the peas and toss for 1 to 2 minutes, then return the potato to the pan and season generously. Toss with the pasta and garnish with chopped parsley. Serve hot with fans of fried baby anchovies (*boquerones*).

ESTOFADO VENADO
VENISON CASSEROLE

SERVES 6–8

Game is used extensively in Spanish cooking, with hare, rabbit and game birds such as partridge, quail and woodcock accounting for much of the meat eaten. However, venison is also popular; its rich, dark meat lends itself well to the casserole style of cooking that is the backbone of Spanish cuisine.

2½–3 lb/1.5 kg venison

2 cups/500 ml/16 fl oz dry red wine

3 bay leaves

6 black peppercorns

2-inch/5-cm cinnamon stick

1 sprig each fresh thyme and oregano

½ cup/60 g/2 oz all-purpose (plain) flour

1 large onion, thickly sliced

½ cup/120 ml/4 fl oz olive oil

4 cloves garlic, chopped

1 tablespoon red wine vinegar

2 cups/500 ml/16 fl oz water

6 small new potatoes, peeled

2 teaspoons paprika

Cut the venison into 1-inch/2.5-cm cubes and place in a glass dish with the wine, bay leaves, peppercorns, cinnamon stick and herbs. Cover and marinate overnight, turning once or twice. Drain, reserving the liquid.

Coat the meat lightly with flour and set aside. Sauté the onion in the oil until lightly colored. Add garlic and cook briefly, then transfer mixture with a slotted spoon to a casserole. Fry the meat in the remaining oil until well browned. Add to the casserole with the vinegar, salt, pepper and reserved marinade. Cook in a 350°F/180°C/ Gas 4 oven for about 1 hour, turning and stirring occasionally. Add the water, stir well and continue cooking for a further 1½ hours. Twenty minutes before the casserole is done add the potatoes and paprika. Serve in the casserole.

TERNERA A LA CONDESITA
VEAL IN ALMOND SAUCE WITH SHERRY

SERVES 4

The subtle tastes of sherry and almonds make this special enough to have become one of my favorites. I was also delighted at the response from my guests when I tried it with veal scallops. It should be finished off on the stove, but if you haven't a suitable pan, arrange the steaks in a casserole and pop into the oven for a quarter of an hour.

8 thin slices veal steak

1 tablespoon lemon juice

½ cup/120 ml/4 fl oz olive oil

5 large cloves garlic, unpeeled

1 cup/150 g/5 oz toasted blanched almonds

¼ cup/60 ml/2 fl oz fino sherry

1 cup/250 ml/8 fl oz veal or chicken stock

1 large egg, beaten

½ cup/60 g/2 oz all-purpose (plain) flour

Flatten the steaks with a meat mallet and place in a wide glass dish. Sprinkle on the lemon juice and 3 tablespoons olive oil and set aside for 10 minutes. Fry the unpeeled garlic cloves in a little oil until the surface is very dark and the cloves feel soft, then remove and cool. Squeeze garlic from the skins into a mortar or food processor. Process with the almonds to a paste, adding the sherry and stock. Drain the steaks and dry with paper towels. Coat with egg, then with flour. Fry steaks in the remaining oil until well colored. Layer in a flame-proof dish and pour on the sauce. Cook over low to medium heat for about 15 minutes until the sauce thickens and the veal is tender. Small triangles of white bread, fried until golden in olive oil, sometimes garnish this dish.

Variation: Substitute 1½ lb/750 g veal scallops/escalopes. Pound the meat to partially flatten and tenderize, cook as above and then arrange side by side in a large casserole with an extra cup of stock. Bake for about 25 minutes. Add sauce and heat through.

CORDERO AL AJILLO
LAMB WITH GARLIC   SERVES 4

2 lb/1 kg lean boneless lamb

1 tablespoon sweet paprika

salt and pepper

2 tablespoons all-purpose (plain) flour

½ cup/120 ml/4 fl oz olive oil

10 cloves garlic, minced

1 small onion, minced

1 cup/250 ml/8 fl oz dry white wine

pinch of saffron threads

2 tablespoons dry sherry

3 slices white bread, crusts trimmed

chopped parsley

Cut the lamb into 1-inch/2.5-cm cubes. Mix half the paprika with salt, pepper and the flour. Roll lamb pieces in the seasoned flour and brown in half the oil. Remove. Fry the garlic and onion briefly in the remaining oil. Add remaining paprika and the wine and return the meat to the pan. Cover and cook gently on top of the stove or in a 325°F/160°C/Gas 3 oven for about 1¼ hours, adding a little warm water to the pan as needed to prevent the sauce from drying up. Toast the saffron threads lightly in a dry skillet. Grind to a powder and mix with the sherry. Splash over the dish and heat for a few minutes. Cut the bread into triangles and fry in the remaining oil. Serve the lamb surrounded by the toast triangles. Sprinkle with chopped parsley.

TERNERA CON ALCACHOFAS A LA CORDOBESA
VEAL AND ARTICHOKES CÓRDOBA   SERVES 4

8 thin veal steaks (each about 3 oz/90 g)

salt and pepper

½ cup/60 g/2 oz all-purpose (plain) flour

¼ cup/60 ml/2 fl oz olive oil

1 medium onion, thinly sliced

2 cloves garlic, chopped

13-oz/400-g can artichoke hearts, drained and quartered

3 tablespoons dry sherry

1 cup/250 ml/8 fl oz veal stock or water

Season the steaks with salt and pepper and coat lightly with flour, reserving remaining flour. Heat the oil in a wide pan and fry the steaks over high heat until barely cooked through. Remove and keep warm. Sauté the onion until softened, add the garlic and cook briefly. Add the artichokes and heat through. Sizzle the sherry in the pan and cook over high heat until evaporated. Sprinkle 1½ tablespoons of the reserved flour into the pan and cook, stirring, for about 2 minutes, then add the stock and stir to make a sauce. Cook gently for 2 minutes, stirring continually. Season with salt and pepper. Serve sauce over the steaks.

Jamón al Jerez
HAM WITH SHERRY
SERVES 4

Jamón York, cooked ham baked with sherry and dried fruit, makes a very special main course (try it next Christmas instead of a standard baked ham). Dried figs or apricots and raisins complement the saltiness of the ham. This dish looks spectacular when surrounded by golden yellow *huevos hilados* — egg yolk threads candied in sugar syrup (see pages 266-7); these are a garnish used in the western regions of Spain and extensively in Portugal to decorate cakes, puddings and occasionally meat dishes. At a wedding, they may be served as a sweet course, draped from edible cookie baskets or stands decorated with colored frosting.

4 lb/2 kg cooked ham

2 cups/500 ml/16 fl oz sweet sherry

$\frac{1}{2}$ cup/90 g/3 oz raisins

1 cup/180 g/6 oz chopped dried figs or apricots

1 cup/250 ml/8 fl oz apricot nectar or water

$\frac{1}{2}$ cup/75 g/$2\frac{1}{2}$ oz blanched, toasted almonds

Using a small, sharp knife, trim away the skin from the ham, leaving a layer of fat on the meat. Score the fat in a diamond pattern, cutting just down to the meat. Place in a roasting pan and pour in the sherry. Cover with aluminum foil and roast in a preheated (350°F/180°C/ Gas 4) oven for 40 minutes.

In the meantime, soak the raisins and dried fruit in the apricot nectar. Remove the foil from the ham, pour in the fruit and liquid and cook a further 40 minutes, basting the ham frequently with the pan juices. When the ham is almost ready, add the toasted almonds to the pan juices. Slice the ham and arrange on a platter, pour on the sauce and serve.

Hígado en Salsa de Naranja
LIVER IN ORANGE SAUCE
SERVES 4

10-oz/650 g calf's or lamb's liver

salt and pepper

$\frac{1}{2}$ cup/60 g/2 oz all-purpose (plain) flour

2 tablespoons olive oil

3 tablespoons butter

1–2 tablespoons Spanish brandy

juice and finely shredded rind of 2 oranges

Cut the liver into very thin slices, season with salt and pepper and dust with flour. Heat oil and butter together in a skillet or sauté pan and sauté the liver until the surface changes color and the liver is very lightly cooked. Remove to a warm plate and set aside. Deglaze the pan with brandy and the orange juice, add the shredded rind and season to taste. Pour over the liver and serve at once.

Pastel de Cabello de Ángel (top), p.63; Brazo de Gitano (front), p.59

Estofado de Rabo de Toro (opposite)

ESTOFADO DE RABO DE TORO
BULL'S TAIL CASSEROLE   SERVES 6

Andalusia is the home of fighting bulls. Bred for weight and strength, they are pampered with an excellent diet so their meat is supremely tender and full of flavor. The day after the bull fights, many restaurants offer a *plato de toro del día* (bull dish of the day). In some of the restaurants specializing in meat from the bullring, the *cocina taurina* — a special "cuisine of the bull" menu — lists the full pedigree and description of the bull along with details of the event and the matador, and offers a variety of dishes created in the kitchens.

3-lb/1.5-kg bull's tail (or 1 large oxtail)

$\frac{1}{2}$ cup/60 g/2 oz all-purpose (plain) flour

salt and pepper

$1\frac{1}{2}$ cups/400 ml/13 fl oz olive oil

2 medium onions, sliced

2 large carrots, peeled and diced

2 small turnips, peeled and diced

4 cloves garlic, chopped

4 large tomatoes, peeled, seeded and chopped

2 teaspoons tomato paste

$\frac{3}{4}$ cup/180 ml/6 fl oz dry sherry

6 oz/180 g small fresh mushrooms

1 bay leaf

1 sprig each thyme and rosemary

2 teaspoons sweet paprika

2 tablespoons chopped parsley

Have the butcher separate the tail at the joints. Blanch in boiling water, drain and dry on paper towels. Season flour with salt and pepper and sprinkle over the tail pieces. Heat oil in a large, heavy pan and fry the meat several pieces at a time until well colored. Set aside. Fry the onions, carrots and turnips until colored, then add the remaining ingredients and stir for a few minutes over medium heat. Return the meat with water to cover. Cover the pan and cook gently for about $2\frac{1}{2}$ hours, or bake in a 325°F/160°C/Gas 3 oven for about 3 hours, adding extra water as necessary and stirring occasionally.

Riñones a la Jerezana
KIDNEYS IN A RICH SHERRY SAUCE   SERVES 6

Being particularly fond of organ meats, I recommend this dish as one of Andalusia's — if not Spain's — most outstanding culinary contributions. The assertive flavors of kidneys and dry sherry complement and highlight each other in this classic, which deserves a good amontillado or fino sherry. I love to surprise guests at a *tapas* meal with this and two other classic organ meat dishes, *hígado frito con orégano* (liver fried with oregano) and *callos a la madrileña* (tripe Madrid style). As tapas, serve with toothpicks and plenty of crusty bread for mopping up the sauce.

2 lb/1 kg veal kidneys

$\frac{3}{4}$ cup/180 ml/6 fl oz milk

1 cup/250 ml/8 fl oz olive oil

salt and pepper

1 cup/250 ml/8 fl oz amontillado or fino sherry

6 cloves garlic, minced

1 medium onion, finely chopped

1 tablespoon all-purpose (plain) flour

1 bay leaf

1 large sun-ripened tomato, peeled, seeded and chopped

$\frac{3}{4}$ cup/180 ml/6 fl oz veal or beef stock

2 teaspoons tomato paste

$\frac{1}{4}$ teaspoon nutmeg

1 tablespoon finely chopped parsley

2 slices white bread, crusts trimmed

Place kidneys in a bowl, cover with the milk and set aside for 2 hours. Drain and rinse. Cut in halves and use kitchen shears to remove the fat. Cut kidneys into bite-sized cubes. Heat $\frac{1}{4}$ cup/60 ml/2 fl oz olive oil in a wide pan until almost smoking. Add the kidneys and sauté until they change color. Add salt and pepper and the sherry. Cook over high heat for 2 minutes, then remove the kidneys with a slotted spoon and continue to boil the sherry until reduced by $\frac{2}{3}$. Pour over the kidneys. Add another 2 tablespoons oil to the pan and fry the garlic and onion until lightly colored. Sprinkle on the flour and cook, stirring, until golden. Add the bay leaf, tomato, stock, tomato paste and nutmeg and bring to a boil, stirring; cook 2 to 3 minutes. Return the kidneys and their liquid, add salt and pepper to taste and half the parsley. Simmer for about 5 minutes, or until the kidneys are tender and sauce is thick. Cut the bread into quarters and fry in the remaining oil. Pile the kidneys into the center of a serving plate and surround with the toast. Sprinkle on remaining parsley.

BRAZO DE GITANO

"GYPSY'S ARM" ROLL   SERVES 8

I have heard several interpretations of the origin of this name for what is essentially a rolled sponge cake. Most appealing is that the roll is as thick as a muscular Gypsy's arm. A creamy custardlike filling is traditional, with rum, caramel and coffee flavors most favored.

6 eggs, separated

$\frac{3}{4}$ cup/180 g/6 oz superfine sugar

1 cup/120 g/4 oz self-rising flour

1 tablespoon cornstarch (cornflour)

$\frac{1}{4}$ teaspoon salt

superfine sugar

custard, rum or coffee cream filling (page 266)

2 tablespoons extra superfine sugar

Preheat oven to 400°F/200°C/Gas 6. Beat egg yolks with the $\frac{3}{4}$ cup sugar until light. Sift flour, cornstarch and salt over the eggs and gently blend in. Whip egg whites to firm peaks and fold in using a large metal spoon; do not overwork.

Grease and flour a 12 x 16-inch baking pan (30 x 40-cm sandwich tin) and line the bottom with parchment paper. Spread the batter evenly in the pan and bake for about 12 minutes, or until lightly golden and the surface springs back when lightly pressed. Invert onto a cooling rack lined with a piece of waxed or parchment paper sprinkled heavily with superfine sugar. Let cool while a filling is prepared.

Carefully remove paper from the bottom of the sponge roll and spread on the filling. Use the sugared paper to assist in rolling the cake around the filling. Place cake on an ovenproof dish and spread the remaining sugar on top. Place under a very hot broiler (grill) to caramelize the sugar. Cool before slicing.

PESTINOS
FRITTERS IN SWEET SYRUP

MAKES 30-40

2⅓ cups/600 ml/19 fl oz olive oil

¼ cup/60 ml/2 fl oz milk

juice and finely grated peel (rind) of 1 lemon

pinch each of ground cinnamon, anise and salt

½ cup/120 ml/4 fl oz anise liqueur or Cointreau

3½ cups/420 g/14 oz all-purpose (plain) flour

½ cup/150 g/5 oz water

confectioners' (icing) or fine castor sugar

In a mixing bowl whisk together ⅓ cup olive oil, milk, lemon juice and peel, the spices and liqueur. Sift flour over and stir in to make a stiff dough. Cover with a damp cloth and set aside for at least 1 hour. Roll out very thinly on a lightly floured surface and cut into 3 inch (10 cm) squares. Heat remaining oil until very hot — it should be almost smoking, then reduce heat slightly. Roll the pastry into cigar shapes and fry several at a time until golden brown. Remove on a slotted spoon and drain on absorbent paper. Make a syrup with the honey and water, boiling gently until it begins to thicken. Add the remaining liqueur and stir in. Dip each of the fritters into the syrup and drain on a rack. Sprinkle with fine sugar or confectioners' sugar while warm. Cool before serving.

POLVORONES SEVILLANOS
SEVILLIAN SHORTBREAD

MAKES ABOUT 20

Because they are so light and crumble easily, these little shortbread-like cookies (biscuits) take their name from the word *polvo* which means a fine dust or powder. There are many variations, many using finely ground almonds. This one is flavored with orange peel and orange liqueur.

1 cup/250 g/8 oz lard or margarine

½ cup/90 g/3 oz confectioners' (icing) sugar

1 egg

1 tablespoon orange liqueur

1 tablespoon finely grated orange peel (rind)

3½ cups/420 g/14 oz all-purpose (plain) flour, sifted

small pinch of salt

Cream the lard or margarine in a mixing bowl and beat in the sugar. Add the egg, liqueur and peel, then slowly work in the flour and salt. Do not overwork the mixture or it will become oily. Turn onto a floured board and roll out to about ⅔ inch/2 cm thickness. Use a floured small round cookie (biscuit) cutter to cut out the cookies. Use up the trimmings by rerolling and cutting out in the same way. Place on a greased and floured cookie (biscuit) pan cook in a preheated hot oven 400°F/200°C/ Gas 6 for about 24 minutes. The cookies should be very lightly browned on top when done. Transfer to a rack to cool.

Tip: Dust with confectioners' (icing) sugar before serving, or pipe on thin lines of chocolate.

HIGOS RELLENOS
STUFFED FIGS   SERVES 6

Dried figs have natural affinity for two ingredients loved by the Spanish, chocolate and almonds. Select moist, light-coloured figs for best results.

18 large dried figs
½ cup/120 g/4 oz sugar
¼ cup/60 ml/2 fl oz Grand Marnier
1 cup/250 ml/8 fl oz water
5 oz/150 g semisweet chocolate
36 whole almonds
1 tablespoon butter

Place the figs in a saucepan with the sugar, liqueur and water. Bring to a boil, stirring to dissolve sugar, then poach figs for 10 minutes. Remove from the heat and set aside for 2 hours. Remove the figs with a slotted spoon and drain on a rack. Boil the liquid until reduced to a thick syrup. Set aside.

Use kitchen shears to remove the stem and make a small incision near the top of each fig. Cut the chocolate into thick slivers. Insert several chocolate slivers and two almonds into each fig. Place on a buttered pan and bake in a preheated hot oven for 5 minutes. Melt the remaining chocolate in a small saucepan, add the butter and stir well. Pour a pool of syrup onto each of six dessert plates. Stand three figs on each plate and pour a little melted chocolate over each. Serve warm.

HIGOS CON DULCE DE MÁLAGA
FIGS IN MÁLAGA WINE   SERVES 4

16 dried figs
1½ cups/400 ml/13 fl oz Málaga wine or tokay, muscat or sweet sherry
2 tablespoons confectioners' (icing) sugar

Snip off the stem from each fig and place figs in a glass dish. Pour on the wine and marinate overnight. Drain, reserving the wine for another use. Sprinkle figs with confectioners' sugar and serve immediately with whipped cream or ice cream.

TOCINO DE CIELO

SERVES 6

This golden brown, toffee-flavored caramel custard flan goes by an intriguing name, which translates loosely into "bacon from heaven." For years there has been much dissension among the experts as to how it got to be so curiously named.

1¼ cups/300 g/10 oz sugar
½ cup/120 ml/4 oz water
12 large eggs*

Pour 1 cup/250 g/8 oz sugar into a non-aluminum saucepan and add the water. Cook over moderate heat without stirring until sugar begins to caramelize; it should be the colour of clear honey. Remove from the heat and cool to room temperature. (If sugar caramelizes too much it will begin to set hard at this stage, making it unusable).

Separate 10 eggs, reserving the whites for another use. Add the two remaining whole eggs to the yolks and beat lightly, then strain into the syrup and beat in well. Spread the remaining sugar in an 8-inch/20-cm cake pan and cook over low heat until it caramelizes. Pour the egg mixture over the caramel and place in a larger pan with warm water to come halfway up the sides of the custard. Bake in a 350°F/180°C/Gas 4 oven for about 25 minutes or until firm to the touch. Cool, then refrigerate until firm. Cut into squares or wedges and serve cold with a frill of piped whipped cream.

*Preferably eggs from free-range grain fed chickens.

DULCE DE BATATA MALAGUEÑO
MÁLAGA SWEET POTATO PUDDING   SERVES 6

The yellow sweet potatoes from the region of Málaga are the best in Spain. They are cooked as a vegetable, made into a jam and used in cookies, cakes and rich puddings like this one, which is flavored with the syrupy sweet wine of Málaga. Because they come into season in late fall, just when chestnuts ripen, the two are often used together.

1 lb/500 g cooked puréed yellow sweet potato (1¼ lbs/625 g unpeeled weight)

¾ cup/180 g/6 oz sugar

¼ cup/60 ml/2 fl oz Málaga wine, tokay or sweet sherry

¾ cup/180 ml/6 fl oz milk

3 eggs, well beaten

1 teaspoon cinnamon

pinch each of salt and nutmeg

Place the potato in a food processor and purée until smooth, adding sugar, wine and milk. Beat in the eggs and seasonings and pour the batter into a buttered 8- to 9-inch (20- to 23-cm) flan or pie dish. Bake in a 350°F/180°C/Gas 4 oven for about 40 minutes or until pudding is set and surface looks dry and firm. Serve warm or cold.

Variation: Use this delightful pudding as the filling for a tart. It's like the best of pumpkin pies.

PASTEL DE CABELLO DE ÁNGEL
SWEET PIE FILLED WITH "ANGEL'S HAIR"   SERVES 6–8

1 recipe puff pastry (page 268)

1 recipe *cabello de ángel* conserve (page 93)

1 egg, beaten

1 tablespoon superfine sugar (optional)

¾ teaspoon cinnamon (optional)

Roll out the pastry and use a little more than half of it to line a pie dish. Fill with the *cabello de ángel* and spread smooth. Cover with the remaining pastry and trim edges. Use the trimmings to make decorations for the top. Brush the beaten egg. Bake in a 425°F/220°C/Gas 7 oven until the pastry is crisp, flaky and golden, about 22 minutes. Brush the surface with a little extra egg or melted butter and sprinkle with the sugar and cinnamon, if used. Cut into wedges and serve hot with sweetened whipped cream.

MURCIA AND VALENCIA
(The Levante)
MURCIA Y VALENCIA

The rice basin of Spain and the home of *paella*. Valencia curves around the Mediterranean coast south of Catalonia, ending abruptly at the twin capes of San Antonia and La Nao, where the Costa Blanca introduces its neighbor Murcia. Valencia, comprising the provinces of Castellón de la Plana, Valencia and Alicante, is a long, narrow coastal strip backed up by a series of uncompromising mountain ranges, so its agriculture, industry and population are concentrated on the lowlands. Murcia includes the inland region of Albacete. Together these two regions have become known as the Levante, the land of the sunrise. South of Valencia city are the swampy, marshy lands surrounding Lake Albufera, a natural habitat of wild ducks and the one grain that appreciates being waterbound, rice — and yielding also vast saltpans for commercial extraction of salt. Valencia too is the land of *huertas*, vegetable gardens abundant with artichokes, salad greens, green beans and potatoes, with peppers, broadbeans and tomatoes, many under gigantic frameworks covered with blue plastic — hothouses growing out-of-season produce. There are also vast plantations of oranges, although the type known as Valencia has largely been replaced by sweeter and juicier navel oranges. The coastal strip is holiday land, the mecca of tourists and sun-seekers from all over Europe. They gather here at beautiful Benidorm, Javea and Denia as much for the white beaches and too-blue-to-believe Mediterranean as for the seafood so readily available in local *tabernas*. The shrimp and *langostinos* are superb, the sea bass (*dorada*) unequaled. Alicante has perfected *dorada a la sal*, baked gilthead fish encrusted with local coarse salt. The Albufera and its rivers are full of *anguilas* (freshwater eels) waiting for the trap, and wild ducks for the hunter and his cookpot.

Valencia is the birthplace of one of Spain's most famous culinary contributions, the *paella*. Originally a peasant dish cooked outdoors in a flat pan over a fire of vine clippings, it was simply a mess of rice and whatever else was on hand at the time to flavor it. That those ingredients happened to be the tastiest of mountain-gathered snails, eels from the lake, onions, garlic, beans and tomatoes from nearby *huertas* tumbled together with the plump round-grained rice of Valencia was happy coincidence. *Paella* was an instant success and remains so today. Named for the pan in which it's cooked, the Latin *paellera*, it developed to become *paella valenciana*, which brings together the best of local seafood: shrimp — small *quisquillas* left whole for flavor, large ones to peel and eat with the fingers; chunky fish, succulent shellfish; a bright red flavorful stock made from tomatoes, onions and garlic simmered in seafood stock, a sprinkling of fresh mountain herbs, a splash of color from peas and beans, some meaty pieces of chicken or pork ... the lot bathed in the golden glow of saffron, enlivened with a splash of sherry and brought to the table steaming hot and bewitchingly fragrant. *Arroz abanda*, from Castellón de la Plana, is another seafood rice combination, simmering the seafoods first, then cooking the rice in the resultant stock and serving the two dishes separately ... literally "rice apart." And in Alicante, they give rice a crusty surface by pouring on beaten egg to brown in the oven. They even use a type of short vermicelli, *fideuá*, to make a dish in the paella style.

Frogs and snails and turtledoves, *fideuá* and *turrón*. Valencia produces large frogs whose tender legs are much in demand for export; the snails are plumper than their counterparts in Catalonia, and sweetly fleshed. Turtledoves, partridges and other game birds are there to hunt and trap on the barren hillsides and grasslands. *Turrón* is a delectable nougat, legacy of Arab times, that is made to perfection in Jijona and Alicante. Finely ground almond meal and honey, laced with hazelnuts and almonds, it's a festive food, a must for Christmas, but now made for sale all over Spain. I find it absolutely irresistible and several boxes of *turrón* (and some delightful little sugared violets I discovered in Madrid) are always stowed in my hand luggage when I leave Spain!

There is Arab influence evident in the crops of almonds, oranges and dates. Elche is the city of date palms, a vigorous, profitable crop. Many local sweets, cakes and biscuits are almond-based, including, of course *turrón*. Like the Catalans, the Valencianos also add surprise ingredients to a dish — pears in a vegetable stew, rabbit and chicken together, sweet tastes in savory foods. They often borrow the *sofrito* and *picada* techniques from their northern neighbor, and the garlicky *alioli*. Their *gazpachos* might be meaty with fish or game, unlike the cooling vegetable blends of nearby Andalusia, and their *ollas* (stews) pack in plenty of local vegetables and flavor them with sausages and pork.

Murcia's hinterland has sloping hills that face the sea — good grape-growing territory, especially around the towns of Yecla and Jumilla.

GUISO DE TRIGO
CREAMY WHEAT POTAGE

SERVES 6–8

1 cup/250 g/8 oz wheat grains

½ cup/90 g/3 oz garbanzos (chickpeas), soaked overnight

1 ham/bacon hock (about 1 lb/ 500 g)

1 lb/500 g shoulder or foreleg of pork, sliced

10 cups/2.5 l/2½ qt water

8 oz/250 g yellow squash, peeled and diced

2 medium potatoes, peeled and diced

1 medium turnip, peeled and diced

1 medium zucchini (courgette), diced

2 teaspoons sweet paprika

salt and pepper

2 teaspoons chopped fresh mint

Soak the wheat for 2 hours; drain. Place wheat, drained garbanzos, ham and pork in a large saucepan and add the water. Bring to a boil and simmer for 2 hours. Add the vegetables and simmer another 1 hour.

Discard ham bone and cut pork into smaller pieces. Return to the soup with the seasoning and heat for 6 to 7 minutes. Sprinkle on chopped mint before serving.

Variations: Use presoaked white beans instead of garbanzos, with sweet potato and white potatoes as the vegetables. In Portugal, coarsely ground chestnuts sometimes replace the wheat.

GAZPACHO DE MERO
GAZPACHO WITH GROUPER

SERVES 4

1 pound/500 g fillets of grouper (or sea bass)

salt and white pepper

¼ cup/60 ml/2 fl oz olive oil

4 large onions, chopped

4 cloves garlic, chopped

2 hot red chili peppers, seeded and chopped

4 large tomatoes, peeled, seeded and chopped

2 bay leaves

½ teaspoon fennel seeds

6 cups/1.5 l/1½ qt fish stock

1 slice day-old bread

¼ cup/30 g/1 oz blanched almonds

Cut the fish into cubes, sprinkle with salt and pepper and set aside. Heat half the oil and fry the onions, garlic and chili until very well colored. Remove about ⅓ of the mixture and set aside. Add tomatoes to the pan and cook until thick and pastelike. Add the bay leaves, fennel and fish stock, bring to a boil and simmer for 20 minutes.

Fry the bread and almonds in the remaining oil until golden. Drain and grind to a thick paste in a food processor with the reserved onion. Add fish to the soup and cook gently for about 12 minutes or until tender. Stir in the puréed ingredients and cook a further 5 to 10 minutes. Serve hot.

EMPANADAS VALENCIANAS
STUFFED SAVORY PASTRIES

MAKES 6

The savory pies the Spanish call *empanadas* are something of a barometer of the Spanish way of life; there is a type to suit every occasion. The *empanada gallega* of Galicia is a large family-sized pie. Some, like this recipe, are a single serving. Smaller ones known as *empanadillas* are eaten in quantity in *tapas* bars all over the country. Fillings are equally variable. Most popular are tuna and *bacalao*, but then the Catalan *samfaina* is delicious encased in pastry, as are braised peppers, cured and smoked ham, bonito, *chorizo* and egg.

1 recipe empanada/empanadilla pastry (page 269)

1 leek, trimmed, rinsed and chopped

1 large clove garlic, minced

2 tablespoons olive oil

2 small very ripe tomatoes, peeled, seeded and chopped

4 oz/120 g *jamón serrano* or other cured ham*, very finely diced

2 hard-boiled eggs, chopped

1 tablespoon finely chopped parsley

salt and pepper

1 egg, beaten

Prepare the dough and set aside. Sauté the leek with garlic in the oil until softened, add tomato and cook briefly. Add the ham and sauté briefly, then remove from the pan and let cool.

Mix chopped eggs and parsley into filling, seasoning to taste. Roll out the dough thinly and use a circular cutter to make 6 rounds of pastry. Place a portion of filling to one side of each, leaving the edge uncovered. Use a small brush to moisten the edges with water, then fold over and pinch or crimp the edges to seal. Prick tops with a fork or skewer. Brush with beaten egg and place on a greased baking sheet. Bake in a preheated 400°F/200°C/Gas 6 oven for about 25 minutes or until the tops are golden brown.

*Or use slightly more *jamón de york* or other cooked ham.

Tip: *Empanadas* can be frozen before baking; bake frozen pastries for about 35 minutes. Make *empanadillas* with a 2½ inch/7 cm cutter; makes about 40.

ANCAS DE RANA REBOZADAS CON SALSA DE TOMATE
FRIED FROGS' LEGS IN FRESH TOMATO SAUCE   SERVES 4

30 prepared frogs' legs

2 cloves garlic, mashed

salt and pepper

1½ cups/180 g/6 oz all-purpose (plain) flour

2 eggs, beaten

2 cups/500 ml/16 fl oz vegetable oil

parsley sprigs

lemon wedges or orange slices

Sauce:

1 small onion, finely chopped

2 tablespoons olive oil

2 large sun-ripened tomatoes, peeled and seeded

1 small red bell pepper (capsicum), seeded and chopped

1 teaspoon sweet paprika

¼ teaspoon aniseed, lightly crushed, or 1 tablespoon Pernod

salt and pepper

For the sauce, sauté the onion in the olive oil until golden. Add the tomatoes and cook until softened; add the pepper and continue to cook until very soft. (It should not be necessary to add liquid, but if the sauce looks too thick or is beginning to stick to the pan, add a little cold water or chicken stock.) Add the paprika, aniseed, salt and pepper and cook for 5 minutes. Pass through a sieve and keep warm.

Rinse and dry the frogs' legs. Make a paste of the garlic, salt and pepper and rub over the legs. Coat lightly with flour. Dip into beaten egg, then coat lightly with flour again. Fry in the oil until golden brown. Remove and drain well. Spoon a pool of the sauce into the center of 4 appetizer plates and arrange the frogs' legs like the spokes of a wheel on top. Garnish with sprigs of parsley and small wedges of lemon or slices of orange. Serve at once.

TORTILLA DE GAMBAS
SHRIMP OMELETTE   SERVES 4

1 small onion, very finely chopped

3 tablespoons olive oil

6 garlic chives, finely chopped

1¼ cups/180 g/6 oz small peeled cooked shrimp (prawns)

6 eggs, beaten

salt and pepper

Sauté the onion in half the oil until it softens. Add the garlic chives and shrimp and cook briefly, then mix with the eggs, adding salt and pepper. Heat an omelette pan with the remaining oil. When very hot, pour in the egg mixture and lower the heat to medium. Cook until the underside is golden, firming the sides of the omelette by running a spatula around the edge several times. Set a plate inside the rim of the pan over the omelette, invert it onto the plate, then slide back into the pan to cook the other side until golden. Cut into 4 wedges to serve.

PIPIRRANA
SALAD OF DRIED SALT COD AND GREENS   SERVES 4–6

8 oz/250 g prepared *bacalao*
(page 266)

1 small head romaine (cos) lettuce

1 medium cucumber, seeded and
sliced

1 medium-size green bell pepper
(capsicum), seeded and sliced

2 green spring onions (shallots/
scallions), trimmed and chopped

2 firm tomatoes, seeded and
chopped

1 fresh hot red chili pepper,
seeded and minced

2 cloves garlic, minced

2 tablespoons red wine vinegar

$\frac{1}{3}$ cup/90 ml/3 fl oz virgin olive oil

salt and pepper

Rinse the *bacalao* and drain; pick out bones and cut meat into small cubes. Rinse lettuce; dry and shred roughly. Mix fish and salad vegetables together in a bowl. Whisk chili pepper and garlic with vinegar, oil, salt and pepper and toss with the salad. Serve chilled.

MEJILLONES AL VAPOR
STEAMED MUSSELS   SERVES 6 AS FIRST COURSE

Fresh scallops (*vieiras*) and clams in the shell can also be cooked this way (scrub shellfish thoroughly with a brush; rinse and drain. Cover with cold water and soak for at least 1 hour). Hot or cold steamed shellfish are served in many ways — simply with a squeeze of lemon and a drizzle of olive oil; in a fresh tomato sauce flavored with wine or sherry vinegar or garlic; or with a classic *romesco*. The top shell is removed and the mussel is loosened from the base, then covered with the sauce and dressed with a sprinkling of chopped parsley. The shellfish should be chilled for at least 1 hour before serving.

30 fresh mussels in the shell

juice of 1 large lemon

2 tablespoons olive oil

$\frac{1}{2}$ cup/120 ml/4 fl oz water

large pinch of salt

chopped fresh herbs

Place the mussels in a large saucepan with the lemon juice, oil, water and salt. Cover tightly and cook over high heat for about 4 minutes shaking the pan frequently to encourage the shells to open. Lift mussels out and transfer to plates. Spoon on the liquid from the pan and dust with a sprinkling of chopped fresh herbs such as parsley or dill. Serve at once.

Tip: Make a creamy white sauce by crushing blanched toasted almonds to a paste with a small piece of white bread, previously soaked in olive oil to soften it, and then adding olive oil, wine vinegar and seasoning to taste. It should be very peppery.

69

Cebollitas al Horno

BAKED BABY ONIONS · SERVES 4

16 small onions, peeled
3 tablespoons olive oil
2 tablespoons dry white wine
1 tablespoon white wine vinegar
3 cloves garlic, finely chopped
$2\frac{1}{2}$ teaspoons sweet paprika
salt and pepper

Cut the tops from the onions and flatten the bases without cutting so deeply that they fall apart. Stand in a small baking dish and add the oil, wine and vinegar. Sprinkle the garlic, paprika, salt and pepper evenly over the onions and cover the dish with perforated aluminum foil. Bake in a preheated 350°F/180°C/Gas 4 oven for about 40 minutes, basting twice and uncovering in the final 10 minutes to crisp the surface.

Guisantes a la Murciana

PEAS MURCIA STYLE · SERVES 6

Green peas are used extensively in the Spanish cuisine. Traditionally peas are not simply cooked by themselves, but with other vegetables or diced meats; they are also added to *paella* and to meat and seafood dishes. A tiny wild white pea known as *guisias* has been eaten in Spain since earliest times and is used in an important Lenten dish, *guinad,* on the island of Ibiza. In Murcia this is a favorite.

1 small onion, minced
1 large carrot, peeled and cut into small dice
5 oz/150 g smoked ham, cut into small dice
2 tablespoons olive oil
3 cups/500 g/1 lb shelled fresh peas
6 dark green outer leaves of lettuce or spinach, very finely shredded
$\frac{1}{2}$ teaspoon sugar
salt and pepper

Sauté the onion, carrot and ham in the oil for 5 to 6 minutes. Add the peas and cook another 1 to 2 minutes, stirring constantly. Add the lettuce, sugar, salt and pepper to the pan, cover and cook over low heat, shaking the pan occasionally, until the peas are cooked, about 15 minutes.

CARDOS FRITOS
FRIED CARDOONS   SERVES 4

This large thistle, related to the artichoke, grows well in the Mediterranean regions. Its long, thick, grey-green stems are fleshy like those of celery, and it can be cooked in the same way — *au gratin* in bechamel or braised with tomato sauce. Or the vegetable can be treated like an artichoke and fried in batter.

2 lb/1 kg *cardo* (cardoon) stems

2 tablespoons lemon juice

1 cup/120 g/4 oz all-purpose (plain) flour

2 eggs, beaten

4 cups/1 l/1 qt olive or vegetable oil for frying

Trim off any leaves from the vegetables and use a vegetable peeler to remove skin and strings. Cut into 2-inch/5-cm lengths. Place in a pan of cold water and add the lemon juice. Let stand for 30 minutes, then bring to a boil and simmer until just tender. Drain. When the cardoons are dry, coat with flour. Heat the oil in a wide pan. Dip the vegetables into the egg and slide into the oil. Fry until crisp. Drain well and serve hot.

PISTO DE CALABACÍN
BRAISED ZUCCHINI (COURGETTES)   SERVES 4

This version of the classic *pisto* emphasizes zucchini (courgettes) instead of red peppers. Serve it with roasted or grilled meats or by itself as a first course, or make it into a main course by adding canned tuna or cooked shrimp (prawns).

1 large red bell pepper (capsicum)

1½ lb/750 g small zucchini (courgettes)

2 medium onions, sliced

½ cup/120 ml/4 fl oz olive oil

2 large sun-ripened tomatoes, peeled, seeded and chopped

1 teaspoon mixed dried herbs

salt and pepper

large pinch of sugar

Roast the pepper in a hot oven until the skin blisters, about 30 minutes, then remove and wrap in a kitchen towel. Cut the zucchini in half lengthwise and place in a heavy saucepan with the onions and oil. Cook over medium heat for about 10 minutes, turning the vegetables to cook evenly. Add the tomatoes, herbs, salt and pepper. Cut the pepper into narrow strips, discarding skin and seeds. Add to the pan. Cover and cook over low heat until the vegetables are very tender. Add the sugar. Serve hot or cold.

ENSALADA VALENCIANA
ORANGE SALAD WITH OLIVES

SERVES 4–6

The groves of golden Valencia oranges are one of the most inspiring sights for the traveler in coastal Valencia, particularly around the city of Castellón de la Plana and the fertile valley of the Mijares River. Naturally oranges are used in the cooking of this region — with braised meat, in creamy desserts and frequently in salads.

4 Valencia oranges

1 small iceberg or romaine (cos) lettuce

1 red Spanish or salad onion

$\frac{1}{3}$ cup/90 ml/3 fl oz virgin olive oil

$1\frac{3}{4}$ tablespoons white wine vinegar

salt and pepper

1 cup/150 g/5 oz small black pitted olives

Using a small, sharp knife, peel the oranges so that the white pith is completely removed. Slice thickly. Rinse the lettuce, shake dry and tear the leaves into manageable sizes. Very thinly slice the onion. Whisk the oil and vinegar together with salt and pepper and pour over the salad. Add olives. Toss well and chill briefly before serving.

Variation: Immediately before serving, add croutons of bread spread with mashed garlic and fried in olive oil.

ENSALADA DE NARANJA Y AGUACATE
ORANGE AND AVOCADO SALAD

SERVES 4

2 Valencia oranges

2 ripe avocados

6 pitted black olives

1 green (spring) onion (shallot/ scallion), salad onion or small brown onion

2 teaspoons chopped fresh herbs (basil, parsley, tarragon)

2 tablespoons extra-virgin olive oil

salt and pepper

Peel and slice the oranges in the same way as for *Ensalada Valenciana.* Peel the avocados carefully and cut into bite-size cubes. Arrange in a salad dish. Slice the olives and finely chop the onion. Mix olives with the onion, herbs, oil, salt and pepper. Pour over the salad and serve.

Variation: Add diced ripe but firm tomato to the dressing.

Empanadas Valencianas, p.67

Dorada a la Sal, opposite

DORADA A LA SAL
GILTHEAD BAKED ON A BED OF SALT

SERVES 6–8

On the coast from the city of Murcia is the *Mar Menor*, the "small sea" landlocked by a narrow peninsula. Northwards to the mouth of the Segura River, just south of the popular beach resort city of Alicante, is an area of shallow lakes and salt flats. Here locally caught seafood and particularly the prized gilthead, a variety of sea bream, is baked or cooked outdoors over an open charcoal fire *a la sal* — in a thick coating of crystalline local salt. This cooking method has been in use for centuries — in ancient China for cooking chickens, in Japan for shellfish, and even the Romans found it an effective way to lock in the natural juices of food while baking.

4-lb/2-kg whole fresh sea bass, grouper, salmon or reef fish

1 lemon, sliced

salt and pepper

4 bay leaves

2 sprigs fennel

2 tablespoons olive oil

7 lb/3½ kg rock/sea salt

extra lemon slices

Clean the fish, scale* and rinse. Drain and dry well. Place several lemon slices in the cavity with salt, pepper, bay leaves and fennel. Drizzle in half the olive oil. Spread half the rock salt in a large oven dish and nestle the fish into it. Drizzle remaining oil over the fish and cover with the salt. Bake in a preheated 400°F/200°C/Gas 6 oven for 35 minutes.

Scrape off the salt and lift out the fish. Place on a serving plate and surround with fresh lemon slices.

*You may choose not to scale the fish; the scales and skin can be easily removed together when the fish is cooked.

ANGUILAS EN ALL I PEBRE
EELS IN PEPPER AND GARLIC SAUCE

SERVES 6–8

3 lb/1.5 kg fresh- or saltwater eel

salt and pepper

¼ cup/60 ml/2 fl oz olive oil

1 tablespoon sweet paprika

4 cloves garlic, chopped

10 threads saffron, toasted

2 oz/60 g toasted blanched almonds

1 tablespoon chopped parsley

Clean the eel and rinse thoroughly. Cut around the head and strip off the skin. Cut into thick steaks and season with salt and pepper. Heat oil in a *cazuela* and add paprika. Immediately add 2 cups/500 ml/16 fl oz hot water. Boil 2 minutes, then add eel.

Grind garlic, saffron, almonds and parsley together. Add to the pan with salt and pepper. Cook, covered, until eel is tender, about 8 minutes. Garnish with more parsley.

SARDINAS A LA MURCIANA
SARDINES WITH TOMATOES IN A CASSEROLE   SERVES 6

24 small fresh sardines, about 1½ lb/750 g

5 large sun-ripened tomatoes, sliced

1 large onion, sliced

1 large potato, peeled and very thinly sliced

1 green bell pepper (capsicum), seeded and sliced

3 cloves garlic, sliced

2 tablespoons chopped parsley

salt and pepper

2 tablespoons olive oil

2 tablespoons fresh breadcrumbs

1–2 teaspoons chopped fresh herbs

Clean and rinse fish thoroughly. Remove fillets, leaving backbones attached to heads; discard bones or reserve for making fish stock. Coat a casserole generously with olive oil. Place ⅓ of the tomato in the casserole, followed by half the onion, potato and pepper. Arrange half the fish evenly over the top. Scatter on garlic and parsley and season generously with salt and pepper. Add more tomato and repeat layering, then spread remaining tomato on top and season with salt and pepper. Drizzle half of the olive oil evenly over the casserole. Bake in a preheated 350°F/180°C/Gas 4 oven for about 50 minutes; after 30 minutes, remove the foil and sprinkle on bread-crumbs mixed with the chopped herbs and the remaining olive oil.

RAPE AL HORNO
BAKED MONKFISH (ANGLERFISH)   SERVES 4

This pugnacious-looking fish, with its large, ugly head and mottled grey skin, inhabits the waters around the coast of Spain in vast numbers. It is prepared in many ways, but is particularly good baked with a sauce. Being rather unappealing in its natural state, monkfish is almost never served whole.

1⅓ lb/650 g monkfish (choose 4 even-sized pieces)

juice of ½ lemon

salt and white pepper

1–2 cloves garlic, minced

1½ tablespoons blanched almonds

1 tablespoon pine nuts

3 tablespoons olive oil

1 large onion, thinly sliced

2 large sun-ripened tomatoes, peeled, seeded and sliced

¼ cup/30 g/1 oz fresh breadcrumbs

1 teaspoon sweet paprika

small pinch of powdered saffron

Place the fish pieces side by side in a greased baking dish and sprinkle on the lemon juice, salt and pepper. Cover with aluminum foil and bake in a preheated 375°F/170°C/Gas 5 oven for 10 minutes.

Sauté the garlic, almonds and pine nuts in the oil until golden. Drain and grind to a paste. Fry the onion until very well colored, then push to one side of the pan and fry the tomatoes until soft. Add the nut mixture, bread-crumbs, paprika and any liquid from the pan in which the fish were cooked. Mix well and stir in the saffron dissolved in a little hot water, milk or fish stock. Spread over the fish and bake for a further 15 to 18 minutes. Serve in the dish.

FIDEUÁ
VERMICELLI WITH SEAFOOD

SERVES 4

1 lb/500 g fresh cod, halibut, bass or other firm white fish

16 medium shrimp (prawns) in the shell

$\frac{1}{3}$ cup/90 ml/3 fl oz olive oil

2 cloves garlic, sliced

1 small hot red chili pepper, seeded and chopped

1 teaspoon sweet paprika

4 sun-ripened tomatoes, peeled, seeded and chopped

12 oz/350 g *fideos* or broken spaghettini, or 4 bundles *fedeli*

6 cups/1.5 l/1$\frac{1}{2}$ qt fish stock

salt and pepper

Cut the fish into bite-size cubes. Fry fish and shrimp in the oil for 3 to 4 minutes, then remove. Fry the garlic, pepper and paprika briefly, then add the tomatoes and cook, stirring, for 3 to 4 minutes. Pour in the fish stock, bring to a boil and simmer for 5 minutes. Add the pasta and return the fish and shrimp. Cook, stirring occasionally, until the pasta is tender. Add salt and pepper to taste and serve in the pan.

Tip: The pan can be placed in a very hot oven for about 10 minutes or until the top is crisped and the liquid absorbed.

TERNERA CON NARANJA
MEDALLIONS OF VEAL IN ORANGE GLAZE

SERVES 6

1$\frac{1}{2}$ lb/750 g veal round or rump roast

1 teaspoon salt

2 cloves garlic, mashed

2 tablespoons olive oil

1 medium onion, sliced

2 large sweet oranges

1-inch/2.5-cm cinnamon stick

1 whole clove

4 black peppercorns

2 bay leaves

1 sprig parsley

1 cup/250 ml/8 fl oz veal stock

$\frac{1}{2}$ cup/75 g/2$\frac{1}{2}$ oz small green olives

Rub the roast with salt and mashed garlic and brown in the oil. Transfer to a casserole. Brown the onion in the remaining oil and place around the meat. Use a vegetable parer to remove the colored part of the rind from the oranges and cut into shreds. Squeeze juice and add juice, rind, spices and herbs to the pan. Add stock, cover and cook for 1 hour. Add the olives and cook a further 15 to 20 minutes or until the meat is very tender.

Remove meat and discard spices and herbs. Thinly slice meat and arrange on a serving plate. Boil sauce until syrupy and spoon over the meat.

CHULETAS DE CORDERO EN AJO CABAÑIL
LAMB CUTLETS WITH GARLIC

SERVES 6

From Murcia comes the favored dish of sliced lamb and potatoes fried in good olive oil, then dressed with a *majado* (rather like the Catalan *picada*) of mashed garlic and paprika sharpened with wine vinegar. Here baby lamb cutlets are served on a bed of sliced potatoes and given this same delicious finale.

12–18 well-trimmed lamb cutlets

$\frac{1}{2}$ cup/120 ml/4 fl oz olive oil

4 medium potatoes, peeled and sliced on a mandolin

4–7 cloves garlic, finely chopped

$1\frac{1}{4}$ teaspoons hot paprika

$1\frac{1}{2}$ tablespoons red wine vinegar

salt and pepper

Fry the cutlets in the oil in a wide pan until evenly browned on the surface and still slightly pink in the center, about 7 minutes. Remove and set aside. In the same pan fry the potatoes until crisp and golden. Arrange the cutlets on top. Mix the garlic and paprika and moisten with the vinegar. Add salt and pepper and pour over the dish. Serve at once.

Tip: If preferred, the garlic can be sautéed in olive oil until just golden.

CORDERO CON ALMENDRAS
LAMB IN ALMOND SAUCE

SERVES 6

4 lb/2 kg leg of lamb

3 tablespoons lard

1 whole head garlic, peeled

5 medium onions, sliced

5 large sun-ripened tomatoes, seeded and chopped

2 bay leaves

2 sprigs fresh thyme or rosemary

1 inch/2.5-cm cinnamon stick

$1\frac{1}{2}$ cups/400 ml/13 fl oz dry white wine

3 cups/750 ml/24 fl oz veal or chicken stock

1 cup/100 g/$3\frac{1}{2}$ oz ground almonds

12 threads saffron

salt and pepper

1 tablespoon chopped parsley

Bone the leg and cut the meat into 2-in (5-cm) cubes. Brown in a large roasting pan in the lard. Add the whole garlic cloves and onions. Cover and roast in a preheated 350°F/180°C/Gas 4 oven for 30 minutes, turning meat and stirring the onions twice. Add the tomatoes, herbs, cinnamon stick, wine and stock and roast a further 1 hour.

Discard herbs and cinnamon stick. Add the almonds, saffron mixed with a little boiling water, and seasoning to taste. Cover and roast 35 to 40 minutes longer. Stir in half the parsley and use the remainder to garnish the dish.

PASTEL DE CARNE MURCIANO
OLD-STYLE MEAT PIE

SERVES 4–6

Like the Cornish pasties of England, this is a peasant-style convenience food. I love to pop a few into a picnic basket with salads and a good bottle of wine. This recipe makes one large pie or can be made into four or even six individual ones.

1 recipe pie pastry (page 269)

1 green bell pepper (capsicum), seeded and chopped

1 red bell pepper (capsicum), seeded and chopped

1 medium onion, sliced

2 tablespoons olive oil

7 oz/200 g *chorizo* sausage, thinly sliced

3 oz/90 g salted *tocino* or other salt pork/bacon, chopped

6 oz/180 g beef or veal steak, cut into thin strips

2 hard-boiled eggs, chopped

2 tablespoons chopped parsley

1 large tomato, peeled, seeded and chopped

salt and pepper

1 egg, beaten

Prepare the pastry and roll out to size: If making individual pies, it should be large enough for four 6-in (15-cm) and four 4½-in (10-cm) circles, or six slightly smaller ones. Otherwise, cut in 2 parts, with one slightly larger than the other.* Press the larger pastry piece(s) into one large or several smaller lightly greased pie dishes covering the sides.

Sauté the peppers and onion in the oil for about 5 minutes or until softened. Layer the meats in the pastry and cover with the peppers and onion. Arrange the eggs over the meats and sprinkle with the parsley. Top with tomato. Season with salt and pepper. Position the top pastry and pinch the edges to seal. Crimp decoratively. Make a slit in the top of the pie(s) and brush the top with beaten egg. Bake in a preheated 375°F/190°C/Gas 5 oven for about 50 minutes or until well browned and crisp. Serve hot or cold.

*An interesting spiral effect can be achieved for the pie top/tops. Cut the rolled-out pastry into strips, wind them into one large or 4 small spirals. Press to flatten and roll out to the required size.

ARROZ ABANDA

RICE AND FISH "SERVED APART"

SERVES 6

While other Valencian rice dishes contain a variety of meats or seafoods, in this classic dish the rice and seafood are served *a banda*, meaning "apart". Saffron-yellow rice cooked in the seafood stock is the first course; then comes the plain boiled seafood with a pot of *alioli*, lemon wedges and crusty bread.

1 lb/500 g white fish fillets, cubed

1 lb/500 g large shrimp (prawns) in the shell

1 lb/500 g clams or mussels in the shell

$\frac{1}{2}$ lb/250 g squid, cleaned

2 bay leaves

1 sprig parsley

1 teaspoon black peppercorns

salt

1 medium onion, chopped

$\frac{1}{2}$ cup/125 ml/4 fl oz olive oil

6 large cloves garlic, minced

3 large sun-ripened tomatoes, peeled and seeded

$1\frac{1}{2}$ teaspoons sweet paprika

12 threads saffron

2 cups/400 g/14 oz short-grain/ round white rice

pepper

$\frac{1}{4}$ cup/70 ml/2 fl oz dry sherry

lemon wedges

Place the seafood in a large pan with the bay leaves, parsley and peppercorns. Add 6 cups/1.5 l/1$\frac{1}{2}$ qt water and 1 teaspoon salt. Bring almost to a boil, then reduce heat and simmer for 12 minutes. Strain liquid into a jug and set aside. Discard herbs and peppercorns. Cover seafood and set aside.

In another pan fry the onion in olive oil until golden, add garlic and fry briefly. Add tomatoes and cook 2 minutes. Add paprika and saffron, ground with a little of the reserved stock. Add rice and stir to coat the grains with oil. Bring 4 cups/1 l/1 qt of the reserved stock to a boil and add $\frac{1}{3}$ to the rice. Cook over high heat for 5 to 6 minutes. Add salt and pepper to taste, then add $\frac{1}{3}$ more liquid and cook, stirring occasionally, until the rice has almost absorbed the liquid. Add the remaining stock and cook until all liquid has been absorbed and the rice grains are separate and tender. Sprinkle sherry over the rice and let stand a few minutes before spooning into a serving dish. Serve seafood separately with a pot of *alioli* and plenty of lemon wedges.

ARROZ NEGRO CON CALAMARES RELLENOS

"BLACK" RICE WITH STUFFED SQUID

SERVES 6

Rice and pasta dishes cooked *al negro* — with the blue/black ink of squid or cuttlefish — are popular all along the Mediterranean coast. The ink, which in the past was used in the production of sepia for photography printing, gives delicate nuances of flavor and a distinct gray-black color. Extra squid ink sacs are needed to give enough color to the rice, as squid expel part of their ink when netted.

For the rice:

12 good-size whole squid, about 2 lb/1 kg

3 cups/750 ml/24 fl oz boiling water or fish stock

1 medium onion, chopped

2 cloves garlic, minced

3 tablespoons virgin olive oil

2 cups/450 g/14 oz short-grain/round white rice

salt and pepper

Filling:

1 small onion, minced

1 clove garlic, minced

2 oz/60 g pork sausage meat

1 teaspoon chopped fresh fennel

2 tablespoons fresh breadcrumbs

1 tablespoon chopped almonds or pine nuts

Remove heads from squid and carefully cut away ink sacs. Place sacs in a fine sieve and pour on 1 cup/250 ml/8 fl oz of the water or fish stock, pressing with a spoon to force the ink from the sacs. Let stand for at least 1 hour.

Very finely chop the squid tentacles and set aside. Clean and rinse 6 of the squid, reserving the others for another recipe. Sauté the onion and garlic in the oil, add rice and stir to coat with the oil. Pour the ink liquid over the rice and cook over high heat for 3 minutes, then add the remaining water or stock with salt and pepper. Set aside.

In another pan sauté the onion and garlic for the filling with sausage meat until lightly colored. Add tentacles, fennel, breadcrumbs and nuts and cook together. Press the filling into the squid without overfilling and secure the tops with toothpicks. Set on top of the rice and partially cover. Cook for 15 minutes or until the rice is tender and fluffy and has absorbed the liquid. Serve at once.

ARROZ CON MARISCOS

SEAFOOD RICE   SERVES 4–6

12 mussels in the shell

6–8 large shrimp (prawns)

1 medium lobster or crayfish,
about 1 lb/500 g

5 cups/1.25 l/40 fl oz water

1 bay leaf

1 small onion, peeled

$\frac{1}{3}$ cup/90 ml/3 fl oz olive oil

4 oz/120 g *jamón serrano* or other
cured ham

5 oz/150 g *chorizo* sausage, sliced

1 medium onion, chopped

1 clove garlic, minced

1 large tomato, peeled, seeded
and chopped

$2\frac{1}{2}$ cups/500 g/1 lb short-grain/
round white rice

1 teaspoon salt

$\frac{1}{3}$ teaspoon pepper

3 small fresh squid, cleaned and
sliced

8 oz/250 g white fish fillets, cubed

4 cooked or canned artichokes,
halved, or 4 fresh asparagus
stalks, cut into thirds

2 tablespoons finely chopped
parsley

10–12 threads saffron

lemon wedges

Scrub the mussels and rinse. Place shellfish in a pan with the water, bay leaf and small onion and bring to a boil. Cook 5 minutes, then drain, reserving the liquid. Cut lobster in half. Heat olive oil in an ovenproof skillet. Fry the ham, *chorizo* and onion for 2 minutes. Add garlic, tomato, rice, salt and pepper and stir over medium heat for 2 to 3 minutes. Reheat the liquid in which the seafood was boiled. Add a little to the saffron and grind to draw out the color. Add both to the rice and cook over high heat for 2 minutes. Add the squid, fish, artichokes or asparagus, half the parsley and the mussels, shrimp and lobster. Cook over low heat for about 15 minutes or until the rice has absorbed the liquid and is completely tender; or stir the seafood into the rice and bake in a preheated 400°F/200°C/Gas 6 oven for about the same amount of time. Sprinkle on the remaining parsley before serving with wedges of lemon.

ARROZ CON POLLO

RICE WITH CHICKEN

SERVES 4–6

3-lb/1.5-kg chicken

salt and pepper

$\frac{1}{2}$ cup/120 ml/4 fl oz olive oil

3 oz/90 g *chorizo* sausage, sliced

2 oz/60 g *jamón serrano* or other cured ham, diced

1 green bell pepper (capsicum), seeded and diced

1 medium onion, chopped

3 cloves garlic, finely chopped

1 small fresh hot red chili pepper, chopped

2 large very ripe tomatoes, peeled, seeded and chopped

1 teaspoon tomato paste

2 cups/400 g/14 oz short-grain/ round white rice

3 cups/750 ml/24 fl oz chicken stock or water

1 cup/250 ml/8 fl oz dry white wine

$\frac{1}{4}$ teaspoon powdered saffron

1–2 tablespoons chopped parsley

Cut the chicken into small serving pieces and season with salt and pepper. Brown in the oil in a wide skillet or *paella* pan for about 8 minutes, then remove. Sauté the sausage and ham briefly, then add the pepper, onion, garlic and chili and sauté until the onion has softened. Add tomatoes and paste and cook for 5 minutes, then add the rice and mix in well.

Bring the stock to a boil and pour over the rice, cooking over high heat for about 3 minutes. Add wine and reduce temperature to low. Cook, stirring to prevent the rice from sticking to the pan, until the liquid is below the level of the rice. Mix saffron with $\frac{1}{2}$ cup/120 ml/4 fl oz boiling water, pour over the rice and stir in with half the parsley. Arrange the chicken over the rice and bake in a preheated 400°F/200°C/Gas 6 oven for about 25 minutes or until the chicken is cooked through and the rice is fluffy. Garnish with the remaining parsley.

ARROZ A LA ALICANTINA
CRISP RICE ALICANTE STYLE   SERVES 4

½ cup/90 g/3 oz dried garbanzos (chickpeas), soaked overnight

12 oz/350 g chicken pieces

5 oz/150 g *chorizo* sausage

1 slice *jamón serrano* or other cured ham, about 3 oz/90 g

6 cups/1.5 l/1½ qt water

¼ cup/60 ml/2 fl oz olive oil

2 thick pork sausages

2 cups/400 g/14 oz short-grain/round white rice

1 tablespoon chopped parsley

1 teaspoon salt

black pepper

2 eggs, well beaten

Cook the chickpeas in boiling water over medium heat for about 2½ hours or until just tender. Separately simmer the chicken, *chorizo* and ham in the water for 40 minutes. Remove the meat, reserving 4 cups/1 l/1 qt of the liquid. Discard chicken bones and skin; cut meat into bite-size pieces. Slice sausage and cut ham into small cubes.

In an ovenproof skillet or pan heat the oil and fry the pork sausages until cooked through and well browned. Remove and slice. Fry the rice in the sausage drippings for a few minutes, then add the meats, parsley, salt and pepper. Pour in the reserved stock and add the chickpeas. Cook over high heat for a few minutes, then reduce to low, cover and cook a further 15 minutes.

Transfer rice to an ovenproof serving dish. Pour the beaten egg evenly over and bake in a preheated 425°F/210°C/Gas 7 oven for 5 to 6 minutes or until the surface is crisp and well colored.

ARROZ CON BACALAO, ALCACHOFAS Y GUISANTES
RICE WITH BACALAO, ARTICHOKES AND PEAS   SERVES 6

8 oz/250 g prepared *bacalao* (page 266)

3 cups/650 g/1¼ lb short grain white rice

1 13 oz/400 g can artichokes in brine

4 tablespoons olive oil

4 cloves garlic, peeled, chopped

3 medium sun-ripened tomatoes, seeded, chopped

salt and pepper

6 cups/1.5 l/1½ qt water

1¼ cups/250 g/8 oz fresh peas

12 threads saffron, ground (or ⅓ teaspoon powdered saffron)

Pick out any bones from the *bacalao* and remove skin. Cut into small cubes. Rinse and drain the rice. Drain the artichokes and set aside. Sauté the garlic in oil in a wide *paella*-style pan until softened. Add tomatoes and cook for 3-4 minutes. Add salt and pepper and half the water and bring to a boil. Simmer for 10 minutes. Add the *bacalao*, rice and peas and cook on very high heat for 10 minutes, stirring frequently to prevent the rice sticking to the pan. Add the artichokes and saffron which has been diluted with a little of the hot broth. Cook on moderate heat until the rice is tender, adding as much of the remaining water as is needed. The liquid should be completely absorbed into the rice leaving it moist, but with grains that are plump and not sticking together.

PAELLA

Paella is named after the *paellera*, a shallow round iron pan used for cooking this classic rice dish — which has become internationally known as the pride of the Valencian cuisine. (The word *paellera* comes from the Catalan language, where it means "skillet" or "frying pan," although this spectacular dish is not from Catalonia but from neighboring Valencia.) The pan is made of metal or earthenware; the latter is preferred by many cooks, as it absorbs a multitude of wonderful flavors from its many visits to the cooking fire, and it holds the heat well when brought to the table. The beaten metal type comes in two main forms. One has high sides and two handles; the other — and this is the one most likely to be placed in front of you in a restaurant, reposed on an iron frame with a receptacle for discarded shells underneath — is shallower, with a looped handle on either side.

The famous *huertas* (vegetable gardens) in Valencia's fertile coastal region, watered by a sophisticated irrigation system, have given rise to a crop of high-quality rice, and the local cuisine has developed around it. The best rice for *paella* is the short-grain variety, similar to the Italian *arborio*, which resembles the rounded type that grows in Valencia. A really good *paella* simply cannot be made without the right rice, but dispute still rages as to exactly what ingredients should accompany the saffron-gilded grains into the classic *paella valenciana*. Historians of gastronomy note that the original *paella* was created with local rice, eels and snails at a lake, *albufera de Valencia*, south of the city. Eel seems to have been replaced by shellfish (shrimp, mussels, squid, clams and the little red *cangrejo de río*) and fish, while the tiny local snails can be an interesting feature. Others enjoy the extra flavor of chicken and pork. Green beans, peas and peppers and the bright yellow of saffron make the dish spectacularly colorful.

Paellas are cooked on top of the stove, often directly over a wood fire. The technique involves adding the water gradually while stirring it into the rice so that it is completely absorbed. Two parts water to one part rice is the general rule, but this depends to some extent on the type of rice being used; some absorb more liquid than others.

PAELLA DE CAZA
PAELLA WITH GAME MEATS

SERVES 6

1 oven-ready partridge, woodcock or wild duck

1 oven-ready small rabbit or hare

4 large sun-ripened tomatoes, peeled and seeded

8 cloves garlic, chopped

2 large onions, thinly sliced

$\frac{1}{4}$ cup/60 ml/2 fl oz olive oil

1 bay leaf

$\frac{1}{2}$ 2-in/5-cm cinnamon stick

1 whole clove

salt and pepper

5 cups/1.25 l/40 fl oz water

2 cups/400 g/14 oz short-grain/round white rice

1 small green bell pepper (capsicum), seeded and chopped

1 small hot red chili pepper, seeded and chopped

$1\frac{1}{2}$ teaspoons sweet paprika

Cut the partridge in half and the rabbit into quarters and place in a saucepan. Fry half the tomatoes, garlic and onion in half the oil for 4 to 5 minutes, then add to the game with the bay leaf, spices, salt and pepper. Add the water and bring to a boil. Cook gently for at least 1 hour, tightly covered.

Remove the game and let cool. Strain the stock, reserving 4 cups/1 l/1 qt. In a *paella* pan, fry the remaining garlic and onion with the green pepper for 3 to 4 minutes, then add the remaining tomato and the chili and fry for 2 to 3 minutes. Add the rice, paprika, salt, pepper and $\frac{1}{3}$ of the strained stock. Cook for about 6 minutes, then add another $\frac{1}{3}$ of the stock.

In the meantime, remove the meat from the partridge and rabbit and cut into small pieces. Place on top of the rice, add the remaining stock and cook until the rice is tender. Stir before serving.

ENSALADA PARA PAELLA
SALAD FOR PAELLA

SERVES 4

3 lettuce hearts, quartered lengthwise, rinsed

1 medium cucumber (unpeeled), cut into chunks

3 small red tomatoes, cut into chunks or wedges

6 small red radishes, halved and soaked in iced water

1 cup/150 g/5 oz small peeled, cooked shrimp (prawns)

1 tablespoon chopped capers

3–4 tablespoons *salsa vinagreta* (page 274)

1 hard-boiled egg, quartered

Drain the lettuce hearts. Toss all of the ingredients together in a bowl and transfer to an oval platter. Serve chilled.

Paella Valenciana
VALENCIA STYLE RICE

SERVES 6

1 lb/500 g chicken meat (preferably from the thigh)

8 oz/250 g lean pork

salt

$\frac{1}{2}$ cup/120 ml/4 fl oz olive oil

1 large tomato, skinned, seeded and chopped

3 cloves garlic, peeled and chopped

$\frac{2}{3}$ teaspoon sweet paprika

$\frac{1}{2}$ cup/90 g/3 oz shelled fresh peas

$\frac{1}{2}$ cup/120 g/4 fl oz sliced green beans

12 prepared fresh or canned snails

2$\frac{1}{2}$ cups/300 g/10 oz short round-grain white rice

6 cups/1.5 l/1$\frac{1}{2}$ qt boiling water*

8–10 threads saffron

salt and pepper

12 clams in the shell, cleaned and soaked

6 mussels in the shell, cleaned and soaked

3 small squid, cleaned and cut into rings

6 small *langostinos* or large shrimp (prawns) or scampi

halved lemons

Cut the chicken into small pieces and pork into bite-sized cubes. Season with salt and brown in olive oil in a *paella* or other suitable large wide flat pan. Add the tomato, garlic and paprika, and stir on medium heat for 2 minutes. Add the peas, beans** and snails, then the rice and cook briefly. Add half the boiling water and cook until it is partially absorbed into the rice. Crush the saffron with 2 tablespoons of the boiling water and stir into the rice with salt and pepper. Add half the remaining hot water (or stock) to the rice and cook until partially absorbed. Place the clams, mussels, squid and *langostinos* or other shellfish on top of the rice and cook until rice is tender, adding the remaining liquid as needed. When the dish is done the rice should still be quite moist and should be chewy-tender. Stir seafood into the *paella* and serve in the pan with halved lemons.

*If you like, the seafood can be briefly poached in the water to add extra flavor.

**Traditionally, the vegetables are very well cooked in this dish. If you prefer them slightly more crisp, add them in the last 5 minutes of cooking.

PAN DE HIGOS
FIG LOG

SERVES 8

This delightful confection uses fleshy local dried figs. It's terrific with after-dinner coffee. Try cutting it into paper-thin slices (use a wet, very sharp knife) and sandwiching between thin leaves of chocolate!

1¼ lb/650 g dried figs

½ cup/90 g/3 oz finely chopped toasted hazelnuts

¼ cup/40 g/1½ oz confectioners' (icing) sugar

1 tablespoon finely grated lemon rind

1–2 tablespoons Pernod or other anise liqueur

2 tablespoons melted chocolate

Stem the figs and chop very finely. Mix in the nuts. Sprinkle with half the confectioners' sugar, the rind and enough liqueur to moisten. Add the melted chocolate and knead until the ingredients are well mixed. Cover a square of heavy-duty aluminum foil with the remaining confectioners' sugar. Shape the fig mixture into a log on a piece of lightly buttered plastic wrap, transfer to the prepared foil, wrap and squeeze gently. Let stand for at least 2 hours before slicing.

Variation: Shape mixture into small balls or ovals and press a whole toasted almond or hazelnut on top, or roll in toasted sesame seeds.

TURRÓN — NOUGAT

Christmas in Valencia is the time for *turrón,* a nougatlike candy made from almonds and honey. It is turned out from literally hundreds of factories and consumed in impressive volume at the year's end. Although it comes in many varieties, the ones from Alicante and nearby Jijona are considered the best. The former is made only with chopped or whole almonds, the latter with a mixture of finely ground almonds and hazelnuts. *Turrón* originated from the Moroccan sweet *jabane,* which is traditionally served during the Mimouna festivities held on the last night of the Jewish feast of the Passover.

TURRÓN DE ALICANTE

MAKES ABOUT 48 PIECES

Thin rice wafers or edible rice paper

1½ cups/500 g/1 lb clear honey

¼ cup/60 ml/2 fl oz water

¾ cup/180 g/6 oz sugar

3 egg whites

2 lb/1 kg blanched almonds, chopped*

1 tablespoon finely grated lemon rind

Line the bottom and sides of a square or rectangular cake tin with waxed paper, then with rice wafer(s). Heat the honey and water in a medium saucepan for 6 to 8 minutes. Add the sugar and heat until dissolved, stirring occasionally. Whip the egg whites to firm peaks and carefully fold into the hot honey mixture. Cook, stirring occasionally, until golden and beginning to caramelize. Stir in the chopped nuts and lemon rind, mixing well. Pour into the prepared pan and smooth the top. Cover with rice wafer(s) and more waxed paper. Place a flat board on top and weight it with several heavy objects. Allow the candy to cool, then slice and store in an airtight container.

*If preferred, toast the almonds until golden before using.

TURRÓN DE JIJONA

MAKES ABOUT 40 PIECES

1 lb/500 g blanched almonds

1 lb/500 g hazelnuts

1 cup/300 ml/10 fl oz clear honey

½ cup/120 g/4 oz sugar

5 egg whites

Prepare a pan as above. Toast the almonds in a medium oven until golden. Remove and crush to a semifine powder. Toast the hazelnuts long enough to loosen their skins. Rub skins off in a kitchen towel, then grind nuts to a semifine powder. (*Turrón* is usually smooth, but if preferred, the nuts can be half ground and half chopped to give the candy a crunchier texture.) Heat the honey and sugar together in a saucepan until the sugar has melted and begun to caramelize. Whip the egg whites to stiff peaks. Fold the nuts into the honey with the egg whites and cook, stirring frequently, for about 8 minutes. Spread into the prepared pan. Leave to firm up, then slice to serve.

CREMA DE CHOCOLATE

CHOCOLATE MOUSSE

SERVES 6

Rich, creamy chocolate mousse is a favorite Spanish dessert. In Valencia it is enlivened with orange.

6 eggs, separated

$\frac{3}{4}$ cup/180 g/6 oz sugar

1 tablespoon cornstarch (cornflour)

$\frac{3}{4}$ cup/180 ml/6 fl oz milk

$\frac{1}{2}$ teaspoon vanilla extract (essence)

2 large sweet oranges

$1\frac{1}{4}$ lb/650 g semisweet chocolate, chopped

3 tablespoons unsalted butter

whipped cream

Beat egg yolks with the sugar until fluffy. Add cornstarch, milk and vanilla and heat gently in a double boiler until slightly thickened, stirring constantly. Finely grate the rind of one orange and add to the custard with the chocolate. Continue to heat gently, stirring, until the chocolate has completely melted. Remove from heat, stir in the butter and let cool to room temperature.

Whisk the egg whites until stiff and glossy and fold into the mousse. Spoon into 6 tall dessert glasses and chill.

Use a vegetable peeler to thinly remove the rind of the other orange and cut into very fine shreds. Boil with 2 tablespoons sugar and 2 tablespoons water until crystallized, about 5 minutes. Remove and separate with a fork and dry on a rack.

Top each mousse with a swirl of cream and garnish with the crystallized orange rind.

ALMENDRADOS VALENCIANOS

VALENCIAN ALMOND COOKIES

MAKES 30

4 cups/420 g/14 oz ground almonds

1 cup/250 g/8 oz superfine sugar

finely grated rind of 2 oranges

$\frac{1}{2}$ teaspoon cinnamon

1 egg

3 egg whites

Mix almonds, sugar, orange rind and cinnamon in a bowl and make a well in the center. Beat the egg and egg whites together and blend into the mixture. Drop by teaspoonfuls onto a greased and floured baking sheet. Bake in a preheated 375°F/190°C/Gas 5 oven for 20 to 25 minutes or until lightly browned. The cookies will still feel slightly soft, but will firm up as they cool.

Arroz Abanda, p.80

Crema de Chocolate (left), p.90; Crema de Naranja (top right), opposite; Pan de Higos (front), p.88

CREMA DE NARANJA
ORANGE CUSTARD   SERVES 4

2 cups/500 ml/16 fl oz milk
½ cup/120 g/4 oz sugar
2 large sweet oranges
5 eggs

Heat milk and sugar together in the top of a double boiler with the rind of half an orange. Cook gently for 10 minutes, then discard rind. Beat 3 whole eggs and 2 yolks together*. Beat in a little of the hot milk, then strain into the remaining milk and add the grated rind of the other orange. Stir over gently simmering water until the custard is the thickness of heavy (thick) cream. Pour into 4 dessert dishes and chill.

Very finely shred the remaining peel and use to decorate the custards.

*The remaining whites can be beaten to stiff peaks and lightly sweetened with sugar. Cook by poaching in gently simmering water or sweetened milk, or pipe in little points onto a baking sheet covered with parchment (silicone) paper and bake in a very low oven for about 40 minutes or until dry and firm. Float on the custards.

Tips: If preferred, omit the grated orange rind and substitute 2 to 3 tablespoons orange liqueur.

Fill *buñuelitos* (page 31) with whipped cream, dust with confectioners' (icing) sugar and float on the custard.

CATALONIA AND THE BALEARIC ISLANDS

CATALUÑA Y LAS ISLAS BALEARES

One of the most enticing Spanish regions is *Cataluña* (Catalonia), in the northeast, encompassing the provinces of *Barcelona, Gerona, Lérida* and *Tarragona*. Curving along the coast from Perpignan in southern France to where it joins the Gulf of Valencia, which announces the border of the Valencia region, it has Spain's largest city, Barcelona, as its capital. Offshore the *Islas Baleares-Menorca* (Minorca), *Mallorca* (Majorca), *Ibiza* and *Formentera*, haven for sun-worshiping holiday makers, are embraced within the boundaries of this region. Catalonia has an area of over 12,000 square miles, spanning a range of diverse terrains from the forest-thatched Pyrenees, bordering France, to coastal Costa Brava and Costa Dorada, and some of the most spectacularly beautiful lake-dotted mountain country inland around Lérida. It's a province of abundance, of plentiful harvests of olives, grapes and grain. Of hundreds of different types of wild mushrooms pushing through the forest floor in myriad spectacular colors, of game to hunt and trap in the hills and seafood to net from the Mediterranean. Its well-fed sheep, cows and goats give rich milk for cheeses, and some of Spain's best are made here in the cool heights of the Pyrenees, for altitude always seems to improve the quality of a cheese. The Ebro river cuts through the southern lowlands to create a fertile valley for fruit, rice and vegetable cultivation, and the raising of excellent pigs.

The cooking of Catalonia has two distinct styles, that of the fishermen on the coast and of the countryfolk inland, where hearty home-style cooking is the order of the day. For despite influence from the Romans, from the Moors and from neighboring France, their cuisine, like any other, is built around availability of ingredients. One of the most prized coastal dishes is the evocative *zarzuela*, an "operetta" of seafood — a steaming pot packed with shellfish and meaty fish pieces swimming in a richly flavored broth. There's the simple pleasure of a *parrillada de mariscos*, succulent seafood spread on a charcoal grill, and giant *langostinos* to dip into garlic-redolent *alioli*. There are beans of many kinds to eat as *entremeses* (side dishes) or with plump white *butifarra* sausages. There is the nutty flavor of roasted red peppers dominating any number of dishes, or served as *escalivada* (roasted peppers) with an oil dressing. Catalan chefs are a mixture of fiercely traditional and searchingly creative. They number among the elite of Spanish chefs in both classic and *nueva cocina* (new cuisine) styles. I was impressed by an inspired salad of several kinds of seaweed, and a carpaccio of horsemeat at one restaurant I visited recently. But equally appealing was a bubbling *cazuela*, a potpourri of fresh wild mushrooms straight from the oven with nought but garlic to grace them. It is something approaching heaven to be in Catalonia in mushroom season. At every roadside junction someone waits to tempt passing traffic with baskets of golden *rovellons*, some the size of soup bowls. The mushrooms are there for the picking, springing up in profusion beneath the trees. Brown bolets, golden cèpes — some are bright orange or inky black like branching coral that has somehow escaped the sea, and there are long-stemmed yellow and buff ones, little rounded cerise ones. Some look disconcertingly dangerous, but the Catalans confirm that all are edible — an assurance that Spaniards from other regions have been known to heatedly dispute.

Catalonia and its history

Once an independent kingdom, after the death of Franco in 1977 Catalonia was again granted regional autonomy with its own local government, the *Generalitat*, a descendant of the body established in the 13th century as the *Corts Catalans*.

The Catalans enjoy a unique culture, an individual language and a cuisine distinct from that of either Spain or France, and with much that proclaims an ancient Roman heritage. They speak the sonorous Catalan here, not a dialect but a language quite distinct from the *castellano* that is the main language of Spain. But most have at least a smattering of *castellano* to assist the visitor, and menus usually come in both languages. It has long been a country of gourmets. The first gastronomic manuscripts in Catalan appeared in the 14th century, and many classic recipes are little changed from these early notations. The Romans instigated large-scale establishment of olive groves — today olive oil from Catalonia remains among the best-produced in the country — and grape orchards, and introduced many of their favorite dishes into the local cuisine. Evidence of Roman tastes is found still in such dishes as grilled red mullet with *salsa romesco*. One of the area's most famed culinary contributions, *romesco* sauce is a classic mixture of crushed almonds, hazelnuts, dried hot peppers and tomato, created in the old Roman capital of Tarragona. Another prized sauce is *all i oli (alioli)*, a potent garlic mayonnaise that is believed to have originated in Egypt and come to Spain, and also France, via the Romans. So from the beginning it was evident that Catalonia was destined to become a major gastronomic center, with Barcelona at its helm.

This vast, majestic and sophisticated port city is Spain's major business center, easily her most cosmopolitan, and a city of restaurants — over ten thousand in all. City squares are fringed with restaurants, their metal tables spilling out onto the squares and sidewalks, where diners can take coffee and a *flan* (egg custard tart), or pick at a plate of *caracoles* (snails) smothered in a piquant sauce beneath a lamp fashioned by the controversial and visionary Gaudí, Barcelona's favorite son of architecture. From humble cafes where you perch on a stool at a wooden table to munch on *pa amb tomàquet* and *jamón*, to the most formal and luxurious restaurant, at lunchtime hardly a seat is vacant. Barcelona is a tourist city, her sites overflowing with visitors from every part of the world. You'll find them munching on a *bocadillo* in the grounds of the magnificent cathedral. Or taking the funicular up Mount Tibidabo to dine in splendor above the expanse that is Barcelona, with a panoramic view of the Pyrenees on one side and the island of Mallorca on the other. Or discovering the wealth of seafood at one of her fish restaurants.

Away from the cities life goes on. The crops are tended, animals fed and families cared for with traditional hearty meals. Hotpots of chickpeas and meat, sausages and beans, plenty of deliciously crusty coarse-grain bread in large round loaves, the occasional rabbit from the trap. There's good wine to drink and olive oil to cook with — for Catalonia produces some of the nation's best.

There are five basic elements in Catalan cooking. The first is *sofrito* (*sofreigt* in Catalan), a slowly sautéed mass of onions with tomatoes, sometimes garlic, peppers and herbs, which is the main flavoring of stocks, sauces, soups and casseroles. *Picada*, which means "pounded," is a mixture of garlic, almonds or hazelnuts, parsley, fried bread and spices, which is ground to a paste to thicken and flavor dishes. *Alioli* (or *all i oli*) is an emulsified sauce of mashed garlic and olive oil similar to a mayonnaise, which accompanies grilled fish and meat. *Samfaina* is rather like the French ratatouille, tomatoes, zucchini, peppers and eggplant slowly sautéed in olive oil. It is a vegetable accompaniment, first course, ingredient of sauces and fillings and all-round multi-purpose dish. *Romesco*, the piquant peppery nut sauce, red with chilis, sweet peppers and tomatoes, enlivens grilled fish and vegetables.

Nestling astride the crest of the Pyrenees is the tiny gem that is Andorra — a principality since the 12th century, a forty-square-mile hiccup in the border between France and Spain. Her people speak both languages interchangeably, but are proudly Andorran. It's a wealthy enclave, snowbound in winter and the mecca of winter sports enthusiasts who flock there as much for the duty-free shopping as the snow sports. And it is a definite must for anyone on a gastronomic tour of Spain. The food is memorable. Here you can have real *cuina de muntanya* (mountain food) — snails, mushrooms, game, superb charcuterie and cheeses in picturesque surroundings reminiscent of Switzerland.

The largest island of the Balearic group lies just over 100 miles from the Spanish mainland, on the same latitude as Valencia. The islands have a history of invasion by Greeks, Romans, Moors, even Barbary pirates, all leaving behind a legacy of cuisine and culture. The food is most akin to that of Catalonia, but they do have their own specialties, such as soft, yeasty sweet buns, or *ensaimada*, shaped in immense spirals, and the pizzalike *coca mallorquina* cooked in brick bakers' ovens. The soft, pepper-spiked *sobrasada* sausage from Mallorca is in demand all over Spain. The islanders make an eggplant casserole similar to the Catalan one, but add fish and meat. The most important contribution of Menorca is the cheese *mahon*.

ESCUDELLA DE PAGÉS
PEASANT SOUP
SERVES 6

Like *Cocido Madrileño*, the hearty three-course meal revered by the people of the nation's capital, this appetizing thick and hearty soup-stew of beans, sausage, bacon and ham with vegetables, rice and pasta is one of the choicest of Catalan country dishes. It is best eaten on the day it is made while the starch vegetables retain their identity and texture. It can be served direct from the pot or separated into a soup of rice and pasta, the beans served with the meat and the sausages with the vegetables. For a lavish event, a giant meatball called a *pelota* of ground/minced meat spiced with garlic and cinnamon is simmered in the broth along with local *butifarra* sausages.

$\frac{1}{2}$ cup/90 g/3 oz dried chickpeas, soaked overnight

$\frac{1}{2}$ cup/90 g/3 oz dried white beans, soaked overnight

1-lb/500-g smoked bacon/ham hock

6 oz/180 g *tocino* (salt pork), cubed

1 bay leaf

1 small onion, peeled

9 cups/2.2 l/2$\frac{1}{4}$ qt water

4 oz/120 g *morcilla* or blood sausage

6 oz/180 g *chorizo* sausage

2 large potatoes, peeled and cubed

2 medium carrots, peeled and diced

1 medium turnip, peeled and diced

1 cup/90 g/3 oz chopped turnip/ beet greens

1 large onion, chopped

$\frac{1}{4}$ cup/60 g/2 oz short-grain/round rice

$\frac{1}{2}$ cup/90 g/3 oz broken egg noodles or pasta (optional)

1$\frac{1}{2}$ teaspoons salt

black pepper

Place chickpeas in a pan with water to generously cover, bring to a boil and simmer for about 2 hours, skimming occasionally. Drain. Place chickpeas, drained white beans, hock, *tocino*, bay leaf and onion in a large saucepan and bring to a boil. Reduce heat and simmer for about 2$\frac{1}{2}$ hours. Remove onion and hock and scrape meat from bone; discard bone and skin and cut meat into small dice. Return to the pan with the remaining ingredients and simmer for about 30 minutes or until very tender, or separate into 3 pots — one for cooking the rice and pasta in some of the broth, one for the vegetables and sausages, the third for the beans and meat. Check seasoning and serve hot.

Sopa de Pescado a la Catalana

FISH SOUP

SERVES 4–6

5 oz/150 g prepared *bacalao* (page 266)

7 cups/1.7 l/1¾ qt water

10 oz/300 g hake or other fish fillets, skinned

1 bay leaf

1 sprig parsley

1 small onion, very finely chopped

3 tablespoons olive oil

2 large tomatoes, coarsely chopped

4 cloves garlic, peeled

20 blanched almonds

½ teaspoon sweet paprika

pinch of ground saffron (optional)

salt and pepper

Place *bacalao* in a saucepan with half the water, bring to a boil and simmer for 10 minutes. Remove, break into small pieces and strain the liquid. Cut fish into cubes. Place in a saucepan with the remaining water, bay leaf and parsley and bring to a boil. Simmer 5 minutes. Sauté the onion in the olive oil until softened, add tomato and cook until soft. Grind the garlic and almonds finely in a mortar or food processor. Add to the tomato mixture and cook for 5 to 6 minutes, then purée in a food processor, adding the liquid from the *bacalao*. Pour into the fish soup, adding the reserved *bacalao*, and bring the soup to a boil. Simmer for 3 to 4 minutes, then add the paprika, saffron, salt and pepper. Heat through and serve with slices of lightly toasted bread.

Sopa de Tomillo

THYME SOUP

SERVES 6

1 large onion, peeled, finely chopped

1 stalk celery, threaded, finely chopped

1 large carrot, peeled, finely chopped

2 medium leeks, trimmed, rinsed, finely chopped

3 tablespoons olive oil

18–24 sprigs fresh thyme

1 bay leaf

6 black peppercorns, cracked

9 cups/2.2l/2¼ qts water or light chicken broth/stock

12 large cloves garlic, peeled

salt and white pepper

1 cup/250 ml/8 fl oz single cream

12 thin slices day-old bread

Sauté the onion, celery, carrot and leeks in a heavy saucepan with 2 tablespoons oil until very well colored. Add half the thyme, the bay leaf, peppercorns and water or stock and bring to a boil. Simmer for 1 hour, then strain the stock into another pan. Add the remaining thyme, the peeled garlic and salt and pepper and bring to a boil. Simmer for 15 minutes. Lift out the thyme and garlic and add cream to the soup. Heat gently. Mash some of the garlic and spread on the bread. Sprinkle on the remaining olive oil. Toast the bread under a hot broiler (grill) or in a very hot oven. Serve the toast separately, or floating in the soup.

CREMA DE ESPINACAS CON SALMÓN AHUMADO

CREAM OF SPINACH SOUP WITH SMOKED SALMON   SERVES 6

3 packages frozen chopped spinach (about 1½ lb/750 g)

1 small onion, finely chopped

1 clove garlic, finely chopped

2 tablespoons butter or olive oil

2 tablespoons all-purpose (plain) flour

4 cups/1 l/32 fl oz chicken stock

salt and pepper

¾ teaspoon freshly grated nutmeg

1 cup/250 ml/8 fl oz light cream

7 oz/200 g smoked salmon, cut into small strips

Place the unthawed spinach in a saucepan, cover and cook gently for 10 minutes or until softened. Drain well and transfer to a food processor. Sauté the onion and garlic in the butter or oil until softened. Sprinkle on the flour and cook until golden, then add the stock and stir to absorb the flour. Boil for 5 minutes, stirring. Add half the liquid to the spinach and purée until smooth. Return to the saucepan and season with salt, pepper and nutmeg. Add the cream and heat gently. Add the smoked salmon immediately before serving.

CARACOLES PICANTES

SPICED SNAILS   SERVES 4–6 (*TAPA*)

Fresh snails have to be purged of any harmful contents before cooking (see page 266).

10 dozen small fresh snails

2 medium onions, peeled

4 sprigs parsley

2 sprigs fresh thyme

2 cups/500 ml/16 fl oz dry white wine

8 cloves garlic, finely chopped

3 tablespoons olive oil

1 tablespoon sweet paprika

½–¾ teaspoon cayenne pepper

½ teaspoon ground cumin

2 large tomatoes, peeled, seeded and finely chopped

salt and pepper

Rinse the snails and drain. Quarter one of the onions and finely chop the other. Place snails, quartered onion, half the parsley, the thyme and half the wine in a saucepan and add water to cover generously. Bring to a boil, then reduce heat and simmer for about 2 hours. Drain well.

Finely chop the remaining parsley and set aside. Fry the chopped onion in a *cazuela* with the oil until lightly colored. Add the garlic and fry for 1 minute. Add paprika, cayenne and cumin and fry briefly, then add the tomatoes and cook for 6 minutes, stirring occasionally. Add the snails, seasonings and water to just cover. Cook over moderate heat for about 30 minutes or until the snails are tender and have absorbed the flavor of the sauce. Serve hot in the *cazuela* and pass toothpicks, plenty of fresh bread and finger bowls.

GARÚM
OLIVE AND ANCHOVY DIP

MAKES 2 CUPS   SERVES 12–20 (*TAPA*)

6 large salted anchovy fillets

1 small slice white bread, crusts trimmed

1½ cups/80 g/6 oz pitted black olives (8 oz/250 g unpitted)

1 tablespoon capers, drained and minced

2 cloves garlic, minced

1 teaspoon finely chopped fresh marjoram

1 teaspoon finely chopped fresh rosemary

2 teaspoons finely chopped fresh thyme

1 tablespoon finely chopped fresh parsley

¾ teaspoon black pepper

3 tablespoons olive oil

Soak the anchovies in cold water for 40 minutes; drain and rinse. Soak the bread in water; drain and squeeze. Blend all of the ingredients in a food processor to a smooth paste. Spoon into dip bowls and garnish each with a sprig of fresh herbs.

Tip: Chop the herbs in the food processor before making the dip.

PURÉ DE CALABAZA GRATINADO
GRATINATED PUMPKIN PURÉE

SERVES 6

This little terrine of puréed pumpkin and eggs can be served in wedges as an accompaniment to meats, as an appetizer on its own, or with other vegetables such as *Judías Verdes con Jamón*.

2 lb/1 kg pumpkin

1 teaspoon salt

1 medium onion, very finely chopped

1 clove garlic, very finely chopped

¼ cup/60 ml/2 fl oz olive oil or butter

1½ cups/750 ml/12 fl oz *salsa bechamel* (page 273)

3 eggs

½ teaspoon freshly grated nutmeg

½ teaspoon black pepper (optional)

½ cup/60 g/2 oz grated cheese or fresh breadcrumbs

Peel and cube the pumpkin and boil in salted water until tender. Drain. Sauté the onion and garlic in the oil or butter and add the drained pumpkin. Toss in the oil for a few minutes, then mash or purée in a food processor. Stir in the bechamel sauce, eggs, nutmeg and pepper with half the cheese. Pour into a buttered pie dish and smooth the top. Sprinkle with the remaining cheese or breadcrumbs. Bake in a preheated 375°F/190°C/Gas 5 oven for about 15 minutes until firm in the center.

TORTILLA ESPINACAS
SPINACH OMELETTE

SERVES 4–6 (*TAPA*)

Spinach omelettes have a pleasing green color and subtle flavor. Serve them cut into narrow wedges as a *tapa*, cook in small pans for individual lunch servings, or serve generous wedges as a vegetarian-style supper dish with a mixed salad.

8–12 oz/250–375 g frozen spinach

1 teaspoon salt

½ teaspoon grated nutmeg

2 tablespoons thick (heavy) cream

1 small onion, peeled, very finely chopped

3 tablespoons olive oil

6 eggs, beaten

Place the spinach in a tightly covered pan without water and cook over gentle heat until thawed (or thaw in a microwave oven), then cook a further 2–3 minutes. Add half the salt and the nutmeg and cream. Set aside. Sauté the onion to golden in half the oil, add the spinach and beaten eggs and mix well. Heat a non-stick omelette pan with the remaining oil. Pour in the batter and cook on moderate heat until the underside is golden and firm and the omelette is very lightly cooked all through. Invert into the pan by turning onto a plate and sliding back into the pan. Cook the other side until the omelette feels firm in the centre. Slide or invert onto a serving plate and cut into wedges.

XATO
CATALAN CHICORY (CURLY ENDIVE) SALAD

SERVES 6

The arrival of bunches of white-green chicory (curly endive) at the Catalan markets announces the onset of winter. This sharply flavored salad with its peppery *vinagreta* is served in huge quantities as a first course with platters of sliced ham and sausage, anchovies and marinated small fish. Add to that a *tortilla* of white beans, potato or onion for a satisfying light meal. The dressing for *xato*, pronounced *char-toh*, is a palate-stimulating combination of ground toasted almonds, garlic and minced red peppers whisked into an olive oil and vinegar base.

3 heads fresh young chicory (curly endive)

3–4 cloves garlic, chopped

1–2 dried red chili peppers, seeded

12 toasted blanched almonds

¼ cup/60 ml/2 fl oz olive oil

2–3 tablespoons white wine vinegar

½ teaspoon sugar

½ teaspoon salt

Thoroughly rinse the chicory, separate leaves and shake or toss in a kitchen towel to dry. Cut leaves into 3-inch/7.5-cm pieces and arrange in a large salad bowl.

Grind garlic, chili and almonds in a food processor to the consistency of fine crumbs. Add the oil, vinegar, sugar and salt and process very briefly to mix. Toss with the greens and serve.

ENSALADA DE HABAS
CATALAN BEAN SALAD

SERVES 4

In February, during the short season of fresh *habas* (broadbeans), this salad appears frequently on Catalan tables. It can be made with frozen broadbeans; peel them to reveal the tender pea-green bean inside.

3 lb/1.5 kg fresh broadbeans in the shell (or 1 lb/500 g frozen beans)

3 oz/90 g *jamón serrano* or other cured ham, cut into paper-thin slices

1 medium onion, sliced

6 cooked or marinated baby artichokes, quartered

2 tablespoons toasted pine nuts

Dressing:

1 tablespoon Dijon-style or other mild mustard

1–1½ tablespoons red wine vinegar

⅓ cup/90 ml/3 fl oz virgin olive oil

salt and pepper

Shell the broadbeans and cook in plenty of salted water until tender, about 8 minutes. Drain and cool under cold running water. Peel if preferred. Cut the ham crosswise into narrow strips. Toss the beans, ham, onion, artichokes and pine nuts in a salad bowl. Whisk the remaining ingredients in a bowl to form a creamy emulsion, then toss with the salad.

ENSALADA VARIADA
MIXED SALAD PLATTER

SERVES 4

1 red bell pepper (capsicum)

4 hard-boiled eggs, cut into wedges

12 cherry tomatoes or 3 medium tomatoes, cut into wedges

¾ cup/120 g/4 oz small green olives

4 small boiled potatoes, quartered

¾ cup/150 g/5 oz sliced cooked green beans

½ cup/60 g/2 oz diced mild cheese

2 small onions, thinly sliced

8 oz/250 g drained tuna, broken into chunks

¾ cup *salsa vinagreta* (page 274)

Roast the pepper in a hot oven for about 30 minutes or until the skin is flecked with black and can be easily removed. Cool and peel, then cut the pepper into small squares, discarding seeds. Arrange the pepper and remaining salad ingredients on a serving platter or 4 plates and pour on the dressing.

ESCALIVADA
CHARCOAL-GRILLED VEGETABLES   SERVES 6

Escalivada in Catalonia means "grilling over charcoal" so this dish is essentially no more than char-grilled vegetables. But the simple process of cooking over an open bed of coals to blacken the skins of sweet local red and green peppers (capsicums) and plump eggplants (aubergines) extracts from these homely vegetables a rich, nutty taste and wonderful aroma. *Escalivada* is one of the backbone dishes of the Catalan cuisine. Serve it as a hot vegetable with grilled meats, as *tapas* or hors d'oeuvre, as an appetizer in the manner of the Italian marinated vegetable *antipasto*, or as a cold salad. Sandwich it with paper-thin slices of cured ham, or pile it on top of grilled sausages. It is incomparable when cooked directly on hot coals, on a grill over an open fire or pushed into cooling embers. But it can be made in the oven, although with a noticeable loss of its unique smoky flavor. Cook the vegetables, turning frequently, until the skins have blackened but are not ashy. Carefully pull away the skins while the vegetables are still hot. Cut the vegetables into narrow strips. To serve *escalivada*, circle the pepper and eggplant in overlapping formation on a platter with the whole tomatoes in the center. Traditionally, a plate of sliced spicy local sausage and thinly sliced local ham should accompany.

3 green bell peppers (capsicums)

3 red bell peppers (capsicums)

4 small purple (Japanese) eggplants (aubergines)

6 small to medium sun-ripened tomatoes

¾ cup/180 ml/6 fl oz virgin olive oil

½–1 teaspoon freshly ground black pepper

1½ tablespoons red wine vinegar (optional)

¾ teaspoon salt

Place the whole peppers and eggplants directly into a gently glowing outdoor fire of wood or charcoal embers, on a barbecue grid or in a hot oven. Cook, turning frequently with tongs, until the skin is very dark and the vegetables are soft to the touch. Cut a cross into the top of each tomato. They can be cooked on the barbecue for about 7 minutes, in a hot oven, or can be gently fried in a non-stick pan with a little olive oil. Remove peppers and eggplant and peel off the charred skin. Tear peppers into strips and thinly slice the eggplant. Arrange on warmed serving plates, and place the tomatoes in the center. Whisk the oil with remaining ingredients and pour on liberally.

Tip: To serve *escalivada* cold, season with salt and pepper and moisten with extra-virgin olive oil. It can be served with *alioli*, although purists maintain that *escalivada* requires no more than a light seasoning of salt, and generous quantities of excellent olive oil.

TUMBRET
MALLORCA VEGETABLE FLAN

SERVES 6

I like to make this tasty vegetarian dish look more attractive by layering the eggplant in the dish, so that the inverted flan is completely covered with overlapping eggplant slices. From the Balearic island of Mallorca, *tumbret* is closely related to the Catalan *samfaina* — a medley of stewed eggplant, tomatoes, peppers and zucchini. In turn, these also closely resemble the original *alboronía* and classic *pisto* of central Spain. A version containing beaten eggs, which more resembles a pie, is equally delicious, as is the seafood version on page 116.

2 medium eggplants (aubergines), thinly sliced

salt

2 large potatoes, peeled and sliced

½ cup/120 ml/4 fl oz olive oil

2 green bell peppers (capsicums), seeded and sliced

5 cloves garlic, peeled and chopped

1 medium onion, chopped

6 sun-ripened tomatoes, peeled and chopped

1 bay leaf

pepper

1 sprig fresh thyme

1 sprig parsley

⅓ cup/40 g/1½ oz fresh breadcrumbs (optional)

lemon slices

Spread the eggplant slices on a cloth and sprinkle with salt. Let stand for 10 minutes, then rinse and dry thoroughly. Fry the potatoes in the oil until golden. Remove. Fry eggplant until the surfaces are well sealed. Remove and overlap in a pie dish with sloping sides. Fry the peppers until softened; remove. Briefly fry the garlic. Layer the vegetables in the pie dish and set aside.

Fry the chopped onion in the same pan until softened. Add the tomatoes, seasonings and herbs and cook to a pulp. Pour over the vegetables. If you do not wish to invert the dish, fry the breadcrumbs in olive oil and sprinkle over the top of the vegetables. Bake in a preheated 400°F/200°C/Gas 6 oven for 15 to 20 minutes. Allow to set for a few minutes, then invert onto a serving plate and garnish with slices of lemon. Serve hot or, if preferred, allow to cool to room temperature.

ESPINACAS A LA CATALANA
SPINACH WITH PINE NUTS AND RAISINS

SERVES 4–6

2 lb/1 kg fresh spinach

⅓ cup/45 g/1½ oz pine nuts

½ cup/90 g/3 oz raisins

¼ cup/60 ml/2 fl oz olive oil

¾ teaspoon salt

freshly ground black pepper

Break off spinach stems and discard. Wash leaves thoroughly and shake to dry. Place in a covered saucepan and cook over low heat for 5 minutes or until softened. Drain well. Fry the nuts and raisins in olive oil until the raisins are plump and nuts are golden. Add spinach and toss quickly over high heat. Season and serve at once.

TOMATITOS RELLENOS DE OSTRAS Y VIEIRAS GRATINADOS
CHERRY TOMATOES FILLED WITH OYSTER AND SCALLOP GRATIN   SERVES 4

An elegant appetizer served on small plates in groups of five, or a novel *tapa* when served on small wooden picks.

20 large cherry tomatoes

20 oysters

20 small scallops

½ cup/120 ml/4 fl oz dry white wine

1 medium onion, very finely chopped

2 cloves garlic, very finely chopped

5 tablespoons olive oil

1 teaspoon finely chopped parsley

1 teaspoon chopped fennel or dill

large pinch of black pepper

small pinch of cayenne pepper

lemon juice

½ cup/30 g/1 oz fresh breadcrumbs

Cut the tops from the tomatoes and use a small spoon to scoop out the centers. Remove oysters from their shells. Simmer scallops in equal parts wine and water for 1 minute. Remove with a slotted spoon. Add the oysters to the cooking liquid and simmer for 10 seconds. Drain. Sauté the onion and garlic in half the oil until soft and golden. Stir in the parsley, fennel, pepper and cayenne, then add the scallops. Toss the mixture to season evenly. Place an oyster in each tomato with a scallop on top. Sprinkle with lemon juice. Fry the crumbs in the remaining oil until lightly golden. Spread evenly over the tomatoes and bake in a preheated 450°C/230°C/ Gas 8 oven for 6 minutes, or place under a hot grill for 1 minute. Serve at once.

HABAS FRITAS
FRIED BROADBEANS   SERVES 4

3 lb/1.5 kg fresh young broadbeans in the shell (or 1 lb/ 500 g shelled beans)*

½ cup/120 ml/4 fl oz olive oil

salt and pepper

2 slices white bread, crusts trimmed

2 cloves garlic, mashed

1 tablespoon butter

Shell the beans and cook with half the oil and 3 tablespoons water, stirring frequently, until tender and the water is absorbed, about 10 minutes. Add salt and pepper to taste. Spread the bread with garlic, cut into small squares and fry in the remaining oil until crisp. Toss beans with the butter, add the croutons and serve at once.

*If the broadbeans are not young, it may be necessary to parboil them before cooking. Pop them out of their gray-green skins for a more attractive and tender dish.

FLANES DE SETAS
MUSHROOM FLANS
SERVES 4

Little flans or "timbales" of vegetables are popular in Catalan cooking. They make delightful first courses and can be served as a vegetable dish. *Rovellóns* give the dish a delicate golden color that is most appealing. Most fresh mushrooms are suitable; otherwise use dried *boletus* mushrooms (*porcini*).

12 oz/350 g fresh *rovellóns* or other mushrooms, coarsely chopped

1 cup/250 ml/8 fl oz heavy (thick) cream

2 eggs

salt and pepper

$\frac{1}{3}$ teaspoon nutmeg

Combine the mushrooms, cream, eggs, salt, pepper and nutmeg in a food processor and purée. Pour into buttered small ramekins or a flan dish and set in a hot water bath. Bake in a 350°F/180°C/Gas 4 oven for about 20 minutes or until set. Unmold onto plates to serve, or cut larger flan into wedges.

Variation: Sauté additional thinly sliced mushrooms in butter. Toss with cream, salt, pepper and parsley and serve as a sauce.

SAMFAINA
CATALAN BRAISED VEGETABLE SAUCE
MAKES 3–3$\frac{1}{2}$ CUPS

Samfaina is one of the cornerstones of Catalan cooking. Akin to the French *ratatouille*, it serves as an appetizer or vegetable side dish or can be spread over meat and seafood as a sauce. It makes an unforgettable canape in small tartlet cases and can be served as a dip with meatballs or crudités. The peppers add a distinctive note by being roasted first to remove the skins and introduce a rich, smoky note. In *Catalan* it can also be called *xamfaina, chanfaina* or *sanfaina*, but whatever the spelling, the components remain incorruptibly unvaried.

4 large red bell peppers (capsicums)

$\frac{1}{2}$ cup/120 ml/4 fl oz extra-virgin olive oil

2 large onions, very thinly sliced

1 large purple or several small Japanese eggplants (aubergines), about 12 oz/350 g

4 medium zucchini (courgettes), about 1 lb/500 g, cubed

4 cloves garlic, minced

3–4 large sun-ripened tomatoes, peeled, seeded and finely chopped

salt and pepper

Roast the peppers on a grill or in a hot oven until the surface is blackened, turning frequently. Wrap in a kitchen towel for 10 minutes, then peel. Discard seeds and cut flesh into narrow strips. Heat the oil in a heavy pan. Add the onions, eggplant, zucchini and garlic. Stir to coat with the oil, then cover and cook gently for about 10 minutes. Uncover and cook over higher heat to evaporate the pan liquids. Add the peppers and tomato and cook uncovered over low heat until the vegetables are all very soft. Season to taste.

Variation: When *samfaina* is to be used as a filling or sauce, continue to cook until very pulpy and ready to caramelize. Mash to a smooth purée if you like.

ALCACHOFAS RELLENAS
STUFFED ARTICHOKES

SERVES 6

Baby artichokes, so tender that they can be eaten whole, are a pre-Christmas treat for the Catalans. They are eaten simply grilled or fried in olive oil, added to sauces, *paella* and *tortilla*, or stuffed to serve as an appetizer.

6 fresh artichokes, each no larger than an apple

1 lemon

8 oz/250 g *butifarra blanca* or large white pork sausages

3 cups/750 ml/24 fl oz olive oil

2 hard-boiled eggs

salt and pepper

$\frac{1}{3}$ teaspoon dried thyme

1 cup/120 g/4 oz all-purpose (plain) flour

2 eggs, beaten

1 clove garlic, minced

3 ripe tomatoes, peeled, seeded and chopped

$\frac{3}{4}$ cup/120 g/4 oz toasted blanched almonds, finely ground

lemon juice

Thoroughly rinse the artichokes and shake dry. Trim stems flat to the base and trim points from the leaves, cutting the tops flat. Discard any tough outer leaves. Squeeze lemon juice into a bowl of cold water and dip artichokes into the acidulated water to prevent them from discoloring during cooking. Drain thoroughly. Spread the leaves to expose the heart, scooping out hairy parts if necessary.

Remove meat from sausage casings and sauté in 2 tablespoons oil until lightly colored. Cool and mash to a smooth paste with the hard-boiled eggs, seasoning to taste with salt, pepper and the thyme. Stuff the artichokes with this mixture. Coat lightly with flour. Dip into beaten egg, then again in flour.

Heat remaining olive oil and fry the artichokes, stuffing downwards, until crisp and golden. Remove and drain well. In the pan in which sausage was fried, sauté the onions until almost caramelized, then add the garlic and tomatoes and cook gently to a pulp. Mix in $\frac{1}{2}$ to $\frac{3}{4}$ cup/ 120 to 180 ml/4 to 6 fl oz water and add the almonds. Season to taste with salt and pepper. Arrange the artichokes stuffing side up in a flameproof casserole. Pour on the sauce and cook over moderate heat for at least 1 hour or until tender, moistening with water as needed. Serve hot.

Habas a la Catalana

BROADBEANS WITH SAUSAGE, CATALAN STYLE

SERVES 4–6

Broadbeans ripen in a short season in February, their large fleshy pods revealing flat, tender, bright green beans sheathed in a firm, pale green skin. At this time of year they are served in salads with a garlic-flavored *vinagreta*, are added to *paella*, are fried in olive oil or simmered in tomato sauce. But perhaps the most favored dish of the Catalan is *habas* cooked with local ham and sausage.

4 oz/120 g *tocino*, salt pork or streaky bacon

8 oz/250 g *butifarra blanca* or other mildly spiced white pork sausages

8 oz/250 g *butifarra negra* or other blood sausages

1 medium onion, chopped

$\frac{1}{4}$ cup/60 ml/2 fl oz olive oil

2 cloves garlic, chopped

1 large tomato, seeded and chopped

$1\frac{1}{2}$ lb/750 g shelled fresh or thawed frozen broadbeans (4 lb/ 2 kg in the pod)

salt and pepper

1 sprig fresh thyme

1 sprig fresh mint

1 bay leaf

3 tablespoons dry sherry

Thickly slice the bacon and cut half into strips. Slice white sausage and leave the other sausage whole. Sauté the onion gently in the oil until softened. Add garlic and tomato and cook to a thick sauce. Add the remaining ingredients with 1 cup/250 ml/8 fl oz water. Partially cover and cook gently until the liquid is absorbed and the beans and meat are tender, about 30 minutes, stirring occasionally. Remove the pieces of ham and chop finely, then slice the whole sausage. Return the meats to the pot, stir and heat through briefly before serving.

Judías Verdes con Jamón

GREEN BEANS WITH HAM

SERVES 4–6

$1\frac{1}{2}$ lb/750 g green beans

salt

4 cloves garlic

6 oz/180 g *jamón serrano* or other cured ham

3 tablespoons olive oil

$\frac{3}{4}$ cup/180 ml/6 fl oz chicken or veal stock

2 hard-boiled eggs, cut into wedges

Cut the beans into $1\frac{1}{2}$-inch/4-cm lengths and boil in lightly salted water until tender. Drain. Sauté the garlic and ham in the oil for 1 minute. Add beans and stock and cook for 2 to 3 minutes. Garnish with the eggs.

Habas Fritas (top), p.105; Judías Verdes con Jamón (middle), opposite; Butifarra con Judías Blancas (front), p.124

Xato (top), p.101; Pa amb Tomàquet (left), p.130; Albondigas con Aceitunas (right), p.113; Escalivada (front), p.103

ACELGAS CON JAMÓN Y PIÑONES
SWISS CHARD WITH HAM AND PINE NUTS
SERVES 4–6

1½ lb/650 g finely shredded Swiss chard (silverbeet) leaves

3 oz/90 g *jamón serrano* or other cured ham, finely diced

½ cup/60 g/2 oz pine nuts

2 tablespoons olive oil

salt and pepper

lemon juice

Soak the chard in cold water for a few minutes, then drain thoroughly. Sauté the ham and pine nuts in the oil until the nuts are golden and ham is crisp. Remove. Cook the chard in the remaining oil, tightly covered, until tender. Return the ham and nuts and add salt and pepper to taste. Toss to mix evenly, sprinkle on a little lemon juice and serve.

CRIADILLAS DE TIERRA
TRUFFLES
SERVES 4–8

Where truffles can be dug straight from the soil beneath oak trees they are delicious simply cooked in butter, or bathed in a wine sauce.

1 lb/500 g fresh truffles

3 tablespoons butter

salt and pepper

Wipe the truffles but do not wash them. Leave whole or slice. Sauté gently in the butter until tender and supremely aromatic. Season with salt and pepper. If liked, splash in 1 to 2 tablespoons of a fine sherry or a ½ cup/120 ml/4 fl oz dry white wine before the truffles are cooked, so that the wine has evaporated by the time they are done.

ROVELLÓNS A LA PLANCHA
GRILLED WILD MUSHROOMS WITH OLIVE OIL AND GARLIC
SERVES 4

24 fresh *rovellóns* or cèpes

2½ tablespoons virgin olive oil

2 cloves garlic, minced

1 tablespoon very finely chopped parsley

½ teaspoon salt

freshly ground black pepper

Wipe the mushrooms and slice thickly. Cook on an oiled griddle, turning frequently, until tender; add garlic in the last few seconds of cooking. Sprinkle on the parsley and salt and toss to mix well. Transfer to a warmed plate and season generously with pepper.

Tip: The mushrooms can be placed in a baking dish with the other ingredients and baked in a preheated 400°F/200°C/Gas 6 oven for about 15 minutes.

ATÚN A LA PLANCHA CON PIMIENTA NEGRA

GRILLED TUNA STEAKS WITH BLACK PEPPER

SERVES 4

4 fresh tuna steaks, 7 oz/220 g each

$\frac{3}{4}$ teaspoon salt

1 tablespoon coarsley ground black pepper

$\frac{1}{3}$ teaspoon sweet paprika

$\frac{1}{4}$ teaspoon dried oregano

2 tablespoons olive oil

$1\frac{1}{2}$ cups *samfaina* (page 106) coarsely puréed

Sprinkle both sides of the fish with salt and let stand for 20 minutes. Mix pepper, paprika and oregano and press one side only of each steak into the seasoning, coating evenly. Grill on both sides until cooked through, about 5 minutes, sprinkling with oil to retain moisture. Serve on warmed plates with *samfaina* and rice.

PULPITOS EN SALSA DE ALMENDRAS Y AJO

BABY OCTOPUS IN GARLIC AND ALMOND SAUCE

SERVES 4–6

$2\frac{1}{2}$ lb/1.2 kg *pulpitos* (very small baby octopus)

9 cloves garlic

$\frac{1}{2}$ cup/120 ml/4 fl oz olive oil

1 slice white bread, crusts trimmed

$\frac{1}{2}$ cup/75 g/$2\frac{1}{2}$ oz toasted blanched almonds

salt and pepper

pinch of cayenne pepper

1 teaspoon sweet paprika

1 medium tomato, peeled and finely chopped

chopped parsley

Turn the octopus inside out, clean and cut away the mouth and eye area. Pull off skin. Rinse well in cold water. Place in a saucepan without additional liquid; cover and cook over low heat for about $1\frac{1}{4}$ hours or until very tender.

Separately fry the garlic in the oil until well browned, then remove and fry bread in the same oil. Grind almonds to a paste in a food processor. Add garlic, bread, salt, pepper, cayenne and paprika and grind until smooth. Fry briefly in a little of the remaining oil. Add tomato and water as needed; cook to a thick sauce. Add the octopus and warm through. Sprinkle with parsley and serve.

ALBÓNDIGAS CON ACEITUNAS
BRAISED MEATBALLS WITH GREEN OLIVES

SERVES 4–6

Butifarra is the most widely used of the sausages traditionally made in Catalonia. *Butifarra blanca* is a white pork sausage, medium to coarse in texture and mildly seasoned. *Butifarra negra*, used in other recipes, is a dark blood sausage, also of medium to coarse texture, which is slightly fatty and mildly seasoned.

1 lb/500 g *butifarra blanca* or other white pork sausage

1 lb/500 g lean ground (minced) beef

5 cloves garlic, minced

2 tablespoons finely chopped parsley

2 large eggs

salt and pepper

1 cup/120 g/4 oz all-purpose (plain) flour

2 cups/500 ml/16 fl oz olive oil

1 large onion, finely chopped

2 large tomatoes, peeled, seeded and chopped

1 small dried hot red chili pepper

1 small cinnamon stick

1 teaspoon sweet paprika

2 cups/500 ml/16 fl oz veal stock or water

1¾ cups/270 g/9 oz pitted green olives

Slit sausages open along their length and remove meat. Mix with the ground beef, garlic, parsley and eggs. Add salt and pepper to taste and knead to a smooth paste. Using wet or oiled hands, form into meatballs a little larger than walnuts. Coat evenly with flour, then reserve ⅓ cup of flour and discard the remainder. Fry the meatballs in olive oil until evenly browned. Remove with a slotted spoon and set aside.

Transfer ½ cup of the oil to a *cazuela*. Fry the onion in it until golden. Sprinkle flour evenly over the onion and cook until lightly browned and very fragrant; take care that the flour does not burn or it will spoil the sauce. Add tomato and chili with the cinnamon and paprika and cook for a few minutes, then add stock or water and bring to a boil. Simmer for 5 minutes. Add the meatballs and olives and partially cover. Simmer for about 30 minutes or until meatballs are very tender and sauce is thickened.

CALAMARES RELLENOS EN SALSA DE AJO

SAVORY STUFFED SQUID IN GARLIC SAUCE   SERVES 4

20 small squid, no more than $2\frac{1}{2}$ inches (6 cm)

4 oz/120 g very finely ground veal or pork

2 small onions, very finely chopped

1 tablespoon finely chopped parsley

8 cloves garlic, finely chopped

3 tablespoons toasted pine nuts

$\frac{3}{4}$ cup/45 g/$1\frac{1}{2}$ oz fresh breadcrumbs

salt and white pepper

2 tablespoons olive oil

18 blanched toasted almonds

2 cups/500 ml/16 fl oz fish stock or water

2 tablespoons dry sherry

$\frac{1}{2}$ teaspoon sweet paprika

1 dried hot chili pepper

1 medium tomato, very finely chopped

8–10 saffron threads

2 tablespoons boiling water

Clean and skin the squid and rinse thoroughly. Drain. Place veal in a mixing bowl. In a food processor grind one onion, the parsley and one clove of garlic together. Add the pine nuts with 2 tablespoons of the crumbs, salt and pepper. Mix well, then blend into the veal. Stuff loosely into the squid (overfilling may cause them to burst during cooking). If desired, secure the openings with toothpicks. Place in a well buttered baking dish, cover and bake in a preheated 350°F/180°C/Gas 4 oven for 15 minutes. Turn and bake uncovered a further 10 minutes.

Fry the remaining finely chopped onion, garlic and breadcrumbs in olive oil until golden. Place in a food processor with the oil and almonds. Grind to a smooth paste, adding a little of the stock and the sherry, then stir into the remaining stock and simmer for a few minutes. Add paprika, chili and tomato and cook to a smooth sauce. Mix saffron with boiling water and stir to extract the color. Add to the sauce and cook briefly. Pass through a sieve, then season with salt and pepper. Arrange the squid in a cartwheel formation on 4 plates and pour on the sauce.

LANGOSTINOS AL ALIOLI

GIANT SHRIMP (PRAWNS) IN GARLIC MAYONNAISE   SERVES 4

16 fresh *langostinos* or large shrimp (prawns) in the shell

1 cup/250 ml/8 fl oz *alioli* (page 273)

Bring a pot of lightly salted water to a boil and drop in the *langostinos*. Boil for about 6 minutes. Lift out in a strainer and place in a dish. Serve the sauce in 4 small bowls. To eat, peel the *langostinos* and dip into the sauce.

MERLUZA CON ROMESCO
HAKE SERVED WITH ROMESCO SAUCE

SERVES 4

4 5- to 6-oz/150- to 180-g pieces of hake*

1 small slice white bread, crusts trimmed

$\frac{3}{4}$ cup/180 ml/6 fl oz olive oil

1 dried red chili pepper

4 cloves garlic, peeled

2 tablespoons toasted blanched almonds

2 tablespoons toasted hazelnuts

2 sprigs parsley

1 medium tomato, peeled, seeded and chopped

1 tablespoon red wine vinegar

Place hake in a non-aluminum pan with water to cover. Bring just to a boil, then reduce to a simmer and cook for about 5 minutes. Drain, reserving a little of the liquid, and set aside.

Fry the bread in the oil until golden; drain well. Fry the pepper and garlic in the same oil until garlic is golden. Place bread, pepper, garlic, nuts and parsley in a mortar or food processor. Sauté the tomato in the remaining oil for 4 to 5 minutes. Add to the ingredients in the food processor with the reserved liquid and chop until almost smooth. Return to the pan and heat for 2 minutes. Add vinegar and cook briefly, then place the fish in the sauce, baste and heat through.

*Preferably cut from the center of the fish. Steaks should be about $1\frac{1}{4}$ inches (3 cm) thick.

PESCADITOS EN ESCABECHE A LA CATALANA
SMALL MARINATED FISH

SERVES 6 (*TAPA*)

12–18 small fresh anchovies or sardines

1 teaspoon salt

$1\frac{1}{3}$ cups/180 g/6 oz all-purpose (plain) flour

3 cups/750 ml/24 fl oz olive oil

1 cup/250 ml/8 fl oz white wine vinegar

8 cloves garlic, halved

3 bay leaves

12 whole black peppercorns

1 sprig fresh rosemary

1 sprig fresh thyme

$\frac{1}{2}$ teaspoon sweet paprika

Clean the fish and rinse thoroughly. Dry with paper towels, then dust with salt and coat lightly and evenly in flour.

Heat $\frac{1}{3}$ of the oil in a wide, flat pan and gently fry the fish on both sides until just cooked, turning carefully with 2 spatulas so skin is not broken. Bring remaining olive oil and vinegar to a boil in another non-aluminum pan, add the garlic, bay leaves, pepper, herbs and paprika. Arrange fish in a glass dish or casserole and pour on the marinade. Cover and let stand in a cool place, preferably not refrigerated, for at least 2 days.

Tip: The marinated fish will keep for several weeks, but is best eaten within a few days of preparation.

TUMBRET DE MALLORCA DE PESCADO

VEGETABLE AND FISH FLAN   SERVES 4–6

This aquatic version of the Mallorcan *tumbret* marries fish with eggplant in a richly flavored dish that hints at Moorish influences.

1–2 eggplants (aubergines), about 1½ lb/750 g

2 teaspoons salt

2 large red bell peppers (capsicums)

2 large potatoes, peeled and thinly sliced

¾ cup/180 ml/6 fl oz olive oil

1 medium onion, thinly sliced

4 sun-ripened tomatoes, chopped

3 cloves garlic, chopped

1 teaspoon sugar

1½-inch/3-cm cinnamon stick

black pepper

⅓ teaspoon ground cumin

1 lb/500 g thick fillets of cod, haddock or sea bass

all-purpose (plain) flour (optional)

½ cup/120 ml/4 fl oz dry white wine

Thinly slice the eggplants and spread on a tray. Sprinkle with the salt and let stand for 20 minutes for the salt to draw out the bitter juices. Rinse and dry thoroughly. Roast the peppers in a hot oven for about 35 minutes or until the skin is blistered. Wrap in a kitchen towel for 10 minutes, then seed and peel. Sauté the potatoes in 6 tablespoons oil until golden and partially tender. Remove with a slotted spoon and set aside. Sauté the onion until softened, then the eggplant; set aside.

Pour ¼ cup/60 ml/2 fl oz oil into another pan. Add the tomatoes, garlic, sugar, cinnamon stick, a large pinch of pepper and the cumin and cook until soft and pulpy. Pass through a sieve or purée in a food processor. Cut the fish into slices and fry in the remaining oil until the surface is sealed, coating lightly with flour first if desired. Pour off the oil and add the wine. Simmer until it has evaporated.

Layer the vegetables and fish in a greased baking dish. Cover with the sauce and finish with a layer of eggplant. Bake in a preheated 375°F/180°C/Gas 4 oven for 20 minutes. Serve in the dish or invert onto a plate.

Variation: Substitute ground (minced) veal for the fish. Sauté until well colored, then add 2 tablespoons brandy, a splash of stock and a few teaspoons of finely chopped fresh herbs.

PARRILLADA DE MARISCOS
CATALAN-STYLE SEAFOOD GRILL

SERVES 6

To eat a lunch of seafood *parrillada* under an umbrella at a casual restaurant in one of Barcelona's picturesque squares is to catch a preview of heaven. The shellfish would be *cigalas, almejas, gambas, cangrejos de río*, the fish steaks of *lubina* and *merluza*, baby *sardinas* and *salmonetes*. A bacchanalian feast of charcoal-grilled seafood requires nothing more than an *alioli* and lemon wedges, and a bottle of local Chardonnay.

salt

6 thick pieces hake, about 4 oz/ 120 g each

6 whiting fillets

6 *cigalas* (scampi/Dublin Bay prawns/langoustines)

6 *langostinos* (large shrimp/ prawns) in their shells

12 clams in their shells, soaked overnight

12 large oysters on the half shell

olive oil

finely chopped garlic (optional)

lemons

Prepare a good bed of glowing charcoal under an iron grill. Sprinkle salt over the fish and let stand for 10 minutes, then brush with olive oil. If you like, cut the *langostinos* down the center backs to extract the dark vein. Brush shellfish with oil. Place the seafood on the grill to cook until tender, turning several times; cooking time will depend on the size of the pieces. Add oysters last as they need only a few minutes to heat.

Separately heat a small pot of good olive oil, adding garlic. Pour over the seafood when it has been arranged on plates and garnish with lemon wedges.

PESCADO A L'ALL CREMAT
FISH IN BURNT GARLIC

SERVES 4

Cremat means "burnt" in Catalan, but actually the garlic is just very well cooked to bring out its flavor — which is more toasty than garlicky in the end! This old fisherman's recipe is still popular in Catalonia.

1 large head garlic, slivered

$\frac{1}{3}$ cup/90 ml/3 fl oz olive oil

3 large sun-ripened tomatoes, seeded and chopped

1 sprig fresh thyme

1 bay leaf

$1\frac{1}{2}$ lb/750 g cod, sea bream or bass fillets

salt and pepper

In a flameproof *cazuela* or casserole, slowly brown the garlic in the oil until very dark. Add the tomatoes with herbs and cook, stirring, until thickened, then add enough water to moisten. Lay the fish on the sauce. Season lightly, sprinkle on a little olive oil to keep the fish moist, then cover and cook gently, turning once, until fish is tender. Serve in the casserole.

ZARZUELA DE MARISCOS
SHELLFISH IN RICH SEAFOOD SAUCE

SERVES 6

The name means "operetta", and this classic Catalan seafood dish is indeed a form of elaborate light entertainment. Midway between soup and stew, *zarzuela* is perhaps the region's most infamous dish. At its best it is almost an embarrassment of riches, a luxuriant blend of seafood flavors. Mussels, clams, lobster or crayfish, fish, squid and shrimp (prawns) supplemented with paprika and saffron give the broth a complexity of flavors, in the typical Spanish tradition, which are enriched by ground almonds and a splash of cognac. But in unscrupulous hands the *zarzuela* pot can become the dumping ground for seafood past its prime, making it one of those dishes best eaten at a recommended restaurant — or at home.

2 lb/1 kg *langosta, bogavante* or *cigala* (lobster)

3 small sole, flounder or other firm-fleshed white fish

$\frac{1}{2}$ cup/60 g/2 oz all-purpose (plain) flour

$\frac{1}{3}$ cup/80 ml/3 fl oz virgin olive oil

1 large onion, chopped

4 medium tomatoes, peeled, seeded and chopped

1 red bell pepper (capsicum), seeded and chopped

1 green bell pepper (capsicum), seeded and chopped

2 teaspoons sweet paprika

2-inch/5-cm cinnamon stick

2 bay leaves

$\frac{1}{4}$ cup/30 g/1 oz toasted blanched almonds, finely ground

6 *langostinos* (large shrimp/prawns) in the shell

12 mussels in the shell

24 clams in the shell

6 medium-size fresh squid, cleaned and sliced

large pinch of saffron threads

$\frac{1}{4}$ cup/60 ml/2 fl oz cognac or dry sherry

salt and pepper

1 tablespoon chopped parsley

lemon juice

Rinse and brush the lobster and drop into a pot of lightly salted water. Boil for 10 minutes, then drain. Cut in half, remove the intestinal vein and thickly slice the meat. Set aside. Return the shell and head to the pot. Cut along the center of the sole and remove the fillets in 2 strips from each side. Set meat aside and place carcasses in pot with the lobster shell. Add 6 cups/1.5 l/1$\frac{1}{2}$ qt water and bring to a boil. Simmer for 10 minutes, then strain the liquid and reserve.

Skin the sole fillets and coat lightly with flour. Fry in the oil until almost cooked; remove and set aside. Fry the onion until golden brown and softened, then add tomatoes and cook for 3 to 4 minutes. Add peppers, paprika, cinnamon, bay leaves and the reserved stock and bring to a boil.

Add ground almonds to the stock and simmer for 20 minutes. Add the shellfish and squid and simmer for about 8 minutes. Mix saffron with a little boiling water; add to the pot with the sole, lobster meat and cognac and simmer 2 to 3 minutes. Discard any shellfish that have not opened. Stir in salt and pepper, parsley and lemon juice to taste. Serve in deep bowls with plenty of crusty bread.

Samfaina y Bacalao a la Catalana
SALT COD WITH *SAMFAINA*   SERVES 6

1½ lb/650 g front part of salt cod, prepared (see page 266)

3 medium-size red bell peppers (capsicums), seeded and diced

1 cup/250 ml/8 fl oz olive oil

2 large onions, diced (about 13 oz/400 g)

4 cloves garlic, chopped

2 small purple (Japanese) eggplants (aubergines), diced (about 10 oz/300 g)

2 medium zucchini (courgettes), diced (about 8 oz/250 g)

4 large sun-ripened tomatoes, peeled, seeded and chopped (about 1 lb/500 g)

salt and pepper

½ cup/60 g/2 oz all-purpose (plain) flour

Drain the cod and cut into 1½-inch (4-cm) cubes. Cover with cold water and set aside. Roast peppers in a hot oven until the skin loosens, about 20 minutes. Seed and peel, cut into strips and set aside. Cook the onion, garlic, eggplant and zucchini in a tightly covered heavy pan with ¼ cup/60 ml/2 fl oz oil until they are very soft. Add the tomatoes and peppers with salt and pepper to taste and cook until the vegetables are well softened.

Preheat the oven to 350°F/180°C/Gas 4. Drain the cod and dry thoroughly. Coat with flour and fry in the remaining oil until golden. Remove and drain on paper towels. Transfer the fish to baking dish and pour the sauce over. Bake uncovered for 20 minutes.

Pollo al Ajillo
GARLIC CHICKEN   SERVES 4

This simple luncheon dish is perfect with a salad, a crusty *barra* (baguette) loaf and a bottle of chilled young red wine.

12 oz/380 g boneless chicken breast, skin on

5–6 cloves garlic, slivered

3 tablespoons olive oil

salt

½ cup/120 ml/4 fl oz dry white wine (optional)

2 teaspoons chopped parsley

Cut the chicken into strips across the fillet. Sauté chicken and garlic in the oil over low heat until the chicken is tender and the garlic has thoroughly impregnated the meat. Add salt to taste. Splash in the wine, if used, and increase the heat until the wine is absorbed. Sprinkle on the parsley and serve.

Pollo en Salsa de Almendras
CHICKEN IN ALMOND SAUCE

SERVES 4

Since Roman times almonds have been enjoyed by the Spanish, who use them frequently in their cooking. The Balearic Islands have extensive almond groves, producing some of the world's finest crop. In the region of Catalonia, ground almonds are a common ingredient in sauces, particularly the classic *romesco*, adding their unique rich flavor and creamy consistency. They are an important element of *picada*, the pulverized ingredients added to a sauce to thicken it. Fried bread, garlic, parsley, saffron and hazelnuts are all prominent *picada* ingredients, as are chocolate and chicken livers when a very rich taste is wanted. This dish, with its diced chicken in creamy almond-enriched sauce, has a marked similarity to the dish known as Circassian Chicken that is enjoyed throughout the Middle East.

3-lb/1.5-kg oven-ready chicken

1 medium onion, halved

4 cloves garlic, peeled

$\frac{1}{2}$ cup/120 ml/4 fl oz olive oil

1 sprig fresh thyme

salt

6 whole black peppercorns

4 slices white bread, crusts trimmed

1 cup/150 g/5 oz toasted blanched almonds

$\frac{1}{2}$ teaspoon cinnamon

pepper

2 teaspoons finely chopped parsley

Cut the chicken in half. Fry chicken with onion and whole garlic cloves in half the olive oil until well browned. Remove to a saucepan and add the thyme, $\frac{1}{2}$ teaspoon salt and peppercorns. Pour in water to just cover and bring to a boil. Reduce heat and simmer for 30 minutes or until chicken is tender.

Make a *picada* for thickening the sauce by frying 2 slices of bread in the remaining oil until golden. Remove, drain and cool, then place in a mortar or food processor with the fried garlic cloves and almonds. Grind to a thick paste, adding cinnamon, salt and pepper to taste.

Remove chicken and drain. Add enough of the liquid to the almond paste to make a thick sauce, then discard the remainder. Heat the sauce gently, stirring. Cut chicken into small cubes, removing skin and bones. Cut the remaining bread into triangles and fry in olive oil until golden. Drain well. Mix chicken into the sauce and spoon into a serving dish, surrounding with the fried bread. Sprinkle with parsley and serve.

Tip: This is delightful as a lunch dish, served cold with a crisp salad.

PATO CON HIGOS
DUCK WITH FIGS

SERVES 4–6

In Catalan this superb dish may be called *ánec amb figues*. It can be made with fresh figs, but the flavor is not so pronounced; supplement them with a handful of raisins.

8 oz/250 g dried figs
1 cup/250 ml/8 fl oz dry sherry
5-lb/2.5-kg oven-ready duck
1 small onion, quartered
1 whole clove
1 large orange
salt and pepper
2 tablespoons orange liqueur

Soak the figs overnight in sherry, or to save time, simmer in the sherry with $\frac{1}{2}$ cup/120 ml/4 fl oz water for 15 minutes.

Cut the duck in half, cutting along both sides of the backbone. Place the backbone, wings, neck and tips of drumsticks in a saucepan with water to barely cover. Add the onion, clove and a strip of the orange rind and bring to a boil. Reduce heat and simmer for 30 minutes. Strain. Cut the duck into 4 pieces and place skin up in a baking pan. Rub with salt and pepper. Roast for 30 minutes in a preheated 400°F/200°C/Gas 6 oven. Drain off the accumulated fat. Add the figs and their liquid and 2 cups/500 ml/16 fl oz of the strained duck stock. Roast at 300°F/150°C/Gas 2 for a further 30 minutes or until the duck is tender.

Remove the duck and figs and keep warm. Boil the sauce until well reduced, then strain into a food processor. Add 6 figs and process to a smooth paste. Return to the pan and simmer for 2 to 3 minutes. Add salt and pepper to taste, the juice squeezed from the orange and the orange liqueur and cook for 2 to 3 minutes. Serve the duck coated with the sauce and surrounded by the remaining whole figs.

PERDICES CON FARCELLETS DE COL

PARTRIDGES WITH CABBAGE CROQUETTES

SERVES 6

Partridge is the most favored hunting bird in Spain. It is generally plentiful in most regions, particularly in the central and northeastern areas. In Catalonia, it is roasted and served with little crisp-tender "croquettes" of blanched cabbage leaves. There are many different methods for preparing the cabbage. Some simply squeeze the blanched leaves into shape; others fold or roll as I have done in this recipe.

6 small oven-ready young partridges (or squab)

¾ cup/180 ml/6 fl oz olive oil

salt and pepper

1 medium onion, halved

6 cloves garlic, peeled

⅔ cup/150 ml/5 fl oz dry white wine

1–1½ cups/400 ml/13 fl oz chicken stock

1 small bay leaf

1 small cinnamon stick

1 large head Savoy or roundhead cabbage

1 cup/4 oz/120 g all-purpose (plain) flour

1 egg, beaten

1½ tablespoons cognac

Rinse and dry the partridges, rub with a little of the olive oil and season with salt and pepper. Place on a low rack in a baking dish. Place the onion and garlic in the pan, add wine and roast in a preheated 400°F/200°C/Gas 6 oven for 15 minutes or until the wine has evaporated. Add 1 cup chicken stock, the bay leaf and cinnamon stick and roast for a further 20 to 30 minutes or until the birds are tender, basting occasionally with the pan juices.

In the meantime, separate the cabbage leaves, cutting away the central rib from each leaf. Bring a large pan of lightly salted water to a boil, add the cabbage and simmer until tender. Remove and drain carefully. Make the croquettes by rolling several leaves together into little parcel shapes. Squeeze gently to firm up the shape, then coat with a film of flour and dip into beaten egg. Coat lightly again with flour. Heat olive oil to moderate and fry the croquettes gently on each side until golden. Drain and sprinkle with salt and pepper. Remove partridges from the pan and cut in halves. Arrange on a serving platter with the croquettes. Pour the cognac into the pan and boil until evaporated. Add the remaining stock and reduce the pan juices by half. Season to taste with salt and pepper; discard bay leaf, cinnamon stick and onion. Mash garlic and stir into the sauce, then pour over the birds. Serve at once.

Tip: These cabbage croquettes go equally well with other roast meats, particularly pork and duck.

PIERNA DE CORDERO RELLENA
STUFFED LEG OF LAMB

SERVES 6–8

5-lb/2.5-kg leg of lamb

3 cloves garlic, slivered

salt and pepper

1 teaspoon dried oregano

3 oz/90 g fatty bacon

1 medium carrot, peeled and very finely chopped

1 medium onion, very finely chopped

1 oz/30 g dried boletus mushrooms, soaked and finely chopped

6 oz/180 g *butifarra negra* or other blood sausage

2 tablespoons toasted pine nuts, chopped

1 slice white bread, crusts trimmed, fried in olive oil

1 cup/250 ml/8 fl oz veal or beef stock

$\frac{1}{2}$ cup/250 ml/4 fl oz dry white wine

Gravy:

1 tablespoon cognac

$\frac{1}{3}$ cup/90 ml/3 fl oz port

2 tablespoons flour

$1\frac{1}{2}$ cups/400 ml/13 fl oz veal stock

salt and pepper

$\frac{3}{4}$ teaspoon red wine vinegar

Cut along the leg bone at the side with the least meat; work the blade of the knife along the bone and remove completely. Turn meat skin side up and pierce in several places, then insert slivers of garlic. Season with salt and pepper. Turn over and season well with salt, pepper and the oregano. Sauté the bacon, carrot, onion and mushrooms together with any remaining fragments of garlic until the onions are well softened. Remove the sausage meat from its casing and sauté lightly, adding the pine nuts. Crush the fried bread and stir into the stuffing, kneading until the mixture is smooth.

Form mixture into a sausage shape and stuff into the meat in the pocket formed by removing the bone. Truss with butchers' twine or strong thread, or close the opening with thin metal skewers. Place on a rack in a roasting pan and add stock and wine. Roast in a preheated 400°F/200°C/Gas 6 oven for 25 minutes, then reduce heat to 350°F/180°C/Gas 4 and roast until done, about $1\frac{1}{4}$ hours. Test in the thickest part with a meat thermometer.

Set the meat aside for 10 minutes, covered with a cloth. Pour off fat from the pan. Pour in the cognac and boil over high heat until nearly evaporated, then repeat with the port, scraping up the pan drippings. Sprinkle on flour and cook until lightly colored, then add the stock and seasonings and boil, stirring frequently, until thickened. Strain through a fine strainer. Stir in the vinegar and boil briefly. Serve over the meat.

CHULETAS DE CERDO EN SALSA DE GRANADAS
PORK CUTLETS IN POMEGRANATE SAUCE   SERVES 4

Pomegranates, introduced by the Moors into the southern parts of Spain and the Balearic Islands, lend their tart-sweet taste to a number of meat dishes, particularly cutlets of pork and veal.

2 tablespoons lard or butter

4 pork chops, about 180 g/6 oz each

1 large onion, sliced

2 ripe pomegranates

½ cup/120 ml/4 fl oz dry white wine

½ cup/120 ml/4 fl oz veal or chicken stock

salt and pepper

Heat the lard or butter in a wide pan, add the chops and cook on both sides until well browned. Remove and keep warm. Pour off half the fat. Sauté onion until golden and softened.

Meanwhile, cut pomegranates in half and scoop out the seeds and pulp. Add to the pan with the wine and cook for 5 minutes. Transfer to a baking dish with the chops, stock and salt and pepper to taste. Cover and bake in a preheated 350°F/180°C/Gas 4 oven for about 40 minutes or until the pork is completely tender.

BUTIFARRA CON JUDÍAS BLANCAS
PORK SAUSAGE WITH WHITE BEANS   SERVES 4

This simple Catalan dish is enjoyed at any time of the day. Any lightly seasoned pork sausages can be used. *Judías blancas* (white haricots) or *alubias* (butter beans) are used here.

1 cup/180 g/6 oz dried white beans

1 medium onion, peeled

1 small carrot

1 sprig each fresh thyme, parsley and rosemary

1 bay leaf

1 clove garlic, peeled

1 whole clove

3–4 whole black peppercorns

5 cups/1.3 l/1⅓ qt water

1½ teaspoons salt

4 thick *butifarras blancas*, or 8–12 thin, mildly spiced pork sausages

¼ cup/60 ml/2 fl oz olive oil

Rinse beans but do not soak. Drain and place in a saucepan with the remaining ingredients except salt, sausages and oil. Bring just to a boil, covered. Reduce heat to very low and cook, tightly covered, for about 2½ hours or until the beans are tender but still retain their shape. Drain, discarding onion, carrot, herbs and spices.

Add salt and set aside. Prick the sausages thoroughly, then grill over medium heat until cooked through. Heat oil in a clean pan and fry the beans over high heat for 2 to 3 minutes, stirring carefully so as not to crush them. Transfer to a serving dish, arrange the sausages on top and pour on the oil from the pan.

SOLOMILLO DE BUEY CON AJOS TIERNOS
BEEF TENDERLOIN (FILLET) WITH GARLIC SHOOTS   SERVES 4

4 beef tenderloin (fillet) steaks

2 tablespoons olive oil

2 bunches (each about 20 pieces) fresh garlic shoots

1 tablespoon Spanish brandy

2 teaspoons all-purpose (plain) flour

¾ cup/180 ml/6 fl oz rich beef stock

salt and pepper

Trim the steaks and brush with oil. Cook in a cast iron pan until well seared on one side. Turn and cook the other side until done to preference. (Do not add salt before cooking, and do not press the steaks with a spatula while they cook.) Remove and keep warm.

Cut the garlic shoots into 2-inch/5-cm pieces. Sauté in the pan until they wilt, then remove. Deglaze pan with the brandy, then sprinkle on the flour and stir to incorporate the pan juices. Add the stock and cook until thickened, adding salt and pepper to taste. Serve the steaks topped with garlic chives and a spoonful of the sauce.

COCA MALLORQUINA
MALLORCA PIZZA   SERVES 4–6

Dough:

1 oz/27 g fresh yeast (or 1 envelope/½ oz/12 g dry yeast)

3 tablespoons lukewarm milk

4 cups/500 g/1 lb all-purpose (plain) flour

1½ teaspoons salt

3 tablespoons olive oil

cold water

Topping:

3 red bell peppers (capsicums), seeded and thinly sliced

2 large sun-ripened tomatoes, sliced

1 large onion, very thinly sliced

2 cloves garlic, very finely chopped

2 teaspoons chopped fresh herbs

1 tablespoon chopped parsley

salt and pepper

12 anchovy fillets in oil

Whisk the yeast into the milk until frothy, then set aside for 10 minutes. Sift the flour and salt into a bowl. Make a well in the center, pour in the oil and add the yeast mixture. Mix in enough cold water to make a soft dough. Knead on a board for about 5 minutes or until smooth and elastic. Return to the bowl, cover with a cloth and set aside at room temperature or slightly warmer to rise for 1 hour.

Knead dough again gently and shape with the fingers into a round or rectangle that fits a large greased and floured baking sheet. Spread the peppers, tomatoes and onion evenly over the dough. Add the garlic, herbs, parsley and a generous amount of salt and pepper. Cut the anchovies lengthwise into narrow strips and arrange in a cross-hatch pattern over the pie. Bake in a preheated 375°F/190°C/Gas 5 oven until the crust is browned. Cut into squares or wedges and serve at once.

Conejo con Ciruelas y Piñones

RABBIT WITH PRUNES AND PINE NUTS
SERVES 6

2 small rabbits, 1½ lb/750 g each

½ teaspoon black pepper

½ teaspoon salt

½ teaspoon dried rosemary

½ cup/120 ml/4 fl oz olive oil

1 large onion, chopped

4 cloves garlic, chopped

5 medium tomatoes, peeled, seeded and chopped

1 slice white bread, crusts trimmed

¼ cup/30 g/1 oz ground almonds

1 tablespoon chopped parsley

4 oz/120 g pitted prunes

⅓ cup/45 g/1½ oz pine nuts

Cut the rabbits into serving pieces and season with pepper, salt and rosemary. Sauté in ⅔ of the oil until evenly colored, then remove. Sauté the onion until softened, then add the garlic and cook briefly. Add tomatoes and cook to a soft pulp, about 6 minutes. Add the rabbits with water to barely cover and cook, covered, for about 40 minutes.

Fry the bread in the remaining oil until golden. Grind to crumbs with the almonds and parsley. Stir into the dish and cook for 20 minutes. In the meantime, simmer the prunes in water just to cover for 6 minutes. Blanch the pine nuts in boiling water for 2 minutes; drain. Add prunes to the dish and cook for 10 to 15 minutes. Add pine nuts. Adjust seasoning and heat through, then serve.

Conejo con Guisantes a la Menta

RABBIT WITH MINTED PEAS
SERVES 4

Supremely tender young rabbits are roasted, then served in a creamy mint-flavored sauce with peas.

2 young rabbits, 1¼–1½ lb/650–750 g each

2 cloves garlic, mashed

½ teaspoon black pepper

1 teaspoon dried thyme

2 tablespoons butter

4 slices fatty bacon

1 cup/250 ml/8 fl oz dry white wine

2 cups/360 g/12 oz green peas

2 tablespoons finely chopped fresh mint

salt

1 tablespoon all-purpose (plain) flour

2 tablespoons heavy (thick) cream

Split the rabbits in half lengthwise. Make a paste of the garlic, pepper, thyme and butter and spread across the inside of each rabbit. Arrange meat down on a rack in a roasting pan and roast in a preheated 400°F/200°C/Gas 6 oven for 15 minutes. Invert rabbits on the rack and lay a strip of bacon on top of each rabbit half. Pour the wine into the pan and roast at 350°F/180°C/Gas 4 for about 30 minutes or until very tender, basting several times with the pan juices.

Boil the peas with half the mint in lightly salted water until tender. Remove the rabbits to a heated plate and keep warm. Sprinkle the flour into the roasting pan and stir until lightly colored. Strain in enough cooking liquid from the peas to make a thin gravy. Cook for 3 to 4 minutes and adjust seasoning. Add the drained peas, remaining mint and the cream. Pour over the rabbits and serve.

Tumbret (top), p.104; Samfaina (front), p.106

Crema Quemada a la Catalana (top right), p.132; Flan (front), p.133

ARROZ CON PASAS Y PIÑONES A LA CATALANA
CATALAN-STYLE RICE WITH RAISINS AND PINE NUTS   SERVES 4–6

2 cups/440 g/14 oz short-grain/ round white rice

3 cups/750 ml/24 fl oz water

$\frac{1}{2}$ cup/90 g/3 oz raisins, soaked and drained

1 tablespoon toasted pine nuts

1 teaspoon salt

$\frac{1}{2}$ teaspoon ground cumin

1 whole clove

Place the rice and water in a saucepan, cover and bring to a boil. Reduce heat and simmer over very low heat for 15 minutes. Stir in the remaining ingredients and cook a further 8 minutes. Serve at once.

FIDEOS EN CAZUELA
VERMICELLI IN CASSEROLE   SERVES 4–6

Pasta in the Italian tradition is becoming more popular in Spain, but the classic Spanish *fideos* remain favorites. In other parts of coastal Spain they are cooked with seafood, but in Catalonia *fideos* become a hearty meal with pork ribs and other meats.

1 lb/500 g pork ribs

$\frac{1}{3}$ cup/90 ml/3 fl oz olive oil

4 oz/120 g salted *jamón serrano* or other salt pork, cut into $\frac{1}{2}$-inch/1.5-cm cubes

6 cups/1.5 l/1$\frac{1}{2}$ qt water

8 oz/250 g chicken (preferably legs)

2 medium onions, peeled

2 cloves garlic, chopped

3 medium tomatoes, peeled and chopped

1 teaspoon sweet paprika

4–5 bundles *fideos* or 8 oz/250 g vermicelli

3 tablespoons toasted blanched almonds, ground

2 tablespoons toasted pine nuts, ground

12 threads saffron or $\frac{1}{3}$ teaspoon powdered saffron

Cut the ribs into 5-cm/2-inch pieces and brown in the oil. Add salt pork and brown. Place in a large *cazuela*, add the water and simmer for 40 minutes. Add the chicken legs, onions, garlic, tomatoes and paprika and simmer for another 40 minutes.

Remove the chicken and discard skin and bones. Tear meat into shreds and return to the pot. Add the pasta. Mix nuts and saffron into 1 cup/250 ml/8 fl oz boiling water. Stir into the dish and heat for a further 20 minutes.

Pa amb Tomàquet

CATALAN TOMATO BREAD

SERVES 4

I have chosen to use the Catalan name *Pa amb Tomàquet*, for this is quite simply the focal point of the Catalan diet. A crusty peasant bread is sliced and perhaps toasted; then the moist, aromatic, soft red pulp and juices of a sun-ripened tomato are rubbed over both sides. Next comes a drizzle of olive oil — the best extra-virgin oil should be aspired to here — and a light dusting of salt. *Pa amb Tomàquet* transcends all social boundaries. It's a midday snack for a farmer in his fields, an after-school munch for a teenager, an accompaniment to appetizers in a fine Barcelona restaurant. It goes equally well with smoked salmon or with smoky mountain ham or firm white cheeses from the Pyrenees, and it's wonderful for breakfast on a sunlit patio.

8 slices fresh or day-old country bread

4 sun-ripened tomatoes

$\frac{1}{3}$ cup/90 ml/3 fl oz extra-virgin olive oil

salt

Slice the bread and toast lightly, if preferred. Cut the tops from the tomatoes. Squeeze and rub the tomato over both surfaces of the bread, then apply a thin spread of olive oil and salt lightly. Eat at once with a platter of sliced ham and sliced *butifarra* sausage, or a spicy salami or *chorizo*, or with oil-preserved anchovies or sardines and thinly sliced hard white cheese.

Pa i All

GARLIC BREAD

SERVES 4

Like its tomato-covered counterpart *Pa amb Tomàquet, Pa i All* is eaten in many situations. The idea may have come from the Italian *bruschetta*, which is a crusty country bread served fresh or toasted, rubbed with mashed garlic, drizzled with a good olive oil and sprinkled with salt. You may like to add a twist from the peppermill. A wonderful culinary tradition of rural Catalonia takes place at year's end, during the pressing of the olives: *La rosta* is the tasting of the first olive oil — warm, yellow-green and fresh from the presses. Bread is toasted, rubbed with garlic and skewered to dip into this nutty liquid gold.

4–5 cloves garlic, smoothly mashed

8 slices crusty country bread

$\frac{1}{4}$ cup/60 ml/2 fl oz virgin or extra-virgin olive oil

salt

Spread the garlic over one side of the bread and drizzle with enough olive oil to moisten without turning the bread soggy. Season to taste.

FLAN DE PASCUAS
CHEESE AND EGG PIE

On the island of Ibiza, *Flan de Pascuas* is always cooked for Easter. It has an intriguing semisweet taste.

1 recipe flan pastry (page 268)

8 oz/250 g well-flavored firm cheese (Pecorino, Gruyere, Jarlsberg), thinly sliced

3 tablespoons sugar

5 eggs

1 tablespoon chopped mint

Roll out the pastry and use to line a prepared flan tin or shallow pie dish. Trim and crimp the edges of the pastry. Arrange the sliced cheese evenly in the pastry. Sprinkle with sugar. Break in 3 of the eggs and sprinkle again with sugar. Beat the remaining eggs with the mint and pour over the pie. Bake in a preheated 350°F/180°C/ Gas 4 oven until the filling is firm and dry to the touch and the edges of the pastry are golden, about 30 minutes.

Tip: I sometimes beat all of the eggs, which gives the dish a quite different taste.

PAN DE SANTA TERESA
SWEET FRIED BREAD CATALAN STYLE

SERVES 4

Sweetened fried bread, in the style of the classic "French toast", is eaten in most parts of Spain. This delightful Catalan version was named for the fascinating and remarkable Santa Teresa of Avila, teacher and writer, whose bold spirit and sense of purpose led her to become the reformer of the Carmelite Order in the 16th century. Her literary achievements were prodigious and unique — and made more momentous by her encroachment into this most male of domains.

8 slices white bread

1$\frac{1}{2}$ cups/400 ml/13 fl oz milk

2 tablespoons granulated sugar

2 strips lemon or lime rind

2-inch/5-cm cinnamon stick

2 eggs

pinch of salt

$\frac{1}{2}$ cup/120 ml/4 fl oz olive oil

2 tablespoons superfine sugar

$\frac{1}{2}$–$\frac{3}{4}$ teaspoon cinnamon

Spread the bread in a wide tray. Bring milk to a boil in a small saucepan, add the granulated sugar, rind and cinnamon stick and let stand for 10 minutes. Pour over the bread and let stand just long enough to absorb evenly.

Beat the eggs with salt in a flat-bottomed bowl. Heat oil in a wide pan over medium heat. Carefully remove bread slice by slice and dip into the egg. Fry 4 slices at a time until crisp and golden brown. Drain and serve at once, sprinkled thickly with superfine sugar and cinnamon.

CREMA QUEMADA A LA CATALANA
CATALAN CRÈME BRÛLÉE

SERVES 4–6

Crema Quemada a la Catalana, translates as "burnt cream", and this Catalan specialty could argue supremacy over that other classic, *crème brûlée*. The custard is coated with sugar, which is then caramelized under a *salamandra* — a heavy metal disk that is heated over a flame or in a very hot oven and held over the pudding until the sugar turns to toffee. It's a tricky business, done more easily though not quite so effectively under a hot broiler (grill).

4 cups/1 l/1 qt fresh whole milk

2-inch/5-cm cinnamon stick

2 5-inch/13-cm strips lemon rind

8 egg yolks

2 tablespoons cornstarch (cornflour)

1¼ cups/300 g/10 oz superfine sugar

Bring 3 cups/750 ml/24 fl oz milk to a boil with the cinnamon stick and lemon rind. Reduce heat and simmer for 5 minutes. Beat egg yolks with half the remaining milk and the cornstarch with the other half. Strain boiled milk through a fine strainer into a clean stainless steel or glass saucepan. Quickly stir in the egg mixture, cornstarch and 1 cup/250 g/8 oz sugar. Stir over low heat until the custard is the consistency of heavy (thick) cream.

Pour custard into 4 to 6 *cazuelitas* or ramekins and let cool to room temperature, then chill. Sprinkle remaining sugar evenly over the top and hold under the *salamandra* or place under a broiler (grill) long enough to caramelize the sugar.

Tip: Push a cigarette-shaped rolled wafer into the edge of the dessert to garnish.

FLAN
CRÈME CARAMEL

SERVES 6

1⅓ cups/320 g/11 oz sugar
2-inch/5-cm cinnamon stick
2 5-inch/13-cm strips lemon rind
6 egg yolks
2 whole eggs

Rinse out 6 small dariole molds or flan dishes with warm water. Arrange them in a baking dish half-filled with warm water. In a small saucepan boil ⅓ cup/80 g/2¾ oz sugar with 2 tablespoons water until the syrup turns a deep golden brown. Quickly pour into the molds, turning the molds and using a spoon to cover the sides. Heat the remaining sugar with ¼ cup/60 ml/2 fl oz water in a small saucepan. Add the cinnamon stick and lemon rind and cook to a thread consistency (230°F/120°C on a candy/sugar thermometer). Discard the cinnamon and lemon and remove from heat. Beat egg yolks and whole eggs together lightly, then gradually pour in the hot syrup, stirring constantly to prevent the eggs from curdling. Strain the mixture through a fine strainer into the molds. Bake in a preheated 350°F/180°C/Gas 4 oven for about 30 minutes or until the tops feel firm. Chill for several hours before unmolding.

MEL I MATÓ
HONEY AND CREAM CHEESE

Burgos is a soft white ewes' milk cheese compacted into little rounds. Instead of being fermented, the fresh cheeses are steeped in brine for 24 hours, which imparts an intriguing saltiness to their otherwise bland taste. The cheese is much appreciated all over Spain, and no less in Catalonia, where it is bathed with honey as a delightful dessert. There are a number of cheeses that can adequately replace burgos: mascarpone is an excellent choice, or select your local specialty — fresh ricotta, mild, soft goats' milk cheese, or good-quality cream cheese, such as neufchatel. Match it up with a well-flavored honey.

POSTRE DE MÚSICO
CATALAN DRIED FRUIT DESSERT

This mixture of whole almonds, walnut halves, toasted hazelnuts, dried figs, raisins and slices of glacé fruit is, rather surprisingly, one of the most popular desserts in Catalonia. Serve a selection of nuts and dried fruits of your choice in individual dessert dishes with small glasses of a good muscat or tokay.

ENSAIMADA
MALLORCAN SWEET BUNS
MAKES 18 SMALL BUNS

These sweet buns are a specialty of Mallorca, where small ones are served at breakfast with hot chocolate or coffee, and larger, elaborately shaped ones are served as a cake or as a dessert with whipped cream. The dough is rolled out and brushed with lard, then layered so the final result is as light as air. It is then formed into a rope and twisted into a spiral to resemble a Danish coffee scroll. *Ensaimadas* are sometimes filled with almond paste or topped with a frosting or *cabello de ángel* (a sweet filling made from spaghetti squash). The dough can also be used to make a festive savoury pie, topped with slices of the local sausage, *sobrasada*.

1 envelope ($\frac{1}{2}$ oz/12 g) dry yeast

$\frac{1}{3}$ cup/90 g/3 oz sugar

$\frac{1}{3}$ cup/90 ml/3 fl oz lukewarm milk

4 cups/500 g/1 lb all-purpose (plain) flour

1 teaspoon salt

2 eggs, beaten

warm milk or water

$\frac{1}{3}$ cup/90 g/3 oz melted lard (or butter)

confectioners' (icing) sugar

Sprinkle the yeast and sugar over the milk in a small bowl and whisk to a froth. Set aside for 10 minutes to activate yeast. Sift $\frac{1}{2}$ cup/60 g/2 oz flour over the mixture and stir in. Sift the remaining flour and the salt into a large bowl and make a well in the center. Add the yeast mixture and eggs, then work in enough warm milk or water to make a soft dough. Turn out onto a floured board and knead until smooth and elastic. Divide into 18 pieces. Roll each out thinly and brush with melted lard or butter. Fold in thirds and roll out again. Repeat twice more, alternating the directions of the folds.

Brush each piece of dough with lard, then roll into a long rope and twist into a spiral. Arrange on a greased baking sheet, allowing plenty of room for expansion. Let rise until doubled in volume, about 50 minutes. Brush with cold water. Bake in a preheated 375°F/190°C/Gas 5 oven for about 12 minutes or until golden. Dust with confectioners' sugar before serving.

POLVORONES
ALMOND SHORTBREAD

MAKES ABOUT 36

As their name suggests, these little cookies are powdery–so fragile that they are sold wrapped in a twist of colored paper. Originally from Seville, they are now made all over Spain in many variations on the original recipe. Some contain orange peel and juice; others are simply made with flour, sugar and eggs. Some are flavored with anise, others with vanilla beans. This nutty, spicy version was one I encountered in Barcelona.

1 cup/150 g/5 oz blanched almonds

2 cups/250 g/8 oz all-purpose (plain) flour

2 teaspoons cinnamon

$\frac{1}{3}$ teaspoon salt

$1\frac{1}{3}$ cups/350 g/11 oz butter or lard

$\frac{1}{2}$ cup/120 g/4 oz sugar

1 egg

$\frac{1}{4}$ cup/60 ml/2 fl oz Cointreau or Grand Marnier

confectioners' (icing) sugar

Spread the almonds on a baking sheet and toast in a moderate oven for about 25 minutes to a rich golden brown. Allow to cool, then grind to a fine powder in a food processor or mortar. Sift the flour, cinnamon and salt into a bowl. Add the almonds and stir in well. Cream butter or lard with sugar until smooth and light, then stir in the egg and liqueur. Work into the flour to make a crumbly dough.

Roll dough out to $\frac{3}{4}$-inch/2-cm thickness on a lightly floured board and cut into small oval shapes. Use a spatula to transfer to a greased and floured baking sheet and prick lightly a few times with a fork. Bake in a preheated 325°F/160°C/Gas 3 oven for about 20 minutes or until light golden. Cool on a wire rack. Coat with confectioners' sugar and wrap in squares of tissue paper.

Variation: Omit the ground almonds and use enough additional flour to form a light, slightly crumbly dough.

PATÉ DE MEMBRILLO
QUINCE PASTE

SERVES 12

Quinces are not eaten raw, but cooked into a purée, made into a clear jelly, cooked as a compote or used in this way. An amber-pink slab of quince "pâté" is found in the display window of many market stalls where *fiambre* and *quesos* (cold cuts and cheeses) are sold. Like a solidified conserve or jam, it accompanies strongly flavored meats, pâtés and cheeses on a cold table.

4 large quinces, peeled, seeded and sliced (1 lb/500 g peeled weight)

2 cups/500 ml/16 fl oz water

$\frac{1}{2}$ cup/100 g raisins

2-inch/4-cm cinnamon stick

$1\frac{1}{2}$ cups/350 g/12 oz sugar

Place the quinces in a pan with the water, raisins and cinnamon stick and cook, tightly covered, until tender. Strain the liquid into another pan and cook with the sugar until well reduced and very syrupy. Purée the quince, or press through a sieve, and return to the syrup. Cook until very thick. Pour into a lightly oiled square pan and allow to cool until set.

ARAGON

ARAGÓN

The ancient land of Aragon covers a vast region, its provinces of Huesca and Zaragoza sweeping from the Pyrenees the full length of Catalonia to Tereul, sandwiched high in craggy mountain ranges between Valencia and the Castilian province of Guadalajara. Her central region is flat and fertile, fed by the Ebro, the large waterway on which sits the city of Zaragoza, named for Caesar Augustus — a city of legends and kings, of glowing gold cathedral domes and Moorish towers, of festivals and mighty battles. Here fruits and vegetables, grapevines and olives provide the foundation for a cuisine hardly changed through centuries. It is food for bitter winters and a simple peasant way of life.

Aragon is medieval, its landscape as dramatic as its history. This old kingdom, once the sovereign state of Spain, has played a pivotal role in Spanish history, with its museum collections and ancient buildings in Zaragoza and Teruel attesting to times of enormous wealth and grandeur. It is bleak terrain of rolling hills, gnarled trees and wind-etched rocky ravines; of ancient stone villages and tiny towns suspended on cliffsides. Her people have been Romans and Moors, have seen the Christian reconquest and fought in the battles that decided much of Spain's history, have scratched a living from the barren soil and tended their flocks of sheep.

The food revolves around lamb, cooked young as *ternasco* (baby lamb) over a wood fire, stewed with tomatoes and a touch of spice, roasted as *paletilla* (shoulder and foreleg) or *pierna* (leg) tiny enough to be a meal for one, grilled as *chuletas* (cutlets) and *costillas* (ribs). No part is wasted; the tails are braised with tomatoes in a dish that has been euphemistically called *espárragos de montaña* (mountain asparagus), the *criadillas* (testicles) fried, the tongues boiled in tomato sauce, the head roasted or grilled, the hocks simmered with garlic and bread to make warming winter soups. *Chilindrón*, lamb braised with red peppers and tomatoes, is the region's most famous dish. Chicken is also much used in Aragon, cooked *al chilindrón*, pan-fried with garlic or grilled over charcoal. The region has earned a reputation for fine charcuterie, using the pigs bred in the mountain regions of Tereul and aging the hams and sausages in the clear cold mountain air. Fat *morcilla* sausages are plump with spiced rice and pine nuts, shades of Moorish tastes from the past.

From here, too, comes *queso tronchón*, a mild, light-colored cheese formed into a dome shape. And game is plentiful. Open season for game hunters begins in the fall, with chamois, red and roe deer and wild boar the prime four-footed targets, while game on the wing includes partridges, quail, woodcocks, pheasant and much more. The catch is jumbled together in meaty, bean-filled thick and hearty soup-stews to eat with wooden spoons, chunks of crusty coarse bread and a good strong wine like the local *cariñena*. One of the traditional rural methods of cooking game is *al entierro*, "interred" or "buried:" the gutted animal, unskinned, is filled with a strongly flavored stuffing of *chorizo*, *tocino*, onions, garlic and herbs, and placed in the earth with a fire kindled on top to slowly cook the beast below. On the snow-capped mountains in Huesca there are five major ski resorts, and there is another on the Sierra de Gudar in Teruel, where winter skiers gather each evening around open fires to dine on more sophisticated fare, sipping warming garlic-flavored soups and eating trout from icy mountain streams flavored with wild rosemary or stuffed with ham, while from hot brick ovens come the tantalizing smells of roasting meats and simmering stews.

Fruit of excellent quality, particularly plump, sweet red-gold peaches, grows in Aragon's lush Ebro valley. A favorite way of serving them is poached *en almíbar*, in a sugar syrup. The Moors have left their mark on the sweets of this region. Almonds and spices go into myriad types of cookies, cakes and confections, and a specialty of the region is glacé fruit, perfectly preserved without loss of color or sugar granulated on the surface, moist, soft and invitingly more-ish. Candied whole baby pears, fat apricots, sliced orange and whole limes go to markets and confectioners' stores all over Spain, lined regimentally in paper-lined trays, tempting with their bright fruit colors. They are a delight to eat with a strong black *café solo*.

SOPA DE PASTOR A LA ARAGONESA
PEASANT SOUP ARAGON-STYLE   SERVES 4

4 thick slices (5-6 oz/150/180 g) crustless day-old country bread

4 cloves garlic, peeled, chopped

½ cup/120 ml/4 fl oz olive oil

6 cups/1.5 l/1½ qt boiling water or stock

salt and black pepper

4 eggs

4 slices *jamón serrano*, prosciutto or cured ham

Break the bread into small cubes. Fry the garlic in olive oil until golden, then remove and set aside. Fry the bread in the same oil until it is well colored, add the water or stock with the garlic and salt and pepper to taste. Break an egg into each of four deep soup bowls and pour on the soup. Add a slice of ham (rind removed) to each bowl and serve at once.

MIGAS A LA ARAGONESA
FRIED BREAD CUBES WITH GARLIC AND HAM

SERVES 4 (*TAPA*)

Migas are small croutons of bread fried in olive oil which are eaten as *tapas*, dropped into soups and stews or served with drinks. They began as a shepherds' dish in central Spain; bread no longer fresh enough to eat was crumbled into hot oil, fried until golden with some chopped garlic and peppers and bits of bacon, sausage or *chorizo*. In Extremadura they add eggs and grapes.

8 large slices bread 1–3 days old

1 teaspoon salt

1½ cups/400 ml/13 fl oz olive or vegetable oil

3 cloves garlic, minced

3 oz/190 g *jamón serrano* or other cured ham, diced

6 oz/180 g *chorizo* sausage, diced

1 teaspoon sweet paprika

Cut or tear the bread into ½-in (1.5-cm) pieces and place in a cloth. Sprinkle with the salt and a little water, wrap and let stand for several hours or overnight.

Heat the oil and fry garlic, ham and sausage for 2 to 3 minutes. Remove from the pan with a slotted spoon. Fry the bread in batches until golden. Drain off the oil. Return the meat to the pan and heat through, sprinkle with the paprika and serve.

BERENJENAS CON SETAS
EGGPLANT (AUBERGINE) WITH MUSHROOMS

SERVES 4

1 large purple eggplant (about 1½ lb/750 g), diced

salt

½ cup/60 g/2 oz all-purpose (plain) flour

½ cup/120 ml/4 fl oz olive oil

1 medium onion, finely chopped

4 cloves garlic, chopped

2 large tomatoes, chopped

1 tablespoon chopped fresh herbs (parsley, thyme, basil, oregano)

1 teaspoon ground cumin

1 lb/500 g sliced fresh wild mushrooms or ½ cup/1 oz/30 g sliced dried mushrooms, soaked

black pepper

cayenne or paprika

Spread the eggplant on a tray, sprinkle with 2 teaspoons salt and let stand for at least 10 minutes for the salt to draw off the bitter juices. Rinse and dry well. Coat lightly with flour and fry in the oil until well browned. Remove with a slotted spoon and place in a casserole.

Fry the onion until softened and lightly colored. Add the garlic and fry briefly, then add the tomato and cook until reduced to a pulp. Add to the eggplant with the herbs, cumin, mushrooms and (if dried were used) their soaking water, plus an additional ½–¾ cup (120 to 180 ml/ 4 to 6 fl oz) water. Cover tightly and simmer very slowly for 1 hour, adding more liquid from time to time if needed. Add salt, pepper to taste and the cayenne or paprika and heat through.

Jamón Serrano con Espárragos Blancos

HAM WITH WHITE ASPARAGUS SERVES 2

Aragon has excellent *charcutería*. Its particularly prized ham, produced in *Teruel*, is teamed with plump white asparagus as an appetizer or light luncheon. Pass a fresh tomato sauce or *alioli*, or serve with a coulis of finely diced tomatoes and a splash of *vinagreta* (vinaigrette dressing).

6 large or 12 smaller paper-thin slices *jamón serrano*, or other cured ham or prosciutto

10 thick white asparagus stalks*

1 tablespoon olive oil

salt and pepper

1 large tomato, peeled, seeded and very finely diced

1½ tablespoons *vinagreta salsa* (page 274)

Spread the ham on 2 dinner plates. Boil the fresh asparagus in lightly salted water until just tender. Drain and splash with the oil, salt and pepper. Place on the ham. Arrange the tomato attractively on the plate. Drizzle a little *vinagreta* on top and serve.

*Canned white asparagus can be used. Drain well and marinate for 10 minutes in *vinagreta*.

Huevos al Salmorrejo

POACHED EGGS WITH SAUSAGES SERVES 4

8 oz/250 g lean pork, preferably tenderloin, coarsely ground

8 oz/250 g thick pork sausages

2 tablespoons olive oil

6 oz/180 g *chorizo* sausage, sliced

4 oz/120 g *tocino*, bacon or *jamón serrano*, cut into narrow strips

1–2 cloves garlic, finely chopped

½ teaspoon hot paprika

1 tablespoon all-purpose (plain) flour

salt and pepper

½ cup/120 ml/4 fl oz dry white wine

¾ cup/180 ml/6 fl oz beef or veal stock

4–8 eggs

Fry the pork and sausages in the oil until just cooked through. Remove sausages and slice. Return to the pan with the chorizo and ham and cook briefly, then add the garlic and sprinkle evenly with paprika and flour. Stir in salt, pepper, wine and stock. Bring to a boil, stirring, then reduce heat and simmer 4 minutes. Divide the mixture among 4 ovenproof serving dishes. Break one or two eggs into each dish and bake at 400°F/200°C/ Gas 6 just until the eggs are set. Serve at once.

Tortilla al Salmorrejo
OMELETTE OF POTATO AND RICE

SERVES 4 (*TAPA*)

Sauce:

8 cloves garlic, chopped

2 tablespoons olive oil

2 large tomatoes, peeled, seeded and chopped

salt and pepper

pinch of dried thyme

Tortilla:

$\frac{1}{3}$ cup/60 g/2 oz short-grain white rice

2 medium potatoes, peeled and very thinly sliced

$\frac{1}{4}$ cup/60 ml/2 fl oz olive oil

1 medium onion, thinly sliced

$1\frac{1}{2}$ tablespoons chopped parsley

$\frac{1}{3}$ teaspoon dried oregano

salt and pepper

5 eggs, beaten

Sauté the garlic in 2 tablespoons oil until very well colored; remove from the pan. Cook the tomatoes with salt, pepper and thyme until reduced to a thick paste. Purée tomato and garlic together and pass through a strainer. Keep warm until needed.

Cook the rice in 2 cups boiling lightly salted water until tender; drain. Sauté the potatoes in the oil until lightly golden; remove. Fry the onion until soft. Drain off excess oil, return potatoes to pan and chop finely. Transfer to a mixing bowl and stir in rice, parsley, oregano and salt and pepper to taste. Stir in the beaten eggs. Lightly oil an omelette pan and cook the mixture until firm and golden underneath. Place a plate over the omelette and invert the pan, then slide the omelette back into the pan to cook the other side. When firm and golden on both sides, transfer to a serving plate and pour on the hot sauce. Serve at once.

Pimientos a la Chilindrón
PEPPER (CAPSICUM) CASSEROLE

SERVES 6

Peppers and tomato are consumed in vast quantities in Spain. Together they form the basis for many different types of sauce or casserole, giving a distinct flavor and pronounced red color to the dish. *A la chilindrón* is Aragon's method of combining these two master ingredients as a sauce for chicken, game and meat — or by itself as a vegetable dish.

6 large red bell peppers (capsicums), seeded

1 medium onion, thinly sliced

8 oz/250 g salted *tocino*, bacon or *jamón serrano*, thinly sliced

$\frac{1}{2}$ cup/120 ml/4 fl oz olive oil

6 large sun-ripened tomatoes, peeled, seeded and chopped

$1\frac{1}{2}$–2 teaspoons hot paprika

salt and pepper

$\frac{1}{2}$ teaspoon sugar

Drop the peppers into a pan of boiling water and blanch for about 4 minutes, then drain and peel off the skins. Cut flesh into narrow strips. Sauté the onion with bacon in the oil until the onion has turned a light golden color, then add the peppers and fry for 3 to 4 minutes. Add tomatoes and cook for about 10 minutes. Add paprika, salt, pepper and sugar and continue to cook, stirring frequently, until the liquid is thickened and the vegetables are tender.

Habas con Salchichas
BEANS WITH SAUSAGES

SERVES 4

This is a quick family meal when broadbeans are in season. Any well-seasoned pork sausages can be used.

1 medium onion, very finely chopped

3 tablespoons olive oil

4 large sun-ripened tomatoes, peeled, seeded and chopped

2½ lb/1.2 kg fresh broadbeans, peeled

salt and pepper

1 tablespoon finely chopped parsley

lemon juice

4–8 spicy pork sausages

Sauté the onion in the oil until golden, add the tomatoes and cook for 2 to 3 minutes. Add the beans, salt and pepper, cover tightly and simmer over low heat until the beans are tender, 15 to 30 minutes depending on their age. Stir in the parsley and sprinkle on a little lemon juice. In the meantime, prick the sausages and cook on a griddle or in a frying pan with a very little oil or lard until cooked through and golden brown. Spread the beans on plates and arrange the sausages on top.

Calabacines Fritos en Salsa Vinagreta
FRIED ZUCCHINI (COURGETTE) SLICES IN VINAIGRETTE DRESSING

SERVES 6
(*TAPA*)

Try this recipe with small green eggplant (aubergines).

6 medium zucchini (courgettes)

2 teaspoons salt

¾ cup/90 g/3 oz all-purpose (plain) flour

1 cup/250 ml/8 fl oz olive oil

1 recipe *salsa vinagreta* (page 274)

4 slices garlic, slivered

¼ cup/15 g/½ oz fresh basil leaves, chopped

½ fresh hot red chili pepper, thinly sliced

Thinly slice the zucchini lengthwise and spread on a kitchen towel. Sprinkle with the salt and let stand for 15 minutes, then rinse, drain and dry thoroughly. Coat lightly with flour and fry in the oil until the surface is crisp. Remove and drain very well.

Prepare the *vinagreta*, adding the garlic, chopped basil and chili. Arrange the zucchini in a glass dish and pour on the sauce. Marinate for at least 1 hour before serving at room temperature.

SETAS A LA VINAGRETA
MUSHROOMS IN VINAIGRETTE DRESSING   SERVES 4–6 (*TAPA*)

1¼ lb/650 g fresh button or wild mushrooms, sliced

1 teaspoon finely grated lemon rind

½ teaspoon freshly ground black pepper

2 teaspoons finely chopped parsley

2 teaspoons finely chopped mint

2 tablespoons red wine or sherry vinegar

½ cup/120 ml/6 fl oz virgin olive oil

1½ teaspoons sugar

salt

Place the mushrooms in a small saucepan and cover tightly. Cook over low heat, shaking the pan frequently, for about 4 minutes or until the mushrooms have softened but have not begun to exude their juices. Remove with a slotted spoon and place in a glass or ceramic bowl. Make a dressing by whisking the remaining ingredients together. Pour over the mushrooms and marinate for at least 2 hours before serving.

CHAMPIÑONES SALTEADOS
SAUTÉED MUSHROOMS   SERVES 4

1 lb/500 g fresh button mushrooms

¼ cup/60 ml/2 fl oz olive oil or butter

1–2 cloves garlic, chopped (optional)

1 tablespoon finely chopped parsley

lemon juice

salt and pepper

In a frying pan sauté the mushrooms in the oil or butter for about 4 minutes. Add the garlic and parsley and cook briefly, then add lemon juice, salt and pepper to taste.

POLLO A LA BRASA
GRILLED CHICKEN   SERVES 6

6 chicken breasts or whole
chicken thighs

$\frac{1}{2}$ cup/120 ml/4 fl oz dry white
wine

$\frac{1}{4}$ cup/60 ml/2 fl oz olive oil

1 teaspoon mashed garlic

$\frac{1}{2}$–1 teaspoon freshly ground black
pepper

$\frac{1}{2}$ teaspoon hot paprika

salt

lemon wedges

alioli (page 273)

Remove the chicken skin if preferred, although the flavor is greatly improved and the chicken remains moister if the skin is left intact. Place chicken in a dish and sprinkle with all remaining ingredients except salt. (Add salt only after the meat is cooked or it draws off the juices from the meat, making it dry.) Let stand for 20 minutes, turning twice.

Prepare a bed of glowing coals and heat the grid. Grill the chicken until the meat no longer feels springy, but has a firm feel when pressed in the center with the fingers. Do not pierce during cooking; use a wooden fork or spoon or a pair of spatulas to turn the meat. Cut the chicken breast into strips and serve with small wooden picks or forks as finger food. Accompany with lemon wedges and *alioli*.

TRUCHAS CON VINO Y ROMERO
TROUT WITH RED WINE AND ROSEMARY   SERVES 4

4 freshwater trout

2 tablespoons olive oil

salt and pepper

1 clove garlic, mashed

4 sprigs fresh rosemary

$\frac{3}{4}$ cup/180 ml/6 fl oz red wine

2 teaspoons chopped fresh mint

Clean the trout and rinse well. Rub with the oil, salt and pepper. Season the cavity with salt, pepper and garlic and place a sprig of rosemary inside each fish. Pour remaining oil into an oven dish and arrange the fish side by side in it. Add the wine and season with salt and pepper. Cover and bake in a preheated 350°F/180°C/Gas 4 oven for about 18 minutes or until the fish can be easily flaked with a fork. Sprinkle with mint and serve.

FRITADA DE CABRITO CON AJILLO

KID FRIED WITH GARLIC   SERVES 4–6

The meat of small young goats, usually the males, is much enjoyed in Spain. Baby lamb can be substituted in most kid recipes.

3 lb/1.5 kg kid meat on the bone*
salt and pepper
2 cups/500 ml/16 fl oz olive oil
2 whole heads garlic, peeled

Season the meat lightly with salt and pepper. Heat the oil in a large pan and fry the meat over high heat for 4 to 5 minutes, turning to seal all surfaces. Reduce heat to moderate and continue to cook, turning frequently, for about 25 minutes or until the meat is tender. Add the garlic and cook a further 10 minutes. Drain off the oil and season the meat with salt and pepper.

*You can probably buy a half kid and select an assortment of tender cuts from leg, shoulder and ribs. Have your butcher cut through the bone into serving pieces.

Tip: This dish is the ultimate garlic experience, so garnish with large sprigs of parsley for nibbling afterwards.

CORDERO AL CHILINDRÓN

CASSEROLE OF LAMB AND PEPPERS   SERVES 4

4 large red bell peppers (capsicums)
1½ lb/750 g lean boneless lamb, cubed
½ cup/120 ml/4 fl oz olive oil
3 cloves garlic, peeled
1 large onion, chopped
4 large tomatoes, peeled, seeded and chopped
2 teaspoons sweet paprika
1 dried hot red chili pepper
salt and pepper
4–8 threads saffron

Roast the peppers in a hot oven for about 30 minutes, until the skin has blackened. Fry the lamb in oil until evenly colored, then transfer to a casserole. Fry the whole garlic cloves until lightly colored; transfer to the casserole. Fry the onion until golden, add tomatoes and fry to a soft pulp. Add paprika and chili pepper and add to the casserole. Peel the peppers and cut into strips. Add to dish and season with salt and pepper. Stir well, cover and cook for about 40 minutes or until the lamb is very tender, adding a little more water if necessary to keep the sauce from drying up (the finished dish should, however, be fairly dry). Crush the saffron with 1 tablespoon boiling water and pour into the dish. Serve hot with potatoes.

Variation: Pitted sliced green or black olives can be added to the dish in the last minutes of cooking.

Champiñones Salteados (top) and Setas a la Vinagreta (right), both p.142.

Lengua a la Aragonesa, opposite

Lengua a la Aragonesa
TONGUE IN PEPPER TOMATO SAUCE   SERVES 6

1 2-lb/1-kg ox tongue or 2–3 calves' tongues, soaked overnight if salted

2 medium onions, peeled

1 medium carrot, peeled

1 bay leaf

2 sprigs fresh thyme

2 sprigs parsley

1 sprig fresh oregano

3 tablespoons olive oil

4 cloves garlic, finely chopped

2 large red bell peppers (capsicums), seeded and sliced

4 large sun-ripened tomatoes, peeled, seeded and chopped

$\frac{1}{4}$ cup/60 ml/2 fl oz dry sherry

6–8 saffron threads, crushed

$\frac{1}{4}$ cup/60 ml/2 fl oz boiling water

$\frac{1}{2}$ teaspoon hot paprika

salt and pepper

Place the tongue/s in a large saucepan with water to cover generously. Add one onion, quartered, the carrot, bay leaf, thyme, parsley and oregano and bring to a boil. Reduce heat and simmer for $2\frac{1}{2}$ to 4 hours or until the tongue/s can be easily pierced with a skewer. Remove and drain, then strip off the skin. Place tongue in a bowl and put a weight on top. Refrigerate for at least 4 hours, preferably overnight.

Finely chop the other onion and sauté in the oil until lightly colored. Add the garlic and peppers and cook 3 to 4 minutes, then add tomatoes and cook until soft. Process to a creamy consistency in a blender or food processor and return to the pan. Add sherry and saffron, which has been dissolved in the boiling water. Simmer briefly, add paprika and check seasoning. To serve hot, slice the tongue, warm in the sauce and serve with boiled potatoes. Or serve cold by slicing the tongue and arranging on a platter dressed with onion rings and parsley. Serve the sauce separately at room temperature.

Melocotones en Almíbar
PEACHES IN SYRUP   SERVES 4

The best fruits of the season poached *en almíbar* — in syrup — are listed as a *postre* (sweet/dessert) on menus all around the country. Clingstone are the most commonly grown peaches in Spain.

8 large fresh peaches, peeled and halved

$\frac{1}{3}$ cup/90 g/3 oz superfine sugar

$1\frac{1}{2}$ cups/400 ml/13 fl oz water

Dissolve the sugar in water in a stainless steel or glass saucepan and add the peaches. Bring just to a boil, reduce heat and simmer until the peaches can be easily pierced. Let cool.

Navarra and La Rioja

Navarra y La Rioja

An important annual event placed Pamplona and Navarra on the tourist route, and has done much for the region's economy. The running of the bulls for the festival of San Fermín, beginning on July 7th each year, sees hundreds of thousands of people thronging the otherwise peaceful streets of this city to witness the enthralling event in which young men prove their masculinity by running the streets before charging bulls. It's a week of festivities, of eating and drinking, dancing and singing, and a week charged with tension, for lives and hopes are often lost as razor horns find home in the flesh of a hapless adventurer.

Navarra is a medieval kingdom, crucial in the history of Spain. It is part of the Basque countries, with which it is closely associated politically, in culture and in tradition, although its food leans more towards that of its southern neighbor Aragón. The ancient city of Tudela was a leading light in the gastronomy of the past, and is best known now for its plump asparagus — which is cooked as *tortilla de espárragos* in an omelette, gratinéed under a blanket of breadcrumbs or steeped in a *vinagreta*. Pamplona, too, offers culinary specialties worth making a trip for, and some of the country's finest *chorizo*. If you travel there from the upper Basque country you'll pass through alpine regions on verdant slopes of the Pyrenees; from the south, the journey takes you the length of the lush Ebro valley or along winding mountain roads lined on either side with the vineyards of La Rioja.

Navarra is pepper country. Her near neighbors in the Basque country were the travelers and adventurers who first sailed to the New World and enjoyed the fruits of discovery back home, among them red peppers. The land and climate of Navarra offered ideal conditions for growing sweet and hot peppers, which became a large rural industry in these parts. Through fall, the women of Navarra's pepper-growing rural villages occupy themselves with roasting the peppers for sale. Peppers roasted over the embers of a wood fire, then peeled, have become an important ingredient in many Spanish dishes from all parts of the country. They add a unique richness of flavor and the distinct bright red color that identifies the dishes as truly Spanish.

Like other regions throughout the densely forested Pyrenees, this is also mushroom country. Bolets and a variety of delectable wild fungi and mushrooms are cooked up with game, particularly small birds such as quail and doves. With them, too, go a specialty of the region, *pochas*, tender beans that mature at the beginning of hunting season. They are slipped from their pods when just mature enough to have flavor, but before they have aged enough to dry for sale as *alubias secas* (dried beans), and they are traditionally cooked with the first quail of the hunt.

Many of Navarra's dishes resemble those eaten in Aragón, particularly the popular *a la chilindrón* dishes. Trout grow plump in icy mountain streams, to be wrapped freshly caught in the brick-red cured raw ham of Navarra and pan-fried. Dishes *a la navarra* are red with tomatoes, chorizo and peppers, and *cochifrito* is a delicate lamb dish seasoned with garlic and lemon. The cuisine makes much use of lamb and game birds, of the spices introduced by the Moors, and of peppers. Other smells emerging from kitchens will be of venison braising in red wine, tender young rabbits simmering with tasty mountain snails, wild boar stewing with chestnuts.

Around the city of Tudela is the rich, intensely cultivated region of La Ribera, where the Ebro and her tributaries flow. This majestic city has a multicultural history that today reflects in the Jewish, Islamic and Catholic elements in her architecture and culture. Many of Spain's leading chefs have developed their repertoire of classic dishes from those borrowed from this region.

La Rioja, tucked into the northeastern side of Castile and neighbor to Navarra and the Basque country, is Spain's most important wine-producing area and the origin of many international award–winning wines, especially reds. The industry centers around the town of Haro, a little northwest of the region's capital, Logrono, with virtually the whole population of the area involved in the business of producing wine. Where there is wine there are usually plenty of festivals, the key one here being *la batalla del vino*, the battle of wines in which everyone is splashed, sprayed, daubed and otherwise thoroughly wetted with the new vintage. La Rioja is known for its full-bodied dishes that go with strongly flavored wines. The food is peppery with paprika, pungent with garlic, hot with chilies, red with peppers. These elements combine to make dishes *a la riojana*, potatoes cooked this way being a staple of the region. Strangely, though, wine does not feature extensively in their cooking, although there is one notable exception — *melocotones al vino*, fat whole peaches poached in red wine.

Much of the food is simply done, in the classic ways of old — chunky hotpots of game, snails and legumes, grills, roasts and charbroils. Strips of roasted red pepper are the classic accompaniment to plainly cooked meats, emerging from metal grids over fires of vine clippings, or from aromatic brick roasting ovens. Vegetables grow in abundance in La Rioja, particularly peppers and finely flavored potatoes, but perhaps most importantly, beans. They come in all sizes and types: fresh slender green beans, plump broadbeans, red, black, white, tiny or huge. Fresh and dried beans are cooked in innumerable ways and enjoyed in some form with most meals. While tender *pochas* are cooked with quail in nearby Navarra, here they are done *a la riojana*, infused in a bright red sauce of paprika and garlic, with perhaps a handful of diced *chorizo* thrown in for extra flavor and its delightfully chewy texture.

GARBURE DE NAVARRA
NAVARRA POTAGE

SERVES 6–8

1 cup/180 g/6 oz dried broadbeans, soaked overnight

1 lb/500 g meaty pork ribs, in 2-inch/5-cm lengths

10 cups/2.5 l/2½ qt water

4 oz/120 g salted *tocino* or other salt pork, diced

2 leeks, white parts only, sliced

2 large potatoes, peeled and cubed

1 cup/180 g/6 oz sliced green beans

1 cup/180 g/6 oz green peas

1½ cups/250 g/8 oz chopped cauliflower

1½ cups/150 g/5 oz shredded cabbage

salt and pepper

1 sprig fresh rosemary

2–3 lightly spiced pork sausages

1 tablespoon olive oil (optional)

Drain broadbeans and place in a large saucepan with the ribs, water and salt pork. Bring to a boil, partially cover and simmer for 2 hours, or until the broadbeans and ribs are both tender. Add leeks and potatoes and cook for 15 minutes, then add the remaining vegetables, seasonings and herbs and cook until the vegetables are tender, a further 15 minutes. In the meantime, fry or grill the sausages in olive oil until cooked through and well browned. Slice thinly and divide among 6 large soup bowls. Check the soup for seasoning and pour over the sausage.

FOIE GRAS CON TRUFAS
GOOSE LIVER WITH TRUFFLES

SERVES 4

10 oz/300 g fresh goose liver (or use duck livers)

2 fresh truffles, trimmed and wiped

2 tablespoons extra-virgin olive oil or butter

1 green (spring) onion (shallot/scallion), chopped

2 tablespoons cognac

¾ cup/180 ml/6 fl oz rich veal stock

salt and pepper

4 small slices white bread, crusts trimmed

vegetable or olive oil for frying

Thinly slice the liver and truffles. Heat the oil or butter and sauté them until the livers just change color. Remove and keep warm. Cook the onion in the remaining oil until softened, add the cognac and cook until it evaporates. Add the stock with salt and pepper and boil until syrupy. Fry the bread until golden. Place a piece of bread on each plate and lay several slices of liver on it; top with the truffles. Spoon on a little of the sauce and serve at once.

MAGRAS CON TOMATE

HAM IN TOMATO SAUCE

SERVES 4

12 oz/350 g *jamón serrano*, *prosciutto* or other cured or smoked raw ham

1 medium onion, minced

$\frac{1}{2}$ cup/120 ml/4 fl oz olive oil

3 cloves garlic, minced

4 large sun-ripened tomatoes, peeled, seeded and chopped

12-oz/350-g can tomatoes, chopped

salt and pepper

1 teaspoon sugar

$\frac{1}{2}$ teaspoon crushed cumin seeds

1 tablespoon red wine vinegar

$\frac{1}{4}$ cup/30 g/1 oz all-purpose (plain) flour

Cut the ham into small cubes and set aside. Sauté the onion in half the olive oil until lightly colored and softened. Add garlic and sauté briefly. Add fresh tomatoes and cook for 6 minutes. Add canned tomatoes, salt, pepper, sugar and cumin and cook uncovered until soft and pulpy. Push the sauce through a sieve, then season with the vinegar. Toss cubed ham in flour, then fry in the remaining oil for about 4 minutes. Add the sauce and heat gently for 10 minutes.

Tip: If preferred, the ham can be sliced instead of cubed. If it is very salty, soak for 20 minutes in milk, then rinse and pat dry before using.

CRIADILLAS DE CORDERO

SHEEP TESTICLES

SERVES 4–6

The testicles of slain *toros* from the *corridas* (bullfights) are highlighted on menus in some of the better restaurants in the towns that have *plazas de toros* (bullrings). However, testicles of veal and lamb have a better flavor and are readily available from the butcher. They are usually sliced and fried to serve as an appetizer.

1 teaspoon salt

$\frac{1}{2}$ teaspoon black pepper

1 teaspoon sweet paprika

1 cup/120 g/4 oz all-purpose (plain) flour

$\frac{3}{4}$–1 lb/375–500 g calves' or lambs' testicles, thinly sliced

2 eggs, beaten

$1\frac{1}{4}$ cups/150 g/5 oz fine dry breadcrumbs

3 tablespoons butter

6 tablespoons olive oil

1 tablespoon finely chopped parsley

Mix the salt, pepper, paprika and flour and coat the testicles lightly. Dip into the egg and coat with crumbs. Chill for 1 hour.

Heat the butter and oil in a sauté pan and sauté the testicles in several batches until crisp and golden. Sprinkle with parsley and serve hot.

Variation: Cook prepared and blanched sweetbreads or brains in the same way.

CARACOLES A LA RIOJANA
SNAILS IN A SPICY SAUCE

SERVES 4

1 small onion, finely chopped

4 cloves garlic, finely chopped

1 red bell pepper (capsicum),
seeded and chopped

1 green bell pepper (capsicum),
seeded and chopped

1 fresh hot red chili pepper,
seeded and finely chopped

3 tablespoons olive oil

2 teaspoons sweet paprika

3 oz/120 g *chorizo* sausage, finely
chopped

1 large tomato, peeled, seeded
and chopped

80 small snails, purged and
prepared (page 266)

salt and pepper

Sauté the onion, garlic, peppers and chili in the oil for 5 minutes. Add the paprika and *chorizo* and cook a further 5 minutes. Add tomato and sauté for 6 minutes. Add the snails with salt and pepper, cover and cook until tender, about 20 minutes.

In Spain snails are never taken from their shells before serving, except when used in small tarts. They are extracted at the table with little pronged picks.

PIMIENTOS RELLENOS CON CODORNICES
RED PEPPERS STUFFED WITH QUAIL
SERVES 6

6 large red bell peppers (capsicums)

6 quail

salt and pepper

6 chicken livers

1 small onion

$\frac{3}{4}$ cup/180 ml/6 fl oz olive oil

1 clove garlic

1 tablespoon Spanish brandy or dry sherry

$\frac{1}{2}$ cup/120 g/4 oz all-purpose (plain) flour

2 cups/500 ml/16 fl oz chicken or veal stock

Cut the tops from the peppers and use a small sharp knife to trim away the internal membranes and seed core. Reserve the tops. Rinse and thoroughly dry the quail and season cavities with salt and pepper. Chop the chicken livers into small pieces. Sauté the onion in 2 tablespoons oil until golden; add the livers and garlic and sauté briefly. Splash in the brandy or sherry and cook until it evaporates. Fill each of the quail with a little of the liver mixture. Season the outside with salt and pepper and coat with flour. Cook in the remaining oil until well browned. Place a quail inside each of the peppers and stand them upright in a casserole. Place the tops in position and pour in the stock. Cook in a preheated 350°F/180°C/Gas 4 oven for about 35 minutes or until the peppers are tender but still retain their shape, and the quail are cooked through. If desired, a gravy can be made with the pan juices.

ESPÁRRAGOS A LA VINAGRETA
ASPARAGUS WITH VINAIGRETTE DRESSING
SERVES 4

20 fresh white asparagus stalks

$\frac{1}{2}$ cup/120 ml/4 fl oz mild virgin olive oil

2 tablespoons red wine vinegar

1 clove garlic, mashed

2 teaspoons Dijon-style mustard

1 tablespoon ground toasted almonds

salt and pepper

pinch of chili powder (optional)

Trim the asparagus and cook in lightly salted simmering water for about 5 minutes or until just tender. Remove from heat, drain and plunge immediately into cold water. Drain again.

In a screw-top jar mix the remaining ingredients, shaking the jar briskly to emulsify. Arrange the asparagus on plates and pour on the dressing. Let stand for 5 minutes before serving.

ALCACHOFAS A LA VINAGRETA

ARTICHOKES WITH VINAIGRETTE DRESSING

SERVES 4 (*TAPA*)

Artichokes done in this way are a palate-stimulating first course, and are enjoyed as a *tapa*. Serve in small dishes with toothpicks.

24 fresh baby artichokes

1 lemon, halved

$\frac{1}{2}$ cup/120 ml/4 fl oz mild virgin olive oil

2 tablespoons red wine vinegar

3–4 cloves garlic, mashed

salt and pepper

1 hard-boiled egg yolk, mashed

2 small to medium onions, thinly sliced

Remove the outer leaves from the artichokes; trim bases flat. Use a sharp knife to trim off tips of leaves, cutting in one motion from bottom to top. Cut off the tops flat. Squeeze lemon into a pan of cold water, drop in the artichokes and soak for 10 minutes. Bring to a boil and simmer for about 25 minutes or until the artichokes are tender; cooking time will depend on their size. (Test by inserting a skewer into the heart; it should pierce easily.) Drain, cool and quarter.

Whisk the oil, vinegar, garlic, seasonings and egg yolk together to make a creamy dressing. Pour over the artichokes and arrange on a serving plate. Separate the onion into rings and place on top of the artichokes.

ESPÁRRAGOS GRATINADOS

ASPARAGUS GRATIN

SERVES 4

Spain is the largest supplier of asparagus to the European markets. Much of it comes from the old gardens of Aranjuez, but superb asparagus also grows in La Rioja.

24 thick fresh white asparagus stalks, or 48 slender young green asparagus stalks

3 slices day-old white bread, crusts trimmed

$\frac{1}{4}$ cup/60 ml/2 fl oz olive oil

3 cloves garlic, finely chopped

$1\frac{1}{2}$ teaspoons sweet paprika

salt and pepper

1 tablespoon red wine vinegar

Trim the asparagus and simmer until tender in lightly salted water. Drain well. Chop the bread to crumbs in a food processor. Fry in the oil until lightly colored. Add the garlic and paprika with a little salt and pepper. Arrange the asparagus in a heatproof dish and pour on the fried ingredients. Place under a hot broiler (grill) to toast the tops, then splash on the vinegar and serve at once.

CALABACINES FRITOS CON UVAS PASAS
FRIED ZUCCHINI (COURGETTES) WITH RAISINS   SERVES 4

6 medium zucchini (courgettes)

2 tablespoons lard or olive oil

$\frac{1}{4}$ cup/45 g/1$\frac{1}{2}$ oz raisins

salt and pepper

1 tablespoon toasted pine nuts

Boil the zucchini in lightly salted water until just tender. Drain and cool. Slice thickly. Sauté in the lard or oil for 1 minute; add the raisins, salt and pepper and cook briefly. Add the pine nuts and serve at once.

Variation: Replace the raisins and nuts with finely chopped sautéed ham and onion, or with chopped apple and slivered almonds.

MENESTRA TUDELANA
VEGETABLE CASSEROLE TUDELA STYLE   SERVES 4

Menestra a la riojana is closely related to its cousin of the Basque provinces, *menestra de verduras*, and similarly the pot is the catchall for the smallest and newest vegetables — the larger the variety the better. The capital city, ancient Tudela, confines itself to a stylish combination of young broadbeans and baby artichokes.

12 baby artichokes

lemon juice or vinegar

2 lb/1 kg fresh broadbeans in the shell (or 12 oz/350 g beans)

2–3 cloves garlic, finely chopped

3 tablespoons olive oil

1 tablespoon ground almonds

$\frac{1}{3}$ cup/90 ml/3 fl oz dry white wine

1 sprig fresh thyme

salt and pepper

1 cup/250 ml/8 fl oz water

5 saffron threads

2 teaspoons chopped fresh mint (optional)

4 hard-boiled eggs, cut into wedges

Trim off the outer leaves and tips of the artichokes. Place artichokes in a non-aluminum pot of cold water acidulated with a little lemon juice or vinegar. Bring to a boil and simmer for 5 minutes, then drain. Boil broadbeans separately in lightly salted water for about 5 minutes. Sauté the garlic in olive oil for 1 minute. Add the ground almonds, artichokes and broadbeans and sauté together for a further minute. Add the wine and thyme with salt and pepper to taste and cook until the wine evaporates. Add the water, cover and simmer for about 20 minutes. Crush saffron and dissolve in a little of the hot liquid from the pot; stir into the vegetables. Add mint and the eggs, warm through and serve.

POCHAS A LA RIOJANA
YOUNG BEANS IN THE RIOJA STYLE

SERVES 4

1 lb/500 g *pochas* or other fresh young beans such as broadbeans

1 small onion, finely chopped

2 cloves garlic, finely chopped

3 oz/90 g *jamón serrano* or other cured ham, finely diced

3 tablespoons olive oil

1 tablespoon sweet paprika

salt and pepper

Rinse and drain the beans. Sauté the onion, garlic and ham in the oil until softened and lightly colored. Add the beans and paprika, cover and cook gently until tender, about 10 minutes, shaking the pan occasionally to turn them. (It should not be necessary to add any liquid, but if they begin to stick add a little chicken stock or water.) Season with salt and pepper.

PATATAS A LA RIOJANA
POTATOES WITH PAPRIKA AND CHORIZO

SERVES 4

The *chorizo* sausage made in La Rioja is one of the best in the country and is used in many dishes. Classic *a la riojana* dishes combine *chorizo* with peppers, tomatoes and onions, cooked with snails, game, tripe, *bacalao* and pork — all meats rich enough to accept the strong flavors of the base ingredients. Potatoes are included in many of these to make a one-pot meal. Here they are a dish in their own right, cooked with enough broth to be almost a soup.

4 large potatoes, peeled and thickly sliced

$\frac{1}{4}$ cup/60 ml/2 fl oz olive oil

8 oz/250 g *chorizo* sausage

1 medium onion, thinly sliced

1 clove garlic, finely chopped

2 teaspoons sweet paprika

1 small hot red chili pepper, seeded and chopped

$1\frac{1}{2}$ cups/400 ml/13 fl oz cold water

salt and pepper

Sauté the potatoes in the oil until lightly colored. Remove and set aside. Fry the whole sausages in the remaining oil until the surface is crisp; remove. Sauté the onion and garlic until golden. Slice the sausage and return to the pan with the paprika and chili. Cook briefly, then add the potatoes with water and salt and pepper to taste. Cover tightly and cook until the potatoes are tender.

TORTILLA DE AJOS TIERNOS Y SETAS
OMELETTE WITH GARLIC SHOOTS AND MUSHROOMS   SERVES 2–4

1 bunch (about 20 pieces) garlic shoots

1 cup/120 g/4 oz thinly sliced small wild or button mushrooms

3 tablespoons olive oil

6 eggs, beaten

salt and pepper

Cut the garlic shoots into 2-inch/5-cm pieces and sauté with the mushrooms in olive oil until the mushrooms begin to exude liquid. Mix in a bowl with the eggs, adding salt and pepper. Reheat the pan and pour in the mixture. Cook until the omelette is firm and golden underneath, firming the edges by pressing all around with a narrow spatula. Invert onto a plate and slide back into the pan. Cook until the whole omelette is firm and golden. Slide onto a serving plate and serve at once, cut into wedges.

TRUCHAS A LA NAVARRA
TROUT NAVARRE STYLE   SERVES 4

This old recipe stuffs freshly caught trout from mountain streams with local cured ham. Some cooks prefer to wrap the fish in thin slices of ham.

4 freshwater trout (about 12 oz/ 350 g each), cleaned

salt and black pepper

1 tablespoon lemon juice

4 long, thin slices *jamón serrano* or other cured ham

$\frac{1}{3}$ cup/45 g/1$\frac{1}{2}$ oz all-purpose (plain) flour

$\frac{1}{2}$ cup/120 ml/4 fl oz olive oil

lemon wedges

Rinse the trout and dry well. Season inside the cavity with salt, pepper and lemon juice and lightly salt and pepper the outside. Place a folded slice of ham in the cavity of each fish, or wrap around the fish and tie loosely with thin string. Coat lightly with flour. Heat oil in a large skillet or sauté pan and fry the fish on both sides until well browned and cooked through. Remove the string and transfer fish to a warmed serving plate. Serve with lemon wedges.

CODORNICES CON POCHAS
QUAIL WITH TENDER BEANS

SERVES 4

At the beginning of the hunting season, a type of small white haricot bean has just formed in the shell but is not yet ready to pick and dry. These tender beans are used in a special dish with the first quail of the season. Small dried white beans, previously soaked and parboiled, can be used.

1½ cups/250 g/8 oz small dried or fresh white (haricot) beans

4 large or 8 small oven-ready quail

5 cloves garlic, peeled

salt and pepper

1 large onion, finely chopped

⅓ cup/90 ml/3 fl oz olive oil

5 oz/150 g *jamón serrano* or other cured ham, finely diced

1 large sun-ripened tomato, peeled, seeded and chopped

1 teaspoon tomato paste

3 oz/90 g *chorizo* sausage, sliced

2 teaspoons finely chopped parsley or other fresh herbs

If using dried beans, cover with cold water, add a little salt and boil for about 1½ hours until just tender. Test occasionally; they are ready when they can be flattened when squeezed between finger and thumb. Drain, reserving 1 cup/250 ml/8 fl oz of the liquid.

Rinse and thoroughly dry the quail. Mash 2 cloves of garlic with salt. Rub over the quail and season with pepper. Set aside. Sauté the onion in 2 tablespoons olive oil until softened, add remaining garlic, finely chopped, and sauté briefly. Add the ham and fry for 4 to 5 minutes. Add tomato and tomato paste and moisten with 1 cup/ 250 ml/8 fl oz water (if using fresh beans), chicken stock or liquid reserved from cooking dried beans. Cook for 6 to 8 minutes.

Brown the quail in the remaining oil. Remove and sauté the *chorizo*. Place the quail in the sauce with the fresh or cooked dried beans, cover and cook gently for about 40 minutes. Add *chorizo* and heat briefly. Sprinkle with parsley and serve.

CODORNICES CON UVAS BLANCAS

QUAIL WITH WHITE GRAPES

SERVES 6

9 small or 6 larger quail

3 tablespoons butter or olive oil

salt and pepper

1½ cups/750 ml/12 fl oz semisweet white wine

1 tablespoon all-purpose (plain) flour

1 cup/250 ml/7 fl oz chicken or game stock

1½ cups/250 g/8 oz white grapes, peeled and halved

1 tablespoon finely chopped fresh mint

Split the quail in half and rub with the butter or oil and salt and pepper. Arrange on a rack in a roasting pan. Add half the wine and ¾ cup/180 ml/6 fl oz water. Roast in a preheated 400°F/200°C/Gas 8 oven for 10 minutes. Baste the birds, reduce the oven temperature slightly and roast a further 10 minutes. Remove the birds and keep warm.

Place the pan over the heat and add the remaining wine. Boil until evaporated, then sprinkle on the flour and stir into the pan juices. Brown lightly, then add the stock and boil, stirring, to thicken. Adjust seasonings, add the grapes and half the mint and warm through. Spoon over the quail and garnish with the remaining mint. Serve at once with shoestring fried potatoes.

CORDERO LECHAL ASADO

ROASTED MILKFED LAMB

SERVES 8

Butchered when they are only a few months old, baby lambs weigh only about as much as a normal leg of lamb. The meat is almost white and very delicate in flavor. Virtually fat-free, it is excellent for those on a low cholesterol diet. It is, however, difficult to obtain in most countries. In Spain, baby lamb is sold whole or split along its length.

1 baby lamb

3 cloves garlic, mashed

salt and pepper

1 cup/250 ml/8 fl oz dry white wine (optional)

Have your butcher deliver the lamb already split in half. Rub with the garlic, salt and pepper and place in an oiled roasting pan with the wine. Roast in a preheated 400°F/200°C/Gas 6 oven for 20 minutes, basting the lamb with the pan liquid. Reduce the heat to 350°F/180°C/Gas 4 and roast about 18 minutes per pound (500 g). Carve and serve.

Tip: Peel and cube potatoes, toss with olive oil and roast with the lamb. Add chopped garlic, fresh herbs and paprika and toss again. Serve the potatoes with the roast and, if desired, make a gravy with the pan juices.

Chuletas de Ternera a la Navarra
VEAL CUTLETS NAVARRE STYLE
SERVES 4

8 small veal loin cutlets

3 tablespoons olive oil

2½ oz/80 g salted *jamón serrano*, bacon or cured ham

1 large onion, chopped

4 sun-ripened tomatoes, peeled, seeded and chopped

2 cloves garlic, minced

salt and pepper

3 oz/100 g *chorizo* sausage, thinly sliced

Fry the cutlets in oil until browned on both sides, then remove to a casserole. Cut the ham into small strips and fry ham and onion in the remaining oil until the onion softens. Arrange on the cutlets. Fry the tomato and garlic to a soft pulp; season with salt and pepper. Pour over the cutlets and bake in a preheated 350°F/180°C/Gas 4 oven for 25 minutes, turning once. Add the chorizo to the dish and return to the oven for 10 minutes. Serve in the dish with sautéed or boiled potatoes.

Variations: Try this recipe also with chicken drumsticks or, a particularly delicious version, with little rolls of very thinly sliced veal.

Chuletas de Ternera a la Riojana
VEAL CUTLETS LA RIOJA STYLE
SERVES 4

4 medium or 12 small veal cutlets

salt and pepper

½ cup/60 g/2 oz all-purpose (plain) flour

¾ cup/180 ml/6 fl oz olive oil

2 red bell peppers (capsicums), roasted and sliced

2 medium onions, sliced

2 cloves garlic, chopped

1½ teaspoons sweet paprika

6 oz/180 g *chorizo* or other spiced sausage, sliced

1 cup/250 ml/8 fl oz prepared tomato sauce or veal stock

Season the cutlets with salt and pepper and flour lightly. Fry in the oil until golden brown, remove and drain. Sauté the peppers and onions until softened, add garlic and paprika and mix well. Transfer half of the mixture to a wide ovenproof dish and arrange the sliced *chorizo* on top. Place the cutlets side by side over this and cover with the remaining peppers and onion. Add the tomato sauce or stock and bake in a preheated 350°F/180°C/Gas 4 oven for about 40 minutes or until the cutlets are tender, add liquid to the pan during cooking, if needed, to prevent it from drying out — although there should not be much liquid remaining when done.

BROCHETA MIXTA DE CARNES

SKEWERS OF MIXED MEAT   SERVES 4

4 small lamb cutlets

4 lambs' kidneys

1 thick slice calf's liver

$\frac{1}{2}$ cup/120 ml/4 fl oz milk

1 thick beef or veal steak

1 *morcilla* or other blood sausage

1 *chorizo* or other spicy sausage (about 6 oz/180 g)

8 small onions, peeled

4 bay leaves

1 small green bell pepper (capsicum), seeded and quartered

8 button mushrooms

$\frac{1}{2}$ cup/120 ml/4 fl oz red wine

3 tablespoons olive oil

$\frac{1}{2}$ teaspoon crushed dried thyme

$\frac{1}{2}$ teaspoon black pepper

$\frac{1}{2}$ teaspoon salt

Trim the cutlets to remove any loose fragments of fat or meat and cut the bone short. Halve the kidneys and remove the fatty core, then cut each in halves again. Cut the liver into cubes. Place kidneys and livers in a dish, pour on the milk and let stand for 10 minutes. Cut the steak into cubes and thickly slice the sausages. Drain the kidneys and livers and dry with paper towels. Thread the meats, sausages, vegetables and bay leaves evenly onto 8 metal skewers. Place side by side in a shallow dish and pour on the wine, olive oil and seasonings. Let stand for 2 hours, turning frequently.

Cook on a grid over glowing charcoal until tender, brushing occasionally with the remaining marinade. Serve at once with charcoal-grilled peppers and tomatoes.

BROCHETAS DE SOLOMILLO A LA RIOJANA

TENDERLOIN BROCHETTES   SERVES 4–6

2 lb/1 kg beef tenderloin

2 cloves garlic, mashed

$\frac{3}{4}$ teaspoon salt

$\frac{1}{2}$ teaspoon sweet paprika

black pepper

1 cup/250 ml/8 fl oz dry red wine

1 bay leaf

1 sprig fresh thyme or rosemary

2 tablespoons olive oil

Cut the beef into 1-inch/2.5-cm cubes and thread onto metal skewers. Mix garlic, salt, paprika and pepper and rub over the meat. Place in a flat dish and pour on the wine. Add bay leaf and herbs and marinate for 2 hours, turning several times.

Remove skewers from the marinade and drain. Brush with oil and cook over glowing charcoal until crisped on the surface but still tender inside. Serve with potatoes.

CHULETAS DE CORDERO A LA BRASA
GRILLED LAMB CUTLETS   SERVES 6

Reared on the lush mountain slopes of the Pyrenees, the long-haired *lacha* sheep of Navarra and of neighbouring La Rioja are lean and superbly flavored. The rib cutlets are often char-grilled over a fire of vine clippings from the local vineyards and served simply with grilled peppers. In Pamplona they bake lamb cutlets under a blanket of chopped tomatoes, covering the dish with slices of the spicy *chorizo* made there (see next recipe).

4 red bell peppers (capsicums)

24 small lean lamb cutlets

salt and pepper

½ cup/120 ml/4 fl oz olive oil

2 cloves garlic, mashed

1 teaspoon wine vinegar

Roast the peppers over a charcoal fire or under the broiler (grill) until their skins blacken. Broil or grill the cutlets, seasoning lightly with salt and pepper and brushing with a little olive oil to keep the meat moist. When almost done, spread with garlic and cook again briefly. Sprinkle with vinegar. Peel peppers. Discard seeds and cut flesh into strips. Sprinkle with salt, pepper and olive oil and serve at once with the cutlets.

Tip: Rub thickly sliced country bread with garlic and toast on the grill until golden. Drizzle with olive oil and serve with the lamb.

CHULETAS DE CORDERO A LA NAVARRA
LAMB CUTLETS NAVARRE STYLE   SERVES 4

12 lamb loin cutlets

3 tablespoons olive oil

4 oz/130 g *tocino* or other cured ham

1 large onion, chopped

4 sun-ripened tomatoes, peeled, seeded and chopped

2 cloves garlic, minced

salt and pepper

3 oz/100 g *chorizo* sausage, thinly sliced

Fry the cutlets in oil until browned on both sides; remove to a casserole. Cut the ham into small strips and fry ham and onion in the remaining oil until the onion softens. Arrange on the cutlets. Fry the tomato and garlic to a soft pulp, then season with salt and pepper. Pour over the cutlets and bake in a preheated 350°F/180°C/Gas 4 oven for 25 minutes. Add the *chorizo* to the dish and return to the oven for 10 minutes. Serve in the dish with sautéed or boiled potatoes.

Variation: Try this recipe also with veal cutlets, chicken drumsticks or with little rolls of very thinly sliced veal.

Chuletas de Cordero a la Navarra, opposite

Menestra Tudelana (top), p.155; Brochetas de Solomillo a la Riojana (middle), p.161; Patatas a la Riojana (front), p.156

CALDERETA RIBEREÑA
LA RIBERA HOTPOT

SERVES 8

The shepherds use a deep potbellied iron pot on three legs for cooking up meals in the open. It is economical to use, as it stands directly over the fire — which need only be made of a few sticks and twigs to give enough heat to cook up a quick stew. In the traditional kitchen, a *caldereta* stands in the hearth over the wood fire. Stews of lamb, fish or this curious mixture of meat and fish with snails are called *calderetas* after this pot. Slow cooking is also done in the *olla*, a tall pot that is narrow at the bottom, widening in the center and narrowing again at the top.

2-lb/1-kg lamb braising chops or neck chops

2 medium onions, quartered

2 cloves garlic, peeled

1 large carrot, chopped

2 large tomatoes, chopped

2 bay leaves

1 teaspoon paprika

$\frac{1}{2}$ teaspoon black peppercorns

$1\frac{1}{2}$-lb/750-g freshwater eel

30 prepared snails (see page 266)

30 small wild or fresh button mushrooms

30 very small onions, peeled

salt and pepper

red wine vinegar (optional)

Cut the chops in halves and place in a large pot with the onions, garlic, carrot, tomatoes, bay leaves, paprika and peppercorns. Add water to cover and bring to a boil. Simmer for 35 minutes. Cut off the eel head; strip the skin from the body and rinse well. Dry, then cut into chunks. Add to the pot with the snails, mushrooms and onions, and cook 25 minutes. Season to taste with salt and pepper, adding a splash of vinegar if needed. Serve with a round loaf of country bread.

COCHIFRITO DE CORDERO
LAMB SAUTÉED WITH GARLIC AND LEMON

SERVES 4

$1\frac{1}{2}$ lb/750 g lean lamb, diced

2–3 tablespoons olive oil

1 large onion, chopped

3 cloves garlic, minced

$\frac{3}{4}$ teaspoon sweet paprika

1 tablespoon lemon juice

salt and pepper

2 teaspoons chopped parsley

Sauté the lamb in hot oil until well browned; remove and keep warm. Sauté the onion until golden brown and softened. Push to one side of the pan, add the garlic and paprika and sauté for 1 minute. Return the meat, add lemon juice and cook, stirring continually, for 4 to 6 minutes or until the meat is cooked, adding salt and pepper to taste. Sprinkle on the parsley and serve hot.

Conejo con Caracoles en Cazuela
RABBIT AND SNAILS IN A CASSEROLE   SERVES 6

2 small fresh rabbits, 1½ lb/750 g each

salt and pepper

½ cup/60 g/2 oz all-purpose (plain) flour

1 cup/250 ml/8 fl oz olive oil

1 medium onion, sliced

3 cloves garlic, chopped

2 cups/500 ml/16 fl oz prepared tomato sauce (page 274)

2 cups/500 ml/16 fl oz veal or chicken stock

1 bay leaf

2 sprigs fresh rosemary

2 cups/400 g/14 oz fresh snails*

Cut the rabbits into serving pieces, season with salt and pepper and coat lightly with flour. Brown in the oil, then place in a *cazuela* or casserole dish. Pour off the oil, reserving 2½ tablespoons. Wipe out the pan and return the reserved oil to it. Sauté the onion until golden. Add the garlic and cook briefly. Add the tomato sauce, stock and herbs and bring to a boil. Pour over the rabbit and add the snails. Place in a preheated 350°F/180°C/Gas 4 oven for about 1 hour, stirring from time to time. Serve in the dish.

*For preparation of snails see page 266. Prepare and cook, then use a small metal skewer to remove the snails from their shells. Alternatively, use a 14-oz/400-g can of prepared snails.

Melocotones con Vino Rioja
PEACHES MARINATED IN RIOJA WINE   SERVES 4

8 large fresh peaches, peeled, halved and pitted

2½ cups/620 ml/20 fl oz dry red wine

⅓ cup/45 g/1½ oz superfine sugar

1 large cinnamon stick

⅓ cup/90 ml/3 fl oz Spanish brandy

whipped cream

Place the peaches in a wide glass dish. Mix all the remaining ingredients except cream, stirring until sugar dissolves. Pour over the peaches and cover with plastic wrap. Set aside in a cool place, or refrigerate, for at least 3 days.

Serve in glass dishes with whipped cream.

BASQUE COUNTRY

PAÍS VASCO

The Basque country of Spain occupies the northernmost corner of the country, meeting with France where the Pyrenees taper towards the coastline. It curves around the Bay of Biscay to Santander, to enclose in its region the coastal provinces of Guipuzcoa and Viscaya and the island provinces of Alava and Navarra. The latter, being a land-locked province more akin gastronomically to Aragón and neighboring La Rioja, has been covered in a separate chapter in this culinary exploration of Spain.

The Basque region extends into France but, aside from common origin and language, the Basques of southern France bear little resemblance to those in Spain, where the men are strong and often stout, hearty drinkers, enthusiastic eaters and skilled cooks. It is not by accident that many of Spain's finest chefs are from this region, for the tradition of gastronomy is deeply rooted. For more than a hundred years, Basque gastronomes have gathered regularly at one of the hundreds of *sociedades gastronómicas*, or *sociedades populares* — gastronomic societies that have been set up in the major cities and many of the prosperous rural towns. The membership has always been exclusively male. In praise of good food, they eat together (often cooking their own meals), buy and cellar excellent wines, and nurture among their members those of the professional set destined to become top chefs. In a region where politics can cause heated debate and heartfelt anger, the societies are apolitical and harmonious; all members enjoy equal status whatever their position in outside life.

Although only a day's journey by express train or an hour or so by plane from Madrid, the Basque Country is set quite distinctly apart from the rest of Spain in many ways. To begin with, there's their native language, *euskera*, an ancient tongue of unknown origin. It may have borrowed partially from Spanish and French, but it has no direct relation to them nor to any other known language. It does have a fascinating preoccupation with the letter X, often in tandem with TX (and pronounced "ch"), which punctuates their words with amazing frequency and to fascinating effect. Names like *txangurro* and *kokotxas*, *txipirones* and *intxaursalsa* are found on the best menus, and indicate some of the finest of Basque dishes. The former is *centolla*, the giant spider crab that they prepare *al horno*, baked in the shell. The meat is so rich and sweet that it's difficult to get through an average-sized crab done in this way, but these magnificent spiny-bodied, long-legged creatures of the sea can grow to a majestic six pounds or so and still remain tender and full of flavorsome meat. *Kokotxas* (pronounced co-CO-chas) are so much in demand in the coastal Basque region that they rarely find their way inland. They are the delicate pendulums of flesh growing in the throat of hake, the very best of which are fished off the Basque coastline. Resembling plump oysters, gray skinned, soft-textured and tasting subtly of the sea, they are prepared *rebozada*, batter-dipped and fried, or in the classic method *en salsa verde*, gently poached in a sauce green with parsley and dotted with asparagus tips and peas.

From the cold Biscayan waters squid is netted in profusion. The small ones are reserved for restaurants offering *txipirones en su tinta*, tiny squid (sometimes stuffed) simmered in their own milky black ink. It's a challenging dish; the flavor is evasive and subtle, the color dramatic and distinct. And it's tricky to eat, as carelessness can leave telltale stains on tie or blousefront.

Intxaursalsa is one of the favorite desserts in the Basque country. Walnuts are not used extensively in Spanish cooking, but one enterprising chef created this wonderful sweet soup of ground walnuts. I particularly enjoyed the version I had on one visit to the Basque country: in a shallow dish of *intxaursalsa* floated two cubes of another Spanish specialty, *leche frita* (creamy cubes of fried custard).

The Biscayan waters yield many surprises, one the treasure of *angulas*, the fry of *anguilas*. These saltwater eels come from the Sargasso sea near the Bahamas and are transported by the Gulf Stream to the Bay of Biscay to spawn and grow (if they can avoid the fishing nets) and later return to their home waters to begin the cycle again. *Al ajillo*, sizzling with garlic, is the most popular way of cooking them. The eels, little more than 2 inches (5 cm) long, are thoroughly rinsed (a wad of local black tobacco is put into the rinsing water, its acidity helping to remove their mucilaginous surface) and dried while olive oil is heated in a *cazuelita*. Chopped garlic and dried chili are tossed into the dish, then the eels. The cooking is no more than the time it takes to carry the dish to the table.

San Sebastián–Donostia is the elegant beachside capital city of Guipuzcoa province, where tourists gather on the beaches by day and gamblers flow into the casino by night. It is a city of sophisticated eating places and atmospheric bars. The old quarter, partially preserved despite the massive fires that razed the city on twelve separate occasions over her long history, has narrow cobbled streets lined with bars offering some of the most spectacular *tapas* in Spain. When the chefs of France invented their *nouvelle cuisine*, it was here in this delightful city, which wraps itself around twin horseshoe bays, that some impressive new Spanish dishes were created — dishes that replaced long-held views with modern ideas, that substituted traditional ingredients with new ones and worked new themes around classic ingredients.

Bilbao is a major fishing port, so naturally its cuisine centers around the fruits of the sea. A visit to the fishmarkets of any of the main ports on the Biscayan waters is a visual treat. Tubs of fat-bellied *rapé*, slender *merluza* graded as *mediana* (medium) and *pescadilla* (small), silvery *kokotzas*, giant tuna and dark-fleshed bonito, *txangurro* and local favorites *gallo*, *chicharro*, *congrio*, and *besugo*, the silvery-pink red bream that is one of the most prized fish in Spain, are all arrayed under a glaze of cracked ice on sparkling white counters. Inland, the Basque regions are a mountainous habitat for game and wild birds, the well-composted soil of the forest floor harboring endless types of wild mushrooms (in the appreciation of which the Basques vie with the Catalans). Well-fed cattle and sheep graze on rich grasslands, providing excellent meat and milk for cheeses; the best known is the smoked ewe's milk cheese *idiazabal*, which is packed in olive oil. Chickens grow plump, and their eggs are cooked as *revueltos* (scrambled eggs) and *pipirrada*, a jumble with sautéed red peppers.

SOPA DE PESCADO A LA VASCA
BASQUE FISH SOUP   SERVES 6–8

2¼ lb/1.2 kg assorted small fish

3 lb/1.5 kg assorted shellfish

olive oil

1 large onion, finely chopped

3–6 cloves garlic, finely chopped

1 large carrot, peeled and diced

1 cup/250 ml/8 fl oz dry white wine

3 slices white bread, crusts trimmed

1 bouquet garni, or sprigs of fresh herbs

salt and pepper

Clean the fish, leaving them whole, and rinse well in cold water. Drain and dry. Thoroughly scrub the shellfish and place in a saucepan. Cover and cook without liquid over low heat, shaking the pan to encourage the shells to open. Remove from heat, remove the top section of each shell and discard those which have not opened. Set aside, reserving any liquid in the pan. Fry the fish in oil for 2 to 3 minutes, then transfer to a deep pan and add 4 cups/1 l/32 fl oz water. Bring almost to a boil and simmer 8 minutes. Remove the fish and separate meat from bones. Break meat into bite-size pieces. Strain the stock and reserve, discarding fish carcasses, heads and bones. Fry the onion, garlic and carrot in olive oil for 3 minutes. Add the wine and heat to boiling, cooking for 2 minutes. Add the bread and 4 cups/1 l/32 fl oz water, bring to a boil and simmer for 15 minutes, then strain through a fine sieve. Push vegetables and bread through the sieve, discarding any that will not pass through. Return the shellfish to the soup and add the herbs, seasonings and reserved shellfish liquid. Bring almost to a boil, then reduce heat and simmer slowly for about 4 minutes. Add the fish and reserved fish stock and heat thoroughly. Season with salt and pepper. Float a little olive oil on top and serve at once.

Variation: If a thicker, more textured soup is preferred, do not sieve the bread and vegetables; soak the bread first in cold water, squeeze and cut into small pieces.

ZURRUKUTUNA

BACALAO AND GREEN PEPPER SOUP   SERVES 6

A robust thick soup that can be served as a complete lunch or supper with crusty bread.

8 oz/250 g prepared *bacalao* (page 266)

6 green bell peppers (capsicums), seeded and chopped

1–2 fresh hot chili peppers, seeded

1 medium onion, chopped

5 cloves garlic, chopped

$\frac{1}{2}$ cup/120 ml/4 fl oz olive oil

3 cups/750 ml/24 fl oz fish stock

3 slices white bread, crusts trimmed

salt and pepper

6 eggs (optional)

Rinse the fish and drain thoroughly. Pick out any small bones and cut the meat into small cubes. Set aside. Place bell peppers in a saucepan with 1 cup/250 ml/8 fl oz water, cover and boil for 20 minutes or until thoroughly softened. Remove from heat. Sauté the chili peppers, onion and garlic in half the oil until golden. Add the fish cubes and cook for 4 to 5 minutes, then transfer to a large saucepan. Add the peppers and their liquid and the fish stock. Break bread into small pieces and fry in the remaining oil. Add to the pan with most of the oil. Simmer together for about 30 minutes, until the soup is thick and full of flavor. Add salt and pepper to taste. Slide the eggs into the soup and cook just long enough to firm up the whites. Carefully transfer to soup bowls and serve at once.

PURRUSALDA

SIMMERED SALT COD WITH POTATOES AND LEEKS   SERVES 6

$1\frac{1}{4}$ lb/650 g prepared *bacalao* (page 266)

5 cups/1.2 l/1$\frac{1}{4}$ qt water

4 young leeks, cleaned and sliced

3 cloves garlic, finely chopped

$\frac{1}{3}$ cup/90 ml/3 fl oz olive oil

4 large potatoes, peeled and cubed

black pepper

4 oz/120 g *chorizo* sausage, finely diced

2 oz/60 g *jamón serrano* or other cured ham, finely diced

1$\frac{1}{2}$ tablespoons chopped parsley

Place the *bacalao* in a saucepan with the water and bring to a boil. Simmer for 15 minutes, then remove the fish, pick out any bones, flake and set aside. Strain the stock and reserve. Fry the leeks and garlic in half the oil until lightly colored and softened, add the potatoes and fry briefly. Pour in the reserved stock and the fish and cook for about 25 minutes or until the potatoes are breaking up. Add pepper to taste; it should not require salt. Fry the chorizo and ham in the remaining oil until crisp. Serve cod in deep bowls garnished with the ham, sausage and parsley.

Variation: Fresh cod can replace the *bacalao*. Add salt to taste and supplement the flavor with a few chopped anchovies.

SHANGURRO AL HORNO
BASQUE STUFFED CRABS

SERVES 4

Shangurro or *centolla* are the large spider crabs caught around the Spanish and Portuguese coastlines. Those from the Bay of Biscay have a particularly fine flavor. In the Basque provinces they are called *txangurro* (pronounced chan gur ro) and can be an impressive sight, the large ones weighing in at over 7 pounds. The classic Basque way of cooking *txangurro* is to bake it piled into an upturned crab shell with spicy seasonings. It's exceedingly rich when the creamy yellow, yolklike *tomalley* is included.

4 cooked crabs, 1–1½ lbs/500–750 g each

OR 1 lb/500 g crabmeat (Alaskan king crab is best)

1 large onion, very finely chopped

1 small carrot, peeled and grated

2 tablespoons olive oil

1 clove garlic, finely chopped

½ small hot red chili pepper, seeded and finely chopped

1 teaspoon sweet paprika

1 large tomato, peeled, seeded and chopped

1 teaspoon tomato paste

½ cup/120 ml/4 fl oz dry white wine

2 tablespoons Spanish brandy or dry sherry

1 tablespoon finely chopped parsley

salt and pepper

⅓ cup/45 g/1½ oz fine dry breadcrumbs

1 tablespoon butter

Cut away the undersides of the crabs, separate meat from the inedible parts and flake. Extract the *tomalley* and set aside with the crabmeat. Scrape and clean the shells; place in a baking dish. Crack claws and extract the flesh. Sauté the onion and carrot in oil for 5 minutes. Add the garlic, chili and paprika and sauté briefly, then add the tomato and tomato paste and cook, stirring occasionally, for about 3 minutes. Add wine and brandy, the crabmeat, parsley, salt and pepper. Cook for 3 to 4 minutes. Stir in the *tomalley*. Pile into the prepared crab shells and smooth the tops. Sprinkle breadcrumbs evenly over the filling and dot with butter. Bake crabs in a preheated 400°F/200°C/Gas 6 oven until the tops brown, about 12 minutes. Serve at once with a green salad.

Tip: Serve this as a first course, cooking in small crab shells, on scallop shells or in individual ovenproof dishes or ramekins for about 8 minutes.

171

ANGULAS AL AJILLO
YOUNG EELS SIZZLED IN GARLIC AND CHILI PEPPER SERVES 6

A few miles from San Sebastián is the coastal township of Aguinaga, famous for its *anguilas*, a type of small edible saltwater eel. The young, or *angulas*, hatch in this area. They are only a few inches long when caught and are exceptionally tender. They can be cooked like whitebait (which make an excellent substitute) by quick frying in olive oil; the boiling oil containing garlic and shreds of hot red chili pepper is poured over them before serving. More classically, they are cooked in heated *cazuelitas*. Many Spanish cooks employ a unique way of cleaning the small *angulas* of their mucilaginous coating by soaking in cold water with a wad of local tobacco. Otherwise they should be blanched and thoroughly rinsed.

2 lb/1 kg *angulas*

1 cup/250 ml/8 fl oz olive oil

1 whole head garlic, chopped

2–3 fresh hot red chili peppers, seeded and thinly shredded

Rinse the eels, drain and dry. Divide the oil among 6 flameproof *cazuelitas* or ramekins and heat until almost smoking. Divide the garlic and chili evenly among them and cook for a few seconds. Toss a handful of the *angulas* into each dish and very quickly fry over high heat for less than 1 minute. Sprinkle with a little cold water and serve in their dishes while the oil is still bubbling.

Variation: Whole large shrimp (prawns) in the shell, cleaned baby squid and small whole fish such as sardines or whitebait are also superb cooked in this way.

GRATINADO DE VIEIRAS
BAKED STUFFED SCALLOPS SERVES 3–6

Serves two for first course, three or four for a main meal.

12 large fresh scallops in their shells

1 tablespoon anise liqueur

1 small onion, very finely chopped

1 tablespoon olive oil

4 oz/120 g crabmeat

1 teaspoon finely chopped dill or parsley

salt and pepper

$\frac{1}{4}$ cup/60 ml/2 fl oz *salsa bechamel* (page 273)

3 tablespoons fine dry breadcrumbs

1 tablespoon butter

Remove the top shells from the scallops and loosen them from the lower shells. Sprinkle with the liqueur. Sauté the onion in the oil until golden. Add the flaked crabmeat and mix well, adding the dill, salt and pepper and bechamel. Spoon over the scallops and smooth the top. Sprinkle with breadcrumbs and dot with butter. Place on a baking sheet and bake in a preheated 450°F/230°C/ Gas 8 oven for about 5 minutes or until the surface is crisp and the sauce bubbling. Serve at once.

PULPITOS A LA VINAGRETA
BABY OCTOPUS IN VINAIGRETTE DRESSING

SERVES 4 (*TAPA*)

1 lb/500 g baby octopus

1 small onion, thinly sliced

$\frac{1}{3}$ teaspoon black pepper

$\frac{1}{2}$ teaspoon salt

$1\frac{1}{2}$ tablespoons red wine vinegar

$\frac{1}{4}$ cup/60 ml/2 fl oz olive oil

Place octopus in a small saucepan, cover tightly and cook over low heat for about 45 minutes or until tender. Drain. Toss with the remaining ingredients and let stand for at least 1 hour before serving. Serve cold.

ALBÓNDIGAS DE PESCADO
FISH BALLS

MAKES ABOUT 24 (*TAPA*)

1 clove garlic, peeled

$\frac{1}{4}$ cup loosely packed parsley leaves

1 lb/500 g hake, cut into cubes

2 slices day-old white bread (crusts trimmed), soaked and squeezed dry

1 egg

salt and pepper

1 cup/120 g/4 oz all-purpose (plain) flour

deep frying oil

In a food processor chop the garlic and parsley. Add the fish and bread and process to a smooth paste. Add the egg, salt and pepper and mix well. Form into small balls and shape into lozenges. Coat with flour and fry in batches in moderately hot oil until golden. Drain and serve hot.

TOMATES RELLENOS CON ATÚN
TOMATOES STUFFED WITH TUNA

SERVES 4 (*TAPA*)

12 large cherry tomatoes

4 oz/120 g canned tuna (or salmon)

3 tablespoons mayonnaise

1 small onion

salt and pepper

lemon juice

Cut the tops from the tomatoes and scoop out the seeds and inner flesh. Break the tuna into 12 pieces. Spoon a little mayonnaise into the tomatoes and fill with a piece of tuna. Add an onion ring on top, season with salt and pepper and sprinkle with lemon juice.

CHIPIRONES EN SU TINTA

SQUID IN THEIR INK

SERVES 4–6 (*TAPA*)

There is an abundance of squid in the Biscayan waters and they could not be enjoyed more than when simmered in their own ink. The very tiny ones go locally by the Basque name *txipirones* (*chipirones*), and may also be called *chopitos* or *calamacets*. They are enjoyed in bars as a *tapa*, where they are served in heated *cazuelitas* with a chunk of bread. The imposing blackness of the dish belies its delicacy of taste. When squid are netted they release much of their black ink, so it is usually necessary to supplement the amount of ink in the recipe by buying extra squid or purchasing the ink separately. In Spain, frozen squid ink is readily available.

2 lb/1 kg baby squid

1½ lb/750 g large squid or 1 tablespoon frozen squid ink*

2 oz/60 g *jamón serrano* or other cured ham, very finely diced

½ cup/120 ml/4 fl oz dry white wine

1 small onion, finely chopped

2 cloves garlic, finely chopped

2 tablespoons olive oil

1 large tomato, peeled, seeded and finely chopped

½ cup/120 ml/4 fl oz fish stock

salt and pepper

Remove heads of squid with ink sacs intact. Clean squid, skin and rinse thoroughly. (The larger squid are needed only for their ink. Set the meat aside for another recipe; it freezes well.) Cut tentacles from small squid, chop and mix with the chopped ham. Press a teaspoon of the mixture into each of the squid. Place the ink sacs in a fine nylon mesh strainer over a jug. Press on the sacs to extract the ink. Pour the wine through the strainer and press again. Repeat this process several times to extract all of the ink. Sauté the onion and garlic in the oil until onion is lightly colored. Add tomato and cook for 4 to 5 minutes, then add the fish stock. Cover and cook over very low heat for 20 minutes. Add the ink and wine mixture, salt and pepper to taste and cook until the squid are tender and sauce is well reduced. *Chipirones en su tinta* is usually served with white rice pressed into a mold and set in the center of the plate with the inky squid surrounding it.

*Where frozen squid ink is available, it will not be necessary to purchase additional squid.

OSTRAS FRITAS

FRIED OYSTERS   SERVES 6 (*TAPA*)

Oysters are greatly enjoyed in Spain, and as they have become more readily available they are served in many ways. The best plump oysters need no more than a squeeze of lemon and are picked straight from their shells and eaten raw. The large, flattish *ostión* or Portuguese oyster, found mainly around the southern coast near Cádiz, is tender and so well flavored that it is excellent when breaded and fried in oil.

36 small fresh oysters in their shells

juice of 1 lemon

1 cup/120 g/4 oz all-purpose (plain) flour

2 eggs, beaten

2 cups/120 g/4 oz fine dry breadcrumbs

3 cups/750 ml/24 fl oz olive oil

lemon wedges

Loosen the oysters from their shells and save the shells. Sprinkle lemon juice over the oysters and let stand for 10 minutes, then pat with paper towels and roll lightly in flour. Dip into beaten egg, coat with crumbs and fry about 10 at a time in olive oil until crisp. Return to the shells and arrange on plates with lemon wedges and crusty bread.

BUÑUELITOS DE BACALAO

SALT COD FRITTERS   SERVES 6 (*TAPA*)

4 oz/120 g prepared *bacalao* (page 266)

1 green (spring) onion (shallot/scallion), finely chopped

black pepper

2 teaspoons lemon juice

2 teaspoons finely chopped mint or parsley

$\frac{3}{4}$ cup/100 g/3 oz all-purpose (plain) flour

$\frac{3}{4}$ teaspoon baking powder

1 whole egg

1 egg white

3 cups/750 ml/24 fl oz olive or vegetable oil

Flake the *bacalao* and mix with the onion, pepper, lemon juice and mint. Sift the flour into a bowl with the baking powder. Beat in the egg and egg white, *bacalao* and enough water to make a thick batter. Set aside for 20 minutes.

Heat the oil in a wide pan and fry spoonfuls of the batter until puffed and golden. Drain on a rack covered with paper towels and serve hot on toothpicks.

ENSALADA DE MARISCOS CON SALSA MAYONESA

SEAFOOD SALAD IN MAYONNAISE   SERVES 4 (*TAPA*)

1½ cups/300 g/10 oz peeled, cooked *quisquillas* (small shrimp/prawns)

1 cup/180 g/6 oz flaked fresh crabmeat

3 cooked *cigalas* (scampi), peeled and diced

4 squid, cleaned, sliced and cooked

10 oz/300 g cod or other thick fish, boiled and cubed

12 small mussels, cooked

3 green (spring) onions (shallots/scallions), chopped

3 celery stalks, thinly sliced

1 cup/250 ml/8 fl oz *salsa mayonesa* (page 273)

1 tablespoon chopped fresh dill

salt and pepper

lemon juice

lettuce leaves

2–3 hard-boiled eggs

parsley or dill

Combine the cooked seafood in a salad bowl. Add the onions and celery. Whisk *mayonesa* with chopped dill, salt, pepper and lemon juice to taste. Stir into the salad, mixing well. Pile onto lettuce leaves and surround with wedges of egg and sprigs of herbs.

Variation: Substitute lightly cooked asparagus tips for celery.

Atún en Adobo con Pimientos

MARINATED TUNA WITH PEPPERS

SERVES 4–6 (*TAPA*)

1 large red bell pepper (capsicum)

1¼ lb/650 g chunk-style canned tuna or cooked fresh tuna

2½ tablespoons white wine vinegar

⅓ cup/90 ml/3 fl oz virgin olive oil

1 medium onion, minced

1 clove garlic, minced

2 teaspoons chopped capers

1 tablespoon finely chopped dill pickle (gherkin)

⅓ teaspoon freshly ground black pepper

salt and sugar

Roast the bell pepper according to the instructions on page 266. When the pepper is well blistered on the surface, remove from the heat and drop into a plastic bag for a few minutes, then peel. Discard stem, seeds and membranes and cut the pepper into narrow strips. Drain the tuna and break into bite-size chunks. Mix with the pepper in a salad bowl. Make a dressing by whisking the vinegar and oil together, then add the remaining ingredients with a small pinch each of salt and sugar. Pour over the salad and let stand for at least 1 hour before serving.

Gambas Rebozadas

FRIED SHRIMP (PRAWNS)

SERVES 4 (*TAPA*)

12 medium-size fresh shrimp (prawns) in the shell

1 cup/120 g/4 oz all-purpose (plain) flour

1 egg

ice water

2 cups/500 ml/16 fl oz olive oil

salt, pepper and paprika

Peel the shrimp, leaving the tails in place. Slit down center backs to reveal the intestinal vein. Devein, then rinse and dry the shrimp. Make a thick but creamy batter with the flour, egg and ice water.

Heat oil in a wide pan. Dip shrimp into the batter, then fry in the oil until golden. Retrieve with a skimmer and drain on paper towels. Sprinkle with salt, pepper and paprika and serve hot.

Variation: Coat shrimp with saffron batter (see page 268).

PIMIENTOS RELLENOS DE BACALAO

PEPPERS STUFFED WITH SALT COD SERVES 6

6 medium-size red bell peppers (capsicums)

1 cup/60 g/2 oz fresh white breadcrumbs

¼ cup/60 ml/2 fl oz milk

1¼ lb/1.2 kg prepared *bacalao* (page 266)

2 medium onions, finely chopped

3 cloves garlic, finely chopped

5 tablespoons olive oil

14-oz/400-g can tomatoes, drained and chopped

2 teaspoons sweet paprika

¼ tablespoon cayenne pepper

2 tablespoons chopped parsley

black pepper

1 egg, beaten

Drop peppers into a pan of boiling water and cook until the skins loosen, about 4 minutes. Remove the skins; cut off tops and set aside. Pull out seed cores. Soak crumbs in milk; squeeze and set aside. Drain *bacalao*, pick out bones and flake the meat. Sauté one onion and half the garlic in 2 tablespoons oil for 3 to 4 minutes. Add tomatoes and cook for 2 minutes, then add paprika and cayenne and simmer for 10 minutes. Purée in a food processor or blender, then pass through a fine sieve. Set aside.

In the meantime, sauté the remaining onion and garlic in 3 tablespoons oil for 2 to 3 minutes. Stir in the crumbs and fish and sauté for a few minutes. Add the parsley, pepper to taste and the beaten egg. Purée in a food processor until very smooth. Spoon into the peppers and place the reserved caps on top. Arrange in a small baking dish and add ½ cup water. Bake in a preheated 400°F/200°C/Gas 6 oven for 15 minutes or until the water evaporates, then add the sauce and heat through. Serve hot.

PIPERRADA

BASQUE PEPPER CASSEROLE WITH EGG AND TOMATO SERVES 4

2 red bell peppers (capsicums)

2 green bell peppers (capsicums)

½ cup/120 ml/4 fl oz olive oil

4–5 large sun-ripened tomatoes, peeled, seeded and chopped

4 oz/250 g *jamón serrano* or other cured ham, sliced

1–3 cloves garlic, minced

1–2 teaspoons chopped fresh basil

salt and pepper

4 eggs, beaten

Drop the peppers into a pot of boiling water and cook until the skins loosen, about 4 minutes. Skin, seed and cut the flesh into strips. Sauté in the oil for at least 20 minutes or until well softened. Add the tomatoes and cook for 10 minutes. Very finely shred the ham and add to the pan with the garlic, basil, salt and pepper. Cook, stirring frequently, until the mixture is soft and pulpy. Add the egg a little at a time, stirring, until the mixture is smooth and fluffy. Spoon onto warmed plates and serve at once.

SALMÓN A LA PLANCHA O PAPILLOTE
SALMON BAKED IN PAPER
SERVES 4

4 salmon steaks, 5 oz/150 g each

2 tablespoons olive oil or butter

salt and pepper

1 lemon, thinly sliced

4 sprigs dill or fennel

4 pieces parchment paper, 12 x 9 inches/30 x 22 cm each

Sprinkle the salmon with olive oil or dot with butter and season with salt and pepper. Place a slice of lemon and sprig of herb on each steak. Brush the parchment paper with oil. Set a piece of salmon on each piece of paper, fold over to encase and fold the edges of the paper together to close. Place on a griddle and cook for about 5 minutes on each side, or bake in a preheated 400°F/200°C/Gas 6 oven for about 12 minutes.

Serve with potatoes boiled with garlic and paprika

CALABACINES RELLENOS CON CIGALAS
ZUCCHINI (COURGETTES) STUFFED WITH CRAYFISH
SERVES 6

I enjoyed these as an appetizer in an elegant restaurant in San Sebastián, three pieces to a plate with a drizzle of creamy crayfish sauce at the side. Or serve them as a side dish with grilled meat or seafood.

3–4 large zucchini (courgettes)

1 small onion, very finely chopped

2 tablespoons butter or olive oil

$\frac{1}{2}$ lb/250 g crayfish (or shrimp/prawn) meat

1 tablespoon Spanish brandy or cognac

1 tablespoon heavy (thick) cream

pinch of sweet paprika

2 tablespoons finely grated hard white cheese or fine dry breadcrumbs

Cut the zucchini into 2-inch/5-cm pieces and use a teaspoon to scoop out some of the seeds from one end of each to make small cup shapes. Place in a pan of lightly salted water and simmer until barely tender. Remove, turn upside down and drain well.

Sauté the onion in butter or oil until softened. Add the seafood and cook briefly, then add the brandy, cream and paprika. Spoon into the zucchini, cover with grated cheese or the crumbs and broil (grill) until golden.

Variation: Make a vegetarian version of this using finely diced green pepper, peas, tomato and hard-cooked egg as the filling, bound with cheese.

BACALAO EN SALSA VERDE
SALT COD WITH GREEN SAUCE   SERVES 4–6

2 lb/1 kg prepared *bacalao*
(page 266), cubed

1 large onion, finely chopped

¼ cup/60 ml/2 fl oz olive oil

1 cup/250 ml/8 fl oz dry white
wine

1 bay leaf

1 clove garlic, finely chopped

2 cups/500 ml/16 fl oz fish stock

3 tablespoons chopped parsley

2 tablespoons potato flour or
instant mashed potato

salt and pepper

Cut the *bacalao* into large cubes, picking out any small bones and removing skin. Sauté the onion in the oil until softened, add the *bacalao* and fry until the surface is sealed. Add the wine, bay leaf and garlic and cook for 3 to 4 minutes. Add the stock and parsley and simmer until the fish is tender. Mix the potato flour or mashed potato with a little of the hot stock, then stir in to thicken the sauce. Season to taste with salt and pepper.

BACALAO AL PIL-PIL
SALT COD SIMMERED WITH PARSLEY AND GARLIC   SERVES 4–6

In Basque cooking, *pil-pil* means "simmered"; it is a technique used here for centuries. The fish is cooked slowly in an earthenware pot — never opened or stirred, but shaken to amalgamate the oil with the cooking liquids. *Bacalao al pil-pil* calls for the more gelatinous cuts of salt cod, taken from near the head.

1½ lb/750 g prepared *bacalao**
(see page 266)

⅓ cup/90 ml/3 fl oz olive oil

2 cloves garlic, minced

1 tablespoon chopped parsley

Place the cod in a pan with water to cover and simmer gently for 20 minutes. Remove and pick out any bones. Break flesh into bite-size pieces and set aside, reserving ½ cup/120 ml/4 fl oz of the liquid.

Heat the oil in an earthenware casserole and cook the garlic until lightly golden. Add the parsley and fish and cook for 3 to 4 minutes, turning once. Add the reserved liquid, close the pan tightly and cook over very low heat, occasionally shaking the casserole gently, for about 7 minutes. Serve in the casserole.

*Use the thick cut of cod from just below the head, or the fatty belly.

Pimientos Rellenos de Bacalao, p.178

Bacalao a la Vizcaina (top), opposite; Merluza a la Vasca (front), p.184

Bacalao a la Vizcaína

BAY OF BISCAY SALT COD WITH ONIONS AND RED PEPPERS   SERVES 4

Originating in the Basque country, this is one of Spain's most famous dishes: dried salt cod cooked in a vibrantly colored, intensely flavored onion and tomato sauce. In Portugal, where it is equally popular, the dish is known as *bacalhau a biscainha*.

1½ lb/750 g prepared *bacalao* (page 266)

2 medium onions, chopped

4 cloves garlic, minced

2–3 tablespoons olive oil

1 medium potato, peeled and finely chopped

6 dried hot red chili peppers (chillies), soaked for 10 hours, or 1–2 chili peppers and 1 red bell pepper (capsicum)

4 large tomatoes, peeled, seeded and chopped

2 slices toasted bread, crusts trimmed

1 bay leaf

1 sprig parsley

salt and pepper

½ cup/30 g/1 oz fresh white breadcrumbs

butter or oil

chopped parsley

Place the cod in a saucepan with water just to cover. Simmer for 20 minutes. Discard any bones and reserve the liquid. Sauté the onions and garlic in the olive oil for 3 minutes; add the potato and sauté for 3 minutes. Slit open the chili peppers and discard the seeds. Cut peppers into fine shreds and cook with the onion and tomato until a soft purée. Add ½ cup/120 ml/4 fl oz reserved fish stock and bread and simmer until mixture is reduced to a pulp. Purée sauce in a food processor and strain. Pour half the sauce into a casserole and place the fish on top, skin side up. Add the bay leaf, parsley, salt and pepper. Cover loosely and bake in a preheated 350°F/ 180°C/Gas 4 oven for about 20 minutes or until fairly dry. Uncover, sprinkle with breadcrumbs and moisten with butter or oil. Bake a further 10 minutes, then sprinkle with parsley and serve.

Tip: There are many interpretations of this classic dish. In one popular version, the onions, peppers, garlic and bread are cooked together briefly, then added in chunky form to the casserole. The dish is stirred several times during cooking. Breadcrumbs on top can be omitted, or replaced by a sprinkling of garlic fried in oil.

Merluza a la Vasca
HAKE WITH GREEN SAUCE

SERVES 4

If you were to order *merluza koskera*, *merluza en salsa verde* or *merluza a la vasca* you would find yourself with a variant of the same dish, a classic dating back to the early 1700s. Meaty pieces of hake, arguably the tastiest fish used in northern Spain, are braised in a *cazuela*. During cooking, the pan is constantly agitated in a circular motion, and the sauce attains a creaminess from the albumen released from the fish. Mashed potato or potato starch is an easier alternative.

4 pieces hake or cod, about 7 oz/ 200 g each

salt

½ cup/60 g/2 oz all-purpose (plain) flour

⅓ cup/90 ml/3 fl oz olive oil

3–5 cloves garlic, finely chopped

1 medium onion, very finely chopped

1 cup/250 ml/8 fl oz fish stock (court bouillon)

½ cup/120 ml/4 fl oz dry white wine

2 tablespoons cooked mashed potatoes*

12 asparagus tips

½ cup/90 g/3 oz frozen green peas

¼ cup/30 g/1 oz finely chopped parsley

12 small clams, or 8 mussels soaked overnight in cold water

2 hard-boiled eggs

salt, pepper and lemon juice

Season the fish with salt and let stand 20 minutes. Coat lightly with flour and fry in the oil to seal the surfaces. Transfer to one large or 4 small *cazuelas*. Drain off half the oil and sauté the garlic and onion until lightly colored. Add the fish stock and wine and bring to a boil; cook 2 minutes. Stir in the potato, asparagus tips, peas and half the parsley. Place 3 clams in each dish and pour on the sauce. Bake in a preheated 350°F/180°C/Gas 4 oven for about 20 minutes or until the fish is very tender (test by piercing with a skewer). Add the remaining parsley and eggs and season with salt, pepper and lemon juice. Serve in the casserole(s).

*Flour can be used to thicken the sauce, but potato gives a creamy consistency.

Tip: See also *kokotxas a la donostiarra*, page 185.

Rape Con Romero
MONKFISH (ANGLERFISH) WITH ROSEMARY

SERVES 4–6

1 medium onion, sliced

2 lb/1 kg monkfish pieces

2 tablespoons olive oil

2 sprigs fresh rosemary

1 lemon, thinly sliced

salt and pepper

Scatter the onion over the bottom of a large baking dish. Place the fish skin side up over the onion. Sprinkle with olive oil and add the rosemary and lemon slices. Season with salt and pepper and cover with foil. Bake in a preheated 360°F/180°C/Gas 4 oven until tender, about 20 minutes, basting twice with the accumulated liquids.

KOKOTXAS A LA DONOSTIARRA
SUPREME OF HAKE COOKED WITH PEAS

SERVES 4

Pronounce them *kokochas,* and recognize them at the fishmonger's as greyish, gelatinous looking morsels the size of a large oyster. They appear in volume in this part of Spain but are as rare as . . . *kokotxas* in other regions. They come from the fish's throat and there is nothing else quite like them, although cod's cheeks are a substitute. *Kokotxas* can be fried in a light flour coating or cooked like *merluza a la vasca,* in a green sauce.

1¼ lb/650 g *kokotxas*

4 cloves garlic, chopped

2½ tablespoons olive oil

2 tablespoons chopped parsley

1½ cups/270 g/9 oz young green peas

½ lb/250 g/8 oz small clams in the shell

Place the *kokotxas* in a saucepan with water to half cover. Cover tightly and simmer for 10 minutes. Remove from the pan and scrape off the skin if desired. Set aside, reserving the liquid. Sauté the garlic lightly in the oil. Add the parsley, peas and clams and cook for 2 to 3 minutes. Add enough of the reserved liquid to thoroughly moisten the dish. Cover and cook gently until the peas are tender and the sauce is thick and gelatinous, about 7 minutes.

KOKOTXAS REBOZADAS
FRIED KOKOTXAS

SERVES 4

I find these even better than oysters when fried in a crisp batter. They can also be tossed in seasoned flour and fried very quickly, calamari style, in very hot oil.

24 *kokotxas* (see previous recipe)

salt and pepper

1½ cups/180 g/6 oz all-purpose (plain) flour

¾ teaspoon baking powder

small pinch of powdered saffron

1 egg white, beaten to soft peaks

a mixture of olive and vegetable oil for deep frying

Season the *kokotxas* with salt and pepper and dust with ¼ cup/30 g/1 oz flour. Sift the remaining flour into a bowl with the baking powder and saffron, adding a little salt. Stir in enough cold water to make a fairly thick batter. Fold in the egg white. Set aside for 15 minutes. Coat the *kokotxas* in the batter and deep fry in the oil until crisp and golden. Serve at once.

Marmitako
TUNA HOTPOT   SERVES 4

1½ lb/750 g tuna steaks

¾ cup/180 ml/6 fl oz olive oil

1 medium onion, finely chopped

2 cloves garlic, minced

4 medium potatoes, peeled and thinly sliced

2 large tomatoes, peeled, seeded and chopped

1 dried hot red chili pepper, seeded and sliced

1 red bell pepper (capsicum), seeded and chopped

1 cup/250 ml/8 fl oz dry white wine (optional)

2 teaspoons chopped parsley

2 slices white bread, crusts trimmed

Fry the steaks in the oil for 30 seconds on each side to seal the surface. Remove fish, pour off half the oil and reserve. Fry the onion in the remaining oil until softened. Add the garlic, potatoes, tomatoes, chili and bell pepper and cook, stirring occasionally, for 6 to 7 minutes. Arrange the tuna on top and add water to almost cover. Add wine if desired (the dish can be thick or soupy as preferred). Simmer gently on top of the stove or cover and bake in a preheated 350°F/170°C/Gas 4 oven for about 1 hour or until the fish is tender and vegetables are soft, basting the fish frequently. Sprinkle with parsley. Cut the bread in halves and fry in the reserved oil until golden, or if preferred, toast in the oven. Serve with the fish.

Pichón con Setas
PIGEONS WITH MUSHROOMS   SERVES 4

4 oven-ready pigeons (or large quail)

salt and pepper

3 tablespoons olive oil

3 tablespoons butter

2 medium onions, finely chopped

2 tablespoons very finely chopped cured ham

1 lb/500 g fresh morels or chanterelles, sliced

1 clove garlic, mashed

1 cup/250 ml/8 fl oz dry white wine

1 cup/250 ml/8 fl oz light cream

1 teaspoon finely chopped parsley or tarragon

Season the birds inside and out and truss with kitchen string. Heat oil and butter and brown each bird thoroughly. Transfer to a casserole. Sauté the onions until softened; add ham and sauté briefly. Push to one side of the pan, add mushrooms and sauté until softened. Add garlic, mix well and cook briefly. Spread mixture evenly around the birds and add the wine. Bake in a preheated 450°F/220°C/Gas 8 oven for about 30 minutes, splashing a little water or chicken stock into the pan as the liquid dries up. Remove the birds and press the sauce through a coarse wire strainer, returning to the pan. Add cream and herbs with salt and pepper to taste. Boil for 3 to 4 minutes. Untruss the birds and serve with the sauce.

Mollejas de Ternera al Oporto
VEAL SWEETBREADS IN PORT SAUCE
SERVES 6

2½ lb/1.2 kg veal sweetbreads

1 teaspoon red wine vinegar

salt and pepper

½ cup/120 ml/4 fl oz olive oil

2 tablespoons butter

¼ cup/60 ml/2 fl oz Spanish brandy

1 small onion, finely chopped

1 small carrot, peeled and finely chopped

1 leek, cleaned, trimmed and sliced

1 celery stalk, chopped

3 medium tomatoes, peeled, seeded and chopped

1 cup/250 ml/8 fl oz ruby port

1 cup/250 ml/8 fl oz veal or beef stock

3 tablespoons light cream

Place the sweetbreads in a saucepan of cold water and add the vinegar. Bring to a boil, then reduce heat and simmer for 2 minutes. Remove from heat and allow the sweetbreads to cool in the water. Drain and dry the sweetbreads, remove skin and fat and cut into thick slices. Season with salt and pepper and sauté in 2 tablespoons oil with the butter until lightly colored. Add the brandy and cook until evaporated. In another pan sauté the onion, carrot, leek and celery in the remaining olive oil for about 6 minutes. Add tomatoes and simmer for 10 minutes. Add the sweetbreads and their liquid, the port and stock and bring to a boil. Reduce heat and simmer for about 30 minutes. Add cream to the sauce and boil quickly to reduce and thicken. Season to taste, pour over the sweetbreads and serve.

Codornices en Hojas de Parra
ROASTED QUAIL IN GRAPE LEAVES
SERVES 4

8 small quail

salt and pepper

2 tablespoons olive oil

24 large white grapes, seeded

8 wafer-thin slices *jamón serrano* or other cured ham

16 grape leaves

½ cup/120 ml/4 fl oz chicken stock

½ cup/120 ml/4 fl oz dry sherry

1 tablespoon cognac

4 slices white bread, crusts trimmed

olive or vegetable oil for frying

black grapes or orange slices

Rinse, dry and season the quail. Brown the quail in the oil and remove. Briefly toss the grapes in the oil, then place 3 in each quail cavity. Drape a slice of ham over breast of each quail. Rinse, drain and dry the grape leaves and brush with olive oil. Place 2 together, slightly overlapping, with the ribs inwards. Set a quail in the center and wrap, leaving the tips of the legs exposed. Tie with string. Repeat with remaining leaves and quail. Place breast up in a roasting pan and add the stock. Roast in a preheated 400°F/200°C/Gas 6 oven for 20 minutes. Remove the quail, untruss and set aside, keeping warm. Add sherry and cognac to the pan and cook over high heat until well reduced. Season to taste. Cut the bread diagonally in halves and fry in oil until golden brown. Drain well. Place a quail on each crouton. Pass the sauce separately. Garnish with fresh black grapes or orange

SETAS

In early October and again in spring the forests of Catalonia and the Basque country take on the musty, sweet-wood smell of fresh mushrooms when hundreds of different varieties of wild mushroom thrust up through soil dampened by fall rains.

Rovellons are thick, meaty golden-yellow mushrooms of full flavor with a hint of tartness. *Ceps* of the *boletus edulis* family are gigantic here, one can be enough for a meal. There are *llano* which resemble *ceps* but are deep brown on the cap. *Rossinyols* are obviously a close cousin of the *chanterelle*, *pies de rata* are like ochre colored coral clusters, and *trompiro* like black branch coral. *Canagroc* have bright yellow long and slender stems with little brown tops. There are *rosinoc, sitake, perrichico* and *seta de marzo, rabassola, hongo negro* and *oronjas*. The more exotic the fungi, the less involved the cooking. Catalonians are fond of combinations of mushrooms and potatoes, such as casseroled potatoes with *morels* and herbs, and cubes of potato sautéed in olive oil with slices of plump fresh *rovellon*. Many are just quickly sautéed or cooked *a la plancha* on a hotplate with lashings of garlic and parsley.

CAZUELITAS DE SETAS
RAMEKINS OF WILD MUSHROOOMS   SERVES 4

This goes well with roasted meats. Pop the *cazuelitas* into the oven when the roast is almost ready and serve separately, spooning the mushrooms and juices over the roast when sliced.

12–14 oz/350–400 g freshly picked cèpes or chanterelles

2 tablespoons butter

8 cloves garlic, thinly sliced

2 green spring onions (shallots/ spring onions), trimmed and diagonally sliced

2 tablespoons olive oil

1 tablespoon cognac or Spanish brandy

1 tablespoon finely chopped parsley

salt and pepper

Wipe the mushrooms and slice very thinly, or dice if they are very large. Heat 4 *cazuelitas* or ramekins, divide the oil and butter among them and heat well. Toss in the garlic and green onions and fry briefly, then add the mushrooms. Stir in the oil. Place the dishes in a preheated 450°F/230°C/Gas 8 oven for 6 minutes. Stir, add cognac and bake for another 2 to 3 minutes. Stir in the parsley, add salt and pepper to taste and serve in the casserole.

Cogollitos de Tudela
LETTUCE HEART SALAD IN GARLIC VINAIGRETTE

SERVES 2

San Sebastián is the birthplace of a number of chefs in the forefront of the *nueva cocina vasca*, the nouvelle cuisine of the Basque country. Salads using baby vegetables are particularly interesting, this one is inspired by a recipe created in the Southern Basque city of Tudela, in Navarra.

6 small hearts of romaine/cos lettuce

3 small red radishes, very thinly sliced

1 medium carrot, peeled and very thinly sliced

8 cloves garlic, very finely chopped

$\frac{1}{4}$ cup/60 ml/2 fl oz olive oil

$1\frac{1}{2}$ tablespoons (or to taste) white wine vinegar

salt

small pinch of cayenne pepper

Halve the lettuce hearts lengthwise; rinse, drain well and dry. Place on plates in a cartwheel arrangement and scatter on the sliced radish and carrot. Whisk garlic, oil, vinegar, salt and cayenne together. Pour over the salad and serve at once.

Revuelto de Setas
MUSHROOM AND EGG SCRAMBLE

SERVES 4

The Spanish usually do not eat eggs at breakfast time, preferring a light breakfast of sweet rolls or pastries. This dish would be served with triangles of fried bread as an appetizer, but with toast it is an appealing breakfast or supper dish. During the mushroom season in the provinces along the foothills of the Pyrenees, mushroom fanatics cook all kinds of wild mushrooms in an egg scramble like this.

1 lb/500 g fresh button, field or wild mushrooms, very thinly sliced

1 clove garlic, chopped

5 tablespoons olive oil

6 eggs, well beaten

salt

2 teaspoons finely chopped parsley

4 slices day-old bread, crusts trimmed

Sauté the mushrooms in a pan with the garlic and half the oil over very low heat for about 10 minutes, shaking the pan occasionally. Pour in the eggs; add salt and half the parsley. Stir over moderate heat until the eggs are set. Fry the bread in the remaining oil and cut each piece in halves. Serve the eggs surrounded by the toast and sprinkle on the remaining parsley.

MENESTRA DE VERDURAS
BRAISED SPRING VEGETABLES

SERVES 4

Harbingers of spring in the Basque country are the mountains of tiny fresh peas, bright green broadbeans and white asparagus stalks spilling from baskets at the vegetable markets. The new potatoes of the season are the size of a walnut. These sweet baby vegetables come together in a famous regional dish, *menestra de legumbres*, which in itself is generous enough to serve as a meal and usually comes with a slice of fried ham and perhaps a poached egg. I enjoy it as a first course with a good amount of sauce, the ultimate chunky vegetable soup!

1 medium onion, thinly sliced

½ cup/120 ml/4 fl oz olive oil

10 oz/300 g *jamón serrano*, *prosciutto* or other cured ham

5 cups/1.2 l/40 fl oz beef stock

20 baby potatoes

1½ cups/270 g/9 oz small peas

16 sugar snap pea pods

4 lettuce leaves, shredded

salt and pepper

3 oz/100 g *tocino* or bacon, diced

1 small onion, minced

1½ cups/260 g/9 oz shelled baby broadbeans*

2 tablespoons all-purpose (plain) flour

16 short stalks young white or green asparagus**

Sauté the sliced onion in 3 tablespoons oil until very well colored. Cut the ham into 4 slices and cut one slice into fine dice. Add diced ham to the onion and fry for 4 to 5 minutes. Add 3 cups/750 ml/24 fl oz stock, bring to a boil and simmer for 30 minutes. Add the potatoes and both kinds of peas with half the shredded lettuce and simmer gently until tender. Add salt and pepper to taste. Sauté the bacon and minced onion in 2 tablespoons of the oil until the onion is soft and well colored. Add 2 cups/500 ml/16 fl oz stock and bring to a boil. Add broadbeans and the remaining shredded lettuce and simmer slowly until tender. Mix flour with a little cold water and stir into the sauce to thicken. Season to taste with salt and pepper. Cook the asparagus separately in lightly salted water. Drain. Fry the sliced ham until crisp and golden on the surface. Arrange the vegetables separately on plates with the slices of ham on top.

Variation: If desired, poach 4 eggs in lightly salted water with 1 tablespoon vinegar added. When cooked but still soft in the yolk, lift out with a slotted spoon and serve with the vegetables.

*If fresh young broadbeans are unobtainable, use peeled frozen beans.

**Use only the top 3 in (8 cm) of the asparagus, reserving the remainder to use in another dish.

Tip: Menestra de verduras can be served garnished with wedges of hard-cooked (hard-boiled) egg.

INTXAURSALSA
WALNUT CREAM

SERVES 6

This creamy dessert, which is a must on Basque tables at Christmas Eve, has been adapted to other serving styles. One of my favorites is to float in it little squares of *leche frita*, but it's equally good with scoops of rich vanilla ice cream. I've even had it with a thin glazed *pastel* of apples. The walnuts should be finely minced, not ground in a food processor.

2 cups/250 g/8 oz walnuts

6 cups/1.5 l/1½ qt milk

3 slices white bread, toasted until golden, crusts trimmed

1 cup/250 g/8 oz sugar

Place the walnuts in a bowl and cover generously with water. Let stand for several hours until the skins loosen, then peel off as much of the bitter buff-colored skin as possible. Partially dry the nuts by spreading on a cloth, then chop very finely. Combine nuts and milk in a saucepan. Chop the bread into fine crumbs, add to the pan with the sugar and simmer for about 30 minutes or until creamy. Serve warm or cold.

PASTEL VASCO
CUSTARD AND ALMOND TART

SERVES 8

Pasteles vascos usually have pride of place in the window of a *pastelería* in Basque cities.

1 recipe *masa quebrada* (shortcrust pastry), page 268

½ cup/120 g/4 oz superfine sugar

1 tablespoon cornstarch (cornflour)

1 cup/250 ml/8 fl oz milk

4 egg yolks

¼ cup/60 g/2 oz butter

½ teaspoon vanilla extract (essence)

1 egg, beaten

½ cup/60 g/1 oz flaked almonds

confectioners' (icing) sugar (optional)

Prepare the pastry and cut into 2 parts, one slightly larger than the other. Use the larger piece to line a prepared shallow pie dish or flan tin and prick the base several times with a fork. Chill until needed.

Mix the sugar and cornstarch in a saucepan, add the milk until it begins to thicken. Add the egg yolks, set over a pan of simmering water and cook until very thick. Remove from the heat and beat in the butter and vanilla. Allow to cool before pouring into the prepared pastry base. Cover with a pastry lid and make an air vent in the center. Pinch and flute the edges. Brush the top with beaten egg and cover with the almonds. Bake in a preheated 350°F/180°C/Gas 4 oven for about 35 minutes or until the pastry is golden brown and the custard is set. Dust with confectioners' sugar, if desired, before serving warm or cold.

PANCHINETA
BASQUE ALMOND TART
SERVES 4

I don't know whether I enjoy *panchineta* best made with puff pastry or the short pastry traditional cooks prefer. They are quite different, so here are both versions. This recipe can be made into one large tart or four tarts of 4-inch/10-cm diameter

1½ recipes *masa quebrada* (short pastry) page 268 or 1 lb/500g puff pastry (page 268)

1 recipe egg custard (page 266)

½ cup/90 g/3 oz toasted slivered almonds

1 egg, beaten

½ cup/90 g/3 oz slivered almonds (untoasted)

confectioners' (icing) sugar (optional)

Grease and lightly flour one large shallow pie dish or 4 smaller ones and line with the short pastry, reserving enough to cover the top/s. If using the puff pastry, cut into 2 rounds as large as possible and place on a greased baking sheet. Prick short pastry in several places. Prick the puff pastry thoroughly, leaving a 1-inch/2.5-cm border around the edge unpricked. Fill short pastry with the custard and cover with toasted nuts. Spread the thick custard evenly over the puff pastry, taking care it does not go on the border. Cover with toasted nuts. Place the other pastry on top. Pinch edges of shortcrust pastry together and flute decoratively, or press edge of puff pastry down with the fingers around the border-line and use the points of a fork to indent a design around the edge.

Brush with beaten egg and cover with the untoasted almonds. Bake in a preheated 350°F/180°C/Gas 4 oven for 40 to 50 minutes or until the pastry is well browned. Sprinkle with the sugar, if used. The puff pastry tart is best served hot, while the other type can be served cold.

CIRUELAS AL ARMAÑAC
PRUNES MARINATED IN ARMAGNAC
SERVES 4–6

1 lb/500 g pitted prunes

2 tablespoons sugar

⅔ cup/150 ml/5 fl oz Armagnac

Place prunes in a small saucepan with water almost to cover. Add sugar and bring to a boil, then remove from the heat and let stand until cool. Pour off half the liquid and add the Armagnac. Let stand for several hours before serving with scoops of icecream or cream.

Old Castile and Leon

CASTILLA LA VIEJA Y LEÓN

The ancient kingdoms of Castilla la Vieja (Old Castile) and León occupy the region north of Madrid, to the Portuguese border in the west and the Cantabrian mountain range to the north. Here is the heartland of Catholic Spain and the birthplace of *Castellano*, the Spanish language. Their provinces and cities are the names of history: *Ávila*, perched high in an imposing mountain range, is where Santa Teresa performed the monumental task of reforming the Carmelite Order in the 16th century; the Roman city of Salamanca is the seat of learning, its vast and ancient university one of the first and finest in the world. Valladolid is where Cervantes, author of *Don Quixote de la Mancha*, lived and Columbus supposedly died. In Segovia the Romans built a massive aqueduct, which stands today as a monument to human endeavor. León, once the capital of Christian Spain, is in high country, as wild and fearless as the rampant lion, its coat of arms, which became the most important insignia of the country's history. Burgos, a province renowned for its cheese, is the home town of El Cid. Zamora, the gateway to Portugal, is a province of medieval castles and age-old culture. And mountainous Soria to the east is where the Basque country and Aragon begin.

Castilla-León is tourist country, dotted with massive castles and ancient fortifications dating to Roman times, with majestic cathedrals and awe-inspiring monuments. It is a series of high plateaus, bleak and austere with vast acreage of wheat plantations, and of mountain ranges in which roam ibex, wild goats and huge flocks of wild birds. The region's cooking reflects the severity of its landscape, almost medieval in its simplicity. It is a cuisine of roasted meats, uncomplex stews and crusty bread. The area is known as the *zona de los asados*, the zone of roasts; chief items on the restaurant menus in this region are baby lambs and suckling pigs, hardly older than three weeks and weighing just a few pounds, with sweet, white and deliciously tender meat. They are split lengthwise and roasted in gigantic brick ovens, along with trays of soft-textured snowy white potatoes and the round loaves of crusty white bread that are another specialty of this region.

Picturesque Segovia, under the shadow of its great aqueduct, is the home of *mesones*, country inns specializing in roasted meats. Some of her well-known restaurants date back more than 100 years. Served anywhere in Spain, dishes *al estilo de Segovia* reflect this classic roasting technique, which produces the crispest skin and most succulent meat. Sepúlveda is only a few hours' drive from Madrid and a little to the northeast of Segovia. It's worth the trip from the nation's capital along a good motorway to try their own style of roasted meats, which many think equals that of Segovia.

In Salamanca many pigs live past their suckling stage to provide their superior meat for the important *charcuteria* industry. *Chorizo de Salamanca*, one of the best in Spain, is a thick sausage of chunky meat and creamy white fat, bright red with paprika and tinged with chili. The best *piernas* (legs) become choice cured hams to grace the counters of delicatessens and *tapas* bars all over the country. *Hornazo de Salamanca* combines the excellent flour of the region (as flaky pastry or yeast-activated dough) with charcuterie and hard-boiled eggs in a deliciously substantial snack.

The Moors brought a touch of spice to the simple Castilian cuisine, sprinkling pungent cumin over eggplant dishes, sweetening desserts and stews with cinnamon, adding paprika and cayenne and refreshing anise. They also introduced the method of *escabeche*, in which foods are marinated in a vinegar solution that partially cooks and pickles them. Trout fresh from the mountain streams gushing from the Cordillera Cantábrica and the Montañas de Leon, and from the ranges just north of Madrid, are gently stewed *en escabeche* to stunning effect. Partridge, quail and other small wild birds are given the same treatment, to eat warm as a main course or to shred into salads.

The Tierra de Campos, north of the great rural metropolis Valladolid, is a fertile farmland of vegetable gardens supplying most of the region with fresh greens and dried beans. Here their famous cheese is known as *pata de mulo*, or donkey's leg, after its characteristic long, cylindrical shape. The soft, mild cheese of Burgos, steeped in brine, is perfectly partnered with honey and sweet fruits. And there are *manchego*-style and soft ewes' milk cheeses almost as good as those from further south.

CONSOMÉ DE HUEVOS AL JEREZ
CONSOMMÉ WITH EGGS AND SHERRY
SERVES 4

4 small eggs

2 teaspoons white vinegar

4 cups/1 1/1 qt rich veal stock or canned consomme

salt and pepper

2 teaspoons finely chopped parsley

$\frac{1}{4}$ cup/60 ml/2 fl oz Amontillado sherry

Separately poach the eggs in gently simmering water acidulated with vinegar. Place one in each bowl. Bring the stock just to a boil and season to taste. Pour over the eggs. Add the parsley and sherry immediately before serving.

Sopa de Bacalao y Patatas
SALT COD AND POTATO SOUP

SERVES 6–8

$1\frac{1}{2}$ lb/750 g potatoes

1 lb/500 g prepared *bacalao* (page 266)

2 medium onions, chopped

2 tablespoons olive oil

2 sun-ripened tomatoes, peeled, seeded and chopped

3 cloves garlic, finely chopped

1 bouquet garni

2 bay leaves

10 threads saffron

Peel the potatoes and cut into small dice. Drain the *bacalao* and pick out any small bones or pieces of skin. Cut into small cubes. Sauté the onion in oil until soft. Add tomatoes and cook for 5 minutes, then add the garlic, herbs, potatoes, *bacalao* and 8 cups/2.5 l/$2\frac{1}{2}$ qt water. Bring to a boil, then simmer until the potatoes are breaking up and the *bacalao* is tender.

Soak the saffron in a little of the hot broth, mashing to extract the color. Add to the soup with salt and pepper to taste. Simmer 5 minutes. Discard the herbs and serve.

Lentejas con Chorizo en Cazuela
CASSEROLE OF LENTILS AND CHORIZO

SERVES 4–6

A simple but delicious *posada* (roadside cafe or inn) dish, served with chunks of crusty bread. Garbanzos can be cooked in the same way after overnight soaking. They require about 3 hours to cook, so should be half-done before adding the other ingredients.

2 cups/350 g/12 oz red or yellow lentils

3 oz/90 g salted *tocino* or other salt pork, diced

1 medium onion, chopped

3 cloves garlic, chopped

$\frac{1}{4}$ cup/60 ml/2 fl oz olive oil

3 sun-ripened tomatoes, chopped

8 oz/250 g *chorizo*

1 tablespoon finely chopped fresh herbs

salt and pepper

1 teaspoon sweet paprika

12 saffron threads (optional)

Rinse the lentils in cold water and drain. In a heavy-bottomed saucepan sauté the salt pork, onion and garlic in the oil for a few minutes. Add the tomatoes and cook for 5 minutes, then add the lentils and whole *chorizos*. Add the herbs and seasonings with water to cover by about $1\frac{1}{2}$ inches/4 cm. Bring to a boil, cover and cook gently for about 30 minutes or until the lentils are tender, check the quantity of water after 20 minutes; the dish should remain moist but not liquid. Remove the *chorizo*, slice and return to the pot. Grind the saffron and dissolve in 2 tablespoons boiling water. Add to the pot with additional salt and pepper as needed.

BACALAO AL AJOARRIERO
SALT COD WITH GARLIC AND EGGS

SERVES 4

Ajo is garlic; *arriero* is a mule driver. This creamy *bacalao* dish is typical country fare.

12 oz/350 g prepared *bacalao* (page 266)

7 cloves garlic, finely chopped

1 small dried hot red chili

3 tablespoons olive oil

1 large red bell pepper (capsicum), seeded and cut into strips

½ cup/120 ml/4 fl oz fresh tomato sauce (page 274)

1 teaspoon sweet paprika

4 hard-boiled eggs

1 teaspoon finely chopped parsley

Drain the *bacalao*, remove skin and bones and separate the flesh into bite-sized pieces. Sauté the garlic and chili in the oil until golden. Add the pepper strips and cook for 2 to 3 minutes, then add the fish and continue to sauté until the pepper is soft. Add the tomato sauce and paprika and simmer gently for at least 10 minutes, until all ingredients are tender. Cut the eggs into wedges, stir into the dish and garnish with parsley.

Variation: I think this dish is even more delicious when potatoes are used instead of the tomato sauce. Add 3 medium potatoes, cut into 1-inch/2.5-cm cubes, to the fish with enough water to cook the potatoes and form a sauce. Cook the dish until the potato has softened enough to make the sauce thick and creamy.

BERENJENAS RELLENAS AL HORNO
BAKED EGGPLANTS (AUBERGINES)

SERVES 4

2 round purple eggplants, each about 6 inches/15 cm long

1 medium carrot, very finely chopped

1 medium onion, very finely chopped

1 large clove garlic, mashed

2 tablespoons olive oil

4 oz/120 g finely ground lamb

2 teaspoons chopped parsley

½ teaspoon each dried oregano and ground cumin

1 teaspoon tomato paste

salt

½ cup/30 g/1 oz fine dry breadcrumbs

½ cup/60 g/2 oz finely grated cheese

Cut the eggplants in half lengthwise and use a spoon to scoop out the flesh, leaving a ½-inch/1-cm layer. Very finely chop the extracted flesh. Sauté chopped eggplant, carrot, onion and garlic in the oil until softened. Push to one side of the pan and fry the lamb until it changes color. Add the herbs and spices, the tomato paste and salt and moisten with a little water or wine. Stuff into the prepared eggplants and smooth the top. Cover with a mixture of breadcrumbs and cheese. Bake in a preheated 350°F/180°C/Gas 4 oven for 15 minutes, then increase the heat to 400°F/200°C/Gas 6 and bake for a further 5 to 6 minutes to crisp the top.

Patatas a la Panadera
OVEN-BAKED POTATOES   SERVES 4–6

6 large potatoes, peeled and
thickly sliced

2 medium onions, thickly sliced

2 tablespoons butter

2 tablespoons olive oil

2 cloves garlic, finely chopped

1 bay leaf

1 small dried hot red chili pepper
(optional)

$\frac{1}{4}$ cup/60 ml/2 fl oz dry white wine
or cider

$\frac{1}{2}$ cup/120 ml/4 fl oz chicken stock
or water

large pinch of sweet paprika

salt

Layer the potatoes and onions in a buttered baking dish and add the remaining butter and oil. Scatter on garlic, tuck the bay leaf and chili among the vegetables, then pour in the wine and stock. Sprinkle with paprika. Cover and bake in a preheated 350°F/180°C/Gas 4 oven for about 30 minutes or until the potatoes are very tender.

Judías Verdes a la Castellana
GREEN BEANS CASTILIAN STYLE   SERVES 4

1 large red bell pepper (capsicum)

1 lb/500 g green beans

1 small onion, finely chopped

2 slices fatty bacon, finely
chopped

1 tablespoon lard or olive oil

2 cloves garlic, finely chopped

salt and pepper

Roast the pepper in a hot oven until the skin blisters. Remove and wrap in a kitchen towel until cool enough to handle. String the beans if necessary and cut into 2-inch/5-cm pieces. Boil in lightly salted water until tender; drain.

Sauté the onion and bacon in the lard or oil until the onion is soft. Peel and seed the pepper and cut into narrow strips. Add to the onion and cook until soft. Add the garlic, beans, salt and pepper and cook for 2 to 3 minutes, stirring continually.

Ensalada de Berenjenas a la Morisca

SALAD OF EGGPLANT (AUBERGINE) IN THE MOORISH TRADITION   SERVES 4–6

1 large purple eggplant (aubergine), about 1½ lb/750 g

salt

⅓ cup/90 ml/3 fl oz olive oil

1 large red onion, chopped

2–3 cloves garlic, finely chopped

1 tablespoon chopped mint

1 teaspoon ground cumin

½ teaspoon crushed dried red chili pepper

1 teaspoon sugar

salt and freshly ground black pepper

2–3 tablespoons red wine vinegar

Thickly slice the eggplant and sprinkle with salt. Set aside for 20 minutes, then wipe the surface. Spread on an oiled baking sheet and brush with some of the olive oil. Bake in a preheated 400°F/200°C/Gas 6 oven until very soft.

Let eggplant cool, then cut into cubes. Place in a salad bowl. Whisk the remaining oil with the chopped ingredients and seasonings. Add vinegar to taste and pour over the eggplant. Toss to coat evenly. Let stand for 30 minutes before serving.

Coliflor Rebozada

FRIED CAULIFLOWER   SERVES 6

Crisply fried cauliflower is a tasty side dish with grilled or roasted meats. Cook whole small zucchini (courgettes), sliced eggplant (aubergine) or slices of tender young pumpkin in the same way.

2 lb/1 kg cauliflower

juice of 1 lemon

1½ cups/180 g/6 oz all-purpose (plain) flour

2 eggs, beaten

2 cups/500 ml/16 fl oz olive or vegetable oil

Divide the cauliflower into flowerets and sprinkle with lemon juice. Drop into boiling water and blanch for 1 to 2 minutes, depending on the size of the flowerets; they should be partially cooked but still quite crisp. Drain well. Coat with flour and then egg. Fry in the oil until crisp.

Hornazo de Salamanca, p.208

Truchas en Adobo con Alcaparras y Anchoas (left), opposite; Bacalao al Ajoarriero (right), p. 196.

OLLA PODRIDA

An *olla* is the earthernware or iron stewpot in which slow cooked dishes are made. Narrower at the top than in the middle, it has two looped handles. *Olla* also means stew, and its partner in this instance, *podrida*, means overripe or overdone, the ingredients in *olla podrida* being cooked very slowly until they are so soft they are falling to pieces. There is a delightful description of *olla podrida* in the mid-eighteenth century diary of the Spanish travels of Alexandre Dumas, author of *The Three Musketeers* in which he lists the innumerable meats that went into a huge *olla podrida*. It included a duck, a chicken, two pigeons, two quails, lamb, beef and ham plus *chorizo* sausages and a mass of garbanzos, and for the vegetables lettuce, carrots, white turnips, artichoke hearts and small onions, followed by green beans, cucumber, asparagus and peas. Cervantes' *Don Quixote* also espoused the merits of a good *olla podrida*. The contents of the *olla* vary from province to province, the pot really being a catchall for the produce of the region. *Chorizo* sausage or *tocino* or belly pork, game birds and garbanzos seem to be the common denominators. These substantial stews, usually served as three courses, also go by other names in different parts, *cocido madrileño* from the nation's capital, *cocido castellano* from the northern plain and *pote gallega* from Galicia. *Olla gitano*, the "gypsy stew" of Andalusia even includes firm pears as an ingredient.

Truchas en Adobo con Alcaparras y Anchoas
MARINATED TROUT WITH CAPERS AND ANCHOVIES   SERVES 6

12 small trout, about 150 g/5 oz each

$\frac{3}{4}$ teaspoon black peppercorns

5 cloves garlic, peeled

2 tablespoons finely chopped parsley

1 cup/250 ml/8 fl oz water

$\frac{1}{2}$ cup/120 ml/4 fl oz olive oil

$\frac{1}{3}$ cup/90 ml/3 fl oz white wine vinegar

2 tablespoons chopped capers

5 anchovy fillets in oil, chopped

salt and pepper

1 medium onion, sliced

1 lemon, sliced

Clean and rinse the trout and place side by side in a pan. Add the peppercorns, garlic, parsley and water with half the oil and vinegar. Cover the pan and simmer gently until the trout are tender, about 7 minutes. Remove with a slotted spoon and place in a glass or ceramic dish. Add the remaining vinegar and oil with the capers, anchovies, salt and pepper. Cover with the onion and lemon slices and let stand for several hours. Serve at room temperature.

GUISADO DE CALABAZA
STEWED PUMPKIN
SERVES 6

2 lb pumpkin or winter squash, peeled and thinly sliced

1 large onion, thinly sliced

2 large tomatoes, sliced

2 cloves garlic, sliced

2 bay leaves

2 sprigs fresh thyme

salt and pepper

Layer the pumpkin in a buttered baking dish with the onion and tomatoes. Scatter on the garlic and push the bay leaves and thyme between the layers. Sprinkle with salt and pepper. Add enough water to just cover. Cover with buttered aluminum foil and bake in a preheated 350°F/180°C/Gas 4 oven for about 50 minutes or until tender, depending on the type of pumpkin used. Serve in the casserole.

LOMBARDA AL MODO SAN ISIDRO
RED CABBAGE IN SAN ISIDRO STYLE
SERVES 4–6

1 large onion, thinly sliced

1 green apple, peeled and coarsely grated

3 tablespoons lard

$1\frac{1}{4}$ lb/650 g red cabbage, finely shredded

2 large potatoes, peeled and sliced

1 bay leaf

$\frac{1}{3}$ teaspoon aniseed

salt and pepper

$\frac{1}{4}$ cup/60 ml/2 fl oz red wine vinegar

$\frac{3}{4}$ cup/180 ml/6 fl oz water

1 slice (about 2 oz/60 g) *tocino* or other cured ham, or fatty bacon

1 tablespoon olive oil (optional)

Sauté the onion and apple in the lard for 3 to 4 minutes. Add the cabbage and toss in the fat until well coated. Arrange the potatoes in the bottom of a casserole. Pile the cabbage mixture on top, adding the lard and the bay leaf. Sprinkle on seasonings and add vinegar and water. Cover and bake in a preheated 350°F/170°C/Gas 4 oven for 1 hour. Finely chop the ham or bacon and fry in the oil, if needed, until crisp. Sprinkle over the cabbage and serve.

PERDICES A LA SEGOVIANA
PARTRIDGE SEGOVIA STYLE   SERVES 4

2–4 oven-ready partridges

salt and pepper

$\frac{1}{2}$ cup/160 g/2 oz all-purpose (plain) flour

$\frac{1}{2}$ cup/120 ml/4 fl oz olive oil

1 medium onion, finely chopped

3 cloves garlic, finely chopped

2 large carrots, cut into small balls

24 small onions, peeled

24 button mushrooms

1 bay leaf

2 sprigs fresh thyme

$\frac{1}{4}$ cup/60 ml/2 fl oz dry sherry

1 tablespoon tomato paste

$\frac{3}{4}$ cup/180 ml/6 fl oz dry or red white wine

1$\frac{1}{2}$ cups/375 ml/12 fl oz chicken stock

4 slices white bread, crusts trimmed

Split the partridges in half. Rinse, dry and season with salt and pepper. Coat lightly with flour, reserving the remainder. Brown in half the oil and set aside. Sauté the onion and garlic until golden, then add the carrots, onions and mushrooms and sauté for a few minutes. Combine the vegetables, herbs and sherry in a casserole. Place the partridges on top and bake in a preheated 400°F/200°C/Gas 6 oven for 10 minutes. Add the tomato paste mixed with wine and stock and return to the oven for 30 minutes or until the birds are tender.

Cut the bread into small triangles and fry in the remaining oil until golden. Transfer the partridges to a serving dish and surround with the toast. Bring the pan juices to a rapid boil and simmer until well reduced. Sprinkle on a little of the reserved flour and stir to thicken. Adjust seasonings and strain sauce over the birds. Serve at once.

PICHÓN EN CACEROLA
SQUAB (PIGEON) CASSEROLE   SERVES 4

4–6 live squab/pigeons

3 oz/90 g salted *tocino* or bacon, diced

2 tablespoons olive oil or lard

1 medium onion, chopped

1 medium carrot, peeled and diced

2 cloves garlic, peeled

1 bay leaf

1 sprig fresh thyme

1 sprig fresh parsley

$\frac{1}{2}$ cup/120 ml/4 fl oz dry sherry

1 tablespoon all-purpose (plain) flour

Kill the birds and drain blood into a container. Pluck and dress, then blanch quickly in boiling water. Drain and dry.

Sauté the bacon in oil or lard with onion and carrot for 5 minutes. Add garlic, herbs and the birds. Add water to half-cover and cook over low heat or in a preheated 350°F/180°C/Gas 4 oven for about 25 minutes, turning twice. Add the sherry. Mix flour with a little of the pan juices and the reserved pigeon blood. Pour into the pan and continue to cook slowly until the birds are done. Strain the sauce. The birds are traditionally served on squares of fried bread, with the sauce poured over and with fried or puréed potatoes on the side.

GALLINA EN PEPITORIA
CHICKEN IN SAFFRON SAUCE
SERVES 4

1.5-kg/3-lb chicken

salt and pepper

¾ cup/90 g/3 oz all-purpose (plain) flour

⅓ cup/90 ml/3 fl oz olive oil

2 large onions, finely chopped

4 cloves garlic, finely chopped

2 bay leaves

1 cup/250 ml/8 fl oz dry white wine

1¾ cups/450 ml/14 fl oz chicken stock

¾ cup/80 g/2½ oz ground almonds

10 threads saffron

chopped parsley

Cut chicken into serving portions, season with salt and pepper and coat lightly with flour. Fry in the oil for about 10 minutes until well colored, then remove and pour off most of the oil. Fry the onions until golden and soft; add garlic and bay leaves and fry briefly. Add wine, stock, ground almonds and chicken, cover and cook over low heat for about 20 minutes, stirring occasionally to keep the sauce from sticking to the pan.

Wrap saffron in a small square of aluminum foil and toast for 2 to 3 minutes in a dry pan. Grind in a mortar, then add 2 to 3 tablespoons boiling water, stir well and pour over the dish. Cook a further 15 minutes. Transfer to a serving dish and sprinkle with parsley.

CACHELADA LEONESA
SAUSAGE AND POTATO CASSEROLE
SERVES 4

The spicy flavor, firm, chewy texture and rich brick-red color of *chorizo* contrast superbly with plain potatoes in one of the simplest yet tastiest dishes from León.

4 large potatoes, peeled and thickly sliced

8 oz/250 g *chorizo* sausage, thickly sliced

1 teaspoon salt

1 cup/250 ml/8 fl oz water

Combine all ingredients in a pot, cover and cook gently for about 25 minutes.

Variation: Garlic enthusiasts will relish this flavorful innovation, which we have borrowed from the Galician dish *Merluza a la Gallega*. Heat ¼ cup/60 ml/2 fl oz olive oil to the smoking point. Add 3 cloves garlic, very finely chopped, and 1 teaspoon sweet paprika and remove from heat. Drain the potato mixture, transfer to a serving bowl and pour on the flavored oil.

CALDERETA DE CORDERO

LAMB CASSEROLE   SERVES 4–6

Caldereta means a stew, or the barrel-shaped cast iron cooking pot on three straight legs in which it is cooked. This practical pot, used outdoors or in traditional kitchens, stands directly in a fire or in glowing coals.

1½ lb/750 g lean boneless lamb

¼ cup/60 ml/2 fl oz olive oil

2 medium onions, chopped

4 cloves garlic, chopped

2 bay leaves

2 sprigs fresh rosemary

3 tomatoes, peeled, seeded and chopped

salt and pepper

1 cup/250 ml/8 fl oz lamb stock

1 teaspoon sweet paprika

4 large potatoes, peeled and cubed

¼ teaspoon powdered saffron

2 tablespoons dry sherry

Cut the lamb into 2-inch/5-cm cubes and brown in the oil. Remove and set aside. Sauté the onions until lightly colored, add garlic and sauté briefly. Add the bay leaves, rosemary and tomatoes and cook for 10 minutes. Return the lamb with salt, pepper, stock and paprika. Bring to a boil, cover and cook gently for about 30 minutes.

Add potatoes and continue to cook until potatoes and lamb are tender, about 45 minutes. Mix saffron and sherry, splash into the dish and cook for 10 more minutes.

Tip: To obtain stock, choose lamb shoulder or leg, bone-in, for the dish. Simmer the bone with water to cover, an onion, a piece of cinnamon stick, salt and a few peppercorns for about 40 minutes. Strain, skim off fat and use for the recipe.

MENESTRA DE CORDERO A LA LEONESA

BRAISED LAMB WITH POTATOES AND PAPRIKA   SERVES 4–6

1½ lb/750 g boneless lamb

salt and pepper

½ cup/60 g/2 oz all-purpose (plain) flour

1 medium onion, sliced

2 cloves garlic, chopped

⅓ cup/90 ml/3 fl oz olive oil

2 bay leaves

1½ lb/750 g potatoes, peeled and cubed

1 tablespoon sweet paprika

1 tablespoon chopped parsley

Cut the lamb into 1-inch/2.5-cm cubes, season with salt and pepper and coat lightly with flour. Sauté the onion and garlic in the oil until lightly colored. Transfer to a *cazuela*. Brown the lamb and place on the onion. Add the bay leaves and enough water to partially cover. Bake in a 350°F/180°C/Gas 4 oven for 30 minutes.

Stir the potatoes and paprika into the pan juices. Cover with aluminum foil and continue to cook until the potatoes and meat are tender. Stir in the parsley and adjust seasonings. Serve in the *cazuela*.

ESTOFADO DE TERNERA A LA ZAMORANA
ZAMORAN VEAL CASSEROLE

SERVES 6

3- to 4-lb/1½- to 2-kg veal roast

salt and pepper

1 cup/120 g/4 oz all-purpose (plain) flour

¾ cup/180 ml/6 fl oz olive oil

6 oz/180 g salted *tocino* or other salt pork, cubed

2 medium onions, chopped

3 cloves garlic, chopped

3 medium tomatoes, chopped

1 teaspoon black peppercorns

2 bay leaves

2 sprigs fresh thyme

1 sprig fresh rosemary

2 sprigs parsley

1 small cinnamon stick

1 whole clove

1 teaspoon ground cumin

1 teaspoon sweet paprika

2 cups/500 ml/16 fl oz dry white or red wine*

24 small onions, peeled

Cut the meat into 2-inch/5-cm chunks, season with salt and pepper and coat lightly with flour. Brown in the oil, cooking about 4 pieces at a time. Transfer to a large baking dish and add the salt pork. Pour off all but about 2½ tablespoons oil and sauté the onions until golden. Add sautéed onions and all remaining ingredients except the small onions to the dish with water to barely cover. Cover and bake in a preheated 350°F/180°C/Gas 4 oven for 1 hour. Add the small onions with salt to taste and cook a further 30 minutes or until the meat and onions are very tender. Serve with creamed or fried potatoes.

*Or use half wine and half water or veal stock.

LENGUAS DE LECHAZO ESTOFADAS
STEWED LAMBS' TONGUES

SERVES 4

16 baby lambs' tongues (about 1¼ lb/650 g)

1 large onion, chopped

¼ cup/60 ml/2 fl oz olive oil

4 cloves garlic, finely chopped

1 green bell pepper (capsicum), seeded and chopped

1 red bell pepper (capsicum), seeded and chopped

1 large tomato, seeded and chopped

1 cup/250 ml/8 fl oz dry white wine

1 cup/250 ml/8 fl oz lamb stock

1 bay leaf

1 sprig fresh thyme

2 sprigs fresh parsley

salt and pepper

If tongues are salted, soak for at least 6 hours; drain.

Place tongues in a saucepan with water to cover generously and bring to a boil. Reduce heat and simmer for 1¼ hours or until the skin feels loose. Drain and rinse under cold water. Strip off the skin and trim the root end.

Sauté the onion in the oil for 3 to 4 minutes. Add the garlic and sauté briefly, then add the peppers and sauté 4 to 5 minutes. Add tomato and cook until soft. Pour in the wine and stock and add the tongues, herbs, salt and pepper. Bring just to a boil, then reduce heat and cook gently on top of the stove or in a preheated 350°F/170°C/Gas 4 oven for about 20 minutes. Discard the herbs. Serve with fried potatoes.

Tip: For lamb stock, boil a lamb shank or lamb scraps with an onion and sprig of thyme for about 40 minutes. Strain.

LECHAZO AL HORNO
MILK-FED LAMB ROASTED IN THE BAKER'S OVEN

SERVES 6–8

Baby lambs are supremely tender even if somewhat bland in taste. They are roasted, in age-old tradition, in large brick ovens over a wood fire. A simple, festive dish, roast milk-fed lamb is accompanied by cubed potatoes baked in the oven or fried in olive oil, and plenty of crusty bread, salad and local wine.

6- to 7-lb/3- to 3½-kg baby lamb

1 tablespoon salt

⅓ teaspoon sweet paprika

2 cloves garlic, mashed

1 teaspoon crushed thyme

½ cup/120 ml/4 fl oz melted lard

1 cup/250 ml/8 fl oz dry white wine

Cut the lamb in half lengthwise. Rub with salt, paprika and the herbs and set aside for 1 hour. Brush with the lard and place skin up on a rack in a large roasting pan. Pour the wine into the pan. Roast in a preheated 400°F/200°C/Gas 6 oven for 45 to 50 minutes. The lamb should be quite pink when done. Baste occasionally with the pan juices.

HORNAZO DE SALAMANCA
STUFFED BREAD
SERVES 8

Castile has been called *tierra de pan*, "land of bread", because of the superior quality of its wheat. In Madrid the standard bread is a long loaf. In other parts of Spain, *pan candeal*, a kind of slightly coarse-grained, round, flat "country style" loaf, is what usually accompanies a meal to the table. The dough of this kind of chewy bread may be filled with chunks of spicy *chorizo*, *morcilla*, cured ham or bacon and hard-boiled eggs. A specialty of the old university city of Salamanca, this is made all over Castile for Easter. The *hornazo* of Zamora, north of Salamanca, is made of ground lamb rolled in cabbage leaves; it is also known as *hornazo a la castellana*. Another version of *hornazo*, and the one more likely to be found in the *pastelería*, is made with golden puff pastry.

1 recipe bread dough (page 270)

3 oz/90 g *morcilla* blood sausage

4 oz/120 g *chorizo* or other spicy sausage

4 oz/120 g cured ham

2 hard-boiled eggs

1 egg

Knead the dough lightly after it has fully risen and press out into a flat rectangle. Cut the sausages, ham and eggs into bite-size pieces. Arrange evenly across the dough. Roll up and form into a loaf shape. Make several slashes diagonally across the top and place on a floured baking sheet. Set aside for 40 minutes. Brush the top with beaten egg. Bake in a preheated 425°F/220°C/Gas 7 oven for about 45 minutes. To test if the loaf is done, turn it upside down and tap on the bottom; it should give a hollow sound. Cool completely before slicing thickly to serve.

HIGOS CON MIEL
FIGS IN HONEY
SERVES 6

In Spain figs grow so abundantly that even after much of the crop is dried, there is still an excess to turn into pig fodder.

18–24 plump dried figs

2 cups/500 ml/16 fl oz ruby port

1 cup/250 ml/8 fl oz orange juice

$\frac{1}{3}$ cup/90 g/3 oz clear honey

whipped cream

Stem the figs and place in a wide non-aluminum pan. Add the port, orange juice and honey and bring almost to a boil. Reduce heat and simmer for about 45 minutes.

Serve hot or cold with whipped cream.

Variations: Add chopped crystallized ginger, or stuff a sliver of ginger or a whole almond into each fig.

YEMAS
SWEET EGG YOLK DESSERT
SERVES 6

Yemas means "yolks" — in this instance, egg yolks that are cooked with sugar into the little golden rolls that are one of the delights of Spanish cuisine. Rich and super-sweet, they come in many variations; some are made with mashed sweet potato, while others, known as *yemas variadas*, have added nuts, dried and candied fruits and peel. But most exquisite are the *yemas de Santa Teresa*, a specialty of Ávila.

½ cup/120 g/4 oz sugar

¼ cup/60 ml/2 fl oz water

2-inch/5-cm cinnamon stick

1 teaspoon finely grated lemon rind

10 egg yolks, lightly beaten

confectioners' (icing) sugar

Dissolve the sugar in water in a small non-aluminum saucepan. Add the cinnamon and boil until the syrup begins to caramelize. Allow to cool. Strain the yolks into the syrup and add the lemon rind. Cook over low heat, stirring, until the mixture is thick and leaves the sides of the pan. Pour onto a slab of buttered marble and let cool.

Cover a work surface thinly with confectioners' sugar. Cut the cooled mixture into squares or sticks and roll into cylindrical or egg-yolk shapes on the sugar. Wrap the *yemas* individually in small squares of tissue or waxed paper, or place into little paper candy cups.

SUSPIROS DE MONJA
"NUNS' SIGHS"
SERVES 6

4 cups/1 l/32 fl oz milk

1 tablespoon vanilla sugar or 1½ teaspoons vanilla extract

½ cup/120 g/4 oz superfine sugar

6 medium eggs, separated

1 cinnamon stick

rind of 1 large orange

½ teaspoon cinnamon

Pour half the milk into a wide pan and add vanilla sugar or extract. Add half the sugar and heat gently, stirring until sugar is dissolved. Set aside.

Beat egg whites to firm peaks. Heat the remaining milk with remaining sugar and the cinnamon stick in the top of a double boiler. Add the orange rind. Remove from the heat and let stand for 10 minutes. Discard cinnamon stick and orange peel. Beat the egg yolks and stir into the flavored milk. Cook over low heat, stirring slowly, until mixture thickens; do not boil. Reheat the first pan of milk to just below a boil. Drop tablespoons of the egg whites onto the simmering milk and cook gently until set. Discard the milk.

Pour the custard into dessert dishes and float several of the meringues on top. Sprinkle with cinnamon and serve hot or cold.

CANTABRIA AND ASTURIAS

CANTABRIA Y ASTURIAS

North of León are the rich pasturelands and forest-clad mountains of Asturias. The province of Orviedo is apple country, where it is said that more than 200 varieties of the fruit are grown.

Apple cider many years ago became the preferred drink in this region. They call it *sidra*, and consume it in vast volume. Enthusiasts imbibe the favored ungasified natural ferment in an almost ritualistic fashion. Small groups gather in *chigres* (the cider-making equivalent of a *bodega*) to literally share a glass. Master in charge of the pouring is the *escanciador* who must pour from the bottle held high above his head into a large glass held near his knees. Only enough for a good swig is poured and the first person drinks this leaving just enough to swill over the rim of the glass to rinse it before handing it back to be refilled and passed on. This tradition of pouring cider from a height has been carried into bars and even into otherwise quite restrained and sophisticated restaurants in many parts of Spain.

It is also cheese country. The cows fattened on the grassy slopes of the *Picos de Europa*, the mountain range separating Asturias from its easternly sister Cantabria, give milk unequaled by those anywhere else in Spain. *Arroz con leche* rivals the region's many sweet, cooked apple dishes as her most famous dessert. It's simple rice pudding, but made with the cream-rich milk for which these parts are legendary.

What milk does not go to the bottling plants and creameries to make Spain's best *mantequilla* (butter) goes towards the production of equally famous cheeses. Mixing cow, sheep and goat milk, a soft creamy cheese is wrapped in chestnut leaves and stored in humid caves, where it invites the invasion of a light green-blue veining to develop its intense taste and aroma. The genuine article, made in the tiny village of Cabrales, is only sold locally, although this superb cheese — known as *queso de Cabrales* or *Cabrales-Picón* — is now produced industrially to meet a huge and growing demand.

Verdant Asturias is also bean and sausage country. Both are encapsulated in the one dish that best exemplifies the food of this region, *fabada*, named after the large dried white butter beans cooked in it. They may be called *fabes*, *faves* or *alubias*, but those grown in Asturias are the best in Spain, delicately nutty in taste and with a soft texture that happily absorbs the flavors of other ingredients. *Fabada* bubbles over the fire right through the bitter Asturian winter, promising a warm respite from biting winds and bone-chilling rains. Winter sustenance also comes from lentils, hams and sausages. Asturias is famous for its cured meats, its dark, plump and soft-textured *morcilla*, its *chorizos* dripping paprika, its *tocino* and bacon salted to just the right degree and wonderfully aromatic.

Vast oak and chestnut forests cover the *Cordillera Cantábrica*, the high mountain range running the length of Asturias and its coastal neighbor Cantabria. This natural division seems to have cut Asturias and Cantabria off from the mainstream of Spanish life and some of its history. To cross them is to cross a border into another land, another culture, almost another time. Here Celtic influence and ancestry is more evident than in any other part of Spain, except perhaps Galicia. They sing their own songs (many with a decided Irish undertone) and dance their own dances, drink their cider in plenty, talk voluminously and accept cheerfully what life offers. Moorish culture did not seep this far north, the Visigothic kings retaining control throughout the occupation, and later the Christians formulated their plans for the reconquest of Spain from these regions.

The rocky, inaccessible coastline of Asturias restricts the access of large fishing vessels, so much of the rich variety of seafood from the Bay of Biscay is transported from nearby. Galicia's chief city, Santander, is an important fishing port where some wonderful fish dishes have been created. The cuisine of Galicia is not a sophisticated one, but then with such riches from land and sea it doesn't have to be. Large, dark-meated tuna and bonito are plentiful and excellent straight from the fishing boats, and the shrimp (prawns) of this region are particularly sweet. *Merluza*, the long, thin, silvery fish loved all over Spain, are caught here in plenty and used in innumerable dishes. *Caldereta* is a hotchpotch of shellfish and fish, a soup-stew of wonderful aromas, delectable textures and flavors.

The *cornisa cantábrica*, the beautiful green coast of Santander province, is on the tourist route connecting directly by rail and motorway to León's Valladolid, en route to Madrid. The croplands through which it travels are dotted with granaries, looking like miniature worker's cottages, where wheat and corn await the miller's wheel. Local bread is crusty and deliciously chewy, and they also love cornbread not unlike that made in Portugal. And from the mountain ranges tumble fast-flowing rivers carrying plump trout and salmon, the surrounding forests offering cover for deer. The venison here is not to be missed, served roasted or richly marinated and braised in red wine. The intrepid hunter might also bag a bear.

CALDERETA DE PESCADO Y MARISCOS

CASSEROLE OF FISH AND SHELLFISH   SERVES 6–8

The cooler waters of the Bay of Biscay offer excellent fishing for many types of firm-fleshed fish, particularly *besugo* (sea bream), *lubina* (sea bass), tuna, bonito, *mero* (sea perch/grouper), as well as enormous schools of those small oily fish so popular throughout Spain and Portugal — anchovies and sardines. The cuisine of the coastal area of Cantabria is so dominated by seafood dishes that one particular tunafish dish has been named *pollo marino* — "sea chicken." A chunky, richly flavored soup-stew in the *bouillabaisse* tradition is a classic of this region.

2-lb/1-kg bream (sea bass)

1 lb/500 g hake, halibut or cod fillets

6 fresh squid

6 fresh mussels in the shell

12 fresh clams in the shell

12 medium shrimp (prawns) in the shell

6 *cigalas* (saltwater crayfish/Dublin Bay prawns)

1 medium onion, chopped

$\frac{1}{3}$ cup/90 ml/3 fl oz olive oil

1 medium-size red bell pepper (capsicum), seeded and chopped

2 large sun-ripened tomatoes, seeded and chopped

1 dried hot red chili pepper

2 bay leaves

2 sprigs fresh parsley

5 black peppercorns

$\frac{1}{3}$ teaspoon powdered saffron

Place the bream and hake in a large pan and add water just to cover. Simmer for 4 minutes, then carefully remove and pick the flesh from the bones. Return bones and head to the pot and cook another 6 minutes, then strain stock into a jug. Clean squid and cut into rings. Rinse the pan and put in all of the shellfish. Add 4 cups/1 l/32 fl oz cold water and bring to a boil. Shake the pan over moderate heat for 3 to 4 minutes until the shells open. Remove from the heat. Strain the liquid into the jug with the fish stock. Discard any shellfish that do not open and remove the top shell from each of the shellfish. Peel shrimp and *cigalas*. Rinse pan again and fry the onion in oil until lightly colored and soft. Add pepper and fry briefly, then add tomato and remaining ingredients except saffron and cook for 3 to 4 minutes. Add the strained stock and saffron and bring to a boil; simmer for 5 to 6 minutes. Return all of the seafood and heat through for 3 to 4 minutes before serving with plenty of crusty bread.

HUEVOS RELLENOS CON ATÚN

EGGS STUFFED WITH TUNA

SERVES 4–6 (*TAPA*)

6 hard-boiled eggs

6 oz/180 g canned tuna, drained and rinsed

1 tablespoon minced green olives

1 teaspoon minced parsley

pinch each of cayenne and white pepper

mayonnaise

1 small dill pickle/gherkin, sliced

12 cooked peeled baby shrimp (prawns)

Peel the eggs and cut in halves lengthwise. Remove yolks carefully with a teaspoon and mash in a mortar or food processor with the tuna, olives, parsley and seasonings, adding mayonnaise to moisten enough to pipe into the eggs. Spoon mixture into a pastry bag fitted with a large star nozzle. Pipe in a tall swirl into the egg whites. Press a slice of pickle and a small shrimp on top and secure with a toothpick.

CROQUETAS CANTÁBRICAS

COD CROQUETTES

MAKES 48 (*TAPA*)

I was so impressed with the julienned potato nests used in one elegant Madrid restaurant to serve bite-size salt cod croquettes that I have done them as a first course this way ever since. For *tapas* pierce each with a toothpick and arrange on a plate surrounded by shredded lettuce and lemon wedges.

6 oz/180 g prepared *bacalao* (page 266)

1 medium onion, very finely chopped

3 tablespoons olive oil

$\frac{1}{3}$ cup/90 g/3 oz all-purpose (plain) flour

$\frac{1}{2}$ cup/120 ml/4 fl oz milk

2 teaspoons finely chopped parsley

salt and pepper

3 large potatoes, boiled and mashed

extra flour

1 egg, beaten

1 cup/120 g/4 oz very fine dry breadcrumbs

$1\frac{1}{2}$ cups/400 ml/13 fl oz olive or vegetable oil

1 lb/500 g potatoes, peeled and julienned (optional)

Prepare the *bacalao* and drain well. Chop in a food processor. Sauté the onion in the olive oil until softened and lightly colored. Stir in $\frac{1}{3}$ cup flour and cook for 1 to 2 minutes on medium heat, then remove from heat and stir in the milk. Cook, stirring continually, until very thick, then add the parsley, salt and pepper, mashed potatoes and fish to form a very thick paste. Form into croquettes with oiled hands. Coat lightly with the extra flour, then dip into beaten egg and coat with bread-crumbs. Fry in olive oil until golden and crisp on the surface. Drain and serve warm or at room temperature.

To make potato nests, blanch the potatoes for 10 seconds in boiling water; drain. Spread in a well-oiled metal strainer or potato nest basket, press another strainer on top to make the shape and place in hot deep oil until the potato is golden. Remove, invert onto paper towels and drain. Surround with shredded lettuce to serve.

TORTILLAS DE BACALAO
SALT COD OMELETTES

SERVES 4-6 (*TAPA*)

Serve these omelettes as a light luncheon dish, as a *tapa*, or as a first course with sun-ripened tomato splashed with wine vinegar.

8 oz/250 g prepared *bacalao* (page 266)

1 small onion, finely chopped

1 clove garlic, very finely chopped

4 tablespoons olive oil

8 eggs

1 tablespoon all-purpose (plain) flour

2 teaspoons chopped fresh fennel

2 teaspoons freshly ground black pepper

Drain the cod, bone and remove any fragments of skin. Flake the fish finely and set aside. Sauté onion and garlic in half the oil until softened; add the fish. Beat eggs in a bowl with the flour, herbs and pepper, add fish and mix in evenly. Heat a small omelette pan and moisten with a little of the remaining oil. Pour in one quarter of the egg mixture and cook until golden underneath, then turn and cook the other side. When just firm, transfer to a baking pan and keep warm. Cook the remaining omelettes, then place under a hot broiler/grill to brown the tops. Serve at once.

Variation: This can be cooked in a larger pan as a single omelette.

HABAS A LA MONTAÑESA
BROADBEANS WITH THYME

SERVES 4–6

3 lb/1.5 kg fresh broadbeans in the shell

¼ cup/60 ml/2 fl oz olive oil

3 cloves garlic, finely chopped

3–4 sprigs fresh thyme

salt and pepper

Shell the beans. Heat oil in a flameproof casserole and add the beans with garlic and thyme. Cook over high heat for 30 to 40 seconds, stirring, then reduce heat and cook slowly until the beans are tender, about 12 minutes, stirring several times. If needed, sprinkle a little cold water over the beans to keep them moist. Season to taste with salt and pepper and serve in the casserole.

Cocido de Lentejas
LENTIL CASSEROLE

SERVES 4–6

Unlike *fabada*, which remains chunky, this lentil stew cooks to a thick, creamy consistency. It makes a satisfying supper dish and goes well as a side dish with roast meats. As a first course I often serve it in that popular Spanish way — over a square of bread rubbed with garlic and fried in oil.

$1\frac{1}{2}$ cups/9 oz/280 g brown lentils

1 medium onion, chopped

8 oz/250 g *chorizo* sausage

1 bay leaf

salt

$4\frac{1}{2}$ cups/1.1 lt/$1\frac{1}{4}$ qt water

pepper

2 slices white bread, crusts trimmed

$\frac{1}{2}$ cup/4 fl oz/120 ml olive oil

4 cloves garlic, minced

2 oz/70 g salted *tocino* or bacon, minced

2 teaspoons sweet paprika

2 teaspoons chopped parsley

Thoroughly rinse the lentils and place in a saucepan with the onion and whole sausages. Add the bay leaf and 1 teaspoon salt. Add water and bring to a boil. Cover and simmer gently for about 30 minutes, until the beans are tender enough to begin to break up. Remove the sausage, slice thinly and return to the pot. Season with salt and pepper to taste. Fry the bread in olive oil until crisp and golden, then chop to coarse crumbs. Fry the garlic and bacon together until crisp. Add paprika and stir in the crumbs. Garnish with the *picada* of fried ingredients and the chopped parsley.

Truchas a la Montañesa
TROUT MOUNTAIN STYLE

SERVES 4

4 fresh trout, 8–10 oz/250 g–300 g each

1 large onion, sliced

2 bay leaves

$\frac{1}{2}$ teaspoon black peppercorns

1 cup/250 ml/8 fl oz dry white wine

1 cup/250 ml/8 fl oz water

salt

4 sprigs fennel

Clean the trout, rinse and dry. Spread half the onion in a fish kettle or other wide, flat pan and place the fish on top. Cover with the remaining onion and add the bay leaves, peppercorns, wine, water and a large pinch of salt. Cover and cook gently for about 12 minutes. Carefully lift the fish onto warmed plates, garnish with fennel and serve with boiled potatoes.

MERLUZA A LA SIDRA
HAKE SIMMERED IN HARD CIDER

Hard cider is an Asturian speciality, and is drunk there more than wine or other alcoholic beverages. *Merluza* (hake) cooked in cider is one of the region's most famous dishes and is often found on menus simply as *merluza asturiana*. Hard cider has a high alcohol content and is very dry, so common cider will not have the same results. The clams are an inspirational addition, but can be substituted with small mussels, or left out altogether.

4 hake fillets (or use cod/ haddock), each 180-200 g/6-7 oz

salt and black pepper

$\frac{1}{4}$ cup/60 ml/2 fl oz olive oil

12 small clams or mussels

1 cup/250 ml/8 fl oz water

1 bay leaf

4 black peppercorns

1 small sprig fresh thyme

1 medium onion, peeled, halved, sliced

2-3 cloves garlic, peeled, mashed

$\frac{1}{2}$ red bell pepper (capsicum), seeded

$\frac{1}{2}$ green bell pepper (capsicum); seeded

1 teaspoon sweet paprika

1 cup/250 ml/8 fl oz hard/dry cider

Season the fish and set aside. Heat 1 tablespoon of the oil in a pan and add the clams or mussels, shake over high heat for 1 minute, then add the water, bay-leaf, peppercorns and thyme with a few slices of the onion. Cook, shaking the pan, until the clams open. Remove clams on a slotted spoon and set aside. Add fish and cook gently for about 9 minutes. Transfer to a large ovenproof serving dish, or place fish in individual ramekins. Arrange the clams or mussels on top. Sauté the onion in the remaining oil until golden, add the garlic and sauté briefly. Cut the peppers into narrow strips and add to the pan. Sauté until well softened.

Drain off excess oil, add the reserved fish stock and cider and simmer until the sauce is well reduced. At this stage the sauce can be puréed in a blender or food processor and passed through a fine mesh sieve to give a smooth sauce, but it is more characteristic to use as it is. Pour the sauce over the fish and place in a preheated moderate oven at 360°F/180°C/Gas 4 for about 15 minutes. Serve in the dish.

Merluza a la Sidra (top), opposite; Tortillas de Bacalao (front), p.214

Caldereta de Pescado y Mariscos, p.212

Pollo con Manzanas
CHICKEN WITH APPLES   SERVES 4–6

3- to 3½-lb/1.5- to 1.8-kg oven-
ready chicken

salt and pepper

½ cup/120 ml/4 fl oz hard cider
(optional)

2 cooking apples, peeled, cored
and halved

2 tablespoons butter

1–2 cloves garlic, mashed

½ teaspoon dried rosemary,
crushed

1 cup/250 ml/8 fl oz dry white
wine

1 cup/250 ml/8 fl oz water

2 teaspoons finely chopped
parsley

Season the cavity of the chicken with salt and pepper and a little of the cider, if used. Push the halved apples into the cavity and close the opening with poultry pins. Push a wooden spoon between skin and breast meat to make a cavity. Mix butter with garlic, salt, pepper and rosemary and press into the cavity, spreading evenly. Rub salt and pepper into the skin and pour on the remaining cider. Place the chicken on a low rack in a roasting pan. Roast in a preheated 350°F/180°C/Gas 4 oven for 20 minutes, then add the wine and water, basting the chicken. Roast a further 1 to 1¼ hours or until the chicken is tender, basting with the pan juices every 15 minutes to keep the meat moist. Remove the chicken and place the pan over direct heat to reduce the liquid, if necessary. Adjust the seasoning and add chopped parsley. Cut the chicken in halves, cutting away the backbone, then cut each half across to give 4 equal portions. Serve each with a half apple and the sauce.

Perdices en Sidra
PARTRIDGE IN CIDER SAUCE   SERVES 4

4 oven-ready young partridges (or
4–8 quail)

salt and pepper

1 tablespoon butter or lard

3 medium onions, thinly sliced

3 oz/100 g smoked bacon, finely
diced

1 bouquet garni or sprigs of fresh
herbs

2 cups/500 ml/16 fl oz hard cider

1 tablespoon all-purpose (plain)
flour

Rinse and dry the birds, truss and season with salt and pepper. Brown them in the butter or lard in an ovenproof dish and set aside. Brown the onions well in the same dish, then fry the bacon briefly. Return the birds and add the herbs and cider. Roast in a 350°F/170°C/Gas 4 oven for about 40 minutes or until cooked through, turning and basting several times. Transfer the birds and onions to a serving platter. Sprinkle flour into the pan and stir over moderate heat until well colored. Add a little extra cider or water if needed and stir until the gravy is thickened. Adjust seasoning, pour over the dish and serve.

ESTOFADO DE BUEY A LA ASTURIANA
BRAISED BEEF WITH VEGETABLES
SERVES 4–6

1½ lb/750 g lean, cubed round beef

½ cup/120 ml/4 fl oz olive oil

1 large onion, chopped

3 cloves garlic, chopped

2 oz/60 g salted *tocino*, salt pork or bacon, diced

1 medium carrot, peeled and diced

1 cup/250 ml/8 fl oz red or dry white wine

3 tablespoons brandy or dry sherry

2-inch/5-cm cinnamon stick

1 bay leaf

1 sprig each fresh thyme, parsley and sage

1 teaspoon sweet paprika

12 small new potatoes, peeled

12 baby turnips, peeled

12 small (pickling) onions, peeled

salt and pepper

Fry the beef in the oil over high heat until all surfaces are seared. Remove and keep warm. Fry the onion until well colored. Add the garlic, *tocino* and carrot and fry for 2 minutes. Add wine and brandy and cook over high heat until reduced by half. Return the meat and add the spices and herbs. Add 1½ cups/400 ml/13 fl oz warm water and bring to a boil. Cover and cook very slowly for 1¼ hours. Add the vegetables and season with salt and pepper, then cook another 15 minutes or until tender. If necessary, remove the meat and vegetables with a slotted spoon and boil the sauce rapidly to reduce, or stir in a little flour mixed to a paste with a teaspoon of butter to thicken. If the stew is too dry, add a little warm water during cooking.

Tip: *Estofado* is greatly improved if prepared a day in advance and reheated. The Catalonians enjoy a slightly sweet and crunchy variation of this dish by adding previously boiled prunes half an hour before serving, and a handful of toasted pine nuts at the last minute.

ARROZ A LA SANTANDERINA
RICE WITH SALMON

1 medium onion, finely chopped

3 cloves garlic, finely chopped

1 bay leaf

2 tablespoons olive oil

2 cups/350 g/12 oz short-grain round/white rice

3 cups/750 ml/24 fl oz hot fish stock or water*

14 oz/440 g tomatoes, chopped

300 g salmon steaks, cubed

Sauté onion, garlic and bay leaf in the oil until the onion has softened but not colored. Add rice and stir to coat the grains with the oil. Add half the hot stock and cook for 5 minutes over fairly high heat. Add tomatoes and cook another 5 minutes, then add half the remaining stock and the cubed salmon and cook gently until rice is tender, adding extra stock as needed.

*If using water, add a fish stock cube to improve the flavor.

ARROZ CON ALMEJAS

RICE WITH BABY CLAMS

SERVES 4–6

1 medium onion, finely chopped

2 cloves garlic, finely chopped

2 tablespoons olive oil

2 large sun-ripened tomatoes, seeded and chopped

1½ tablespoons tomato paste

2 cups/350 g/12 oz short-grain round white rice

1¼ teaspoons salt

12-oz/300 g can baby clams

2¼ cups/550 ml/18 fl oz water or fish stock

2 tablespoons chopped parsley

lemon wedges

Sauté the onion and garlic in the oil in a *paella* pan or other suitable pan until lightly colored. Add the tomatoes and cook for 5 minutes, then add tomato paste, rice and salt and mix well. Add the liquid from the canned clams and cook over high heat for 5 minutes, stirring occasionally. Add the water or stock, cover tightly and cook over fairly low heat for about 15 minutes. Stir in the clams and parsley and continue to cook, stirring frequently, until the rice has completely absorbed the liquid. Serve in the pan with wedges of lemon.

Using fresh clams: Soak 1½–2 lb/750 g-1 kg fresh clams overnight in cold water and drain well. Place in a saucepan, cover tightly and cook over moderate heat until the shells open. (Shake pan occasionally to help them open.) Discard any unopened shells. Remove top shell of each clam if desired.

ALUBIAS CON ALMEJAS

WHITE BEANS WITH CLAMS

SERVES 4–6

It is the creamy texture of the white *alubias* that is the essence of their popularity. However, other dried white beans can be used in their place, particularly Italian cannellini or large white haricots.

2 cups/1 lb/500 g fresh *alubias*, or dried *alubias* soaked overnight

1 medium onion, quartered

1 medium carrot, peeled and halved

1 sprig fresh thyme or rosemary

1–2 cloves garlic, peeled

1 bay leaf

2 lb/1 kg fresh clams in the shell, soaked overnight

3 tablespoons olive oil

2 cloves garlic, finely chopped

salt and pepper

Cook the beans with water to cover generously and the onion, carrot, herbs, whole garlic and bay leaf until the beans are tender. Cooking time can vary from 1½ to nearly 3 hours depending on the age of the beans. (Fresh beans will cook in a fraction of that time.)

Drain beans discarding herbs and vegetables. Steam the clams until they open, then pick off the top shells, or remove clams completely from their shells. (Discard any that do not open.) Heat oil in a large sauté pan and sauté the garlic briefly. Add beans and sauté for about 3 minutes, then stir in the clams and heat through. Season to taste and serve hot.

Fabada Asturiana

SERVES 8

You don't need to experience the bitter cold of an Asturian winter to understand why a simple bean stew has become one of Spain's classic dishes. *Fabes* or *faves* are a type of white butter or lima bean growing abundantly in this region, as well as in the Basque country and Catalonia, where they may be called *alubias*. They are cooked with a *compagno,* a mixture of *morcilla* (the richly flavored blood sausage), spicy *chorizo* sausages and various cuts of pork, to create a hearty one-pot meal that has a strong affiliation with the *cassoulet* of France. Purists maintain that *fabada* should only be made from beans grown in Asturias.

2 cups/350 g/12 oz butter beans or lima beans (or use Boston/haricot/navy beans)

1 ham/bacon hock

1 pork hock/pig's foot/trotter

6 oz/180 g salted *tocino*, salt pork or bacon

1 lb/500 g fresh bacon/belly pork, sliced

4 pieces (about 1¼ lb/650 g) veal shank/shin

12 oz/350 g *chorizo* sausages

10 oz/300 g *morcilla* or other blood sausages

1 large onion, thinly sliced

1 whole head garlic, peeled

1 dried hot red chili pepper

2 bay leaves

2 sprigs fresh thyme

Rinse the beans and drain; place in a very large pot with the ham or bacon hock and pork hock. Cover with water and bring to the boil. Simmer for 10 minutes, then drain. Cover with warm fresh water, adding the bacon, sliced pork and veal pieces. Bring to a boil and simmer for 1 hour. Add the sausages, onion, garlic, chili and herbs and simmer slowly for another 1½ hours, adding warm water from time to time as needed.

Remove the ham and pork hocks, pick off any meat and return it to the pot. Discard veal marrow bones, if preferred. Slice the *tocino* and sausages or leave whole as desired. Serve in a deep dish with plenty of crusty bread.

Tip: Like many stewed dishes *fabada* improves with keeping, so prepare in advance and reheat.

PASTEL DE MANZANAS
CARAMELIZED APPLE TART
SERVES 6

2½ lb/1.2 kg cooking apples

¼ cup/60 g/2 oz packed brown sugar

2-inch/5-cm cinnamon stick

2 tablespoons water

¼ cup/60 g/2 oz granulated sugar

1½ tablespoons water

1 cup/250 ml/8 fl oz milk

1 teaspoon grated lemon rind

5 eggs, beaten

Peel, core and thinly slice the apples and place in a saucepan with the brown sugar and cinnamon stick. Add 2 tablespoons water, cover tightly and cook gently until very tender. Remove the cinnamon stick and pass half the apple through a sieve or purée in a food processor; set the remaining apple aside. In a small saucepan combine the granulated sugar with 1½ tablespoons water and boil gently, without stirring, until caramelized. When it has turned a rich golden brown, pour into an 8-inch/20-cm piepan and tilt the dish so the caramel covers the base and sides. Set aside.

Bring the milk with grated peel to a boil in the top of a double boiler. Add the eggs and stir over simmering water until thickened. Stir in the apple purée. Arrange the remaining sliced apple in a spiral on the caramel; pour on the apple custard. Place in a larger pan with water to come halfway up the sides of the piepan. Bake in a 400°F/200°C/Gas 6 oven for about 25 minutes or until the tart is firm and a thin skewer inserted in the center comes out clean. Let cool, then invert onto a plate and serve with whipped cream.

SORBETE DE MANZANAS CON CALVADOS
APPLE SORBET FLAVORED WITH CALVADOS
SERVES 4–6

1 recipe poached apple purée (see *Pastel de Manazanas*)

⅓ cup/90 ml/3 fl oz Calvados

1½ cups/400 ml/13 fl oz sugar syrup

Sugar Syrup:

½ lb/250 g superfine sugar

1½ cups/400 ml/13 fl oz water

Prepare the apple purée following the previous recipe. Pass through a sieve or blend in a food processor, then sieve to make a very smooth purée. In an ice cream maker churn the apple purée with Calvados and sugar syrup according to manufacturer's instructions. Serve at once in tall glass dessert dishes, or transfer to a dish, cover with aluminum foil and freeze until needed.

In a heavy-based saucepan dissolve the sugar in the water. Simmer gently, without stirring, for 10 minutes.

Arroz con Leche

RICE PUDDING   SERVES 6–8

This verdant northern province produces the best milk in Spain, creamy rich and high in butterfat. The countryside is dotted with factories that make a vast variety of superb cheeses. Although it is found on menus in almost every part of Spain, *arroz con leche* is the pride of Asturias. Its literal translation, "rice with milk," profoundly understates this sublime rice pudding dessert when made with local milk. Taken to the New World it became a firm favorite with the introduction of milk and rice into the diet, and today it remains one of the most popular desserts in Mexico.

1½ cups (330 g/11 oz) short-grain/round white rice

2 cups /500 ml/16 fl oz cold water

3-inch/7.5-cm cinnamon stick

rind of 1 lemon

2 whole cloves

1 cup/120g/8 oz sugar

large pinch of salt

6 cups/1.5 l/1½ qt milk

1 teaspoon vanilla extract (essence)

cinnamon (optional)

Cook the rice with water over moderate heat until the water has been absorbed. In another pan combine the cinnamon stick, lemon rind, cloves, sugar and salt, pour in the milk and bring to a boil. Simmer for 6 minutes, then strain over the rice, adding the vanilla. Cook until the rice is tender enough to be easily mashed. Sprinkle on the cinnamon and serve hot or cold.

Variation: Add 2 beaten eggs to the cooked pudding, pour into a buttered baking dish and sprinkle with cinnamon. Bake at 350°F/180°C/Gas 4 until the top is golden brown. Or add ½ cup/60 g/2 oz raisins with the milk.

Frixuelos con Manzanas

CREPES WITH APPLES   SERVES 6

1½ cups/180 g/6 oz all-purpose (plain) flour

3 eggs

2 tablespoons softened butter

2 cups/500 ml/16 fl oz milk

2 tablespoons cognac or brandy

2 teaspoons sugar

4–5 cooking apples, peeled and cored

¼ cup/90 g/3 oz clear honey

¼ cup/60 ml/2 fl oz water

½ teaspoon cinnamon

cream, whipped

almonds

For crepe batter beat the flour, eggs, butter, milk, cognac and sugar together until smooth and creamy, then set aside for 30 minutes.

Slice the apples. Heat the honey and water in a saucepan and add the apples and cinnamon. Poach gently, turning occasionally, until the apples are tender. Set aside.

Rub an omelette pan with a piece of buttered paper and warm over moderate heat. Cook the crepes, stack when done and cover with a cloth to keep warm. Fill crepes with the apples, or roll and arrange the apples on top.

Serve warm with whipped cream and garnish with almonds.

GALICIA

GALICIA

If you can speak Portuguese, you can speak Galician with a little prompting on colloquialisms. Galicia, in Spain's northwest, seems hardly to belong to the same country. It saw none of the dramatic changes wrought by the invasion of the Moors. It is a region where Christianity has been the dominant force, where pilgrims trekked to the ancient city of Santiago de Compostela to worship at the Shrine of St James, patron saint of Spain. It was in the early part of the 9th century that the remains of the Apostle Santiago were discovered and interred, and the pilgrimages began. The reward for the arduous journey was dispensation from all crimes or sins.

The *camino de Santiago*, the pilgrims' route, has had a profound effect on this region. Receiving pilgrims from many parts of Europe meant an exchange of ideas and knowledge, and the import of new foods and customs. The elegant fan-shaped sea scallop that the Galicians call *vieira* proliferates on these rocky coastlines. The pilgrims collected them for food, keeping the shells as proof that they had seen their journey through, and the shells became known as *concha peregrina* — the pilgrim's shell.

Vieiras have retained their importance, but now gastronomically rather than spiritually. Here they are sweeter and plumper than in any other part of Spain. They may be eaten straight from the water with a squeeze of lemon, or baked on their shells in a splash of local Albariño wine or with a coating of crumbs and spices. Here, too, the fascinating *percebes* offers its sweet bite of meat beneath a shell that looks like the miniature foot of some prehistoric, elephantine creature. And the oysters of Galicia are prized. The favorite way of preparing them — if they are not simply eaten raw — is to dip them into cornmeal and fry them for just a few seconds in olive oil; or they might go into a creamy soup.

The coastline of Galicia is spectacular — green, windswept, indented by estuaries or *rías* for deep- and shallow-water fishing. The rocky shorelines hold mollusks of myriad kinds and provide a secluded habitat for a variety of delectable crustaceans. The shellfish of Galicia is much in demand all around Spain, so superb in flavor that it is usually cooked simply to enhance rather than disguise its quality.

Galicia has the provinces of Pontevedra on its west coast, La Coruña on its northwestern extremity (the site of Santiago de Compostella gets the full brunt of fierce Atlantic storms) and Lugo tipping the north coast at the Bay of Biscay and neighboring Asturias. Octopus inhabit the deep bay waters; the tenderest come to the table as *pulpo gallega* or *pulpo al fiera* (festive style), beaten and boiled to tenderize them, then sliced and dressed with oil and paprika. It is a popular *tapa* dish, usually served on a flat wooden plate. Baby octopus, not more than about 12 inches (30 cm) from rounded gray head to tip of tentacle, are simple to cook and supremely tender, requiring none of the tedium of preparation that the older ones demand.

Many of the dishes claimed by the Galicians are reflected in the cuisine of Portugal, where rich seafood soups and stews are the focal point of their coastal cuisine. The Galician housewife grills fresh sardines outside her kitchen on pot-bellied grills like those of her Portuguese neighbor, using vine clippings if she can for fuel to give that special flavor.

The lush green inland province is Orense, where rich pastures feed plump dairy cattle and grain crops green the landscape, where vegetables thrive and game meats fill the stewpot. *Lacón con grelos* — cured pork shoulder (*lacón*) slow-cooked with *grelos*, the bitter greens of young turnip plants — is the pride of the inland cuisine. *Empanada gallega* is a sort of highly magnified version of the small snack pastry eaten elsewhere in Spain. Here the pastry is a yeast-risen dough that wraps around layers of sliced meat, peppers and tomato. It emerges smoothly golden-glazed from the oven to cut into thick wedges. Rigorous winters demand warming foods, provided in the pot by *pote gallega* and *caldo gallega*. The former is a chunky stew of local *chorizo* and *morcilla* (some of the best in Spain), root vegetables, white beans and tangy greens. The latter is a thinned-down, souplike version of the *pote*.

Well-fed cows give rich milk, which goes into some of Spain's finest cheeses. Galicia's best are *tetilla* or "little breast," named for its characteristic rounded shape, and *San Simón*, pear-shaped, delicate and creamy, smoked over birchwood to a reddish orange rind.

Galicians do not indulge in their neighbors' love of cider, but make wines in the style of the Portuguese *vinho verde* — light, crisp and greenish, with a hint of spritz. These cannot, however, surpass the wines of Albariño from the demarcation region of Rías Bajas. But to finish a meal, the Galician turns away from wine to *aguardiente*, a potent grape liqueur that is flamed in a pottery bowl as *quemada* or "witch's brew." It's fierce on its own, deliciously warming in coffee.

CALDO GALLEGO
GALICIAN BROTH

SERVES 6–8

The pride of the cuisine of the inland parts of this northwestern region of Spain is *caldo gallego*, a thick broth that transposes into its stewlike cousin *pote gallego*. The superb local pork, in the form of a smoky cured bacon, many kinds of vegetables — for they grow here in plenty — and dried beans are the ingredients for this humble and hearty meal in a pot.

The peppery local green vegetable *grelos* (turnip tops) can be replaced by beet greens (beetroot tops), giant radish greens or collard greens (silverbeet). Generous and outgoing, the Galicians traditionally serve *caldo gallego* after an already copious main course at a banquet dinner.

1 cup/180 g/6 oz haricot (navy) beans, soaked overnight

6 oz/180 g *chorizo* sausages

1 ham (bacon) hock

3 thick slices (about 200 g/7 oz) smoked bacon or ham

8 cups/2 1/2 qt water or beef/veal stock

1 lb/500 g potatoes, peeled and cubed

2 medium turnips, peeled and chopped

1 medium onion, chopped

1 large carrot, peeled and chopped

2 cups/200 g/7 oz chopped cabbage

2 cups/200 g/7 oz chopped turnip or other greens

3 cloves garlic, chopped

salt and pepper

Place beans, whole *chorizo*, ham hock and sliced ham in a pot with the water. Bring to a boil and reduce heat; simmer for 2½ hours, skimming the surface from time to time. Remove meat. Slice sausage, remove ham from hock and chop, dice the smoked ham, and return to the pot. Add vegetables and garlic and continue to simmer until they have become very tender and are starting to break up and thicken the broth, adding more water or beef/veal stock as needed. Check for seasoning, adding salt and pepper. Serve hot with warm, crusty rolls.

Tip: A little virgin olive oil floated on the surface of the soup adds extra flavor and is said to aid digestion.

Vieiras Gratinadas a la Gallega

SCALLOPS AU GRATIN

SERVES 4 AS A FIRST COURSE (*TAPA*)

12 large fresh scallops in their shells

2–3 cloves garlic, finely chopped

1 medium onion, finely chopped

3 oz/90 g *jamón serrano* or other cured ham, finely chopped

2 tablespoons olive oil

½ cup/30 g/1 oz fresh white breadcrumbs

3 teaspoons chopped parsley

salt and pepper

lemon wedges

Loosen the scallops from their shells and place the shells on baking pans. Sauté the garlic, onion and ham in olive oil until lightly colored. Add the breadcrumbs, parsley, salt and pepper and mix well. Spoon onto the scallops and spread evenly. Place in a preheated 425°F/210°C/Gas 7 oven for about 12 minutes or until the surface is crisp and golden brown. Serve at once with wedges of lemon.

Tip: If scallops in the shell are unobtainable, purchase 20 oz/300 g sea scallops with or without coral. Place them in buttered individual or one large ramekin and cover with the topping. Bake until crisp.

Vieiras al Albariño

SCALLOPS POACHED IN ALBARIÑO WINE

SERVES 4 AS A FIRST COURSE, 2 AS A MAIN COURSE

Albariño de Fefiñanes, the aristocrat of Galician wines, is produced at the palace of Marqués de Figueroa using *albariño*, the best white grape of the district. Other wines made across the border in Portugal with the same grape have a typical hint of effervescence, characterizing them as *vinho verde*. They are used to poach shellfish and fish, and are particularly good with sole.

20 large sea scallops, with coral

1½ cups/400 ml/13 fl oz *albariño* or other light white wine

1 small carrot, peeled and sliced

1 small onion, sliced

2 cloves garlic, chopped

1 bay leaf

2 sprigs parsley

½ teaspoon salt

4 black peppercorns

2 teaspoons cornstarch (cornflour)

2 tablespoons light cream

1 teaspoon finely chopped parsley

lemon juice

Rinse the scallops and drain. Mix the wine, vegetables, herbs and seasonings in a stainless steel or glass saucepan. Bring to a boil and simmer for 6 to 7 minutes. Reduce heat, add the scallops and poach for 2 to 3 minutes. Remove with a slotted spoon and keep warm. Strain the sauce and return to the pan. Boil until reduced by half. Mix cornstarch with the cream and stir into the sauce. Simmer gently until thickened, stirring frequently. Adjust seasonings, adding chopped parsley, lemon juice and salt and pepper to taste. Serve on scallop shells or on a bed of rice.

CIGALAS
SALTWATER CRAYFISH

SERVES 4

The French call them *langoustines*, which is not to confuse them with the large shrimp the Spanish call *langostinos*. *Cigalas* are saltwater crayfish, and may also be called Dublin Bay prawns. Looking like a miniature lobster with a coral-colored shell and two large white-tipped claws, they are usually served simply boiled in salted water; the meat extracted from tail and claws is dipped into a garlicky *alioli*. Freshwater crayfish are *congrejos del rio*.

12 *cigalas*

1½ teaspoons salt

¾ cup *alioli* made with egg (page 273)

Bring a large pan of water to a boil, add *cigalas* and salt and boil for 10 minutes. Remove with tongs and drain on rack. Break off tails and claws and arrange on a plate with crab crackers. Serve the *alioli* in small dishes for dipping.

Tip: The *cigalas* can also be poached in wine; see *Vieiras al Albariño* on page 228.

ALMEJAS A LA MARINERA
CLAMS STEAMED IN WINE

SERVES 4

All shellfish respond to this treatment, gentle steaming in white wine with herbs, but it is particularly good with clams and mussels. They should first be soaked in cold water overnight so they expel any sand. The beards should be removed from the mussels.

2½ lb/1.2 kg fresh clams (or mussels), soaked overnight

1 medium onion, very finely chopped

2 tablespoons olive oil

2 large sun-ripened tomatoes, seeded and chopped

4 cloves garlic, chopped

1½ cups/350 ml/12 fl oz dry white wine

1 teaspoon sugar

salt and pepper

1 tablespoon finely chopped parsley

lemon wedges

Drain the clams (or mussels) and scrub if necessary under running cold water. In a large pan cook the onion gently in the oil until golden and softened. Add the tomatoes and cook to a thick pulp. Add the garlic, wine, sugar, salt, pepper and 1 cup/250 ml/8 fl oz water. Put in the shellfish, cover the pan tightly and cook over high heat, shaking the pan to encourage the shells to open. Remove shellfish as they open, continuing to cook the remaining ones; discard any that do not open. Boil the liquid briskly until well reduced. Strain over the shellfish and add the parsley. Serve with wedges of lemon.

PULPO Á FEIRA
OCTOPUS FESTIVE STYLE

SERVES 6 (*TAPA*)

This simple Galician dish of stewed octopus is often enjoyed by Spanish families on festive occasions. It is one of the most popular *tapa* dishes, when it is known as *pulpo a la gallega*. This traditionally uses a 5- to 6-lb octopus, which must be tenderized by beating and then simmered for several hours. But whole baby octopus, weighing about 4 oz/120 g, can be cooked in the same way and served as a first course. The dish is excellent on a lunch buffet.

3-lb/1.5-kg octopus (or use the same weight of baby octopus)

5–8 cloves garlic, finely chopped

2½ teaspoons sweet paprika

salt and pepper

½ cup/120 ml/4 fl oz olive oil

chopped fresh herbs (parsley, dill)

1 medium onion, sliced

Turn the body part of the octopus inside out and trim away the inedible parts, then cut away eyes and mouth sections. Rinse thoroughly. Place the octopus in a heavy saucepan with 1 cup/250 ml/8 fl oz water, cover tightly and cook over very low heat for about 1½ hours or until it is tender enough to be easily pierced with a knife. (Small octopus does not require water and will be tender in about 35 minutes.)

Remove the pan from the heat and set aside until completely cold. Drain octopus and rinse under running cold water, rubbing off any fragments of skin. Cut into bite-size serving pieces. Mix the garlic, seasonings and oil and pour over. Garnish with chopped fresh herbs and onion rings and serve cold.

Tip: A sprinkle of red wine vinegar or lemon juice gives a tang to the dressing.

PERCEBES
ROCK BARNACLES

Percebes, pronounced per-thay-bes, are a most unusual type of rock barnacle found along the northwestern coast of Spain. They are about 4 inches (10 cm) long, shaped like the long toes or fingers of some prehistoric animal. They are eaten quickly boiled in salt water, or raw with an oil, garlic and lemon dressing.

Mix ½ cup/120 ml/4 fl oz good olive oil with 2 to 3 cloves garlic mashed to a paste with salt. Add lemon juice to taste. Break open the *percebes* and dip into the dressing before eating.

EMPANADA GALLEGA
GALICIAN PIE

SERVES 6

Where *empanadas* elsewhere in Spain are small crusty pies rather like the Cornish pasty of England, or even little bite-size canapes to eat as *tapas*, *empanada gallega* is a hearty family-sized pie. Fillings are many and various, but most popular is the meaty combination of *chorizo*, cured ham, veal and pork, or *bacalao* cooked with red peppers and onions. In Galicia most housewives make this *empanada* large enough to provide leftovers to serve cold.

1 recipe *empanada* dough
(page 269)

2 large onions, chopped

½ cup/120 g/4 oz lard

1 red bell pepper (capsicum),
seeded and chopped

1 green bell pepper (capsicum),
seeded and chopped

1 small hot red chili pepper,
seeded and finely chopped

1 clove garlic, finely chopped

salt and pepper

10 oz/300 g *chorizo* sausages, diced

3 oz/90 g *jamón serrano* or other
cured ham, diced*

8 oz/250 g lean pork or veal,
finely diced*

3 hard-boiled eggs, peeled and
sliced

2 tablespoons chopped parsley

1 large tomato, thinly sliced

¼ teaspoon powdered saffron

1 small egg, beaten

Prepare the dough and chill. Cook the onions in the lard over low heat until lightly colored and soft, about 15 minutes. Add the peppers and garlic and cook until partially softened, adding salt and pepper to taste. Divide the pastry in 2 parts, one slightly larger than the other. Roll the larger one out to fit a 10-inch/25-cm deep pie dish. Layer the *chorizo*, ham and veal on the pastry. Add the fried onions and peppers, the sliced hard-boiled egg and chopped parsley. Arrange the sliced tomato on top and season generously with salt and pepper. Roll out the remaining pastry and use to cover the top. Trim the edges and flute them decoratively. Make a small slash in the top to release steam.

Mix saffron with beaten egg and brush over the top of the pie. Bake in a preheated 375°F/190°C/Gas 5 oven for 50 minutes. Cut into wedges and serve hot or place on a rack to cool, then chill slightly.

Tip: A quick version of *empanada gallega* can be made by cooking the filling in advance for about 40 minutes, leaving out the hard-boiled egg. Use a short pastry cut into two rounds, one about 12 inches/30 cm in diameter and the other about 15 inches/38 cm. Pile the cooked ingredients on the smaller pastry with the sliced eggs on top. Cover with the larger pastry and pinch the edges together. Brush with egg and bake in a very hot oven for about 18 minutes.

*The *jamón serrano* and meat can be replaced with cooked ham.

EMPANADILLAS DE CEBOLLA Y ANCHOAS
ONION AND ANCHOVY TARTS

MAKES 24 (*TAPA*)

3 large onions, finely chopped

2 tablespoons olive oil

black pepper

2 cloves garlic, finely chopped

8 fillets salted anchovies, soaked in cold water for 1 hour, drained and finely chopped

2 tablespoons drained capers or chopped black olives

1 recipe *empanada* dough (page 269)

Sauté the onions in the oil over low heat for about 1 hour or until caramelized, adding pepper and garlic in the last few minutes. Add the anchovies and capers or olives and mix well. Roll out the dough very thinly, cut into 2-inch/5-cm rounds and use to line tartlet pans. Prick each one several times with a fork, then bake in a preheated 350°F/180°C/Gas 4 oven for 6 minutes. Place a spoonful of the filling in each pastry case. Return to the oven for a further 6 minutes, then serve at once.

CACHELADA GALLEGA
OCTOPUS CASSEROLE

SERVES 6–8

4-lb/2-kg octopus

2 large onions, chopped

5 cloves garlic, chopped

3 tablespoons olive oil

6 large sun-ripened tomatoes, chopped

black pepper

$\frac{1}{2}$ teaspoon cayenne pepper

$\frac{1}{2}$ teaspoon fennel seeds

1 cup/250 ml/8 fl oz red or dry white wine

12 small potatoes, peeled

12 clams in the shell, soaked overnight

1 cup/180 g/6 oz green peas

$\frac{1}{2}$ teaspoon powdered saffron

1 teaspoon sweet paprika

Clean the octopus (see recipe for *Pulpo à Feira*, page 230) in a saucepan of cold water. Bring to a boil; simmer for about 2 hours or until almost tender. Drain and rub under cold running water to remove any fragments of skin. Cut into chunks and set aside. Sauté the onions and garlic in the oil. Add tomatoes and cook for 6 minutes. Add pepper, cayenne, fennel seeds and octopus. Add the wine with 2 cups/500 ml/16 fl oz water and bring to a boil. Add the potatoes and simmer for 15 minutes. Add the clams, peas, saffron and paprika and simmer until the octopus is tender and sauce is thickened. Adjust seasoning and serve.

MERLUZA A LA GALLEGA
HAKE GALICIAN STYLE WITH POTATOES

SERVES 4

4 medium potatoes, peeled

2 medium onions, peeled

1 teaspoon salt

4 thick slices hake or cod, 180 g–220 g/6–7 oz each

3 tablespoons olive oil

6 cloves garlic, finely chopped

1 teaspoon sweet paprika

Thickly slice potatoes and onions. Place in a large saucepan with water to cover generously and add salt. Bring to a boil, reduce heat and simmer for about 18 minutes or until the potato can be easily pierced with a fork. Place the fish on the vegetables and push under the liquid; cover and cook gently for a further 7 to 8 minutes. Strain off the liquid (it can be used in a seafood soup) and place the vegetables and fish in a serving dish. Heat the olive oil to very hot. Toss in the garlic and paprika and cook only for a few seconds, as paprika burns easily and takes on a bitter flavor. Pour the flavored oil over the dish and serve at once.

MERLUZA CON ACELGAS
HAKE WITH CHARD LEAVES

SERVES 4

4 thick pieces hake, about 180–200 g/6–7 oz each

salt and pepper

all-purpose (plain) flour

5 tablespoons olive oil

1 small onion, finely chopped

1 clove garlic, chopped

1 large sun-ripened tomato, seeded and chopped

2 cups/500 ml/16 fl oz water or fish stock

3 cups/250 g/8 oz finely shredded Swiss chard (silverbeet) leaves

2 hard-boiled eggs, quartered

2 teaspoons finely chopped parsley

Cut the hake in halves, season with salt and pepper and coat lightly with flour. Fry in 3 tablespoons of the oil until golden, then remove and set aside. In another pan sauté the onion and garlic in the remaining oil until golden. Add the tomato and cook until pulpy. Add water or fish stock and the chard, and bring to a boil. Add the fish, season with salt and pepper and simmer for 10 minutes. Transfer to a serving dish, add the eggs and parsley and serve.

CALLOS A LA GALLEGA
TRIPE CASSEROLE WITH GARBANZOS AND HAM
SERVES 6

1 cup/180 g/6 oz garbanzos (chickpeas), soaked overnight

1¼ lb/650 g tripe, soaked

1 large onion, sliced

5 cloves garlic, sliced

½ cup/120 ml/4 fl oz olive oil

6 large tomatoes, chopped

2 sprigs fresh thyme

2 bay leaves

2 dried hot red chili peppers, seeded

1½ teaspoons salt

1 teaspoon black pepper

1 ham/bacon hock

6 oz/180 g *tocino*, bacon or cured ham

1 large green bell pepper (capsicum), seeded and chopped

8 oz/250 g *chorizo* sausages, sliced

2 tablespoon finely chopped parsley

Drain garbanzos and tripe. Cut tripe into small squares. Sauté the onion and garlic in half the oil for 4 minutes. Add tomatoes and cook briefly. Add the garbanzos, tripe, herbs, seasonings, ham hock, *tocino* and enough water to just cover. Bring to a boil and simmer for about 3 hours or until tripe and garbanzos are both tender, adding extra water as needed. Remove hock and ham. Skin the hock and cut the meat and ham into small pieces; return to the pot. Sauté the green pepper and *chorizo* in the remaining oil and add to the pot in the last half hour of cooking, together with half the parsley. Check seasoning and continue cooking until done. Sprinkle on remaining parsley to garnish.

FIDEOS CON ALMEJAS
SPANISH-STYLE NOODLES WITH BABY CLAMS
SERVES 4–6

2 medium onions, finely chopped

olive oil

4 large sun-ripened tomatoes, peeled, seeded and chopped

2 cloves garlic, chopped

12 oz/375 g *fideos* or other fine noodles or vermicelli

3 cups/750 ml/24 fl oz fish stock

3 lb/1.5 kg venus clams, soaked overnight in cold water

Sauté the onions in oil, then add the tomatoes and garlic and cook to a thick paste. Boil the *fideos* in lightly salted water until almost tender, drain and place in a pot with the tomato sauce. Heat the fish stock in another pan, add the clams and cook until they open. Add to the pasta and tomato sauce, adding as much of the fish liquid as is desired to make the dish thick or soupy. Cook together for a few minutes, season to taste and serve.

Empanada Gallega, p.231

Lacón con Grelos (top), opposite; Pulpo á Feira (front), p.230

LACÓN CON GRELOS
PORK WITH TURNIP GREENS

SERVES 6–8

Tender young *grelos*, the shoots of young turnips are enjoyed as a vegetable, being simply boiled in salted water. Equally good are those from beets (beetroot), giant white radish (Japanese daikon) and miniature plants of the *brassica* (cabbage) family.

  Galicia is renowned for its *grelos*. Their slight astringency is a perfect balance to the richness of pork. Although sometimes eaten alone as a vegetable, *grelos* are more customarily cooked with *lacón*, the smoked or salted foreleg of pork for which the area is also famous. As *grelos* will obviously be hard to come by in other countries, they can be replaced by very young beet greens. The shoots of giant white (icicle/daikon) radish are also ideal for this dish.

3 lb/1.5 kg *lacón* (smoked/salted foreleg of pork)*

12 oz/350 g *chorizo* sausages, cubed

2lb/1 kg *grelos*, beet greens, silverbeet or mustard greens, lower stems removed, leaves chopped

salt and pepper

4 medium potatoes, peeled and cubed

Place the pork in a large pan with water to cover. Bring to a boil and reduce heat. Cook for 1½ hours. Add *chorizo* and *grelos* with salt and pepper to taste. Cook a further 30 minutes. Add potatoes and simmer gently until they begin to break up. Adjust seasoning. Serve in a deep dish with crusty bread.

* Pickled or salted pork can replace *lacón*.

FILLOAS
GALICIAN CREPES

1 recipe egg crêpe batter (page 267)

1 cup (250 g/8 oz) soft cream cheese

2 tablespoons confectioners' (icing) sugar

1 cup (250 ml/8 fl oz) cream

1 tablespoon anise liqueur or Pernod

2-3 tablespoons flaked toasted almonds

Prepare the batter mixture and set aside. Heat a non-stick or omelette pan over moderately high heat. Dip a ball of kitchen paper into vegetable oil or softened lard and rub the surface of an omelette pan until it shines. Reduce the heat slightly and cook thin crepes, stacking when done. Make the creamy filling by beating the cheese with the sugar until light and smooth. Whip the cream to soft peaks and fold in adding the liqueur. Stir in the nuts or use to garnish. Fill the crepes, roll and serve.

Tip: Delicious simply sprinkled with sugar, or serve with fresh or poached fruit.

QUEIMADA
"WITCHES" BREW

With a name that translates loosely as "fire drink," this is made with a Galician distilled spirit — *aguardiente de orujo* — that is similar to the French *marc* or Italian *grappa*.

Queimada is made in an earthenware bowl that has been well warmed. Stir 1 tablespoon sugar into $\frac{1}{4}$ cup/ 60 ml/2 fl oz of *aguardiente*. For effect, douse the lights. Lift up a spoonful of the spirit, light it and return it to the bowl so the remaining spirit ignites. Let it burn off. Drink when cool enough, or make into a potent nightcap by adding to freshly brewed black coffee.

TARTA DE SANTIAGO
ALMOND TART

SERVES 6

This classic tart is delicious served hot with whipped cream or crème fraîche, or cold in thin slivers with strong coffee. The cinnamon in the pastry gives it a rich brown color and heightened flavor.

1 recipe cinnamon pastry
(page 268)

1 lb/500 g blanched almonds

6 eggs, beaten

1 cup/250 g/8 oz sugar

1 teaspoon cinnamon

grated rind of 1 lemon

confectioners' (icing) sugar

Prepare the pastry and use to line a 9-inch/23-cm pie dish with sloping sides. Trim and flute the edge. In a food processor chop the almonds finely. Beat eggs and sugar together until creamy; add the cinnamon, rind and most of the almonds. Pour the mixture into the pie shell and sprinkle the remaining almonds evenly on top. Bake in a preheated 375°F/190°C/Gas 5 oven for about 45 minutes or until well browned. Sprinkle with confectioners' sugar and serve.

TORTA DE ACEITE
OLIVE OIL CAKE

2 cups/250 g/8 oz self-rising flour

$\frac{3}{4}$ cup/180 g/6 oz sugar

$\frac{3}{4}$ cup/180 ml/6 fl oz olive oil

2 eggs

$\frac{1}{2}$ cup/120 ml/4 fl oz milk

$1\frac{1}{2}$ teaspoons caraway seeds

Sift flour into a bowl and add sugar. Beat oil, eggs and milk until smooth and stir into the batter with caraway seeds. Pour into a greased and floured 9-inch (22.5-cm) round tin lined in the bottom with waxed paper. Bake in a preheated 350°F/180°C/Gas 4 oven until the cake feels firm and springy when touched in the center, and is golden brown on top, about 35 minutes. Remove and invert onto a rack. Remove the tin but leave the paper in place until the cake is cool. Slice to serve.

TAPAS AND TASCAS

What separates a *tasca* from a bar elsewhere in the world is its *tapas*. The delightful tradition of serving small snacks with drinks is found all over Spain, but attains its greatest heights in the major cities of Madrid, Barcelona, Sevilla, Santiago de Compostela and the smaller, sophisticated San Sebastián. *Tapa* means a cover or lid, and the association with appetizers is thought to have come from the old habit of placing a slice of bread or a piece of ham on top of one's wine glass (probably to keep out insects). This edible "lid" was the precursor of modern-day *tapas*, which now number in the hundreds in variety. One bar in Madrid offers over eighty different *tapas* on the menu! *Tapas* are tiny appetizers, no more than a mouthful or three, and can range from the most basic — a sliver of ham or cheese — to quite elegant and sophisticated hors d'oeuvre and canapes. Any small serving of food can be classed as *tapas*. A single grilled quail, two little fried croquettes, a bowl of *nécoras* (small crabs) in paprika sauce, a toothpick loaded with cubed cheese and pickle, an anchovy rolled around a pickled chili, a single marinated artichoke heart, one perfect large scallop lightly cooked on the griddle.

Tapas are intended as appetizers, as a nibble before the meal, not as a meal in themselves. But I find myself drawn to this way of eating and often prefer a leisurely evening at different *tascas*, to dinner at a conventional restaurant. What then is a *tasca*? It's essentially the bar where Spaniards gather before lunch or dinner for a drink, a chat and *tapas*. The gregarious Spanish love to talk just about as much as they love to eat and drink, and are drawn to crowds where they can loudly, and often passionately, air their views on the world and its ways. In Spain you simply do not drink without eating, even if it is just the little dish of small olives or roasted nuts they promptly pass across with your glass of wine as soon as you've squeezed into a position at the bar. Wine, beer and cider are the usual *taberna* drinks, but many are happy to serve spirits and nonalcoholic drinks. *Tascas* are usually not elegant, but functional and atmospheric. They are often small, with standing room only and space for no more than thirty and a limited number of specialty *tapas* on their menu. But some can be quite cavernous, filling up with a hundred noisy patrons at peak hours and fashionably abuzz with action and noise. You're not meant to dine, simply to snack, so most *tascas* do not have seating or tables. Most people have their favorite *tasca*, where they can be sure to find familiar faces and their favored *tapas*. But many choose to go *de tapas*, barhopping from one place to another in search of the best *tapa* in each. They may find bowls of stewed snails dripping with chili, garlic and paprika-laden sauce in one, to mop up with coarse and crusty bread; in another, elegant *vol au vents* filled with creamed salmon; further afield, crunchy boiled shrimp fresh from the sea or *chipirones* (minuscule squid) in a wash of inky sauce. They may know that one tiny corner bar does the very best *callos a la madrileña* (braised tripe) in town, or that the ham in another bar has just that edge of flavor over all the others, or that the *empanadas* are crisp and fuller than anywhere else, or that a *flamenco* busker is likely to be around a certain bar if you're there at the right time. You can tell at a glance if a *tasca* is a popular one, not by the number of habitués, as the clientele is a floating one — crowded one minute, virtually empty the next awaiting a new influx — no, rather by the condition of the floor. Eating with the fingers is an essential part of the fun of snacking in *tascas*. Normal table habits are forgotten as bar floors disappear under a snowy sea of abandoned tiny paper napkins and used white wooden toothpicks, and acquire a crunchy overlay of shrimp shells, discarded bones and ends of rolls.

The accounting systems employed in these busy bars are various and often quite ingenious. Some use colored markers, others slips of paper to indicate how many plates have gone to a particular table or group. Some have a board on which they mark each customer's "score" of dishes. Some trust to the honor system, the clients simply telling the waiter what has been eaten from the food on display. In others you pay as you eat.

Tapas are easy to cook at home and wonderful for entertaining. Serve the more substantial ones as first courses, the bite-size ones and finger foods as hors d'oeuvre. And they are great party food. Go for variety; many can be made in advance and reheated in the oven. Mix and match from my collection, or use them for inspiration and invent your own. The only restriction is your imagination. In each regional chapter we have also designated dishes which can be served as *tapas*.

CALAMARCETS CON AJO Y PEREJIL
BABY SQUID SAUTÉED WITH GARLIC AND PARSLEY

1 lb/500 g fresh baby squid

½ cup/120 ml/4 fl oz extra virgin olive oil

2 teaspoons coarse salt

5 cloves garlic

2 tablespoons chopped parsley

Clean, rinse and dry the squid. Heat the oil in a sauté pan and add the salt. Heat briefly. Add squid and sauté for about 30 seconds, then add the garlic and parsley and cook just long enough for the squid to turn white.

OSTIONES A LA GADITANA
OYSTERS CÁDIZ STYLE

24 fresh oysters

1 teaspoon very finely chopped garlic

1 teaspoon very finely chopped parsley

$\frac{1}{3}$ teaspoon freshly cracked black pepper

$\frac{1}{4}$ teaspoon hot paprika

3 tablespoons fine dry breadcrumbs

olive oil

lemon wedges

Remove the top shells from the oysters and loosen oysters from their lower shell. Arrange on a baking sheet. Evenly dress them with garlic, parsley, pepper and paprika, then cover each with a fine coating of breadcrumbs. Add a few drops of oil and place in a very hot oven or under the broiler/grill until they are well warmed. Serve with lemon wedges.

GAMBAS AL JEREZ
SHRIMP (PRAWNS) IN SHERRY

The strong flavor of sherry goes well with fresh shrimp. Use this recipe also for crayfish and scallops.

12 medium-size fresh shrimp (prawns) in the shell

2 tablespoons olive oil

3 tablespoons dry sherry

salt and white pepper

$\frac{1}{3}$ teaspoon Tabasco sauce

1 tablespoon chopped parsley

Peel the shrimp, leaving the tails in place. Slit down center backs and remove the intestinal vein. Rinse the shrimp and dry. Sauté in the oil until they change color, then add the sherry and cook on high heat until the liquid has almost evaporated. Add salt and pepper to taste, the Tabasco and chopped parsley. Serve at once with toothpicks or in small dishes over saffron rice or plain white rice.

GAMBAS AL AJILLO
GARLIC SHRIMP (PRAWNS)

24 medium-size shrimp (prawns) in the shell

$\frac{2}{3}$ cup/150 ml/5 fl oz mild olive oil

5-6 cloves garlic, finely chopped

lemon wedges

Remove heads from shrimp if desired, although usually they are left whole. Heat oil to smoking point. Sauté the shrimp with garlic over fairly high heat until they turn pink, about 2 minutes. Serve immediately with bread for dunking or on a bed of boiled rice. Garnish with lemon wedges.

CHANQUETES FRITOS
FRIED MINIATURE ANCHOVIES

1 lb/500 g *chanquetes* or whitebait

1 teaspoon salt

1 cup/120 g/4 oz all-purpose (plain) flour

3 cups/750 ml/24 fl oz mild olive oil

Rinse and thoroughly dry the fish. Mix salt and flour in a paper or plastic bag, add the fish and shake the bag until the fish are evenly coated. Heat olive oil to smoking point, then reduce heat slightly. Pick out the fish, discarding excess flour. Fry in handfuls until crisp and golden, drain well and serve at once.

CRISP FRIED SARDINE BONES

2 teaspoons lemon juice

24-30 fresh sardine or anchovy backbones

1 teaspoon black pepper

2 teaspoons sweet paprika

1 teaspoon salt

$\frac{3}{4}$ cup/90 g/3 oz all-purpose (plain) flour

3 cups/750 ml/24 fl oz frying oil*

Sprinkle lemon juice over the backbones and let stand for 20 minutes. Mix the pepper, paprika and salt and sprinkle evenly over the bones, then coat lightly with flour. Heat the oil and fry the bones in batches until crisp and well browned. Drain on paper towels and serve hot.

* Do not waste good olive oil on this dish as it will become too "fishy" to use again.

Tip: They are delicious served with a slightly sweet chili sauce.

SOLDADITOS DE PAVÍA
FRIED SALT COD STICKS

Lined up on a plate, these golden sticks of *bacalao* are like little Roman soldiers on parade.

1 lb/500 g prepared *bacalao* (page 266)

2 tablespoons lemon juice

1$\frac{1}{2}$ teaspoons sweet paprika

2 tablespoons olive oil

$\frac{1}{4}$ teaspoon black pepper

1 recipe saffron batter (page 268)

4 cups/1 l/32 fl oz olive or vegetable oil

Cut the *bacalao* into fingers and place in a dish. Mix the lemon juice, paprika, olive oil and pepper, pour over the *bacalao* and let stand for 20 minutes. Prepare the batter and set aside for 20 minutes.

Heat the oil in a wide pan. Dip the fish into the batter and slide into the hot oil. Fry until the *soldaditos* are puffed and golden. Drain on a rack covered with paper towels and serve hot.

Tip: Can be made with fresh cod or other thick white fish fillets.

BUÑUELOS DE BACALAO
SALT COD FRITTERS

MAKES 36

There are many interpretations of this dish. Some cooks prepare a batter rather like that of *croquetas*, using mashed potato or a thick bechamel sauce to thicken it; others simply batter little cubes of prepared *bacalao*. In still other recipes the fish is flaked and stirred into a light batter of egg whites.

1 small onion, very finely chopped

1 tablespoon olive oil or butter

2 cloves garlic, mashed

6 oz/180 g prepared *bacalao* (see page 266)

1½ cups smoothly mashed cooked potato

2 eggs, separated

1 teaspoon finely chopped parsley

1 cup/120 g/4 oz self-rising flour

salt

6 cups/1.5 l/1½ qt oil for frying

Sauté the onion in the oil or butter until softened. Add the garlic and sauté briefly. Drain and flake the fish; stir in the onion and potato with the egg yolks and parsley. Add the flour and salt to make a very thick batter. Whisk the egg whites well and fold into the mixture. Heat the oil. Drop tablespoons of the mixture into hot oil to dry until golden and floating on the surface, turning twice during cooking to color evenly. Drain on a rack covered with paper towels and serve very hot.

CALAMARES FRITOS
FRIED SQUID

10-12 fresh squid, skinned, cleaned

1 teaspoon sweet paprika

⅓ teaspoon cayenne pepper

1 teaspoon salt

¼ teaspoon black pepper

1 cup/120 g/4 oz all-purpose (plain) flour

2 eggs, beaten

3 cups/750 ml/24 fl oz olive or vegetable oil

lemon wedges

Cut the squid into narrow rings and dry on paper towels. Place paprika, cayenne, salt, pepper and flour in a paper bag. Add squid and flour lightly and evenly, then remove, dip into egg and flour again. Heat oil to smoking point, then reduce heat slightly. Fry the squid in small handfuls for about 20 seconds only, and remove on a slotted spoon or strainer. Drain well on absorbent paper before serving hot with lemon for squeezing.

ANCHOAS FRITAS A LA CATALANA
FRIED SALTED ANCHOVIES CATALAN STYLE

The anchovies fished off the coast of Catalonia are plump and excellent to eat grilled or shallow-fried in olive oil. Many are canned in oil or salt for domestic consumption or export sales. Salted anchovies are preferred for this dish, although oil-packed ones can be used if they are drained and well rinsed. Cooked in this airy wine batter, their crisp saltiness makes an appetizing companion to drinks.

24-36 small salted anchovies

½ cup/60 g/2 oz all-purpose (plain) flour

1 cup/250 ml/8 fl oz dry white wine

4 cups/1 l/32 fl oz olive oil

Soak the anchovies in cold water for 1 hour to remove salt; rinse well and drain. Dry on paper towels. Beat the flour and wine together to make a light, thin batter. Heat the olive oil to very hot. Dip the anchovies one by one into the batter and slide into the oil. Cook about eight at a time until crisp and golden brown, turning once. Remove with a slotted spoon and drain well before serving.

GAMBAS REBOZADAS
FRIED SHRIMP (PRAWNS)

12 medium-size fresh shrimp (prawns) in the shell

½ cup/60 g/2 oz all-purpose (plain) flour

1 large egg, beaten

ice water

4 cups/1 l/32 fl oz deep frying oil

salt, pepper and paprika

Peel the shrimp, leaving the tails in place. Slit down center backs and remove the intestinal vein. Rinse and dry the shrimp. Make a thick but creamy batter with the flour, egg and ice water. Heat oil in a wide pan. Dip shrimp into the batter, then fry in the oil until golden. Remove with a skimmer and drain on paper towels. Sprinkle with salt, pepper and paprika and serve hot.

PESCADITOS REBOZADAS
FRIED SMALL FISH

24 small fresh sardines or 1½ lb/ 750 g fish fillets

salt

1 cup/120 g/4 oz all-purpose (plain) flour

6 cups/1.5 l/1½ qt deep frying oil

1 recipe saffron batter (page 268)

Gut the sardines and rinse well. Dry thoroughly, salt lightly and dust with flour. Heat the oil to moderately hot. Dip the fish into the batter and slide into the oil. Fry until puffed and golden.

If using fish fillets, cut crosswise into narrow fingers and cook in the same way.

MARISCOS
SHELLFISH

With an abundance of fine seafood at their disposal, Spanish restaurants and *tabernas* can offer a wide choice of the freshest of local shellfish, plus others imported from Portugal. Where seafood is featured at a *tasca* there will invariably be the strangely prehistoric looking Portuguese *percebes* and their fine *ostiones*, plus local *ostras*. Other shellfish are *navajas*, the long, slender razor clams; *mejillones* (mussels); *vieiras* (scallops); *almejas* (clams); and occasionally even spiny *crizos de mar* (sea urchins). Crustaceans — *gambas* and *camarones*, *cigalas* and little *nécoras* — are served simply boiled, to be eaten straight from their shells. Cold seafood is arranged appealingly on large trays packed in ice and dressed with lettuce and kale leaves, lemon and the usual staging of fish nets, glass floats and ships' lamps.

Don't be dismayed by the crunch of seafood shells underfoot at a bar specialising in seafood snacks. It's usually a sign that business is brisk, and that means freshness!

OSTRAS FRITAS
FRIED OYSTERS

24 oysters

1 tablespoon lemon juice

1$\frac{1}{2}$ cups/200 g/7 oz cornmeal

3 cups/750 ml/24 fl oz olive or vegetable oil

lemon wedges

Remove oysters from shells, or drain bottled oysters and sprinkle with lemon juice. Coat thickly with cornmeal.

Heat the oil in a wide pan and fry the oysters in two batches until golden; do not overcook or they will toughen and become bitter. Remove with a skimmer, drain and serve hot with wedges of lemon.

SARDINAS EN ESCABECHE
MARINATED SMALL FISH

12 fresh anchovies or sardines

3 tablespoons olive oil

$\frac{1}{2}$ cup/120 ml/4 fl oz white wine vinegar

1 cup/250 ml/8 fl oz water

1 teaspoon black peppercorns

bay leaves

1 sprig fennel

Slit behind the head of each anchovy or sardine and pull away the fillets. Save the backbones to fry separately (see Crisp Fried Sardine Bones, page 242). Fry briefly in hot oil, then place in a dish. Pour on the remaining oil. Heat vinegar with water, peppercorns, bay leaves and fennel and pour over the fish. Let stand for at least 6 hours before serving.

TORTILLA
SPANISH OMELETTE

5 tablespoons olive oil

3 large potatoes, peeled and thinly sliced

1 medium onion, very thinly sliced

6 eggs, lightly beaten

salt and black pepper

In a non-stick 9-inch/23-cm pan heat half the oil and fry the potatoes until tender and only very lightly colored; it is vital that the potatoes do not become crisp and dry at the edges. Remove or push to one side of the pan. Fry the onion until soft and lightly golden. Remove from the pan with a slotted spoon and mix the potatoes and onion into the eggs, adding salt and pepper. Reheat the pan with the remaining oil and, when it is very hot, pour in the *tortilla* mixture. Reduce the heat and cook gently until the underside is golden and firm. Use a spatula no more than 1½ inches/4 cm wide to shape the edge of the *tortilla* as it cooks so that it is of even thickness right across, not tapering off at its perimeter. Select a plate the same size as the tortilla, fitting inside the rim of the pan. Place it directly on the *tortilla*. Invert the pan so the omelette is transferred to the plate, then return the pan to the heat. Slide the omelette back in to cook the other side; cook gently until it feels firm to the touch. Invert again or slide onto a serving plate and cut into wedges to serve.

EMPAREDADOS DE PAN Y JAMÓN
LITTLE FRIED SANDWICHES

4 small, thin slices cooked ham

4 slices white bread (crusts trimmed), soaked in milk and squeezed dry

salt and pepper

1 large egg, beaten

1 cup/250 ml/8 fl oz olive oil

Place the ham on the bread, fold over and press down firmly with a weight. Let stand for 2 to 3 hours. Cut in halves and secure each with a toothpick. Sprinkle with salt and pepper and dip into the egg. Fry in hot oil until crisp and golden.

Tip: Replace the bread with very thin slices of veal, coat with flour and then egg and fry as above, or dust with crumbs and fry until golden.

ALBÓNDIGAS DE TERNERA O CORDERO
MEATBALLS OF VEAL OR LAMB

MAKES 24–30

1 lb/500 g finely ground (minced) lean veal or lamb

1 small onion, very finely chopped

1 clove garlic, finely chopped

2 tablespoons finely chopped parsley

½ teaspoon dried oregano, crushed

1¼ teaspoons salt

black pepper

1 egg

½ cup/60 g/2 oz all-purpose (plain) flour

1 cup/250 ml/8 fl oz olive oil

Sauce:

1 small carrot, diced

1 celery stalk, diced

1 small onion, diced

1½ tablespoons all-purpose (plain) flour

2 cups/500 ml/16 fl oz veal stock

In a bowl combine the ground meat with onion, garlic, parsley, oregano, seasonings and egg and knead to a smooth paste. Form into walnut-sized balls with wet hands. Roll in flour, then fry in ¾ cup/180 ml/6 fl oz oil until browned on the surface and cooked through, about 5 minutes. Remove and keep warm.

Pour off the oil and wipe out the pan. Heat the remaining oil and sauté the diced vegetables until golden. Sprinkle on flour and brown well, then pour in the stock and stir over high heat to make a sauce. Return the meatballs and simmer for 4 to 5 minutes. Serve hot.

HIGADITOS
LITTLE LIVER STICKS

12 oz/370 g calves' liver

salt and pepper

1 teaspoon sweet paprika

1 tablespoon dry sherry

1 cup/120 g/4 oz all-purpose (plain) flour

2 cups/500 ml/16 oz olive or vegetable oil

1 dried red chili, seeded and very finely chopped

1 teaspoon chopped garlic

2-3 teaspoons chopped parsley

Cut the liver into bite-size cubes, peeling off any fragments of skin. Season with salt, pepper and paprika, then sprinkle on the sherry. Roll in flour.

Fry in the oil until golden brown and cooked through. Drain off the oil and toss the liver with chopped chili, garlic and parsley for a few seconds. Serve.

BUÑUELITOS DE JAMÓN
HAM FRITTERS

4 oz/120 g *jamón serrano*, very finely diced

1 tablespoon olive oil

1 small onion, very finely diced

2 teaspoons chopped parsley

pinch each of salt and pepper

½ cup/60 g/2 oz all-purpose (plain) flour

½ teaspoon baking powder

2 egg whites, beaten to a froth

⅓–½ cup/90–120 ml/3–4 fl oz water

2 cups/500 ml/16 fl oz olive or vegetable oil

Sauté the ham in the oil until well colored, add the onion and fry until golden. Remove from the heat and stir in the parsley and seasoning. Beat flour and baking powder with the egg whites and water to make a smoother batter of pouring consistency. Let it stand for 20 minutes. Stir in the ham. Heat the oil almost to smoking point, then reduce heat slightly. Drop spoonfuls of the batter into the oil to fry until golden, turning once. Remove with a slotted spoon and drain well. Serve hot.

EMPANADA DE MOLLEJAS
SWEETBREAD PATTIES

2 lb/1 kg sweetbreads

2 eggs, beaten

1 cup/120 g/4 oz fine dry breadcrumbs

3 cups/750 ml/24 fl oz olive or vegetable oil

2 cups/500 ml/16 fl oz fresh tomato sauce

1 teaspoon hot paprika (optional)

2-3 teaspoons chopped parsley

lemon wedges

Soak sweetbreads in cold water for 2–3 hours, then drain. Place in a saucepan of cold water and bring to a boil. Remove from heat and allow to cool in water. Drain and trim away membranes. Place in pan of water and bring to a boil. Reduce heat and simmer for 20 minutes, then cool and drain. Cut into bite-size pieces. Dip sweetbreads into the egg, then coat with crumbs. Fry in hot oil until crumbs are golden. Arrange in a dish. Heat the tomato sauce, adding paprika and parsley. Pour over the sweetbreads and garnish with lemon wedges.

PALITOS DE QUESO FRITOS
SKEWERS OF FRIED CHEESE

½ lb/250 g firm cheese

all-purpose (plain) flour

1 egg, beaten

3 cups/750 ml/24 fl oz olive oil

salt

Cut the cheese into bite-size cubes and roll in flour. Dip into egg, then roll in flour again. Thread several pieces each onto small wooden skewers and fry until the surface is crisp and golden; do not overcook or the cheese will become tough and chewy. Serve hot, sprinkled with salt.

CIRUELAS RELLENAS
STUFFED PRUNES   SERVES 6

24 unpitted prunes

1 small onion, very finely chopped

90 g/3 oz bacon, very finely chopped

1½ tablespoons olive oil

3 chicken livers, chopped

salt and pepper

1½ teaspoons very finely chopped parsley

6 very thin slices *jamón serrano,* bacon or prosciutto

Make a slit in one end of each prune and squeeze out the pit. Sauté the onion and chopped bacon in the oil until softened. Add the livers and sauté until they change color, mashing with the back of a spoon. Add salt and pepper with parsley and mix well. Press a small amount of the filling into each prune. Cut the ham or bacon slices in half lengthwise, then cut each piece in half crosswise to make 24 pieces. Wrap a piece around each prune and secure with a toothpick. Place on a baking sheet and bake in a preheated 425°F/220°C/Gas 8 oven for about 5 minutes if using ham, 7 to 8 minutes if using bacon. Serve hot.

HUEVOS DUROS RELLENOS CON CREMA DE SALMÓN
EGGS STUFFED WITH CREAMED SALMON

6 hard-boiled eggs

6 oz/180 g canned salmon, well drained

1 tablespoon capers, very finely chopped

1 tablespoon very finely chopped onion

1-2 tablespoons mayonnaise

pepper (optional)

1 small slice smoked salmon or 12 small cooked, peeled shrimp (prawns)

2 slices lemon, cut into tiny wedges

Peel the eggs and cut in half lengthwise. Remove the yolks and mash three of them with the salmon, capers, onion and mayonnaise. Add a little pepper if desired. Spoon or pipe into the egg whites and decorate each with a sliver of smoked salmon or a shrimp and a wedge of lemon.

TORTA DE VERDURAS
VEGETABLE TART

1 small onion, finely chopped

1 clove garlic, finely chopped

3 tablespoons olive oil

2 cups/400 g/13 oz diced cooked vegetables (potato, carrot, green beans, cauliflower, zucchini)

½ cup/45 g/1½ oz cooked green peas

1 tablespoon finely chopped parsley

2 teaspoons finely chopped fresh herbs (parsley, thyme, oregano)

1 cup/250 ml/8 fl oz *salsa bechamel* (page 273)

3 eggs, well beaten

salt and pepper

Sauté the onion and garlic in the oil until softened, add the vegetables and sauté for a few minutes. Remove from the heat and add the parsley, herbs and bechamel. Stir in the beaten eggs with salt and pepper. Pour into a buttered 9-inch (22.5-cm) pie dish and bake in a preheated 375°F/190°C/Gas 5 oven for about 15 minutes until firm in the center. Cool and cut into small wedges or squares. Serve with a fresh tomato sauce or *salsa mayonesa* (see page 273).

ALCACHOFAS A LA VINAGRETA
ARTICHOKES IN VINAIGRETTE DRESSING

12 medium-size fresh artichokes

1 lemon

salt

¼ cup/60 ml/2 fl oz white or red wine vinegar

½ cup/125 ml/4 fl oz olive oil

1-2 teaspoons finely chopped parsley

Trim stems of artichokes flat with the base and rub with the cut lemon. Trim off tops of leaves. Place artichokes in a large saucepan with the lemon; add water to cover and 1 teaspoon salt. Bring to a boil and simmer for 45 minutes. Remove and drain well.

Cut artichokes into quarters. Whisk vinegar and olive oil together, adding parsley and salt. Arrange the artichokes on a plate and pour on the dressing. Serve cold.

PURÉ DE PIMIENTOS
RED PEPPER PURÉE

Roasted red peppers purée to vivid orange-red cream which makes a novel dip. Use it also as a sauce for grilled steaks and for pizzas.

4 large red bell peppers (capsicums)

4-5 large cloves garlic, unpeeled

¾ teaspoon salt

1 teaspoon ground cumin

½ teaspoon cayenne pepper

⅓ teaspoon black pepper

¼ cup/60 ml/2 fl oz heavy cream or olive oil

Roast the peppers and garlic in a hot oven until the skin of the peppers is blackened and blistered, without charring the flesh, and the garlic is soft to the touch. Wrap peppers in a kitchen towel for a few minutes, then peel and tear or cut the flesh into strips. Pass peppers and garlic through a sieve or purée briefly in a food processor (do not overprocess, or the mixture will become too aerated and the texture will be spoiled). Add the remaining ingredients and beat to a smooth paste. To serve as a dip, pour into a shallow dish and garnish with a design of finely chopped parsley, mint or basil. Serve with thinly sliced bread or crisp crackers.

To use as a pizza topping, spread the purée over raw pizza dough that has been sprinkled with olive oil. Dot with black olives, sliced *chorizo* or other spicy sausage, strips of anchovy fillet, sautéed onions and sliced tomato. Add a sprinkle of salt, crushed rosemary and a little grated cheese (optional). Bake in hot oven until the dough is crisp.

CROQUETAS DE JAMÓN YORK
HAM CROQUETTES   MAKES 24–30

½ lb/250 g *jamón de york* (cooked ham)

3 oz/90 g *jamón serrano* (cured ham or bacon)

½ teaspoon black pepper

2 hard-boiled eggs, chopped

2 tablespoons chopped parsley

1 egg

all-purpose (plain) flour

3 cups/750 ml/24 fl oz deep frying oil

Cut both types of ham into small cubes and chop in a food processor. Add pepper and hard-boiled eggs and chop until reasonably smooth. Add the parsley and whole egg and blend until smooth. Fold in enough flour to make a smooth paste, then form into small balls and coat with more flour. Fry in moderately hot oil until golden brown. Remove, drain well and serve hot with toothpicks.

Variation: Substitute chicken for the cooked ham.

TAPAS A LA PLANCHA

Snacks *a la plancha* (on the griddle) are popular, and many *tabernas* have a large metal *plancha* on which they prepare toasted sandwiches and griddle-cooked foods.

PESCADITOS A LA PLANCHA CON AJO Y PIMIENTA

Prepare small fish such as sardines by removing the backbone, as in *sardinas en escabeche*, page 245, or cut thick white fish fillets into strips and coat lightly with flour, brush with olive oil and cook on the griddle. In a small pan on the side of the griddle fry plenty of finely chopped garlic and a little chopped hot red chili pepper in olive oil. Pour the hot oil over the fish and serve immediately.

SARDINAS A LA PLANCHA

Allow about four 6-inch (15-cm) fresh sardines per serving. Gut by cutting away the whole stomach section; rinse and dry. Sprinkle with salt and set aside for 20 minutes. Brush with olive oil and cook on the griddle for about 40 seconds on each side. Serve with wedges of lemon.

OSTRAS, ALMEJAS Y VIEIRAS A LA PLANCHA

Fresh sea scallops, clams and large oysters in their shells are great cooked on a griddle. Place on the hot griddle long enough for the shell to spring open, then lift up the top shell and remove. Sprinkle a little lemon juice and olive oil onto scallops and cook until they turn white. Allow about 3 per person.

GAMBAS A LA PLANCHA

Large fresh shrimp (prawns) cooked *a la plancha* are unforgettable. Leave them unpeeled but slit them down the center back cutting through the shell. Pull out the dark intestinal vein. Cook about 1 minute on each side, depending on their size. Serve with lemon wedges.

CIGALAS/CANGREJOS DE RÍO A LA PLANCHA

Scampi (sea crayfish) and freshwater crayfish can be cooked whole on the griddle. Cook for several minutes on each side, until the shells develop a whitish look and feel fragile. Remove, split open and extract the cooked tails. Alternatively, slit in half lengthwise, brush with olive oil and cook cut side down for about $1\frac{1}{2}$ minutes, depending on size. Serve with lemon.

SETAS A LA PLANCHA

Large fresh mushrooms cook beautifully on a griddle. Splash on a little oil and toss the mushrooms on the hot surface until they begin to exude juices. At this point add chopped garlic, salt, pepper and lemon juice and cook briefly. Use a flat spatula to scoop them onto a plate.

A selction of tapas: black and green olives (top); Jamon Serrano (middle), p.261; Alcachofas a la Vinegreta (middle left), p.154;
Roasted marinated red peppers (front left); Queso Manchego (middle right), p.262; Boquerones en Adobo (front right), p.255

A selection of tapas: Calamares Fritos (middle left), p.243; Buñuelitos de Jamón (top), p.248; Gambas al Ajillo (front), p.241

BOQUERONES EN ADOBO
WHITE ANCHOVIES

30 fresh anchovies

1½ cups/375 ml/12 fl oz white vinegar

1 teaspoon salt

¾ cup/180 ml/6 fl oz olive oil

2-3 cloves garlic, very finely chopped

2-3 teaspoons finely chopped parsley

lemon juice

Cut off the anchovy heads; use the point of a knife to push the meat back from the end of the backbone and grasp it firmly. Hold the end of the fish and pull sharply backwards towards the tail. The backbone should come out cleanly, leaving the two fillets attached at the tail. Separate if preferred. Rinse and dry, place in a wide shallow dish and evenly pour on the vinegar. Add salt, cover with plastic wrap and let stand in a cool place overnight. Drain, rinse to remove excess vinegar and place in a serving dish with the remaining ingredients, adding lemon juice to taste.

CROQUETAS DE PESCADO A LA VALENCIANA

VALENCIAN FISH CROQUETTES

MAKES 18–24

1 lb/500 g thick white fish fillets (cod or haddock), cubed

2 green (spring) onions/shallots or scallions, very finely chopped

1 tablespoon chopped fresh dill

3 slices white bread (crusts trimmed), soaked and squeezed dry

2 eggs

1 tablespoon anise liqueur (optional)

1–2 tablespoons potato flour or dehydrated flaked potato

salt and pepper

½ cup/60 g/2 oz all-purpose (plain) flour

1 cup/120 g/4 oz fine dry breadcrumbs

2 cups/500 ml/16 fl oz olive or vegetable oil

Combine the fish and onions in a food processor and process to a smooth paste. Add the dill, bread, 1 egg, liqueur and potato flour and process to a thick paste, seasoning to taste with salt and pepper. Form into small croquettes. Coat with flour, then dip into the remaining egg, which has been well beaten. Coat with crumbs and chill for 1 hour. Fry in shallow oil until golden.

CANAPÉ DE FIAMBRES

Hors d'oeuvre of many kinds are offered in *tabernas* with drinks, and are served in the home with cocktails. Thin slices of fresh bread cut from baguette-style rolls, little cubes of day-old bread fried in olive oil, baked rounds of crisp pastry and commercial bite-sized *vol au vent* cases house the fillings. Allow 4 to 5 canapes per person.

1 small baguette

2 tablespoons mayonnaise

choice of *jamón serrano, lomo de cerdo, chorizo*

sliced pickles, stuffed olives, roasted pepper

Slice the baguette and spread one side of each slice with mayonnaise. Using a sharp round pastry cutter the same size as the bread, cut the meats and place on the bread. Garnish with a small piece of pickle, stuffed olive or roasted pepper pierced on a toothpick and inserted into the center of the canape.

CANAPÉS DE ROQUEFORT Y JAMÓN

1 small baguette

3 oz/90 g *queso cabrales*, roquefort, or other soft blue cheese

very thinly sliced *jamón serrano* or prosciutto

halved stuffed olives

Slice the baguette and spread thinly with the cheese. Cut the ham into narrow strips and roll up. Pierce a half olive with a small wooden pick, then insert into the ham and place in the center of the canape.

CANAPÉS DE FIAMBRES

1 small baguette

olive oil (optional)

24 anchovy fillets in oil, drained

strips of pimiento, drained

Slice the baguette and toast or fry in olive oil. Roll each anchovy around a strip of pimiento and pierce with a toothpick. Place on the toast and serve.

CANAPÉS DE CAVIAR Y HUEVOS DUROS
CANAPES OF CAVIAR AND BOILED EGG

1 small baguette

butter

4 hard-boiled eggs, sliced

2 oz/60 g black or red caviar

3 lemon slices, cut into tiny wedges

parsley sprigs

Thinly slice the baguette and spread with butter. Place an egg slice on each and top with a little of the caviar. Garnish with a small wedge of lemon and a tiny sprig of parsley.

TARTALETAS Y BARCOS

Can be served with cocktails or predinner drinks. Use either the Savory Pastry on page 269 or *masa para tartalets o barcos* on page 269. Or for simplicity, use purchased tartlet shells or vol au vent cases.

TARTALETAS DE GAMBAS
SHRIMP (PRAWN) TARTLETS
MAKES 36

36 medium shrimp (prawns) or 72 smaller ones, peeled

4 tablespoons butter

2 cloves garlic, very finely chopped

$\frac{3}{4}$ teaspoon freshly cracked black pepper

1 tablespoon finely chopped parsley

pinch of sweet paprika

1 tablespoon Spanish brandy

$1\frac{1}{2}$ tablespoons all-purpose (plain) flour

1 cup/250 ml/8 fl oz fish or chicken stock

parsley sprigs

Prepare the pastry and roll out thinly. Line 36 small tartlet tins with pastry and prick each one twice. Bake in a preheated 375°F/190°C/Gas 5 oven for about 12 minutes or until golden.

Sauté the shrimp in the butter until they change color; remove from pan. Add the garlic to the pan and sauté briefly, then add pepper, parsley and paprika and cook briefly. Add brandy to the pan and cook until evaporated. Sprinkle in the flour and cook until lightly colored. Add the stock and boil, stirring, until thickened. Return the shrimp to the pan and mix in evenly. Fill the tartlet shells and garnish with small sprigs of parsley. Serve immediately.

BARCOS DE JAMÓN
HAM BOATS
MAKES 36–48

1 recipe tartlet pastry (see page 269)

$\frac{1}{2}$ cup/120 ml/4 fl oz mayonnaise

1 cup/250 g/8 oz very finely chopped ham

$1\frac{1}{2}$ tablespoons finely chopped dill pickle (gherkin)

2 teaspoons finely chopped parsley

2–3 teaspoons finely chopped canned pimientos or stuffed olives

Prepare the pastry and form tartlet shells following the directions in the tartlet recipe. Mix the remaining ingredients together, spoon into the shells and serve.

PAN, BOCADILLOS Y TOSTA
BREAD, ROLLS AND TOAST

Traditional Spanish bread is of a firm, chewy and crusty style, wonderfully aromatic when baked in old-fashioned brick ovens. In general, bread is shaped into baguettes and round, flattish country-style loaves, but this varies from province to province. Spanish bread is made of freshly milled flour made from local wheat, and it is this freshness that is the key to its unique taste. In the country, rye and corn (maize) flour may be added to wheat flour to make a wonderful coarse bread such as that enjoyed by the Catalans as *pa amb tumàquet* (*pan con tomate*), or tomato bread. Spanish bread is almost never served with butter (the exception is in bigger hotels and restaurants where they cater to international taste, and perhaps in the far north where the butter is too delicious to avoid). Bread instead is eaten plain or drizzled with a good olive oil, with perhaps a sprinkle of salt.

Traditional Spanish bakers use no preservatives, so the bread stales quickly. Hence we find innumerable uses for "day-old" bread in Spanish cooking. *Migas* are fried breadcrumbs served as a breakfast dish. Fried squares or (more traditionally) triangles of bread are a common garnish, and breadcrumbs and croutons, either fresh or fried, are used to enrich and thicken sauces and soups, or to sprinkle on top of them.

In most *tabernas* (taverns), "open sandwiches" are available on request. Thick slices of baguette or enormous oval slices cut from a country loaf are topped with slices of ruby-colored local ham, cheese or whatever takes your fancy.

Bocadillos are fine-textured, crisply crusted white rolls and one of Spain's most popular snacks. I think the one that intrigues me most is the *bocadillo de tortilla*: a thick wedge of *tortilla española*, potato omelette, sandwiched in a plump roll. *Bocadillos* also come filled with *jamón serrano* and *quesos* (cheeses), type and quality dictating price. Or with sliced *chorizo*, with marinated anchovies, mackerel or bonito, with tenderloin of pork or grainy *morcilla*, with shellfish, or *mixto* — with several fillings together.

Tostas are thick slices from a round country-style loaf. They are topped with a variety of ingredients, led by salty anchovies.

Catalan tomato bread (see page 130) and other types of tostas (toasts) served in tabernas are made either with fresh bread or with lightly toasted older bread. Garlic-impregnated bread toasted over an open fire is delicious, as is the unusual *pan de costa al ajo* — a specialty of Málaga in which bread is spread with a paste of garlic, oil, orange juice and sweet pepper.

BOCADILLOS

Bocadillos de jamón are the indisputable leaders in Spanish snack foods. They are munched on trains and buses, at the bar of a *taberna*, under a tree outside a *posada*, at the beach, trekking in the mountains, as a midday snack in the fields. The roll should be fresh and crusty, with light-textured bread, no butter, and the ham the finest *jamón serrano* (cured ham) affordable — at least three slices stacked into the split roll. If your taste is towards something a bit more flavorsome, then *chorizo de salamanca*, a chunky salami-style Spanish sausage, is the choice, or several slices of *queso manchego* — or perhaps a roquefort style of cheese. And if your appetite demands it, there is the king of all snacks, the *bocadillo de tortilla*: sandwich a wedge of *tortilla española* (see page 39) into the split roll with no other embellishments.

TOSTA

From a flat, round, country-style loaf cut thick slices and toast lightly. Brush with a well-flavored olive oil or rub with the cut side of a very ripe tomato half so that the top is thinly covered with tomato pulp and is soft and moist. Top with several thin slices of *jamón serrano* (cured ham) or prosciutto, *queso manchego* or another cheese of your choice, or combine ham and cheese on one *tosta*. My favourite topping on toast smeared with cut tomato is neatly arranged oil-packed anchovies. It's a strong taste that demands an accompanying drink. Flaked tuna garnished with strips of roasted red pepper or canned pimiento is a welcome taste combination, as is a topping of the *puré de pimiento* on page 251. Or simply sprinkle on a quality olive oil, add a little salt and a squeeze of tomato.

PIMIENTOS CON PAN
PIMIENTO OPEN SANDWICH

MAKES 8

2 large red bell peppers (capsicums)

1½ tablespoons mayonnaise

8 slices baguette

2 teaspoons finely chopped capers

8 small onion rings

Roast the peppers in a hot oven for about 35 minutes or until the skin has darkened and blistered. Remove from the oven and wrap in a kitchen towel for a few minutes, then peel off the skins. Cut each pepper into four pieces, discarding seeds and internal membranes. Spread a little mayonnaise on one side of each bread slice and top with a piece of pepper. Pipe lines of mayonnaise over the top and garnish with the capers and onion rings.

PAN CON ENSALADA DE GAMBAS
SHRIMP SALAD ON OPEN SANDWICHES

MAKES 8

1½ cups/300 g/10 oz small peeled cooked shrimp (prawns)

1 small onion, very finely chopped

6-inch/15-cm celery stalk, very finely chopped

1 hard-boiled egg, chopped

1 tablespoon very finely chopped dill pickles (gherkin)

1 teaspoon very finely chopped capers

3 tablespoons mayonnaise

salt and pepper

8 slices fresh baguette

sliced lemon

parsley or dill

In a bowl mix the shrimp with the onion, celery and egg. Add pickles, capers and mayonnaise with salt and pepper to taste. Mound on the bread, smoothing at the edges. Garnish with slivers of lemon and little sprigs of parsley or dill.

PAN CON ROQUEFORT Y JAMÓN

OPEN SANDWICH OF BLUE CHEESE AND HAM

MAKES 8

2 oz/60 g roquefort or other soft blue-veined cheese

1 tablespoon sour cream

8 slices fresh baguette

8 small, thin slices *jamón serrano* or other cured ham

8 very small dill pickles (gherkins)

Mash the cheese with sour cream and spread over the bread. Wrap a piece of ham around each pickle and pierce with a toothpick. Place on top of the bread.

PAN CON SALMÓN AHUMADO

OPEN SANDWICH WITH SMOKED SALMON

MAKES 8

8 slices smoked salmon

8 slices fresh baguette

2 tablespoons mayonnaise

3 lettuce leaves, finely shredded

1 small onion, thinly sliced

1 tablespoon chopped capers

$\frac{3}{4}$ teaspoon finely grated lemon rind

Trim the salmon to fit the bread. Spread each piece of bread on one side with mayonnaise and cover with lettuce. Arrange a slice of smoked salmon on each and garnish with onion rings, chopped capers and lemon rind.

BANDERILLAS

Banderillas are the long darts, wound with colorful fringed fabric or paper, that are pierced into the back of the bull in the early stages of a bullfight. Little wooden skewers of food are given this same name in the *tabernas*, although in some parts they might be called *palitos*. Almost any food can be threaded onto these skewers to serve as *banderillas*. Popular choices are *jamón york, jamón serrano, chorizo, cheese, tuna or bonito in cubes with squares of roasted red pepper, marinated button mushrooms with salmon, quartered hard-boiled egg with pitted olives, marinated artichokes with onion, rolled anchovies with pickled hot peppers, and dill pickles (gherkins) with smoked eel.* Cut into $\frac{3}{4}$ inch (2 cm) cubes and thread about three pieces onto each skewer. Start and end the skewer with a cube of firm white bread.

RACIONES
COLD PLATTERS

Cold platters are one of the most popular snacks taken with drinks. Each bar has its own specialty. One may boast the very finest *jamón ibérica*, another the tastiest *queso manchego*. One may have perfected a pâté unlike any other and serve it in a thick wedge with crusty *pan*. Some may go upscale, offering *salmón ahumado* and *ostres*.

JAMÓN SERRANO

Indisputably the most important snack food in Spain is local ham. Like the Italian prosciutto, *jamón serrano* is salt-cured before undergoing a lengthy drying process that turns the meat a deep red-brown, interlayered with translucent white fat. Though originally made from the long, lean haunches of the native *cerdo ibérico*, a black pig, loss of much of the herd and a heavy demand has meant that the ham is now processed from other breeds of pig. Some *tabernas* specialize exclusively in hams, covering the ceilings of their establishments with row upon row of hams suspended from their hocks and decked underneath with little plastic umbrellas to catch the drippings. Aficionados covet the tender, intensely flavored *jamón de jabugo*, made only from *cerdo ibérico* fed on acorns in the province of Huelva, where they are reared in the Sierra de Aracena — the mountain range north of the Gulf of Cádiz. Hams of quality are now officially awarded *denominaciones de origen*, including the best from Aragón and Salamanca, from Granada and Cáceres. Price is usually indicative of their quality, a *jamón de jabugo* being as much as four times more expensive than some others. Local demand means that genuine *jamón serrano* is rarely available outside of Spain, but prosciutto or the smoked hams, such as the European Bayonne and Westphalian and American Smithfield, do just as well. Slice them thinly enough to be almost transparent, and arrange in an overlapping cartwheel formation on a flat plate. Serve with crusty rolls and olives.

CHORIZO

The spicy cured sausage that is the salami of Spain is a popular appetizer. Two of the best are the chunky *chorizo de Salamanca* and the finer-textured *chorizo de Pamplona*, but from there the range spreads into many types of thick or thin, light or dark, strong or mild-tasting cured sausages with names like *salcichada blanca Asturiana*, *sobrasada*, *longaniza*, *puro de lomo*. And with them in any display of good *charcutería* will be *lomo* — cured pork tenderloin compressed into a thick sausage shape, the surface red with paprika. Again, the best is made from *cerdo ibérico*.

Select a variety of well-flavored salamis and cured sausages, slice thinly and arrange in overlapping formation on a flat platter. Pile olives in the center and serve with crusty rolls.

TABLA VARIADA

Tabla variada is a plate of assorted cold cuts, known also in Spain as *fiambre*. *Jamón serrano*, *chorizo*, the dark crumbly *morcilla* or *morcón* (a rich blood sausage filled with whole-grain rice), *lomo* and *chicharrones Ibericos*, a sausage resembling a meaty "head cheese", are arranged together on a plate with olives. Serve with crusty bread.

QUESO MANCHEGO

When one speaks of cheese in Spain, what is meant is often simply *queso manchego*. One of the finest of the Spanish cheeses and quite possibly the most commonly eaten, it is only one of the many great Spanish varieties. *Queso manchego* was originally a ewes' milk cheese made by hand by shepherds in La Mancha, where the high plateau is home to hundreds of herds. Today it is mass-produced in many parts of Spain, and not always with ewes' milk, but modern techniques have meant that there is no loss of the characteristic sharpness of flavor that pronounces a fully ripened *queso manchego*.

   Queso manchego is served thinly sliced, arranged in cartwheel fashion on a plate, accompanied by bread and a dish of small olives. See page 281 for more on Spanish cheeses.

QUESO EN ACEITE

Certain Spanish cheeses, like the *pedroches* of Cordoba, the tasty *idiazábal* from Guipuzcoa province, and *Málaga* goats' cheese, are preserved in oil. Others are marinated in oil to serve as a snack dish with bread. A well-flavored salty cheese works best; it should be steeped in a good-quality olive oil. A sprinkling of dried herbs, a little black pepper and a bay leaf or two add their own taste dimension, as does a sliced clove of garlic.

   Slice cheese and cut into 2-in/5-cm squares. Place in a dish and cover with oil. Add the other ingredients and macerate for several hours before serving.

TABLA DE QUESOS

Tabla de Quesos is a platter of mixed cheeses, a popular choice in a *tapas* bar early in the evening or later in the night. The selection will be dictated to some extent by location and by the whim of the chef, but it usually includes a semi-cured or matured *queso manchego* or a *grazalema*, something creamy or mild which will probably be a goats' milk cheese, and perhaps a tangy or smoky cheese like *idiazábal*, a delicious ewes' milk cheese from the Basque country with the smoky flavor of hawthorn and beech. If you're lucky there will be a wedge of *cabrales*, the Spanish equivalent to roquefort, the best of which comes from Asturias. Prepare a selection of cheeses and serve with a good sherry. See page 281 for more on Spanish cheeses.

SALMÓN AHUMADO

Spain is renowned for its seafood dishes and produces a number of its own smoked specialties. Atlantic and North Sea smoked salmon are major imports enjoyed in many better restaurants and served by discerning *taberna* managers. As a *racion* the presentation is simple: chunky slices of salmon spread on a plate with wedges of lemon. Where the *nueva cocina* has established a foothold, *salmón ahumado* teams up imaginatively with seaweeds, with exotic salad greens, with cold shellfish and in hot soups in recipes found elsewhere in this book.

TABLA DE AHUMADOS

Tabla de Ahumados are selected cuts of smoked salmon, shellfish, trout, *anguila* (eel) and *mojama* (tuna) arranged with cooked shrimp and marinated mussels. Select your choice of smoked seafoods and arrange on lettuce with lemon wedges. *Alioli* or a chunky tartar-style sauce can accompany.

NUECES
NUTS

Spain is one of Europe's major nut-producing countries and in particular has extensive almond groves, so little wonder they appear so frequently in the cuisine. Delicious straight from their shells, nuts as a snack are also roasted if they are to go with drinks. At a *tapas* bar a small plate of nuts, and often of olives as well, usually accompanies your first drink.

ALMONDS

Whole almonds in their shells can be roasted in a slow oven, which takes about 40 minutes and calls for frequent tasting in the last stages as there is no outward indication of their readiness.

Shelled almonds can be roasted by spreading on a baking sheet and roasting in a slow oven for about 40 minutes, shaking the pan occasionally to turn them. Or roast in a microwave for about 5 minutes (depending on how many nuts are done in one batch). They tend to turn a deeper color inside than on the surface, so it is wise to check by breaking one open when it is nearly time. The brown skin can be rubbed off the hot roasted almonds if desired.

Blanched roasted almonds are made by first boiling the nuts for a minute, then leaving them in the hot water until the skins loosen. Rub the skins off under running cold water and spread the nuts on a tray to dry. Roast in a slow oven until they are dry and golden.

Glazed almonds are deliciously salty. Toast shelled almonds, then brush with a little olive oil and toss in fine salt until coated. Dry on a fine mesh rack.

ENTREMESES
MIXED PLATTERS

Entremeses are the Spanish equivalent of the Italian antipasto — a platter of cold foods served at the start of a meal. They are not usually served at *tascas*, unless there are tables where one can sit to dine. Many are salads, and any of the salads throughout this book could be served in this way. But generally the *entremés* is a platter of different components. Chopped vegetables in mayonnaise, such as in the following recipes, might be mounded in the center and surrounded by sliced cold meats and sausage, a few olives, and marinated or pickled vegetables such as beets, cucumber, cauliflower or artichokes. Larger platters to serve several diners might also include some crisply fried sardines, a few stalks of asparagus or fresh cooked shrimp (prawns), some roasted red pepper, a couple of *albóndigas*.

ENTREMÉS DE FIAMBRES
AN APPETIZER OF COLD CUTS

For each person allow:

1 cup/250 g/8 oz cold mayonnaise-dressed salads (see page 376)

4–6 slices cold cuts such as ham, *chorizo*, salami, roast pork

Press the salad into a small bowl and invert in the center of a plate. Surround with the cold meats. Serve chilled.

ENTREMÉS MIXTO
MIXED APPETIZER

For each person allow:

1 slice *jamón serrano* or other cured ham

1 slice *jamón york* or other cooked ham

1 slice *chorizo* or other spicy sausage

1 cup/250 g/8 oz mayonnaise-based salad

4–6 green olives

2 marinated artichoke hearts

2 slices dill pickle (gherkin) or pickled cauliflower

2 peeled cooked shrimp (prawns)

Overlap the cold meats on one side of the plate. Press the salad into a small bowl and invert onto the center of the plate. Arrange the olives, artichokes and pickles on the other side, and place the shrimp on top. Serve chilled.

JAMÓN CON HIGOS
HAM WITH FIGS

With its distinct flavor and slightly chewy texture, *jamón serrano*, the well-flavored brick-red ham of Spain, is a favored ingredient for *entremeses*. It is thinly sliced and arranged slightly overlapping on a flat dinner plate, partnered with all manner of fresh fruits, vegetables, salads and other smoked, cured meats and cold cuts. Sliced melon is also a natural partner to ham. In Spain there is *ogen* in April, *cantaloupe* in May, the aromatic *melón reticulado* and honeydews midyear, *tendral* and *elche* from October on.

For each person allow:

5 thin slices *jamón serrano* or prosciutto/pancetta

3–4 fresh figs, halved or quartered depending on their size

Arrange the ham and figs attractively on a plate. Serve lightly chilled.

Variation: Substitute sliced avocado or melon for the figs.

Basic Recipes

Picada

Makes about $\frac{1}{2}$ cup

Picada *is a preparation of ground ingredients used to flavor, thicken and enrich a sauce, casserole or stew. There are hundreds of variations, but the basic ingredients are garlic, nuts (almonds and hazelnuts), fried bread and parsley. Much like a good Italian* pesto, *the ingredients should first be pounded in a mortar or spice mill so that the nuts and bread are pulverized together and no longer grainy in texture. Then, if desired, it can be finished off in a food processor.*

1 slice day-old white bread, crusts trimmed

$\frac{1}{4}$ cup/60 ml/2 fl oz olive oil

3 cloves garlic, peeled

20 toasted, blanched almonds

10 toasted, blanched hazelnuts

3 small sprigs parsley

large pinch of salt

olive oil

Fry the bread in oil until golden. Drain and cut into small pieces. Pound in a mortar with the garlic and nuts until pulverized. Chop the parsley in a food processor or blender with the salt. Add the pulverized ingredients and slowly add oil, pulsing the motor to process to a smooth, thick paste. Store in an airtight container in the refrigerator for up to a week.

Fried Bread

Day-old bread is called for in many Spanish recipes. Country-style coarse-grain bread without preservatives is the preferred kind; the bread should be yesterday's, so that it has lost some of its moisture, making it less oil-absorbent when fried. If using bread containing preservatives, partially dry the slices in the microwave oven or leave out overnight to dry before use. A slice as required in these recipes would be from a loaf of standard size; if using a large, round country-style loaf, cut each slice in two. Remove crusts and cut bread into $\frac{1}{2}$-inch (1.2-cm)-thick slices. Fry in hot oil until golden brown. Drain and use as required. Use standard square slices of white bread, dried overnight and with crusts removed, for making the fried toast triangles used to garnish many dishes. For effect, dip the point or one edge into very finely chopped parsley as soon as the bread is removed from the oil.

Sofrito

Makes about 4 cups

The Catalans call this sofregit *and use it extensively. It derives from a Catalan word that means "to lightly fry", but in fact is a technique of very slowly frying ingredients until they are reduced to a pastelike consistency, which is then used to flavor and thicken a sauce. The traditional components are onions and tomatoes, although this medieval procedure actually began only with onions and leeks. Sometimes ham or salt pork and red peppers are added. Sofrito is the foundation of a dish; the longer it cooks, the more intense its flavor. An acceptable sofrito can be made in 20 minutes or so, but slow, gentle cooking gives it a depth of flavor that takes the taste from ordinary to rhapsodic. It can be made ahead of time and stored in the refrigerator in a screw-top jar, with a film of oil covering the surface of the* sofrito *to prevent it from discoloring.*

olive oil

4 large onions, very finely chopped

6 sun-ripened tomatoes, seeded and grated*

Pour about 1 cup/250 ml/8 fl oz oil into a large, heavy-based pan and heat gently. Add the onions and cook over very low heat. Stir only occasionally and continue to cook until the onions are golden and beginning to caramelize, spooning off any excess oil. Add the tomato and cook until it has cooked to a pulp and the liquid has evaporated.

*If preferred, skin the tomatoes, squeeze the flesh into a sieve and push through to remove seeds.

Variations: Other ingredients, such as garlic, herbs, leeks and/or bell peppers (capsicums), can be added after the onions have caramelized. Experiment with various ingredients until you find a combination that appeals.

BACALAO PREPARATION

Soak dried salt cod for 24 to 48 hours in cold water to cover generously, changing the water several times. Alternatively, soak overnight in cold water, drain, cover with fresh water and bring to a boil. Drain and repeat twice. Drain the fish and pull away the skin and any remaining bones (use tweezers if necessary).

At this stage the fish will be completely rehydrated, only slightly salty and ready for cooking.

SNAIL PREPARATION

To prepare the snails, ensure they have been purged by placing in a tray of cornmeal for several days, during which time they expel anything harmful in their digestive tract. This can also be achieved by fasting the snails. Rinse in cold water and drain. Place in a pot with cold water to cover, bring to a boil and simmer for a few minutes. Drain and cover with water again, adding aromatics such as quartered onion, sprigs of fresh herbs, a cup of white wine or a splash of brandy, and a pinch of pepper. A cinnamon stick also helps give a good final flavor. Bring to a boil and simmer for about 2 hours, then drain.

ROASTING PEPPERS

Roasted peppers (capsicums) are used in many Spanish dishes. They can be done in several ways. 1: Place on a rack in a very hot oven; 2: Set under a broiler (grill); 3: Pierce with a long-handled fork and hold over a flame or glowing charcoal; 4: Place on the grid of a charcoal barbecue. Cook, turning frequently, until the peppers are charred on all sides. The skin should be deeply colored, wrinkled and lifting from the flesh, but not blackened to the point that the pepper begins to burn. Remove and wrap in a kitchen towel or drop into a plastic bag until cool enough to handle. Peel off the skin, cut out the stem and its connecting ball of seeds, and trim away any internal white ribs. Use in salads and sauces, and as a side dish with roasted and grilled meats.

CREMA QUEMADA
CUSTARD CREAM FILLING

2 cups/500 ml/16 fl oz milk

peel (rind) of $\frac{1}{2}$ lemon

1 vanilla bean

$\frac{1}{3}$ cup/90 g/3 oz sugar

3 egg yolks

1$\frac{1}{2}$ tablespoons butter, softened

$\frac{1}{4}$ cup cornstarch (cornflour)

Pour milk into a saucepan and add lemon peel and split vanilla bean. bring to a boil, then remove from the heat and stand for 10 minutes. Cream the sugar with egg yolks until thick and smooth, add the butter and cornstarch, then slowly stain on the milk. Cook, stirring constantly, on low heat until the mixture is very thick and golden in color. Allow to partially cool.

CREMA QUEMADA
COFFEE/RUM FILLING

2 cups/500 ml/16 fl oz milk

1 vanilla bean

3 egg yolks

$\frac{1}{2}$ cups/120 g/40 oz sugar

$\frac{1}{4}$ cup/60 ml/2 fl oz dark rum or strong black coffee

2 tablespoons unsalted butter, softened

$\frac{1}{4}$ cup cornstarch (cornflour)

Heat milk with split vanilla bean until almost boiling, then remove from heat and stand 10 minutes. Cream egg yolks in a small saucepan with sugar, then add rum or coffee and butter. Work in thoroughly and add cornstarch. Strain on milk and cook over low heat, stirring constantly, until the filling is very thick. Partially cool before using.

HUEVOS HILADOS
EGG THREADS

Ovas reais, ("royal eggs" — also known as fios de ovas), are said to have been invented centuries ago by nuns who pierced eggshells to allow the egg to run into a thin stream into hot syrup, a slow process justified by the impressive result. Today, the beaten egg is passed through a funnel with a series of small holes, to make the process faster.

12 egg yolks

2 egg whites

3 cups/750 g/1$\frac{1}{2}$ lb fine white sugar

1 cup/250 ml/8 fl oz water

Beat the yolks and whites together, then pass several times through a fine nylon sieve. This removes any albumen and other impurities which might prevent the egg running freely through the funnel.* Make a syrup with the sugar and water in a wide pan and cook to the thread stage (32-34° Baume). Pour the egg into the funnel and hold over the pan. Allow the egg to run from the container into the syrup in thin streams, swirling them over the syrup. Use slotted spoons to remove the egg from the syrup and drape over a large strainer upturned over sheet of paper to dry. Occasionally sprinkle cold water into the syrup to prevent it thickening. Use wet hands to separate the egg threads and when using them to decorate a dish. If serving as a dessert, the threads can be dipped into a thin sugar syrup first.

* Use a funnel with several small holes in the bottom to pour the egg into the syrup. An improvised funnel can be made by piercing the bottom of a empty food can in several places with a thin nail. (Pierce from inside so the jagged rim of each puncture is on the outside of the can where it cannot prevent the flow of the egg.)

RICE COOKING

Spanish rice is quite different from the short- and long-grain rices used in other parts of the world. The rice fields of Valencia, vast marshes where the bulk of the Spanish crop is grown, produce a grain that is round and very white. Italian rice is similar, as are other short-grain rices, particularly Australian and Japanese. For *paella*, long-grain rice should never be used; and the rice should not be rinsed before using unless the recipe so specifies. *Paella* is cooked in a wide, shallow pan that is kept uncovered to prevent the rice from steaming and becoming mushy. Shallow metal *paella* pans are the most typical choice, but earthenware casseroles no more than 2 inches (5 cm) deep are also good.

Rice can be cooked on top of the stove, using two burners or hot plates and moving the pan frequently to equalize the heat. Do not cook over a single burner or the heat will be concentrated in the center, which will burn before the outer parts have cooked. The various meats and the ingredients which will flavor the rice, such as onions and tomatoes, are cooked or partially cooked first, then the rice is tossed with them until heated through and slightly opaque before adding the liquid.

The general rule is to use two parts liquid to one part rice. The liquid can be water or a well-flavored stock, and it should be boiling hot. It is added in one or two lots to the rice and cooked over moderate heat until absorbed, then on slightly lower heat until the rice is almost tender. The rice should be removed from the heat just before it is done and allowed to stand for 10 minutes before serving.

Saffron is not used in all Spanish rice dishes, but it is indeed common. And it's not just for color. Saffron imparts a wonderfully subtle flavor as well as a golden hue, so don't cheat yourself and your guests by adding artificial color, or, heaven forbid, turmeric. Use saffron threads, wrapped in a square of aluminum foil and lightly toasted in a dry pan, then ground in a mortar with a little boiling water to bring out their fullest qualities.

BATTERS, PASTRIES, DOUGHS AND BREADS

EGG CREPE BATTER

Makes about 12 thin crepes

2 eggs

1 cup/250 ml/8 fl oz milk

¾ cup/90 g/3 oz all-purpose (plain) flour, sifted

pinch of salt

1 tablespoon melted butter

In a bowl beat eggs, half the milk, flour and salt until smooth. Add the remaining milk and the butter and beat well. Cover and set aside for at least 20 minutes.

To cook crepes, rub the inside of a nonstick, seasoned cast iron or omelette pan with a paper towel dipped in oil or softened butter. Heat to moderately hot. Add a portion of the batter, allowing just enough to spread into a thin crepe of about 7 inches (18 cm) diameter. Cook, shaking the pan occasionally, until the edges lift and the underside is golden brown. Flip over or turn with a spatula and briefly cook the other side. Keep the heat to moderate, and rub pan with oil after cooking each crepe. Stack and cover with a cloth when done.

CREPE BATTER

Makes about 12 thin crepes

This batter can be used for sweet or savory crepes. Add sugar for sweet crepes, pepper for savory ones. For additional flavor add liqueur, cinnamon, ground anise or vanilla to sweet crepes. Savory crepes can have finely chopped fresh or dried herbs, finely grated cheese, cracked pepper or creamed vegetables such as spinach or pumpkin added to the batter.

1 cup/120 g/4 oz all-purpose (plain) flour

1 egg, beaten

1½–1¾ cups/375–430 ml/12–14 fl oz milk

2 tablespoons vegetable oil or melted butter

⅓ teaspoon salt

large pinch of white pepper (for savory crepes) or

1 tablespoon superfine sugar

Sift the flour into a bowl and make a well in the center. Add the egg and half the milk and mix in smoothly. Add the remaining milk and oil or butter, beating to remove any lumps. Add seasonings as required. Cover and set aside for at least 20 minutes before using.

SAFFRON BATTER

1¼ cups/150 g/5 oz all-purpose (plain) flour

½ teaspoon salt

2 teaspoons baking powder

⅓ teaspoon powdered saffron

2 tablespoons Spanish brandy or dry sherry

2 tablespoons olive oil

Sift the flour, salt, baking powder and saffron into a mixing bowl. Add brandy or sherry, oil and enough water to make a smooth, reasonably thick batter.

MASA QUEBRADA

SHORT PASTRY

2 cups/250 g/8 oz all-purpose (plain) flour

1 tablespoon sugar

½ teaspoon salt

¾ cup/180 g/6 oz cold butter

1 egg yolk

1 teaspoon lemon juice

Sift the flour, sugar and salt into a mixing bowl. Cut the butter into small cubes and rub into the flour until the mixture resembles fine crumbs. Add the egg yolk and lemon juice with enough cold water to make a stiff dough. Wrap in plastic and chill for 1 hour before rolling out.

FLAN PASTRY

Makes 1 flan case

1½ cups/180 g/6 oz all-purpose (plain) flour

⅓ teaspoon salt

1 tablespoon superfine sugar

⅓ cup/90 g/3 oz butter

1 egg, beaten

1 tablespoon peanut oil

ice water

Sift the flour with salt and sugar into a mixing bowl. Cut the butter into small cubes, add to the flour and work in with the fingers until the mixture resembles fine crumbs. Beat the egg and oil together and work into the dough, adding enough ice water to make a firm dough. Knead briefly, then wrap in plastic and chill for 30 minutes before using.

CINNAMON PASTRY

FOR SWEET PIES AND TARTS

Makes 1 shell

The cinnamon gives the pastry a darker appearance. If you like, add plain or toasted finely ground almonds to the dough.

1½ cups/180 g/6 oz all-purpose (plain) flour

1 teaspoon cinnamon

small pinch of salt

6 tablespoons unsalted butter

¼ cup/60 g/2 oz superfine sugar

1 egg, beaten

ice water

Sift the flour into a bowl with cinnamon and salt. Cut the butter into small cubes and rub into the flour until the mixture resembles fine crumbs. Add the sugar and egg and work in enough ice water to make a smooth, firm dough. Roll out and press into a tart tin or shallow pie dish. Chill for 1 hour before using.

PUFF PASTRY

Enough for one 8- to 10-inch/20- to 26-cm pie

3 cups/375 g/12 oz all-purpose (plain) flour

1 tablespoon lemon juice

1½ cups/375 g/12 oz butter

¾ teaspoon salt

ice water

Sift the flour into a bowl and sprinkle on the lemon juice, then rub in ¼ of the butter until the mixture resembles fine crumbs. Add salt with enough ice water to make a very firm dough. Knead for a few minutes, then roll out thinly. Soften the remaining butter so that it is pliable but not melted. Spread across the center of the pastry and fold in the 4 corners to make an envelope shape, completely enclosing the butter. Roll out to a rectangle and fold in thirds. Turn and roll out again. Chill for at least 1 hour. Repeat this process 5 or 6 times, chilling well in between. Wrap in plastic and chill before use.

Tip: Puff pastry should be baked in a preheated hot to very hot oven to encourage it to rise and become crisp.

SAVORY PASTRY

Makes about 30 small tart/canape shells

2 cups/250 g/8 oz all-purpose (plain) flour

½ teaspoon salt

⅓ cup/90 ml/3 fl oz olive oil

½-¾ cup/120-180 ml/4-6 fl oz ice water

Sift the flour onto a board with the salt. Make a well in the center and pour in oil and ½ cup water. Mix in more water as needed to make a smooth but firm dough. Knead lightly, then wrap in plastic and refrigerate for 1 hour.

MASA PARA TARTALETAS O BARCOS

PASTRY FOR TARTLETS AND "BOATS"

Makes about 30 shells, 1¾ inches/4 cm in diameter

1½ cups/375 g/12 oz butter, margarine or lard

3 cups/375 g/12 oz sifted all-purpose (plain) flour

1½ teaspoons salt

1 tablespoon olive oil

1 egg

ice water

Cut the butter into small cubes and rub into the flour, adding the salt and olive oil. Work in the egg and enough ice water to make a firm dough. Wrap in plastic and refrigerate for 1 hour.

Roll dough out very thinly and press into small tartlet or barquette pans. Trim edges and prick the bases. Bake in a preheated 350°F/180°C/Gas 4 oven for about 9 minutes or until dry to the touch but not browned. Remove, cool and store in an airtight container until needed.

PIE PASTRY/DOUGH

Enough for 1 large savory pie empanada

4¼ cups/600 g/1⅓ lb all-purpose (plain) flour

1¼ teaspoons salt

¼ cup/60 ml/2 fl oz olive oil

¾ cup/180 ml/6 fl oz (approximately) ice water

Sift the flour and salt into a mound on a work surface and make a well in the center. Pour in the oil and add most of the water. Work to a smooth dough, adding more water as needed. Knead until smooth, then wrap in plastic and chill for about 30 minutes before using. Roll out very thinly, then fold the pastry 3 times, roll and fold again. Repeat this 3 or 4 times to make a light, layered pastry.

EMPANADA DOUGH

Enough for 6 large or 36–48 small empanadas

2 cups/250 g/8 oz all-purpose (plain) flour

½ teaspoon salt

1 tablespoon Pernod

⅓ cup/90 ml/3 fl oz olive oil

ice water

Sift the flour and salt onto a board and make a well in the center. Add the Pernod and olive oil, cover with flour and work partially in. Add enough ice water to make a smooth but reasonably firm dough. Knead lightly, then wrap in plastic and set aside for at least 1 hour before using.

YEAST EMPANADA DOUGH

1 tablespoon/35 g/1.4 oz fresh yeast, or 2 teaspoons dried yeast mixed with 1 tablespoon warm water

3½ cups/420 g/14 oz all-purpose (plain) flour

¼ cup/60 ml/2 fl oz olive oil

1¼ teaspoons salt

¾ cup/180 ml/6 fl oz water, or milk and water mixed

Dissolve the fresh yeast in 2 tablespoons lukewarm water, then stir in 2 tablespoons of the flour. Let stand for 10 minutes for yeast to activate. Sift flour onto a board, and make a well in the center. Add the yeast mixture, and mix in lightly. Add oil and salt, cover with flour and mix in lightly again. Add the water to make a smooth dough, kneading for a few minutes. Place in an oiled bowl and cover with a cloth. Let rise for 1 hour. Roll out very thinly, fold into quarters and roll again. Repeat this 3 or 4 times to make a pastry with a light, layered texture. Wrap in plastic and chill for up to 2 hours. Often this pastry is glazed with beaten egg tinted with saffron.

PASTA DOUGH

Serves 4–6

4 cups/500 g/1 lb all-purpose (plain) flour

1½ teaspoons salt

4 eggs, beaten

Sift the flour and salt onto a work surface and make a well in the center. Slowly add the egg, incorporating into the flour with the fingers. When all of the egg has been added, if the dough looks dry, add cold water little by little to make a dough that is soft but not sticky. (When the dough is of the right consistency it can be kneaded on an unfloured board without sticking.) Knead for 10 minutes, then wrap in plastic and set aside for 10 minutes. Knead again lightly, shape into a rectangle of the required width and pass through a pasta machine, or roll out very thinly and cut as required.

BREAD DOUGH

Makes 1 large country-style loaf

1½ lb/1.2 kg all-purpose (plain) flour

1¼ teaspoons salt

2 teaspoons dry yeast

1 teaspoon sugar

1¾ cups/460 ml/15 fl oz lukewarm milk

2 tablespoons butter, melted and cooled (optional)*

1 egg, beaten (optional)*

Sift the flour and salt into a large mixing bowl. Sprinkle yeast and sugar over ¼ cup/60 ml/2 fl oz of the milk and whisk with a fork until frothy. Set aside for 10 minutes for the yeast to activate. Make a well in the flour and pour in the yeast mixture. Add the remaining milk, butter and egg and knead until smooth and elastic, about 10 minutes, adding more flour or milk as needed to make a soft but not sticky dough. Shape into a ball and return to the bowl. Cover with plastic wrap and let rise at room temperature or slightly warmer for about 2 hours.

Punch dough down and knead for a few minutes. Form into a ball and allow to rise again before using.

Shape into a thick round, place on a floured baking sheet and bake in a preheated hot 425°F/

210°C/Gas 7 oven for about 20 minutes, or use for such recipes as *hornazo de salamanca*.

*The butter and egg make the dough richer, and can be omitted when baking a plain loaf. Add extra milk as needed.

PAN DE PAYES

PEASANT BREAD

Makes 2 loaves

In Catalonia this is called *Paa de Pages*. Use it for *Paa am Tomaquet* (tomato bread). Make dough in the same way as above. Shape into 2 round mounds and flatten slightly. Use a very sharp knife to make several slashes diagonally across the top, or make 3 or 4 cuts straight across in opposite directions for a cross-hatch effect. Let rise 1 hour, then bake as above, but brush or spray with cold water before placing in the oven.

PAN DE PUEBLO

COUNTRY BREAD

Makes 2

2 teaspoons dry yeast

1 teaspoon sugar

¼ cup/60 ml/2 fl oz lukewarm water

1¼ cups/310 ml/10 fl oz milk or a mixture of milk and water

2 teaspoons salt

4 cups/500 g/1 lb unbleached all-purpose (plain) flour

2–3 tablespoons fine cornmeal

In a small bowl whisk the yeast and sugar into the water until dissolved. Set aside for 10 minutes for yeast to activate. Warm the milk or milk and water to body temperature. Sift the salt and flour into a bowl and make a well in the center. Pour in the yeast mixture and cover with flour. Let stand for 10 minutes, then stir into the rest of the flour, slowly adding the milk to make a soft dough. Turn out onto a large board and knead for at least 10 minutes. Wipe out a large bowl with an oiled cloth and place the dough in the bowl. Cover with a piece of oiled plastic wrap and set in a warm place away from drafts for at least 2 hours or until the dough has doubled in volume.

Punch the dough down and knead again lightly for about 4 minutes, then roll into a large square.

Tarta de Santiago, p.238

Ciruelas al Armanac (top left), p.192; Intxaursalsa (top right) and Pastel Vasco (front), both p.191

Cut in half crosswise or diagonally and roll up (a diagonal cut will result in loaves that are higher in the center like large croissants). Sprinkle a baking sheet with the cornmeal and place the bread on it seam side down. Make several slashes across the top of each loaf with a sharp knife. Let rise for 1 hour.

Bake in the top third of a preheated 450°F/220°C/Gas 8 oven for about 12 minutes. Brush the tops with cold water and return to the oven for about 8 minutes. When done, the loaves should give off a hollow sound when tapped underneath. Cool on a rack before slicing.

Tip: Placing a dish of water in the oven with the bread for the first 6 to 7 minutes of baking helps to prevent the tops from cracking.

SALSAS (SAUCES AND DRESSINGS)

ALIOLI
CATALAN GARLIC MAYONNAISE
Makes ¾ cup

The Catalans are justifiably proud of their alioli, *the whipped froth of garlic and olive oil that defies all laws of chemistry by staying — at least in the hands of a master — a creamy, homogeneous mass. They've been working at it for 10 centuries, since the Romans introduced this idea for a sauce for fish, meat, vegetables and salads. The Romans, in turn, probably learned the technique from the Egyptians. It is most definitely not a mayonnaise, but simply an emulsion of mashed garlic and the finest of mildly flavored extra-virgin olive oil. Purists abhor what has become the easy way to make* alioli, *by adding egg yolks, though this is how it is done now in all but the finest of Spanish restaurants.*

Alioli can be made perfectly if a few basic rules are applied. First, the ingredients must be at room temperature. The garlic must be mashed to a smooth paste with the salt, not homogenized as happens in a food processor — so be prepared to work at this by hand with a good mortar and pestle. The oil should be added very gradually, while being stirred constantly and evenly in the same direction. If the emulsion does break, the damage can be circumvented by adding to the emulsion a lightly beaten egg yolk and continuing the process — thus resulting in the "inferior" variety of alioli, *but at least not in despondency and waste of time and ingredients. It can be kept for several days in the refrigerator.*

4 large cloves garlic, peeled

⅓ teaspoon salt

about ⅔ cup/150 ml/5 fl oz mild extra-virgin olive oil

In a mortar mash the garlic with the salt to form a smooth, thick paste. Add the oil a few drops at a time, working in one direction. Continue working until a creamy white emulsion is formed. When this is achieved, do not add further oil; the garlic has reached its capacity to emulsify with the oil, and to continue would cause the sauce to break down and separate.

Food processor (egg) version:
Mash garlic and salt together as above; do not grind in the food processor. Transfer to the processor with the yolks of 2 small eggs. With the machine running, slowly add the oil and blend to the right consistency.

Tip: You may care to add a few drops of lemon juice or wine vinegar to cut the cloying richness of the sauce. Do this at the last moment and stir in gently.

SALSA BECHAMEL
Makes 3 cups

3 tablespoons butter

3 tablespoons all-purpose (plain) flour

2½ cups/650 ml/20 fl oz milk

½ teaspoon nutmeg

salt and pepper

Melt the butter in a saucepan and stir in the flour. Remove from the heat and stir in the milk. Return to the heat and cook until thickened, stirring continually. Add the nutmeg, salt and pepper.

SALSA MAYONESA
MAYONNAISE
2 egg yolks

2 cups/500 ml/16 fl oz olive oil

about 1 tablespoon wine vinegar or lemon juice

Beat the egg yolks in a bowl until creamy. Very slowly incorporate the oil, beating constantly to make a thick sauce. When it is not possible to add any more oil (you will notice that it floats on the surface and does not want to be incorporated), add vinegar or lemon juice to taste. Bottle and store in the refrigerator for a week or two.

SALSA ROMESCO
CATALAN PEPPER SAUCE
Makes about 1 cup

This tangy, peppery sauce is a specialty of the province of Tarragona, where there are extensive almond groves. It began life as part of a classic fish stew from that region, and evolved to become essentially a sauce for cooked fish. But it also does wonders for vegetables or a simple grilled lamb chop. It combines ground toasted almonds with sweet red peppers, garlic, bread (either plain or fried in olive oil), tomatoes and a type of dried sweet local pepper known as a nyora *or* ñora.

2 large dried red bell peppers (capsicums)*

1 dried hot red chili pepper

1 cup/250 ml/8 fl oz olive oil

2 tablespoons blanched almonds

1 slice day-old white bread, crusts trimmed

3 cloves garlic, finely chopped

1 teaspoon sweet paprika

½ teaspoon hot paprika

½ teaspoon sugar

salt and pepper

about 2 tablespoons red wine vinegar

Fry the peppers and chili in half the oil until well colored. Remove. Fry the almonds and bread until golden. Remove and let the oil cool. Cut open the peppers and chili and scrape the flesh into a food processor or blender, discarding seeds and skins. Add the nuts, bread and garlic and grind to a paste. Add paprika, sugar, salt and pepper and grind smoothly. With the machine running, gradually add the remaining oil to make a smooth dressing. Add vinegar to taste; the sauce should be slightly tangy and the consistency of heavy (thick) cream. Chill slightly before serving.

* If dried sweet peppers are unobtainable, use oven-roasted red peppers, see page 266.

SALSA VINAGRETA
VINAIGRETTE (OIL AND VINEGAR) DRESSING

2 tablespoons white or red wine vinegar

6 tablespoons olive oil

large pinch of salt

Whisk all ingredients together until creamy, or shake in a screwtop jar. Can be stored in the refrigerator for several weeks.

SALSA VINAGRETA CON AJO
VINAIGRETTE WITH GARLIC

1 recipe *salsa vinagreta*

1 teaspoon finely chopped parsley

1–2 cloves garlic, mashed

Make the *salsa vinagreta* and whisk in the parsley and garlic.

SALSA DE TOMATE
FRESH TOMATO SAUCE
Makes 3–3½ cups

1 large onion, very finely chopped

3 tablespoons olive oil

3 cloves garlic, very finely chopped

5 large sun-ripened tomatoes, peeled, seeded and chopped

1¼ teaspoons salt

⅓ teaspoon black pepper

1 tablespoon chopped fresh herbs (parsley, rosemary, thyme, oregano)

Sauté the onion in the oil until soft and very lightly colored. Add the garlic and sauté briefly, then add the tomato and cook slowly until reduced to a pulp. Season with salt and pepper and add the herbs. Simmer briefly, then pass through a sieve or purée in a food processor or blender if a smooth sauce is desired. Can be frozen.

Variation: To make a **spicy tomato sauce**, add hot paprika or cayenne to taste. Also add extra garlic as desired.

SALSA HISTORIADA
SALSA MOSTARDA WITH EGGS

2 hard-boiled eggs

1 recipe *salsa mostarda*

1 tablespoon chopped parsley

extra oil to taste

Mash the egg yolks, discarding whites. Whisk into the *salsa mostarda*, adding the parsley and enough extra oil to make the dressing creamy.

SALSA MOSTARDA
VINAIGRETTE WITH MUSTARD

1 recipe *salsa vinagreta*

1 tablespoon whole-grain mustard

Whisk the *salsa vinagreta* with the mustard until creamy. Add a little extra oil if needed.

BEVERAGES

HORCHATA
VALENCIAN SUMMER BEVERAGE

¼ lb/250 g/8 oz *chufa* nuts (or blanched almonds)

4 cups/1 l/1 qt water

3 tablespoons superfine sugar

cracked ice

cinnamon

Wash the nuts under running water. Soak overnight in water to cover, changing the water twice. Drain. Purée in a food processor with as much of the water as is necessary to keep the machine from clogging. Add the remaining water and set aside for 4 to 5 hours. Strain through a sieve lined with a clean cloth. Sweeten with the sugar and serve over cracked ice with a pinch of cinnamon.

SANGRÍA
RED WINE PUNCH

A pitcher of sangría, *a loaf of bread, a wedge of cheese and a shady tree. Summer afternoon bliss! The tourists probably love this red wine punch more than the Spanish do. It's hardly the right drink to have with a meal, being slightly too sweet, but it's cooling and refreshing — and decidedly more alcoholic than its mild taste suggests! I don't know that there is an absolute original recipe for this punch; I've tried innumerable so-called "authentic" versions. Some contain only red wine, brandy and a little sliced fresh fruit. Others include fruit macerated in brandy; sugar or fruit syrup; orange liqueur or orange juice; soda water or sparkling mineral water. My Sunday lunch recipe is for orange and lime slices macerated in brandy for 2 hours, thoroughly chilled light-bodied red wine, a dash of soda water and a good splash of orange juice. I float a little orange liqueur on top of each filled glass and garnish with a slice of orange on the side. I don't expect to work in the afternoon!*

Here is still another version.

4 cups/1 l/1 qt light-bodied red wine, well chilled

¾ cup/180 ml/6 fl oz Spanish or other brandy

½ cup/120 g/4 oz superfine sugar

2 cups/500 ml/16 fl oz soda water or lemonade*

1 orange, sliced

1 lemon, sliced

6–8 strawberries, halved

Mix wine, brandy and sugar, stirring to dissolve sugar. Chill well. Just before serving add the soda water or lemonade and fruit.

*You may want to add slightly less sugar if using lemonade.

THE SPANISH KITCHEN

Spanish cooking is, in general, uncomplicated, requiring few special utensils. You will need a good mortar and pestle, for many sauces are based on a mixture of ground ingredients. The Spanish call theirs *almirez* and prefer a brass set, but granite or heavy porcelain will do. It gives a better result than a spice grinder or blender, although for large grinding jobs these may be used. Food processors, too, are making their appearance in Spanish kitchens, and are proving to be great time savers.

The pots and pans already in your kitchen can be used for Spanish cooking, but if you plan to cook *paella*, a special paella pan gives the best results. Choose a flat pan of heavy metal with a shallow looped handle on each side, and purchase a thick woven cane mat on which to set the pan at the table.

Spanish cooks like to make their stews and simmered dishes in earthenware pots. The flavors seem somehow to develop with more complexity and smoothness, so it is worth the investment. *Cazuelas* are the popular thick earthenware casserole dishes, glazed only on the inside. They can be used on top of the stove and in the oven. New ones should be soaked overnight before use to prevent cracking or crazing when heated, but once "seasoned" they will last for years — provided they are heated slowly at the beginning of the cooking. If placed directly onto high heat they may break in two. *Cazuelitas* are smaller versions, used for individual servings. An *olla* is a tall and deep, terracotta pot narrower at the bottom and top than in the middle; a large heavy-based saucepan can take its place. For *tortillas*, an omelette pan is absolutely necessary as it is imperative that the omelette doesn't stick, which makes turning impossible. Choose either a pan with a nonstick coating or a heavy cast iron pan that has been well seasoned; before use, always rub it with an oiled cloth until the inside shines. If the pan is made of a light metal such as aluminum, cook the tortilla at a slightly lower temperature in order to avoid a burned spot in the center. Any other utensils or equipment needed can be improvised with what you already have in your kitchen, or from the suggestions given with the recipe.

THE SPANISH MARKETS

The food markets in Spain are more than just a place to buy food. They are the venues for friends to meet for a morning chat, to linger over coffee while contemplating the hubbub of the crowd and the marketers, to bathe in the sweet smells of fresh fruit and feast the eyes on a profusion of vegetables, charcuterie, seafoods and fruit. The Spanish love their food fresh, and usually choose to buy what's in season. Every marketplace, from the smallest in a rural village to the grand markets of Barcelona and Madrid, is thronged with shoppers from early morning. Restaurateurs haggle volubly over prices and housewives wander from stall to stall comparing quality, price and freshness, seeing what's new, and remonstrating with a stall holder at any attempt to pass off yesterday's goods at today's prices. The *Mercamadrid* on the outskirts of Madrid — which replaced the old central market, the *Mercado Central de Legazpi* — is scrupulously hygienic and so vast it can take a day to cover the whole area. Its counterpart in Barcelona, affectionately known as *La Boquería* but officially as the *Mercat de Sant Josep* (or *Mercado de San José* in Castellano), is equally vast and wondrously atmospheric. La Boquería is located off the fascinating *Ramblas* mall, a pedestrian precinct shaded by huge trees and edged by stalls where caged birds, exotic flowers, magazines and books are sold, where retirees rest on plastic chairs and hopeful poets recite their latest endeavors from upturned fruit cases. The market's dimly lit wrought-iron entrance is set back from the street, and only the brightly hued cascade of fruit from the stalls just inside the entrance distinguishes it from a railway station of times past. Inside, it opens to a maze of passageways between clustered stalls offering merchandise from all parts of Spain. To be there in mushroom season is particularly rewarding if you're a devotee of fungi. The selection has to be seen to be comprehended: *rovellons* so bright in their burnished bronze that they appear to be painted; *trompero* looking like branching black coral; *canagroc* with long yellow stems and tiny brown tops, recalling the Japanese *enokitake*; *russinyols*, which are the French chanterelle; *pies de rata*, like ochre-colored coral formations; *rosinoc*, big fluted yellow mushrooms; *llano* like a pale *cèpe*; and of course *bolets*, the *cèpes* of France and *porcini* of Italy, with their wonderful earthy flavor.

The seafood stalls are always inviting, packed with the freshest fish air-transported or overnight-hauled from Galicia, the Andalusian and Basque coasts. *Bacalao* is set apart from the fresh seafood and sold in many different preparations, from huge whole dried fish, sun-stiffened and thickly salt-encrusted, to portion-sized cuts, shreds for soups, stuffings and *croquetas*, and de-salted *bacalao* in plastic tubs.

The fruit is always magnificent. Tiny sweet pineapples and fat bananas from the Canary Islands, sweet-fleshed persimmons, huge black figs, profusions of berries — *groselas, moras, fresons, frambuesas*. Apples from Asturias, oranges from Valencia, grapes from Andalusia. *Granadas* and *aguacates, melocotones* and *mandarinas*, exotic custard apples they call *chirimoya*, pears of myriad types and massed melons of the sweetest yellow flesh. The vegetable stalls impress just as much. Chains of plump pink garlic, bunches of sweet white, pink-red and yellow onions, serried rows of *endibias* (white endives), jumbles of green, mottled pink or cream *alubias*, purple eggplants, long, slender green wild asparagus, strings of scarlet chili peppers, and box upon box of fresh green and red peppers, firm tomatoes and tiny *tomatitos*.

The markets include *charcuteria* (cured meats) and *quesos* (cheeses) from most parts of Spain, displayed hygienically in refrigerated glass counters. You can rely on freshness, as the turnover is huge and there is strong competition between the merchants to supply the best. I can't think of a better snack than the one I had when I last wandered these passageways — a few slices of *jamón de Jabugo* in a freshly baked roll and a juicy black fig that only the day before was being picked from its tree.

OLIVES

Olives are an ancient fruit. The gnarled, twisted greyish trees look like they have been around since the beginning of time, and many almost have. It is not unusual to find an olive tree that is as much as a thousand years old, still standing, producing its annual crop, still braving summer heat and winter chill. Andalusia has some of the largest olive plantations in the world. Growing in a soil that is so grey-green in color it appears to have absolutely no fertility left to offer, the trees flourish and spread their branches of spindly leaves wide enough to almost touch the next in their neatly planted rows. They grow up the sides of mountains, in areas that are hardly accessible; they require little to nourish them and little care. Branches are pruned so the tree can concentrate on fruit production, and the soil beneath is raked of any other foliage that may draw off precious moisture or in which the falling olives may be lost. In September the soil is ploughed to trap the fall rains, vital to the maturation of the olives. When ripe, the fruit are almost a violet color.

Most olives are still harvested by hand. Sheets are spread over the soil to catch the fallen fruit, the harvesters using long poles to shake the branches so they release the olives. But the olives you nibble as hors d'oeuvre don't come straight from the tree. Fresh olives are extremely bitter and must be processed and fermented for eating. It is not a lengthy or complicated process, and is easily done at home with fresh olives bought from the market. In most olive-growing countries villagers have their own trees, producing enough fruit for family consumption. If they are blessed with more than a few trees, it is not unusual for someone from the village to pick the olives and return with olive oil and cured olives for the owner, in exchange for keeping enough for themselves.

Commercially, the process of curing olives is expedited by steeping the fruit in a lye solution for about a week, compared with the traditional method of soaking them in water for a month to draw off the bitterness. They are then steeped in a strong brine solution.

Cured Olives

Select firm, unblemished and unbruised fresh olives and make a slit along the length of each, or crack by hitting with a hammer or heavy pestle. Place in a large earthenware or glass container and cover with water. Let stand in a cool place, changing the water every second day, for three weeks. At this point test an olive to see if it is no longer bitter; allow extra soaking time if it is.

Make a strong brine solution using 1 cup/ 250 g/8 oz salt for every $3\frac{1}{2}$–4 cups/875 ml–1l/ 28–32 fl oz of cold water. Add thyme and fennel sprigs and several peeled cloves of garlic. Add the olives, cover and set aside for about 10 days. Give the olives added flavor by including sliced lemon or hot chili pepper in the brine. Transfer to airtight jars to store.

Marinated Olives

Drain cured olives and add finely shredded carrot and onion which have been pickled in 8 parts vinegar, to 1 part each sugar and salt. Add dried mixed herbs, black pepper, crushed dried chili and garlic. Add a few caraway and cumin seeds and a splash of olive oil. Mix well and keep chilled.

Olives in Oil

I like to store my olives in oil. Drain off the brine and replace with olive oil. Add sliced garlic, crushed dried thyme, peppercorns, a sprig of rosemary, sometimes a small dried hot chili pepper. As the olives are eaten, I use the oil in salad dressings.

Olive Oil, the Liquid Gold of Spain

The Romans brought the art of olive oil production to Spain, but they must in turn thank the Egyptians for the skill. Small-production oil is still made by the age-old method of a grinding stone. Large-scale production is merely an elaboration of this method, for why change something that works perfectly? The olives must be kept clean and cool before and during processing to prevent rancidity and oxidizing of the oil.

Olive oil is the only vegetable oil that can be used without refining. The first press produces the finest oils, *extra virgen* and *fino* or *virgen* — classified by their degree of acidity, which is tested by their percentage of oleic acid. *Denominación de origen* classifications have been introduced by the Spanish Department of Agriculture to classify the better oils, allowing them to be marketed for export at handsome prices to an appreciative clientele. These are strongly flavored oils, to be used as dressings, and in moderation. The better-quality, but not virgin, olive oils are generally labelled *aceite de oliva puro*. Pure olive oil can be a good-quality second pressing, or may have a percentage of virgin oil added, but it must be within the prescribed acidity rating. It can be used for cooking as well as salad dressings, as it has a less pronounced fruit flavor. The pulp remaining after pure olive oil is extracted requires refining to make it into an edible oil. This will be the lowest-grade and therefore lowest-priced olive oil, and may in fact be labeled vegetable rather than olive oil.

One of the added joys of using olive oil in cooking — for the obvious first pleasure is its wonderfully distinct taste — is its health-promoting properties. In a time of cholesterol consciousness, this is one product that can be relied on as cholesterol-free.

For cooking, olive oil does have some limitations. It has a distinct flavor that can overpower more subtle tastes. (For frying sweet pastries, for instance, a bland vegetable oil is generally preferred.) But it is a taste that can become addictive. I float olive oil on soups, drizzle it over bread and vegetables, cook all but Chinese food and curries with it (it simply does not go with these) and add it to all sorts of cake and biscuit recipes where a moist texture is needed. Like all oils, it can become rancid if not used within a certain time of opening, or if allowed to become too warm. Only buy in large quantities if you intend to use it generously. Otherwise, choose a smaller glass or metal (never plastic) container and keep it in a cupboard away from light and heat. In very hot climates it may even be best in the refrigerator. Even if the cold solidifies the oil, its flavor will not be affected if the container is sealed.

CALCOTADA

Valls, in the province of Tarragona on the southern strip of Cataloni, celebrates a unique annual festival, that of the *calcotada*. It began as a harbinger of spring and warmer weather to come, with a family feast in the fields — the meal starting with roasted onions plucked straight from the soil and cooked over a fire. These onions are in themselves unique. During winter the shoots that sprout from onions are removed along with the little bulbs they have formed. These are planted, watered just once and grow into *calcots*, which resemble bulbous green (spring) onions.

Eating roasted *calcots* is a messy business, but this is all part of the fun. It became such a thing to manoeuver a visit to relatives in the area to coincide with the *calcotada* that it has developed over the years into a tourist attraction, which today celebrates the festival in *tabernas*, restaurants and farmhouses as a commercial enterprise. Diners are sheathed in large paper aprons or bibs and the mountains of plump onions are roasted on charcoal grills. *Calcots* are served with a sauce for dipping; *alioli* is ideal, but a spicy tomato-based sauce will also do. The trick in getting the blackened onion to release its tender white heart is to gently but firmly pull the green sprout, while pinching the base of the onion with the other hand.

CHARCUTERIE

Cured meats and sausages are enormously important to the Spanish diet. Major commercial producers and many small rural producers turn out dozens of different types of hams and sausages for local consumption and some export trade. *Jamón serrano*, the Spanish cured ham of which *jamón de Jabugo* is the most sought after, can be found suspended on hooks from the ceiling of delicatessens, butcher's shops, grocers and bars all over Spain, each with its little plastic umbrella underneath to catch any drips of fat that may exude from the meat. Spanish cured hams (the rear haunches with trotter intact) and the foreleg and shoulder are first salt-cured for several days, then washed, dried and hung to mature in large cellars similar to those used for wine. The remainder of the pig goes to the sausagemakers.

The Spanish Ministry of Agriculture has developed a program of classifications to which pork producers must subject their produce before it can be marketed. Meats are classified with a series of colored markings for quality and point of origin. These *denominaciones de origen* take the guesswork out of buying ham. You can expect to pay most for the best, made with meat of the *jamón ibérico*. *Jamón serrano*, or "mountain ham", is best from the mountain regions, where its curing process is slower at cooler temperatures, so that it acquires a greater intensity of flavor. The small village of Jabugo is nestled high in the western peaks of the Sierra Morena ranges, the mountains covered with massive oak trees, a natural combination for quality ham production.

Salamanca, Aragón and Huelva are the provinces known to produce the best hams, while Granada and Cáceres follow closely behind with some of their production.

La matanza is the traditional killing of the pig, which takes place on the 10th or 11th of November every year to provide food for the winter months ahead. A vital part of Spanish rural life, it is the annual ritual of the slaughter, dissection and processing of the meat into hams and sausages. Many villagers still participate enthusiastically in this and many other old practices as their ancestors did before them. In Catalonia, the slaughter is called *matança de porc*. The actual killing is done by a *matador*, not of the bullring in pink stockings, skintight trousers and heavily embroidered jacket, but of a bloodstained apron, by trade a killer of animals at a butchery. Pig slaughter is timed for after the fall of the acorns, on which the pigs are allowed to feast for several weeks to build up their fat and add that certain quality of flavor to the meat that distinguishes Spanish ham from any other.

Chorizos are the best-known of the many types of Spanish cured sausage. They come in numerous forms, each region having its own style to distinguish it from the other. It stands to reason that those provinces where the best hams are produced also produce excellent sausages. The thick, large, brick-red, paprika-flavored *chorizo* of Salamanca has meaty chunks. Pamplona's best is finer-textured, resembling a good quality salami and with a superb strong flavor. *Chorizo blanco* has lighter meat and whole peppercorns, while *chorizo puro de lomo* is a pork tenderloin flavored with paprika and compressed into a sausage casing. *Lomo ibérico* or *lomo embuchado* is similarly pure pork tenderloin, which may be cured or smoked and compressed into a sausage casing. *Lomo adobado* is also a pork tenderloin, marinated and smoked but uncured so that it must be cooked before eating.

Cured sausages, which can be eaten without cooking or added to dishes for flavor, are *salchichón* or *longaniza*. They vary in size and thickness from region to region, maker to maker. Fresh sausages of the link variety are *salchichas*. Made of pork, they can be bland and very lightly seasoned or quite spicy. The Catalan *butifarra blanca* is a plump white link sausage that is excellent for grilling. Blood sausage of the French *boudin noir* style is manufactured in many parts of Spain. Pig's blood is the main ingredient, with pork, garlic and spices supplementing it. To give it the slightly grainy texture the Spanish enjoy, seasoned rice and sometimes pine nuts are added. In Asturias *morcilla* sausage is a vital ingredient in the hotpot they call *fabada*. The sausages are hung in the chimney to smoke which gives them an intense flavor. The Catalan blood sausage is *butifarra negra*, which omits the grain but may use bread soaked in the pig's blood, and adds mint. *Morcilla blanca* is a chicken-and-fat bacon sausage, pale in color and supplemented with egg and parsley, lightly seasoned. In the Emporda region of Catalonia they produce an unusual sweet sausage, *butifarra dolça*, the pork cured with sugar instead of salt, and flavored with cinnamon.

The sausage native to the Balearic Islands but eaten all over Spain is *sobrasada*, a finely ground soft pork link of excellent quality, flavored with paprika. *Tocino* is pork fat, used to add flavor to many slow-cooked hotpot style dishes and to moisten lean meats like veal. It may be salted or fresh and can be substituted by any salted or fresh fat pork, or the Italian *panceta*. Bacon is relatively new to the Spanish cuisine and will be called *bacon* or *beicon*, the smoked variety suffixed by *ahumado*.

CHEESES

Queso manchego is the monarch of Spanish cheeses. Originating in La Mancha, where the shepherds made it by hand from ewes' milk, it traditionally had a yellow rind and a firm texture with slight saltiness. As demand grew, it became necessary to commercialize its production, so that large discs of *manchego* are now sold all over Spain. Although it is not always made with ewes' milk today, there has been no loss of the original sharp flavor that brought it into popularity. The rind may be yellow or black. The cheese is sold in various stages of maturation, the youngest being soft, pale yellow and deliciously smooth. As it ages, it develops to become brittle and crumbly and it acquires the characteristic full-bodied taste that makes it unbeatable. Italian *pecorino* can be substituted in recipes requiring *queso manchego*, as can a low-salt *feta*.

Spain's cheese manufacture has expanded from a cottage craft to a large commercial enterprise servicing export as well as domestic markets. Many of Spain's best cows' milk cheeses come from Asturias, where the milk is exceptionally rich and creamy. Some of the more exclusive cheeses can only be obtained at their point of origin, often a tiny village high in the mountains where the business of cheesemaking has been carried on by one family for generations. A typical example is the cone-shaped cheese called *afoga el pitu* from Oveido in Asturias. I have listed some of the popular cheeses below; others can be found in the glossary.

Ansó is a creamy white cheese from Pyrenean sheep, made in the valley of Huesca.

Beyusco from Asturias mixes goats' and ewes' milk for a slightly sharp-tasting, lightly smoked cheese.

Burgos was made to eat with honey. It is a semisoft white, rindless, unfermented cheese of ewes' milk. The round cakes are steeped in brine for a day to give a contrast of flavors.

Villalón, affectionately known as *pata de mulo* (mule's leg) for its peculiar cylindrical shape, is another mild white cheese that goes well with sweet tastes. Buy it *con sal* or *sin sal*, with or without salt. The Catalans use a soft fresh white cheese known as *mató*, made from goats' and cows' milk, to make one of their best desserts, *mel y mató* — honey with *mató*, a delicacy beyond compare.

Puzol is another unfermented soft white cheese, this one made in Valencia, meant to be eaten fresh.

Cabrales, Spain's best blue-vein cheese, became such an important commodity that its manufacture is now industrialized. The best is Cabrales-Picon, from the village of Cabrales in the Cantabrian mountains, which rivals Roquefort for quality although it is slightly more acidic. The cheese is wrapped in chestnut leaves and stored in caves to develop its blue-green veining and creamy consistency. Another cheese matured in natural caves in Asturias is *gamonedo*, a mixed-milk type that is smoked before maturation. It develops small holes, blue veins, white flesh and a distinctly tangy taste.

An excellent marriage is made in Cádiz with local sherry and their *cádiz*, a strongly flavored goat cheese. From the same region is *grazalema*, of the *manchego* style.

The cheeses of Navarre are of high quality, and popular, although not produced in vast quantity. *Roncal* is considered one of Spain's best. A hard ewes' milk cheese full of tiny holes, it has a hard buff-colored rind. *Idiazábal*, also made in the Basque province of Guipuzcoa, comes to the market fresh and tasting considerably milder than when it develops to maturity in 3 or 4 months.

Pedroches, a sheep's milk cheese from Córdoba, is strong, salty and tangy. It is sometimes preserved in vats of oil.

SEAFOOD

A visit to a Spanish fishmarket is a joy to the "foodie". Their displays are grandly ostentatious, meant to impress and catch the eye. Cascades of ice and decorative green leaves display long, silvery *merluza* looped tail in mouth; fat *rape* upturned to reveal their tender bellies with their ugly bearded heads beneath; *cigalas* with pincers raised in mock battle; *bogavantes* with antennae twitching, their flat pincers restrained with twine. Leaf-lined baskets hold *cocochas* (*kokotxas*) and *ostiones*, tiny *nécoras* and prehistoric *percebes; gambas* and *camarones* are arranged regimentally; fillets and small whole fish are aligned with precision on wide trays. Fresh salmon and tuna repose in tubs of ice at the foot of display counters. All is clean, fresh, wet and inviting.

The variety of fish and shellfish caught off the coast of Spain is immense. Little wonder that so much of the cuisine is based on seafood. But the fish that takes precedence over all is not even fished from Spanish waters. Spanish fishermen travel vast distances into the cold northern waters to catch the gigantic cod they call *bacalao*. And it rarely reaches the market fresh. Instead, *bacalao* is salted and the large white carcasses are stretched out on racks to catch northern sunshine to dry into cardboard caricatures of their former selves. You'll find them whole or dissected into pieces of different grade in markets all over Spain. The salting process develops a distinct strong flavor revered by all, and the fish is the basis of many of the classic Spanish dishes. Hake (*merluza*), of the same family, is a long, thin, silvery fish with fine-textured flesh. One of the most commonly used fish in Spanish cooking, it does not keep well so should be used quickly after purchase. Smaller hake are *pescadilla*, the fillets delicious simply floured and lightly fried. They are often displayed at the fishmongers' with their tails caught in their jaws.

Anchovies (*boquerones, anchoas*) and sardines (*sardinas*) are prolific. The former are snapped up by canneries for canning in oil or salt, and by restaurants for pickling in vinegar to serve as *tapas*. Small fresh anchovies can be fried and eaten whole. Sardines fresh from the water are superb straight from the grill, with a squeeze of lemon or a splash of hot oil impregnated with garlic and paprika. Filleting these small fish is simple: cut around the head, grasp it and the top of the spine firmly between knife blade and fingers, and tug sharply towards the tail. The backbone will separate from the fillets, leaving them attached at the tail. It's fascinating to see a fishmonger preparing even the smallest of anchovies in this way.

Tuna (*atún*) and bonito (*bonito*) are of the tuna family, large meaty fish with dark flesh that is excellent eaten fresh, simply grilled as steaks, or stewed. Much of the catch goes to the cannery.

Many members of the bream family are found in Spanish waters. Along the coast of Valencia, particularly near Alicante, the biggest and best gilthead (*dorada*) are caught. They are nestled into a pan of local coarse salt to bake *a la sal*. You'll find red bream (*besugo*) on many menus, often simply charcoal-grilled. Dentex (*dentón*) is similar, but silvery-blue; one of its family, *urta*, is the specialty of Rota across the bay from Cádiz. Various members of the rascasse family are eaten in Spain, particularly the scorpion fish (*cabracho*) and *rascacio*. Red mullet (*salmonete*) are one of the most popular Mediterranean species. They are added to fish stews, fried or grilled whole.

Sea bass (*lubina*) will be found on most good menus. It's a pricey fish and one of the best, although grey mullet (*lisa*) is sometimes substituted by unscrupulous restaurateurs as it has a similar coloring but is decidedly less expensive. Grouper (*mero*) is another popular meaty fish.

One of the ugliest fish is also one of the most sought after. The angler or monkfish (*rape*) makes quite delicious eating, with a sweet flesh reminiscent of lobster. It's grey-skinned, with a large triangular head bristling with soft spines, wide shoulders and a slim tail. The strange-looking flatfish with their faces on one side, turbot (*rodaballo*) and sole (*lenguado*), are popular eating, as are John Dory (*pez de San Pedro*) and black pomfret (*palometa negra*), which have similar flat bodies, but with eyes on both sides and little beaklike mouths.

Of the other fish eaten in Spain, swordfish (*pez espada* or *emperador*) is worth mentioning; its steaks are wonderful when grilled by a careful cook who ensures they do not end up dry. And the wide triangular wings or flaps of skate or stingray (*raya*) are similarly good eating. Tiny *chanquetes*, the minuscule fry of the goby fish, were an annual treat off the Málaga coast. Overfishing has severely depleted their numbers and now if they appear on a menu — cooked like whitebait, quickly fried and crisp — they will probably be the fry of another kind of fish, as their netting is today under strict control.

Eels of both fresh- and saltwater varieties are much enjoyed. *Anguilas* are cooked whole or sold in chunks for stewing; their spawn are *angulas*, which at around 2 inches (5 cm) long are a delicacy much sought after. They are cooked by dropping into *cazuelitas* of hot oil flavored with garlic and chili.

Fast-flowing icy rivers in the north and trout hatcheries elsewhere provide a plentiful supply of pink-fleshed trout, while salmon (*salmon*) is both locally hatched and imported.

SHELLFISH

In Spain you can expect to be surprised by the variety of shellfish in the markets. Seafood restaurants proudly display immense trays of shrimp (prawns) of many sizes and types. What looks like miniature lobster are *cigalas* or Dublin Bay prawns. Crabs range from tiny square-bodied *nécoras* to massive *centolla* crabs, which can weigh more than 5 pounds. There are mollusks of endless variety — the long *navaja*, looking like an immense fingernail; cockles, mussels, scallops and clams in all shapes, colors, sizes and delicacy of taste. There are long, flat *ostiones* and plump *ostras*, spicy whelks and urchins, plump grey-pink squid and cuttlefish. No one bothers with elaborate shellfish preparations; they are too good just as they are, straight from water to pot to boil briefly, perhaps with an *alioli* for dipping, or a squeeze of lemon. But you will find various shellfish popping up in unexpected places, like clams with salt cod and asparagus or squid in a rabbit stew and that's the fun of this unique cuisine.

Barnacles (rock or goose barnacle), *percebes*, are found clinging to the rocks around the northwestern coast in the province of Galicia, and all along the Portuguese coast. They are a delicate mollusk rather like the English winkle, growing inside a strange outer casing. They are popular in seafood *tapas* bars.

A number of different types of clams, *almejas*, are eaten, and they come in sizes from thumbnail to as large as the palm of the child who digs them from the sand on the retreating tide. *Almejas* have a ridged shell. Venus clams (*cochas finas*) are red-brown and smooth, the flesh deliciously meaty and tasting of the sea. Often found in cooked dishes are *coquinas*, or wedge-shaped clams of a buff-yellow color. All are delicious in seafood soups. Buy clams fresh and purge them for at least several hours in several changes of cold water. Boil or steam until they open, discarding those that do not. The Portuguese have a pan called a *cataplana* for cooking shellfish, resembling two Chinese woks hinged at one side with looped handles that fit together on the opposite side. It steams them gently, and can be shaken without spillage to encourage shells to open. *Cataplanas* are sometimes used in the Spanish provinces bordering Portugal.

Cockles, *berberechos*, have deeply ridged shells enclosing well flavored meaty mollusks that can be eaten straight from the sea.

King of the crabs in Spain is the *centolla*, or spider crab, with long legs, narrow claws and a spiny, knobbly back. Some of the biggest weigh many pounds and provide meat for several diners. But the average crab does not quite provide one good serving. Known as *txangurro* or *shangurro* in the Basque country, where they are a feature of all good menus, the most popular way to eat them is baked in the shell. The meat is finely textured and sweetly rich, so is often added to fillings for superb flavor. *Nécora* is a tiny square-shaped crab that you'll find often in *tapas* bars, dripping with sauce and messy to eat, but irresistible. *Buey de mar* (meat of the sea) has a smooth round shell and smallish claws. Crabs may also be known as *cangrejo*. Freshwater crayfish, *cangréjos de río*, has a delicate flesh like the finest shrimp. Best bought live, to cook by plunging into lightly salted boiling water.

Cuttlefish, *jibia*, is not as elegant of body or as tender of flesh as squid, but can be used in the same recipes.

Dublin Bay prawns (sea crayfish) are called *cigalas* by the Spanish, *scampi* by the Italians, *langoustines* by the French. They have bodies like large shrimp (prawns) with pincers disproportionately large for their size. Hard shells make the meat a little difficult to extract, but worth the effort.

The black-green *bogavante* or lobster of Spain is the *homard* of France, the flat pincers yielding thick, sweet meat. *Langostas* are spiny lobsters, with no pincers but a sweet thick tail. The *cigarra* or sea cricket is a strange-looking flat lobster of smallish size with a squared head and no pincers. Its flesh is acceptable but not as well flavored as the other kinds of lobster cooked in Spain.

Black-shelled mussels, *mejillones*, are the ones usually found at Spanish fishmongers'. A type of brown mussel called *dátil de mar* (sea date) is also eaten. Treat them like clams, purging before use to expel sand. Boil or steam only until the shells open. Mussels *en escabeche*, marinated in vinegar with herbs, are a delicious appetizer.

Octopus, *pulpo*, is an inexpensive and greatly enjoyed seafood. The larger ones can be tough and require tenderizing by beating to break down the muscular tissue before slow simmering to tenderize. Baby octopus, *pulpitos*, can be cooked in much the same way as cuttlefish, requiring only a half hour to tenderize. They are delectable marinated. *Pulpo á feira*, stewed octopus in paprika, is a festive dish; *pulpo gallega*, sliced stewed octopus with garlic and paprika, is a favorite *tapa*.

The large, flat long *ostiones* found only along the rockeries near southern Cádiz are amongst the world's finest oysters, highly regarded — and accordingly priced — in Spain. The common *ostra* is also very good. Usually eaten "au naturel" with a squeeze of lemon, but also tasty coated with cornmeal or a saffron-tinted batter and deep-fried.

The pilgrims to Santiago de Compostela chose the attractive flute-edged scallop shell as their symbol, and the Galicians named them *vieira* or *concha del peregrino*, "pilgrim shell".

Serve them on their shells, which can withstand the few minutes in a hot oven that it takes to cook these delectable white mollusks with their sweet orange coral.

The meat of spiny shelled sea snails or whelks, *caracola*, tastes like snails, so they are called by the same name. Like snails, they must be wriggled out of their shells with a little spear.

Sea urchin, *erizo de mar*, is usually eaten raw, scooped from the split shell with a spoon. The creamy coral-colored contents make a delectable sauce for other seafood dishes or chicken.

Shrimp in general are called *gambas*. The smallest, called bay prawns or shrimp in some parts, are *quisquillas*, which appear unshelled in *paellas* and soups to eat if you can bother peeling them, or simply for flavor. Common shrimp are *camarones* or *gambas*, while the larger ones with deep red shells are *carabineros*. If you want grilled shrimp you will probably be served *langostinos* of enormous size, split lengthwise, brushed with oil and cooked in their shells over charcoal to eat with a squeeze of lemon.

Squid — *calamar, chipirones, chopitos, calamarcets* — requires only the briefest of cooking; otherwise its rubbery flesh turns to leather. Pull away the head and tentacles and cut below the eyes to remove the stomach and inedible beaklike mouth. Pull off the pink-grey skin and side flaps. Cut across the tubular body into rings, or open flat and cut into strips or squares. Spanish cooks often stuff squid with finely chopped ingredients and braise them in a sauce, or simmer them in their own black ink. You can buy extra ink to supplement the dish and provide adequate color, as netted squid tends to expel most of its ink. The smallest squid are called *chipirones, chopitos* or *calamarcets*. They take just seconds to deep-fry, which is the best way to serve them.

USING THE MICROWAVE

The microwave is now as much a part of the modern domestic Spanish kitchen as it is of the commercial one. It makes short work of many of the chores that originally made certain dishes lengthy and involved. We have not given microwave cooking times for the recipes in this classic collection, but the following points may be useful.

Roasting peppers: Roasting peppers over charcoal is the only way to produce the characteristic rich, smoky flavor, but they can be done in the microwave. Cut them in half and trim away the inner white membranes and the stem and seed segment. Place skin side up on a paper towel. Microwave on HIGH for $1\frac{1}{2}$ minutes, turn and microwave on HIGH for $1\frac{1}{2}$ minutes. Continue turning and cooking until the flesh feels tender and the skin has loosened and begun to wrinkle; the time will depend on the size and the thickness of the pepper. Remove, wrap in a cloth or a plastic bag and let stand for a few minutes before peeling.

Dried hot chili peppers: Fresh hot red chili peppers can be dried in the microwave. Place whole peppers on paper towels. Microwave on HIGH or MEDIUM HIGH for about 2 minutes, turning twice. Once they begin to feel dry, remove from the oven and allow to cool. If they require further drying, return and cook on HIGH. Overcooking will burn them.

Almonds and other nuts: Nuts toast well in the microwave. Spread on a microwave-safe plate, preferably not a plastic one as nuts become extremely hot when microwaved. They tend to cook from the inside out, so take care they are not overdone and burnt on the inside. Cook on HIGH, stirring every minute, until they turn a light golden brown. Remove (use an oven mitt as the plate usually becomes very hot) and leave on the plate to complete their cooking. They become darker as they cool. When cold, store in an airtight container if not using immediately.

Bread, croutons and toast: Many Spanish recipes require day-old bread. If unavailable, sliced fresh bread can be dried in the microwave. Place on a double thickness of paper towels and microwave on HIGH for 1 minute. Turn and repeat cooking in half-minute cycles until the bread is dried to the desired stage.

Fried bread: Microwave-dried bread can be "fried" in the microwave and will become a light golden color. Pour a film of oil into a microwave-safe plate and place bread in the oil. Brush generously with oil and microwave on HIGH, turning several times, for about $2\frac{1}{2}$ minutes until the bread is golden and crisp.

Pasta and rice: These generally take as long to cook in the microwave as on the cooktop, so follow traditional methods.

Vegetables: The Spanish traditionally cook vegetables until they are very tender, almost mushy. If preferred, microwave them by the usual methods, cooking them to the desired stage of tenderness.

Meat and poultry casseroles: Casseroled meats should be floured and browned in oil according to the recipe; then they can be microwaved with the usual methods applicable to braised meats, using one-third to one-half less water than the recipe recommends. Use a microwave-safe dish, covered with its lid or plastic wrap pierced in one corner. Cook on MEDIUM HIGH or MEDIUM and, in general, allow one-quarter to one-third the cooking time of the traditional recipe. Turn meats frequently to prevent exposed parts from overcooking and becoming dehydrated.

Fish and seafood: Poached fish and shellfish can be cooked in the microwave oven on MEDIUM HIGH with only a few tablespoons of the liquid required in the recipe (unless it is needed for a sauce). Cover tightly and cook for about one-quarter of the recommended cooking time. Test after 2 minutes, then more frequently after that.

Fried onion, garlic and tomato: These three ingredients, often with red peppers added, form the *sofrito* that is the basis of most Spanish dishes. They can be cooked in the microwave, although I do not find it any great advantage as it takes as long as in a pan and the flavor is less distinct. In a microwave-safe dish heat olive oil for 30 seconds. Add finely chopped onion and microwave on HIGH for 1 minute. Stir and microwave on HIGH a further one-half to 2 minutes, depending on the volume of onions. Add the garlic and microwave for 20 seconds, then add tomato and/or peppers, finely cut. Cover and microwave on HIGH for 1-minute cycles, stirring in between, until the mixture is thick and pulpy. Pass through a sieve or food processor/blender to purée if needed.

Reheating: Microwave reheating has become standard practice in *tascas* and *tabernas* for many kinds of *tapas* — unfortunately, I think, to the detriment of the food. Pastry-covered snacks such as *empanadas* and the various crisply fried *tapas* like *croquetas* and coated seafoods can become chewy and indigestible, their quality sadly diminished. Use only for reheating moist dishes — not those that are bread-based or that should have a crisp surface.

Eggs: For the most part the egg dishes in this book will not respond well to microwave cooking. A *tortilla*, for example, can be microwaved but will not have the appetizing appeal of one done in the pan by the traditional method. Poached eggs for adding to soups can be made by the microwave method of breaking them separately into little oiled dishes, pricking both whites and yolks several times and cooking for about 30 seconds on HIGH, or longer on MEDIUM HIGH, until the whites have firmed up and the yolks are still liquid.

GLOSSARY

Ajos tiernos: Garlic shoots, the slender flowering stems of garlic plants, have a delicate garlic flavor and crunchy texture. I discovered these delicious stems in their favorite habitat, *tortilla de ajos tiernos*, on the lunch menu during a train journey from Madrid to Barcelona and have pursued their brief season ever since. The fresh ones may not be around for long, but they are sold canned, and the garlic chives sold by Chinese greengrocers are a good substitute.

Almonds: *almendras* The Romans brought them to Spain, the Moors planted them in groves and taught the Spanish how to cook with them. They even replaced flour at one time of shortage and a new dish was invented, *mazapán*. Some of the world's best almonds are grown in Spain but few see the export market; the demand is too high at home. The Spanish nibble them in *tapas* bars, grind them for *turrón* and a variety of confections, cakes and biscuits. The Catalans could not make their famous *romesco* sauce or *picada* without them.

Aniseed: *matalahuva* Small seed spice resembling caraway with a strong anise flavor, used extensively in cakes, sweets and confections. Also flavors a liquor, *aguardiente de anises*, used in cooking.

Apples: *manzanas* An important crop in Asturias, where many different varieties are grown, mostly absorbed into the production of *sidre* (cider).

Apricots: *albaricoques*

Artichokes: *alcachofas* The fruits of a thistle, of which only the heart and ends of the leaves are edible, although the whole bud can be eaten if picked very young. Artichokes grow profusely in the Mediterranean region of Spain. The globelike fruit, pale green in color and faintly purple-tinged, should have tightly packed leaves and feel heavy and firm. Larger artichokes offer so little to eat that they are hardly worth the time it takes to cook them. Trim the stem level with the base and use a sharp knife, cutting upwards from the base, to remove the tips of the leaves. Plunge immediately into cold water acidulated with lemon juice or vinegar to prevent discoloration; untreated they turn an unappealing gray. Boil

until a knife can be plunged into the center. The Spanish add them to many dishes, including paellas and stews, or cook them in sauce, which makes for messy eating. Marinate small cooked artichokes in oil and vinegar with onion and herbs to serve as a *tapa*. To eat, pluck off the leaves one by one, dip the fleshy end into a sauce or dressing (*alioli* is a good match) and pull between the teeth to remove the tiny portion of edible flesh at the base of the leaf. When you reach the center, spoon out and discard the fuzzy "choke" and slice the tender heart.

Asparagus: *esparragos* Several types of asparagus grow in Spain — the plump cultivated white stalks of the type grown in Belgium and Germany, the common green asparagus and two wild varieties. *Esparragos trigueros* is so called because it springs up wild in wheat (*trigo*) fields, and *esparragos amargueros* is named for its bitter taste. They both have long, thin stems, with slightly thorny heads, and must be eaten young. Spain is one of Europe's largest cultivators of asparagus, the best of which grows near Aranjuez and in La Rioja.

Atún: (tuna) Sold in steaks for grilling, baking or stewing. Canned tuna is used in *tapas* and *entremeses* and in some cooked dishes. *Mojama* is strips of cured tuna.

Avocados: *aguacates*

Bananas: *plátanos* Mostly grown in the Canary Islands.

Bacalao: Bacalao is cod, and it is also dried salt cod, one of the mainstays of the Spanish cuisine. Large thick-fleshed cod fished from the cold Atlantic waters are slit lengthwise, flattened, thickly encrusted with coarse sea salt and dried. See page 266 for details of desalting *bacalao*.

Bay leaves: *laurel* The aromatic dried laurel or bay leaf is an important flavoring in soups and stews.

Beans, dried: *alubias secas* Dried beans are a good protein source, are inexpensive and can be stored indefinitely. They are one of the staples of the diet in isolated areas in wintertime, when they are cooked up in warming stews such as the *fabada asturiana* and the many different types of *ollas*, *cocidos* and *pucheros* with bits of meat and an assortment of vegetables. Many types of beans are used — substantial, creamy yellow *garbanzos* (chickpeas), tender *judías blancas* (white beans), *judías negra* (black beans), *judías rojas* (red beans), *faves* or *fabes* (haricot beans), *habas* (broadbeans), *judías pintas* (borlotti beans), *judías del barco* (butter beans), *lentejas* (lentils).

Beans, green: *judías verdes, habichuelas* Extensively used in Spain. Serve them as a first course, cooked up with shreds of ham or nuts. They are sliced into paellas, salads and the stewpot.

Beef: *carne de buey* or *carne de vacuno* Beef is not eaten much in Spain. *Ternera* (veal) is preferred, which is not veal in the true sense but is from animals that are at least a year old. Veal or yearling has a less pronounced taste, is decidedly more tender and is less fat than meat from older animals. Beef from fighting bulls is called *carne de lidia*. It is a deep-red color, almost gamey in taste. Butchers are obliged to display it separately from their other meats. *Ternera lechal* or *ternera de Ávila* is real veal, milk-fed calf no more than 12 months old. *Solomillo* is tenderloin (fillet); *lomo alto* and *lomo bajo* are the loin cuts; *chuletas* are rib steaks using the meat cut from between the ribs, while *chuletas de solomillo* are the chops including the loin and tenderloin of veal, a quite delicious cut; *cadera* is round (rump) steak. Remaining cuts correspond roughly to standard butchery methods to make cuts suitable for pot roasting, braising and stewing.

Beets (beetroot): *remolacha* Baby beets cooked whole, or larger beets boiled until tender and sliced, are made into salads or pickled to serve with *entremeses*. The greens of young beets are a tasty spinachlike vegetable.

Bell peppers (capsicums): *pimientos* If you're cooking Spanish food, you need to ensure a good supply of sweet green and red peppers. They come in many varieties and are used endlessly, particularly the red ones — which are the matured green ones and are milder and sweeter in taste. Red peppers are usually roasted and peeled (see page 266). Canned small sweet red peppers (*pimiento marrón*) are useful as a garnish. Dried sweet peppers are *nyoras* or *pimientos choriceros*, an essential ingredient in the Catalan *romesco* sauce. They are usually soaked or roasted and the flesh scraped from the skin. See also *chili*.

Brains: *sesos* Used as an ingredient in some meat pies to give a creamy texture, also cooked in various ways as *tapas*.

Breadcrumbs: *pan rallado* Finely ground crumbs used for breading.

Broadbeans: *habas* Plump, large pods that house about six square, flat, pale green beans which arrive in the markets at springtime. When very young they can be cooked in their pods, or the pods can be shredded to cook separately as a vegetable dish. The beans should be shelled immediately before cooking and boiled in lightly salted water. The skin of older beans turns hard and grayish, but can be slipped off to reveal the tender bright green bean inside. Do not cook broadbeans in aluminum or iron pans as the beans discolor.

Broccoli: *broculi, brecol*

Brussels sprouts: *coles de Bruselas*

Butter: *mantequilla* (also *margarina*) Not used a lot in Spain, olive oil doing most of the work that butter might do in other countries. The best is from the northern region of Asturias. Sold *sin sal* (unsalted) and *con sal* (salted).

Cabbage: *col, repollo, lombarda* (red cabbage)

Capers: *alcaparras* Used on dishes of the *escabeche* or marinated style.

Cardoons: *cardo* This relative of the artichoke has long, thick stalks that should be peeled and cooked until tender. They taste vaguely of celery, which can be substituted. When cut, cardoons should be soaked in acidulated water to prevent them from darkening. In many parts of Spain *cardo* is served on Christmas Eve.

Carrots: *zanahorias* As a vegetable carrots are superb with a sweet glaze, the Spanish favorite being *dulce de Málaga* — the sweet Málaga wine. Shred carrot finely, steep in ice water to crisp, and add to salads for delicious crunch.

Cauliflower: *coliflor*

Celery: *apio*

Chard: *acelgas* Swiss chard or silverbeet has long, thick white stems with deep green leaves resembling overgrown spinach. The stalks can be cooked separately and covered with a white sauce, or braised in butter. They may also be battered and fried like *cardo*. The leaves are treated in exactly the same way as spinach.

Cheese: *queso* Cheesemaking is a major industry in Spain. There are many interesting varieties made; see more details on page 282.

Cherries: *cerezas*

Chicken: *pollo*; stewing hen is *gallina*.

Chili (hot chili peppers): *pimientos picantes* or *guindillas*. The smallest are the hottest. Use fresh or dried; the latter can be stored indefinitely in a dry place. Thread fresh red chili peppers on a string and hang in the kitchen away from moisture to dry.

Chocolate: *chocolate* As a cooking ingredient use unsweetened baking chocolate. Chocolate for drinking is *chocolate a la taza*, which contains a thickener.

Chufa (*Cyperus esculentus*): The nutlike tuba, which grows on the knotted roots of a type of sedge common to the area of Valencia. They are brown on the outside, white and sweet within. Eaten raw or roasted as a nut, but more popularly in Spain they are ground into a milky sweet drink known as *horchata*, which tastes slightly like coconut milk. *Horchata* is sold in bars all over Spain as a refreshing summer drink.

Cidra: A member of the squash family with bright orange skin and flesh, which when cooked separates into fine strands. It is made into a thick sweet conserve or jam known as *cabello de ángel* (angel's hair) and used to fill small sweet *empanadillas* or tarts. Other conserves, particularly marmalade or apricot, can be substituted, although a quite acceptable jam can be made with mature, deep orange pumpkin.

Cinnamon: *canela* A cinnamon stick is popped into many stews and braised dishes, and is an invaluable flavoring in many stewed sweets. Ground cinnamon adorns innumerable desserts and is sprinkled over some drinks.

Cloves: *clavos* The word means "nail", and that is how the clove bud looks. Its strong flavor should be treated with respect; in moderation it adds subtle overtones to all kinds of dishes sweet and savory. Overuse simply numbs the palate.

Coriander: *cilantro* The whole spice and the fresh green leaves, known as Mexican or Chinese parsley, are both used in Spanish cooking. The leaves have a distinctly pungent aroma that is not always liked, but it diminishes when cooked.

Add it to salads and soups or use the delicate fronds as a garnish.

Corn: *maíz*

Cornmeal: *maíz molido* This makes bread and gruel and is used for a similar thick, pastelike porridge the Italians call *polenta*. Use cornmeal also for breading, particularly oysters. Finely milled cornstarch (cornflour) is *harina fina de maíz*.

Courgette: see Zucchini.

Cream: *nata* in Spain is a heavy whipping cream.

Cucumber: *pepino* A basic ingredient in *gazpachos* and salads, this cooling summer vegetable can also be lightly sautéed. Use to make edible containers for salad by cutting into sections or removing a slice from the top and scooping out the seeds.

Cumin: *comino* The Moors introduced their favorite spice, cumin, to the Spanish, who readily absorbed it into their cuisine to add its slight pungency to many braised and baked dishes. A little touch of it in tomato sauce and soups is a masterful addition.

Curly endive: *escarola* A slight misnomer here. Actually escarole is Batavian endive, which is not as curly as the very curly-leafed lettuce the Spanish mean to describe by this name. Curly endive is used extensively in Spanish salads, particularly the Catalonian specialty *xato*. The lettuce should be picked while young and light green in color, and the best part is the tender heart. See also Endive.

Custard apples: *chirimoyas*

Dates: *datils*

Duck: *pato*

Eggplant: *berenjenas* These came to Spain with the Moors, who also knew how to make the most of them in the kitchen. They range from tiny clusters through long, thin, pale green ones to gigantic purple globes that should be sliced and sprinkled with salt before cooking to draw off any bitter taste.

Endive: *endibia* Belgian endive or witloof is a winter vegetable with long white-tipped, cream-green leaves compacted into cone shapes. The leaves, which have a slightly bitter taste, are separated and used whole or shredded in salads, or the vegetable is quartered lengthwise and braised. Individual leaves can be filled with tangy cheese or salmon cream to serve as canapes. The English call it chicory, which confuses it with another salad green — a type of lettuce, the French *chicorée frisée* or curly endive, see above.

Fennel: *hinojo* Fennel grows wild in the Mediterranean regions. Its anise flavor complements seafoods and the bulbous layered root can be sliced into salads to give a fresh taste and appealing crunch. Fennel seeds have a natural affinity with seafood and lend a superb flavor to soups and stews. Simmer them in the stock, and strain before adding seafood. Fennel is also used in curing olives, see page 279.

Figs: *higos* This delectable, delicate fruit grows on gnarled, stunted gray trees with broad, rough-surfaced gray-green leaves. Requiring little from nature, fig trees push up between rocks in barren terrain, cling to steep, dry hillsides and canyons, emerge between flagstones on a patio to offer an abundance of their sweet, plump fruit. The early summer crop is the black variety, followed by the brown-purple common fig. Eat them straight from the tree, skin and all, or slice onto salads, fruit salads or cheese platters. They are delicious with *jamón serrano* sliced wafer-thin. Much of the crop is dried and pressed to meet a demanding market. Cook both fresh and dried figs with a little sugar to make compotes and pie fillings and a wonderful, grainy conserve.

Fish: see page 283.

Flour: *harina de trigo* All-purpose (plain) flour is what is used for breadmaking and in most recipes, unless otherwise specified. Cake flour is *harina para repostería*, and a coarse flour, *harina para rebozar*, is literally "flour for frying," used for breading fried foods, although cornmeal is sometimes used for this.

Game: *caza* Spain has plenty of hunting reserves avidly attended by game shooters. Various types of game birds are taken (they are listed here under their different names), and game meats include wild boar (*jabalí*) and deer (*ciervo*) of several kinds. *Venado*, venison, is sold by specialist butchers.

Garbanzos (chickpeas): *garbanzos* These nutty-tasting dried peas are an invaluable protein source and a major ingredient in Spanish cooking, blending well with the strong tastes of tomato, *bacalao*, *chorizo* and peppers. The hardest of the dried beans, they should be soaked overnight before slowly cooking for several hours (a pressure cooker speeds up cooking but take care not to overdo them and end up with mush). They are added to soups, omelettes and all kinds of stews.

Garlic: *ajo* Buy firm, plump heads and store in a cool, dry part of the kitchen away from moisture. A single clove is a *diente*, but rarely are they used on their own. They are reputed to be excellent for improving the quality of the blood, so do as the Spanish do and add them in quantity to most dishes. Cooked garlic is far less pungent than the raw garlic added to salad dressings. Combat the latter by chewing parsley after the meal.

Goose: *oca*

Grapes: *uvas* Grapes have been an important crop in Spain for many centuries. Numerous varieties are grown, providing plump black and white table grapes as well as the raw material for the wine producers. One of the most famed, and appreciated for the table, is the sweet Málaga grape, *moscatel*.

Grelos: Shoots of young turnip plants used as a vegetable, particularly in Galicia. Young leaves of giant white (icicle) radish or young beet leaves can replace them. Cook in same way as spinach.

Guinea hen/guinea fowl: *pintada* These probably came to Spain from Africa where they were native. Any recipe for partridge or pheasant can be made with guinea fowl, the hens being more tender than the cocks.

Ham: *jamón*, see page 281.

Kid (baby goat): *cabrito* The slightly gamey taste of kid is much appreciated. Substitute it in any recipe for lamb.

Kidneys: *riñones* A prized dish from Andalusia is *riñones al jerez*, in which diced kidneys are braised in sherry. Grilled kidney on skewers is a popular *tapa*.

Lamb: *cordero pierna* is the leg; *chuletas* are cutlets of chops; the shoulder is *paletilla* or *espaldilla*, the inexpensive breast or flap is *pecho*. Most prized is *cordero lechal*, milk-fed baby lamb no more than three months old. The flesh is white and delicate in flavor. They are split lengthwise or sold whole. Roast baby lamb is a special feature at all kinds of festive get-togethers. In many villages the local baker takes charge of the roasting in his large brick oven, in a tradition that has continued for many centuries.

Leeks: *puerro* An ancient member of the onion family, leeks grow wild in many parts of Europe including Spain. They have a more delicate flavor than onions, making them more suited to some soups and sauces. They should be trimmed at the root, slit lengthwise and thoroughly rinsed of grit before use.

Lettuce: *lechuga* The native lettuce is a loose-leafed type similar to, although darker than, romaine or cos, which can be used instead. Otherwise *escarola* or curly endive is the most frequently used salad lettuce. Rinse thoroughly in cold water and avoid overhandling, which bruises the leaves.

Liver: *hígado* The Spanish use pork, lamb, veal and beef liver, the former having a strong flavor that responds well to strong seasonings. A popular pig's liver dish is *chanfaina*, in which the blood is also used.

Melons: *melones* Introduced to Spain by the Moors, they are a popular summer dessert. Several types are grown and come to market through the year; *ogén* and cantaloupe in spring, the *melon reticulado* covered with a fine tracery of white veins, and honeydew midyear. *Elche* or *tendrel* melons, with their green and yellow thick-furrowed skins, arrive at the markets in October for eating right through winter. They are particularly delicious served with thinly sliced *jamón serrano*.

Milk: *leche* Cows', sheep's and goats' milk are all sold in the Spanish markets, often direct from the churn.

Mint: *hierbabuena* It means "good weed" in Spanish and they love its fresh flavor, adding it to soups, rice and noodle dishes, fish soups and stews. It does wonders to a *gazpacho*.

Mushrooms: *setas* *Setas* describes all types of edible wild mushrooms found in Spain, of which there are many, many varieties. Mushrooms are not widely eaten, but where they grow in profusion, they are consumed with passion — in the Basque country, in Catalonia and in Galicia.

Hongos, a name often associated with mushrooms, actually means edible fungus, and is used to describe certain of Spain's wild mushrooms. *Champiñones* are cultivated button mushrooms.

Mustard: *mostaza*

Nutmeg: *nuez moscada*

Nuts: *nueces* The most important to Spanish cooking are almonds and pine nuts, which are listed separately. Peanuts (*cacahuetes*) grow well and are a popular snack food but rarely used in cooking. Hazelnuts (*avellanas*) are used in *turrón* and other confectionery and the toasted ground nuts are added to sauces, particularly in Catalan cooking. Chestnut (*castaña*) trees grow in several parts of Spain, particularly in the Pyrenees, and are used in cooking. Fall means the appearance of vendors on streetcorners and the enticing smell of freshly roasted chestnuts to nibble on the way home from work.

Oils, cooking: *aceite* Olive oil is the one we most commonly associate with Spanish cooking, however they manufacture a number of other high-grade vegetable oils. *Aceite de girasol* is sunflower oil, made from the seeds harvested from the vast plantations of sunflowers that occupy central Spain. *Aceite de cacahuete* (peanut oil) and *aceite de cártamo* (safflower oil) as well as *aceite de soja* (soybean oil) and *aceite de maiz* (corn oil) are all locally made, but not necessarily cheaper than olive oil.

Olive oil: *aceite de oliva* Olive oil comes in different grades, the best being *aceite de oliva virgen* or *extra virgen* (virgin or first-press olive oil), unrefined and straight from the presses. *Aceite de oliva puro* is pure olive oil, which is usually a blend of virgin and refined olive oil, while the lower-grade, more refined oil is *aceite de orujo*.

Olives: *aceitunas* Spain produces masses of olives in many varieties. See page 279.

Onions: *cebollas* A large part of Spain's cultivated land is devoted to growing onions. It is the sweet yellow variety that is chopped and cooked until caramelized to make *sofrito* and to flavor all kinds of sauces, soups and stocks. But also grown are tiny, flattish, pink-red onions called *cebollas francesas*, which are perfect for salads, and round green ones. Spring onions have a delicate flavor. Their bulbs are braised as a vegetable and the green tops eaten raw with some dishes, or chopped into salads and soups. Shallots are *chalotas*, chives are *cebollinas*. In Tarragona there is the annual ritual of the *calcotada*, where young onions are roasted over charcoal fires (see page 280).

Oranges: *naranjas* When the Moors brought oranges to Spain they named them for the Sanskrit word *naranga*, meaning sublime fruit. The trees, hardy and adaptable, with their shiny dark leaves and richly perfumed waxy white blossoms, were planted as ornamentals around many of the important new Moorish buildings, including the Alhambra Palace at the edge of Granada city and in the square of the Great Mosque in Córdoba. They were of the bitter orange variety, the fruit fragrant but inedible. The fruit from many of the thousands of bitter orange trees that line the streets of Sevilla is still sent to the United Kingdom to be processed into marmalade — some for re-export to Spain. Bitter orange juice is used in some Spanish dishes for flavoring, but it can be replaced by sweet orange juice balanced with vinegar or lemon juice. Sweet oranges were introduced from the Far East, the Spanish naming them *chinas*.

Oregano: *orégano* A must to add to marinades and many braised dishes, and to sprinkle fresh over salads.

Palm heart: *cogollo de palmito* The heart of the palmetto palm is canned to eat as a salad ingredient. It has a mild, indistinct flavor and agreeable crunchy texture. Sold canned, they are simply drained for use. Excellent in combination with seafood and cured ham. Substitute artichoke hearts or asparagus.

Paprika: *pimientón* Made from a type of bell (capsicum) pepper, this richly red-colored spice comes in hot and strong *fuerte* and sweet *dulce*. It, more than any other ingredient, adds the strong red color to many Spanish dishes and most Spanish cured sausages.

Parsley: *perejil* It is the flat-leafed type that is used in Spain, similar to the Italian variety. Add it generously to most of your savory dishes or chop it finely to sprinkle over the top.

Partridges: *perdices* (*perdiz* singular) One of the most popular game birds in Spain. There are two types hunted for the kitchen, common or gray and red-legged partridge. They appear on menus in most parts of the country. This relative of the pheasant is best roasted when young, and braised if older. Generally they are hung for three to four days, depending on their age and size; half to one bird makes a serving. Grouse, woodcock or pheasant can substitute. In certain recipes, baby chickens can replace partridge.

Peaches: *melocotones* Peaches ripen in midsummer to the delight of many Spanish, particularly in the eastern provinces, where they are much enjoyed as a dessert — simply poached in syrup or marinated in sweetened red wine. But nothing can beat biting into a cold, sweet, tree-ripened peach and washing it down with a glass of icy champagne. Freestone and clingstone varieties are both grown, as well as nectarines.

Pears: *peras* Many different types are on the market, from enormous pale-skinned ones with soft, sweet flesh to smaller, firm types ideal for cooking. For the recipes in this book, choose the latter type, which have crisp, almost potatolike flesh. Japanese pears (*nashi*) are a good substitute in these dishes.

Peas: *guisantes* You'll find peas turning up in quite unexpected places when eating Spanish food. They add a bright green contrast in *paella*, scrambled eggs, fish stews, veal pot roasts. In fact, you're more likely to find them as an ingredient than as a vegetable. If using frozen peas, add them towards the end of cooking so they won't be overdone.

Pepper: *pimienta* Not to be confused with sweet peppers, which are *pimiento*. Crush whole peppercorns in a mortar or peppermill immediately before use. Black is most commonly used, but white (*pimienta blanca*) and green (*pimienta verde*) are available, the latter sold in small tins for use in sauces to accompany steaks or fish.

Peppers: see Bell peppers.

Pheasant: *faisán* The cock, although blessed with distinctive plumage, has less appeal on the table than the hen which is plumper and generally more tender. Pheasant should be hung unplucked from 4 to 10 days. Pheasant can be used in any recipe for partridge.

Pigeon (squab): *pichón, paloma*

Pineapples: *piñas*

Pine nuts (pine kernels): *piñones* One of the priciest nuts on the market, these tiny golden points are the kernels of pine cones. Raw they have a bland, slightly saplike taste; roasted they are pleasantly nutty, with a creamy texture. Pine nuts have become a popular addition to salads, stuffings, batters and coatings for fried foods, confections and sweet dishes. They are readily available where nuts and health foods are sold. Store in an airtight container and use within a few months or, like all nuts, they develop a rancid taste.

Plums: *ciruelas: ciruelas pasas* are dried plums or prunes.

Pomegranates: *granadas* What could be more Spanish than this red, globe-shaped fruit named for one of the country's major cities — but strangely, they are not often found in Spanish markets. Look for these firm, red-skinned fruits in season during early fall. Scatter the tiny, rubylike, juicy seeds onto fruit salads, over ice cream, into sauces to accompany fish or pork. Their tart-sweet taste is a pleasing contrast. The juice is very refreshing but you need a lot of fruit to extract a small amount.

Pork: *solomillo de cerdo* is tenderloin (fillet); *lomo* is boned loin; *chuletas* are cutlets or chops; *paletilla* is the shoulder or picnic hand; *pierna* or *jamón* is the leg or ham; *panceta* is the belly or fresh bacon; *costillas* are the spareribs, and *manos* are the hocks. *Cochinillo* is whole suckling pig. If you can get one killed at about 4 weeks old and weighing about 4 lb (2 kg) it is just big enough for a small family meal and will be supremely tender. It will take just minutes to roast, the flesh turning white and very succulent, the skin crisp and richly flavored. Spanish butchers usually slit suckling pigs along the length, leaving the head in one piece. For a crowd I buy a pig of about 20 lb (10 kg), which roasts over a charcoal spit in about $2\frac{1}{2}$ hours.

Potato: *patata* Thanks to Christopher Columbus, this vegetable appears on all European tables — including Spain's — more than any other food. *Patatas fritas* (French fries) are a favorite, but there is nothing quite like the flavor of a plain boiled white potato in Spain. Garlic and paprika are frequently partnered with potato, as is *chorizo* cut into chunks.

Prickly pears: *chumbo* An import from the New World, a cactus with flat paddlelike leaves covered with imposing spines produces soft-fleshed, juicy fruit with a pleasant, resinous taste. They should be carefully peeled using two knives, avoiding hand contact with the fruit as the skin is covered with hairy spines. A nice addition to fruit or vegetable salads.

Pumpkin: *calabaza* Bright orange pumpkin, from the squash family, is cooked as a vegetable, but you'll more often find it adding sweetness to soups and stews. A particular kind of squash known as *cidra* in Spain, and elsewhere as "spaghetti squash," is used to make jam. See *cidra*.

Quail: *codornices (codorniz* singular) Quail abound in Spain and appear frequently on Spanish menus. One plump bird makes a small serving, but two is generally better. They are excellent grilled or roasted, the meat has a fine texture and a mildly gamey flavor. Care should be taken in cooking to keep them moist by brushing with oil or covering the breast with fat bacon.

Quince: *membrillo* This yellowed applelike fruit has never appealed as a table fruit and is usually cooked. Bake, stew or poach quinces to make compotes, jams and jellies. Quince jelly is the sliced fruit boiled with sugar, then strained through muslin; it firms into a jelly that can be sliced. An inspirational addition to the cheese board, with either salty firm cheeses or the softer creamier types.

Rabbit: *conejo* You'll frequently find rabbit dishes on Spanish menus. They are raised domestically for the kitchen, and also taken as game. Best when young at no more than 3 lb, when the meat is tender and delicate. They can be fried or grilled, and are often braised. Use in any recipe for chicken. *Liebre* is hare, much larger and stronger in taste. It should be marinated before cooking.

Radishes: *rabanos* Small bright red radishes are used in salads, thinly sliced, quartered or decoratively cut. Refrigerate before use, and steep in ice water for 20 minutes after preparation to crisp them.

Raisins: *uvas pasas* Dried sweet grapes (raisins) are used in many Spanish meat dishes.

Raspberries: *frambuesas*

Rice: *arroz* The bulk of the Spanish rice crop is grown in the marshy hinterland of Valencia. It is of the short variety, with a round grain. Rice from this region has the best flavor of any grown in Spain, and is preferred by most cooks. Long-grain rice is not a substitute. See page 267 for more information.

Rosemary: *romero* This fragrant herb, with its spiky leaves and purple flowers, grows wild in most Mediterranean countries, and Spain is no exception. Branches of rosemary are used on the fire when grilling meat to impart a distinct flavor and are use in wood-fired bread ovens. The Spanish do not cook with it extensively, but try adding a sprig to stews and braised dishes, and to just about anything containing lamb, to which it has a natural affinity.

Saffron: *azafrán* The most expensive spice in the world, and little wonder, as each tiny stigma of the saffron crocus has to be hand-picked. The whole stigmas or "threads" are best, as saffron loses its delicate aroma when ground to a powder — and is often supplemented by fillers to make it less expensive, and therefore less effective in a dish. Its ability to impart a bright golden yellow color to foods makes it as appealing as the subtle taste it also lends. *Paella* would not be the same without saffron (although unfortunately for economy, an artificial colorant is often used). The threads should be wrapped in a square of aluminum foil and toasted briefly in a hot oven or dry pan before grinding in a mortar, adding a little boiling water to help release the color.

Salt: *sal*

Sausages: *embutidos, chorizos, salchichones*; see page 281.

Shellfish: *mariscos*, see pages 245 and 284.

Spinach: *espinacas* Fresh spinach should be very thoroughly washed before use to remove grit. Cook it quickly in a covered pan with only the water remaining on the leaves from washing. The Catalans like to add raisins and pine nuts to cooked spinach. Substitute Swiss chard (silverbeet) leaves. Frozen spinach can be used in soups and stuffings.

Strawberries: *fresas*

Sugar: *azúcar*

Sweetbreads: *mollejas* The pancreas and thymus glands, usually of beef or veal, which are a meat delicacy. They should be soaked and blanched before using. They have the consistency and taste of brains, although firmer in texture.

Sweet potato: *batata, boniato*

Testicles: *criadillas* beef and lambs' testicles are sold by Spanish butchers. They are cooked simply, usually breaded or floured and quickly fried in oil.

Thyme: *tomillo* This fragrant herb with delicate small leaves grows wild. It is used when curing olives, and extensively in marinades and to flavor stews and stuffings.

Tomalley: yellow yolk-like fat inside shellfish.

Tomatoes: *tomates* I am always surprised in Spain to find insipid crunchy green-pink tomato on my plate. Tomatoes are such an intrinsic part of Spanish cooking that one expects the salad tomatoes to be as they would be in Italy — bright red, sweet and fleshily soft. It seems that the former are preferred for eating fresh, the well-ripened red tomatoes being reserved for cooking, to give good color and flavor to *gazpacho* and *sofrito* and the many dishes into which tomatoes go. And of course, for smearing over coarse country bread in Catalonia to make *Pa amb Tomàquet*. Tomatoes for cooking are always peeled, which is easily done by floating them in boiling water for about 8 seconds (if they are very ripe, longer if not). And they are seeded by slicing in half and squeezing out the seeds. For dishes where the tomato needs to be finely chopped, this process can be simplified by seeding and grating the flesh. I like to buy tomatoes when they are well priced, allow them a few days in a warm part of the kitchen to fully ripen, then store them in the freezer already peeled and seeded. Do the same with caramelized onions so you have an instant *sofrito*.

Tongue: *lengua* Beef, veal, pork and lamb tongues are all used fresh or salted. Salted tongues should be soaked for several hours, or overnight, to reduce saltiness. Cook in unsalted water until they can be easily pierced, then pull off the tough outer skin and trim the root section, removing the small bones at the end. Strong tomato and pepper-based sauces go well with the unique taste and texture of tongue.

Tripe: *callos* I know of no other countries except England and China where tripe is eaten quite as much as it is in Spain. And little wonder it is so enjoyed, they cook it so well. *Callos a la madrileña*, braised spicy tripe, is one of the highlights of a visit to a Madrid *tapas* bar. In many regions tripe and garbanzos are partnered in a rich and sustaining hotpot.

Turnips: *nabos* Baby turnips are delightful raw and braised as a vegetable dish, otherwise Spanish cooks add them to the stewpot. Their shoots are *grelos*, prized in Galicia as a tender green vegetable.

Vinegar: *vinagre* Wine vinegar, both white (which is actually a pale amber color) and red, is used except when otherwise specified. Sherry vinegar, a specialty of Jerez, is strong with a distinct fragrance. Cider vinegar may be used if preferred.

Zucchini (courgettes): *calabacines* Small squash (marrows) resembling cucumbers. Zucchini has a delicate flavor and can be cooked skin and all as a vegetable. Try it sliced, floured and deep fried, or steamed. Cut into sections and scooped out it makes an attractive side vegetable or appetizer, stuffed with seafood or diced vegetables.

A-Z SPANISH/ENGLISH GLOSSARY

Abadejo: haddock, codfish

Aceite: oil

Aceituna: olive

Acelgas: Swiss chard, silverbeet

Adobo: marinade; *adobado*, marinated

Afoga el pitu: a type of cheese, dry and cone-shaped

Agua: water

Aguacate: avocado

Aguadiente: distilled liquor

Ahumado: smoked

Ajo: garlic

Ajoarriero: mule-driver's style, descriptive of a *posada* dish

Albóndiga: meatball

Alcaparras: capers

Alella: wine demarcation region

Alicante: wine demarcation region; a type of soft, unaged white goat's cheese

All i oli (alioli): Catalan garlic mayonnaise

Almejas: clams

Almendra: almond

Almendras garrapiñadas: sugar-coated almonds

Almíbar: sugar syrup

Alubia: haricot bean

Ampurdán-Costa Brava: wine demarcation region

Anca de rana: frog's legs

Anchoa: anchovy (also *boqueron*)

Anguila: eel

Angula: baby eel no more than 2 inches (5 cm) long

Anís: anisette, a strong grape spirit flavored with aniseed

Anso: cheese produced in valley of Huesca from Pyrenean sheep's milk, creamy and mild

Arenque: herring

Armada: a type of semihard, slightly bitter cheese from León

Arroz: rice

Asado: roast (*asar*, to roast)

Atadito de hierbas aromáticas: bouquet garni

Atún: tuna, tunnyfish

Avellana: hazelnut

Azafrán: saffron

Azahar: orangeflower water

Azúcar: sugar

Azúcar tamizado: confectioners' (icing) sugar

Bacalao: cod (fish) and dried salt cod

Banderilla: an appetizer on a skewer

Baño-maría: bain marie (cooking utensil)

Barbacoa: barbecue

Batata: sweet potato

Becada: woodcock

Berenjena: eggplant, aubergine

Besugo: red bream (fish)

Beyusco: an Asturian cheese of mixed ewes' and goats' milk. Hard and amber skin, may be smoked

Bizcochos: cakes of light texture, various kinds

Blanquear: to blanch

Bocadillo: sandwich (usually made on a crisp white roll)

Bogavante: lobster

Boleto: boletus mushroom

Bollo: bread roll or bun

Bonito: bonito (fish), similar to tuna

Boquerones: anchovies (fish)

Brasa: charcoal embers; *a la brasa:* charcoal grill

Bota: leather wine bottle

Brasear: to braise

Buey: beef; also a type of crab

Bullabesa: fish stew similar to French bouillabaise

Buñuelo: fritter, *buñuelito:* small fritter

Burgos: a type of soft ewes' milk cheese, widely available and much enjoyed. Good as a dessert cheese with nuts and fruit. Not fermented but submerged in brine for 24 hours

Butifarra: Catalan sausage (*blanca* is white, *negra* is black)

Caballa: mackerel (fish)

Cabello de angel: angel's hair. A sweet squash jam

Cabracho: scorpionfish

Cabrales: a type of blue cheese of excellent creamy quality

Cabrito: kid (baby goat)

Cacao: cocoa bean

Cacahuete: peanut

Cacerola: cooking pot, casserole, saucepan

Cádiz: a type of cheese, fresh, white and full of tiny holes, made from goats' milk

Café: coffee — *café con leche* is coffee with milk; *cortado espresso* with a little milk; *solo* is black

Calabacín: zucchini (courgette), squash, marrow

Calabaza: pumpkin, squash

Calamar: squid (calamari), also *chopitos*, *calamarcets*

Calcotada: grilled spring onions, see page 280

Caldereta: stew, stewpot

Caldo: stock

Callos: tripe

Calostro: a type of cheese

Camarón: small shrimp (prawn)

Camerano: a type of goats' milk cheese from Rioja

Canaillas de la isla: pointed-shelled whelks

Canelones: canneloni

Canela: cinnamon

Cangrejo: crab

Cangrejo del río: crayfish

Caracol: snail

Cardo: cardoon

Carne: meat; beef is *carne de vacuno* or *vaca*, veal is *carne de ternera*

Carne picada: ground (minced/chopped) meat

Castaña: chestnut

Caviar: caviar

Cayena: cayenne pepper

Caza: game; *la caza* is the hunt

Cazuela (cazuela de barro): casserole of earthenware, usually glazed internally

Cazuelita: small version of the above for individual or small servings

Cebolla: onion

Cebollita: small or bulbous spring onion

Cebrero: a type of cheese, tangy and mushroom-shaped

Cena: dinner or supper, the evening meal

Centolla: spider crab (also *shangurro*, *txangurro*)

Cerdo: pork, pig

Cerdo ibérico: Spanish black native pig

Cervecería: bar

Cervera: a type of cheese from Valencia, made from sheeps' and cows' milk, unaged

Cerveza: beer

Cigala: Dublin Bay prawn, saltwater crayfish

Cilantro: coriander leaves

Ciruela: plum

Clavo: clove

Cochinillo: suckling pig

Cocido: a meal-in-a-pot, stew or hotpot. A cooking method of slow simmering in a pot

Cocina: cuisine; kitchen

Cocochas: see *Kokotxas*

Codorniz: quail

Cogollo: heat or core

Col: cabbage

Coliflor: cauliflower

Comida: meal; food, lunch

Comino: cumin

Coñac: cognac

Concha: a type of shellfish or clam

Conejo: rabbit

Confitería: confectionery shop

Confitura: preserve, conserve, jam

Congrio: conger eel

Cordero: lamb

Costilla: rib

Crema: cream (as in soup or covered with cream sauce)

Crema pastelería: cream-filled pastries

Criadillas: testicles

Criadilla de tierra: truffle

Croquetas: small fritters or croquettes

Cuaresma: Lent

Champiñon: button mushroom

Chanquete: small fry of the goby fish

Charcutería: curing meat; delicatessen where cured meats are sold

Chicarro: horse mackerel (fish)

Chilindrón: a spicy sauce from Aragón

China: a strainer

Chipirón: small squid (*calamarcet*), also *txipirones*

Chirimoya: custard apple

Choco: small cuttlefish

Chocolate: chocolate

Chocolatería: chocolate shop (cafe)

Chorizo: cured sausage of pork and paprika

Chuleta: chop or cutlet

Churros: fried doughnutlike pastries eaten at breakfast

Dátil: date

Datil de mar: sea date, a type of dark brown mussel

Denton: dentex fish

Desayuno: breakfast

Despojos: offal, variety meats

Diente de ajo: clove ("tooth") of garlic

Dorado: gilthead (fish)

Dulce: sweet

Dulce de membrillo: quince paste or jelly

Eglefino: haddock (fish)

Embutido: sausage

Empanada: pastry-covered pie

Empanadilla: small pie

Empanado: breaded

Emperador (pez espada): swordfish

Endibia: endive

Ensalada: salad

Entremeses: hors d'oeuvre, starter platter

Erizo de mar: sea urchin

Escabeche: marinade (*en escabeche* is pickled)

Escalope: a thin slice of meat

Escarola: curly endive

Esparragos: asparagus

Especias: spices

Espinacas: spinach

Estofado: stew; *estofar:* to stew

Estrellita: a type of star-shaped pasta

Fabes, faves: dried butter beans

Faisán: pheasant

Fiambre: cold cuts (sliced meats); pâté

Fideo: vermicelli

Flamear: to flambé

Flan: a tart or baked pudding like a caramel custard

Foie-gras: goose liver

Freír: to fry

Frito: fried

Gallego: Galician cows' milk cheese

Gallina: hen, stewing hen

Gallo: cock

Gambas: shrimp, prawns

Gamonedo: a type of cheese from Asturias

Garbanzo: chickpea

Garúm: a type of fish sauce, and anchovy spread

Gazpacho: a soup, usually served cold

Girasol: sunflower

Gorbea: a type of cheese from Gorbea mountains in Viscaya

Granada: pomegranate

Gratinado: "au gratin"

Grazalema: a type of cheese from Cádiz made of ewes' milk

Grelos: turnip greens

Guarnición: garnish

Guindilla: chili pepper

Guisantes: peas

Habas: broadbeans

Habichuelas: beans (green or dried)

Harina: flour

Helado: ice cream, iced

Hierbabuena: mint

Hígado: liver

Higos: figs

Hinojo: fennel

Hojaldre: flaky and puff pastry

Hongo: wild mushrooms, edible fungus

Horno: oven; *al horno* is baked

Huevo: egg

Idiazábal: a type of cheese made in Navarra and Guipuzcoa of ewes' milk

Jabalí: wild boar

Jamón: ham (*jamón serrano,* mountain ham; *jamón de Jabugo,* the best type of Spanish ham; *jamón de York,* cooked ham)

Jarabes: sugar syrup, almost caramelized, for making sweets

Jerez: sherry (amontillado and fino — dry; oloroso — slightly sweet)

Judías: beans (*judías verdes,* green beans; *judías secas,* dried beans)

Jumilla: a wine demarcation region

Kokotxas: a gelatinous part, the size of an oyster, found in the throat of certain large fish, considered a delicacy in the Basque country, where it is fried and cooked in a light sauce

Lacón: cured pork shoulder, pickled (salt) pork

La Mancha: a wine demarcation region

Langosta: spicy or rock lobster

Langostino: large shrimp (prawn)

Lardear: to lard or bard (add fat to dry meats to keep moist during cooking)

Laurel: bay leaf

Lechal: milk-fed; *lechazo* is baby lamb or milk-fed lamb

Leche: milk

Lechuga: lettuce

Legumbre: vegetable of the legume type such as pulses and roots

Lengua: tongue

Lenguado: sole (fish)

Lenteja: lentil (brown, green, red or yellow)

León: a type of cows' milk cheese

Levadura en polvo: baking powder; *levadura prensada* is fresh yeast

Liebre: hare

Lima: lime

Limón: lemon

Lombarda: red cabbage

Lomo: fresh loin of pork, also a type of cured pork loin stuffed into sausage skins and dried

Longaniza: a type of thin sausage

Los Santos: All Saints' Day, November 1st. Typical treats for the day are *huesos de santo,* little pastries shaped like bones, and *panellets.*

Lubina: sea bass (fish)

Mahón: a cheese from the Balearic Islands

Maíz: corn

Málaga: a type of white goats' cheese molded in *esparto* forms

Manchego: Queso manchego is Spain's best-known cheese (see page 282)

Manteca: lard

Mantequilla: butter

Manzanas: apples

Manzanilla: sherry, the dried camomile flower used as an infusion, and a type of small olive

Margarina: margarine

Mariscos: shellfish

Masa: dough or pastry; *masa quebrada* is rich flan pastry

Matanza, La: the annual slaughter of the pigs

Mató: a type of cheese

Mayonesa (or *mahonesa*): mayonnaise

Mazapán: marzipan

Mejillón: mussel

Mejorana: marjoram

Melocotón: peach

Melón: melon

Membrillo: quince
Menú del día: menu of the day
Mercado: market
Merienda: late afternoon snack
Merlo: wrasse (fish)
Merluza: hake (fish)
Mero: grouper (fish)
Miel: honey
Migas: fried breadcrumbs
Mollejas: sweetbreads
Morcilla: blood sausage, blood pudding
Morella: goats' cheese from Castellón
Morón: a type of cheese
Mostaza: mustard
Mujol: gray mullet (fish)
Nabos: turnips
Naranja: oranges
Nata: cream
Navaja: razor clam
Navidad: Christmas
Nécora: small boxlike crab
Nueva cocina or *Nueva cocina vasca:* The new style of cooking, a Spanish version of *nouvelle cuisine* led by the chefs in Catalonia and the Basque Country
Nuez (pl. *neuces*): nuts
Nuez moscada: nutmeg
Nyora: sweet dried red pepper
Oca: goose
Olla: stewpot
Orduña: a sheep's milk cheese from Alava
Oregano: oregano
Oropesa: sheep's milk cheese like Manchego
Ostión: Portuguese oyster
Ostra: oyster
Paella: a classic rice dish cooked in a wide, flat pan
Paellera: the pan used for cooking paella
Paletilla: shoulder (meat cut)
Palmito: heart of palm
Paloma: pigeon (squab) or dove
Palometa: pompano (fish)
Palometa negra: black pomfret (fish)

Panadería: bakery: *a la panadera* refers to food cooked in a baker's oven
Pan: bread
Pan dulce: sweet bread and buns
Pan rallado: breadcrumbs
Panceta: streaky bacon, fatty pork
Pargo: type of dentex fish
Parrilla: grill (*a la parrilla* means cooked on a grill or grid over charcoal)
Pasas: dried, as in fruit (*uvas pasas,* raisins; *ciruelas pasas,* prunes)
Pascua: Easter
Pasiego: cows' milk cheese from Santander
Pastelería: pastry shop
Pastel: pie or pastry
Pata: leg or hock (meat cut)
Patata: potato
Pato: duck
Pavo: turkey
Pedroches: a type of sheep's milk cheese from Córdoba
Pepinillo: dill (cucumber) pickle or gherkin
Pepino: cucumber
Pera: pear
Percebes: rock or goose barnacles
Perdiz: partridge
Perejil: parsley
Pescadilla: small hake (fish)
Pescado: fish
Picada: ground ingredients used in Catalonia to thicken a sauce
Picante: hot, spicy
Pichón: pigeon
Pierna: leg (meat cut)
Pimentón: paprika
Pimienta: pepper (spice); *pimienta en grano* (peppercorns)
Pimiento: sweet bell (capsicum) pepper
Piña: pineapple
Pinchos: Small kebabs served as a *tapa,* also known as *morunos*
Piñones: pine nuts, pine kernels
Pintada: guinea fowl

Plancha: griddle (*a la plancha,* cooked on a griddle)
Plátano: banana
Pochas: type of dried beans
Pollo: chicken
Polvo: powdered
Porrón: long-spouted drinking vessel used instead of a glass
Priorato: a wine demarcation region
Posada: roadside cafe or inn
Potaje: potage, thick soup
Puchero: boiled dinner, hotpot, stockpot
Puerros: leeks
Pulpo: octopus
Pulpitos: baby octopus
Puzol: a type of unfermented white cheese from Valencia
Queso: cheese
Quesucos: a smoked cheese also called *Lebena,* made in Santander
Quisquillas: small shrimp (prawns)
Rábano: radish
Rabo: tail (meat cut)
Rape: angler or monkfish
Rascacio: rascasse
Raya: ray or skate
Rebozado: batter-dipped and deep- or shallow-fried
Remolacha: beet (beetroot)
Repollo: cabbage
Ribeiro: a wine demarcation region
Ribera del Duero: a wine demarcation region
Riñones: kidneys
Rioja, La: a wine demarcation region
Rodaballo: turbot (fish)
Rombo: brill (fish)
Roncal: one of the best Spanish cheeses, made from ewes' and cows' milk
Rosco: a type of doughnutlike cake
Rovellón (Robellon): a type of wild mushroom gathered in Catalonia, ochre in color. May

be known as *níscalo* or *seta de pino* (pine mushroom)

Rubio: gurnard (fish)

Sal: salt

Salamandra: tool used for glazing the top of sugared desserts and cakes. The original was a heavy metal disc that was heated in the oven. Now a grill or electric/gas salamander is used.

Salchicha: fresh pork sausage; *salchicha blanca asturiana* is one of the finest

Salchichón: cured pork sausage

Salmón: salmon

Salmonete: red mullet

Salmorejo: a tart sauce; a type of *gazpacho*; a dish involving rice, eggs and sausages; or a dish of partridge breasts in a creamy custardlike sauce

Salsa: sauce

Salteado: sautéed

Sangre: blood

San Pedro: John Dory (fish)

San Simón: a type of cheese from Galicia

Sangría: wine punch

Sardina: sardine (fish)

Sargo: bream (fish)

Sartén: frying pan

Seco: dry or dried

Sepia: cuttlefish

Serena: a type of ewes' milk cheese from Badajoz

Serrano: of the mountains

Sesos: brains

Seta: mushrooms, wild mushrooms

Shangurro: centolla crab, also *Txangurro*

Sherry: the wine of Jerez, wine demarcation region

Sidra: cider, the best of which comes from Asturias

Sobrasada: a sausage from the Balearic Islands

Sociedades Gastronomicas: gastronomic societies in Basque cities

Solomillo: tenderloin (fillet) of meat

Sofrito: caramelized onion and tomato base for sauces, stews and soups

Sopa: soup

Soria: a type of goats' milk cheese, lightly salty, made in Soria

Suizos: sweet and fancy breads

Taberna: a tavern

Tapas: appetizers, small snacks, hors d'oeuvre

Tarragona: a wine demarcation region

Tarta: cake or tart

Tascas: bars serving drinks and *tapas*

Ternera: young beef or veal

Tetilla: a type of cone-shaped cheese (may be called *petilla*)

Tocino: fresh pork fat or salt pork

Tomate: tomato

Tomillo: thyme

Torta: round flat bread or cake

Tortilla: omelette; *tortilla español* is an omelette of potato, often with onion

Tostado: toast or toasted

Trigo: wheat

Tronchón: a ewes' milk cheese from Tureul

Trucha: trout

Trufas: truffles, also known as *criadillas de tierra* "earth sweetbreads"

Turrón: nougat

Ulloa: a soft cows' milk cheese from Galicia

Uvas: grapes

Urta: fish similar to dentex

Vainilla: vanilla

Venado: venison

Verduras: green vegetables

Vieiras: scallops (shellfish)

Villalón: a cheese shaped like a mule's foot and given the name *pata de mulo*. Good with fruit and honey

Vino: wine

Yemas: egg yolks

Zanahorias: carrots

Zarzuela: a type of seafood stew

INDEX